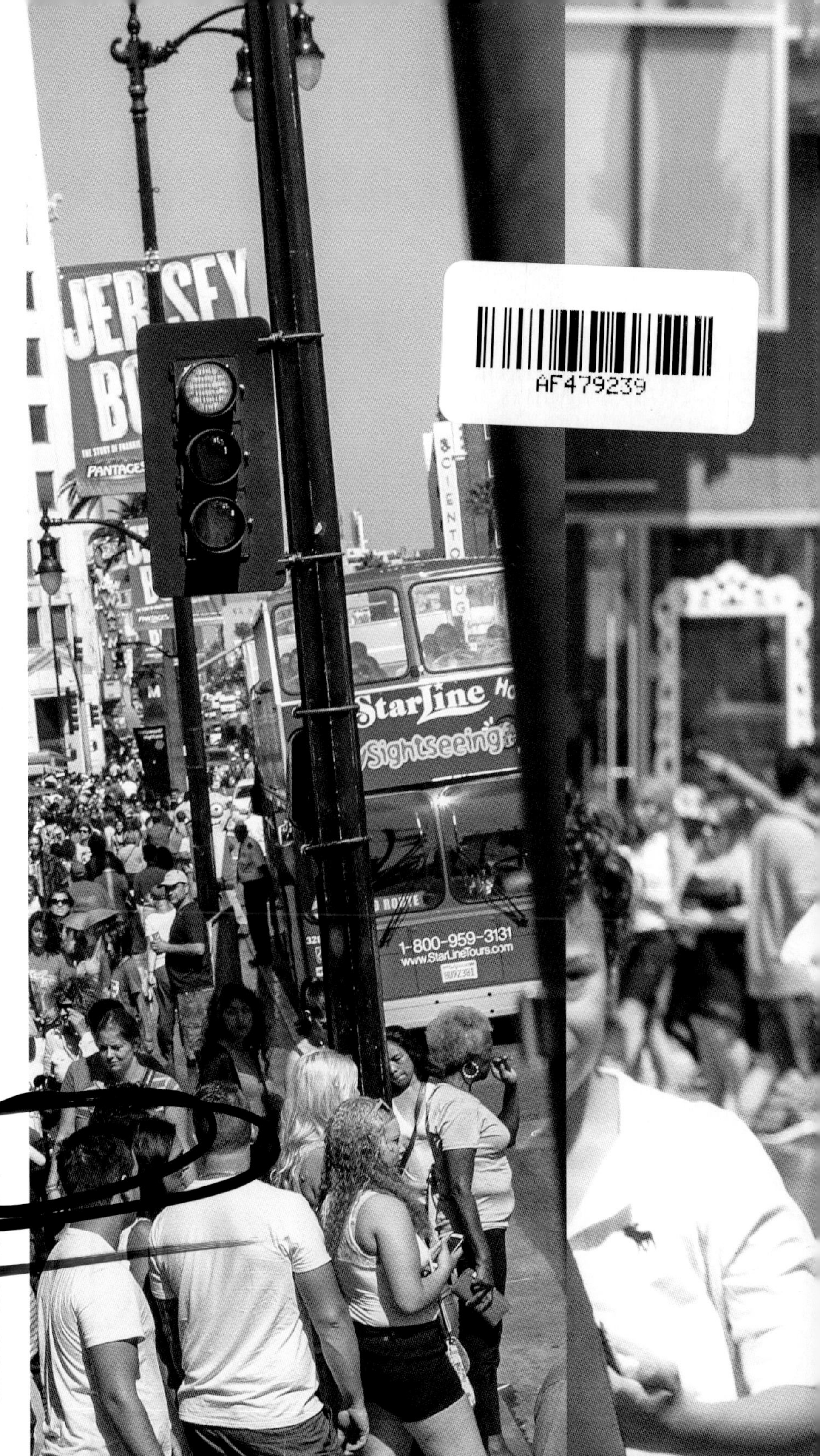

JER SEY
B
THE STORY OF FRANKIE
PANTAGES
StarLine Ho
Sightseeing
1-800-959-3131
www.StarLineTours.com
AF479239

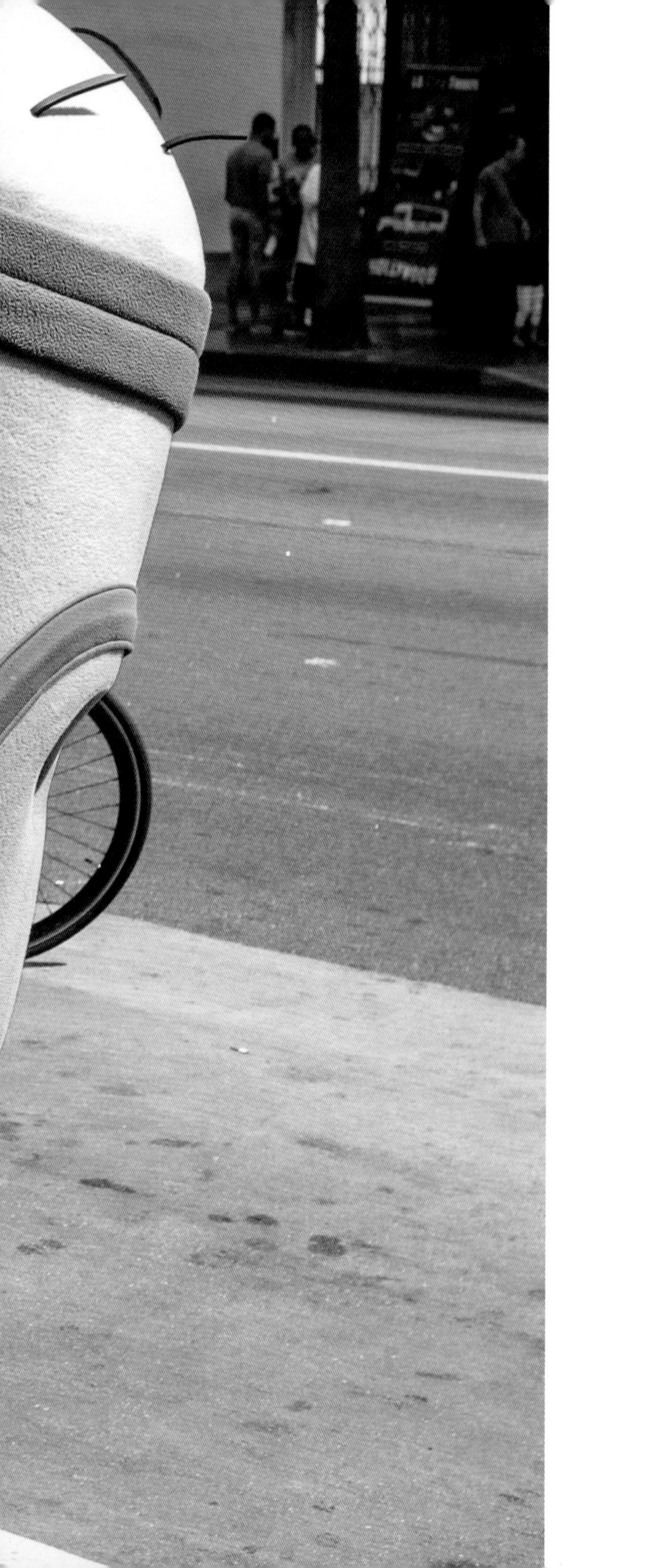

KATHRYN ANDREWS   STRIP

UCCA / KOENIG BOOKS, LONDON

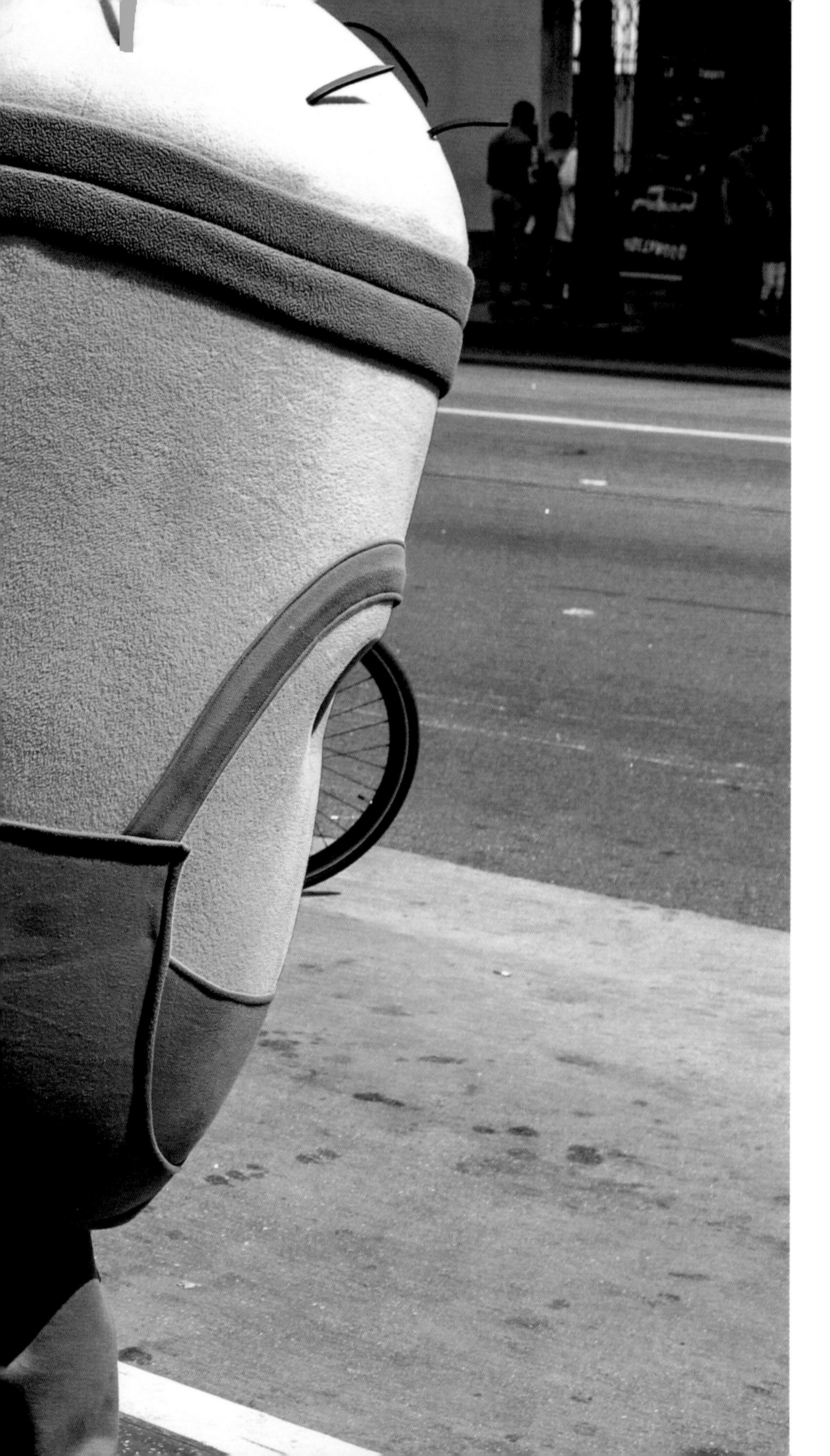

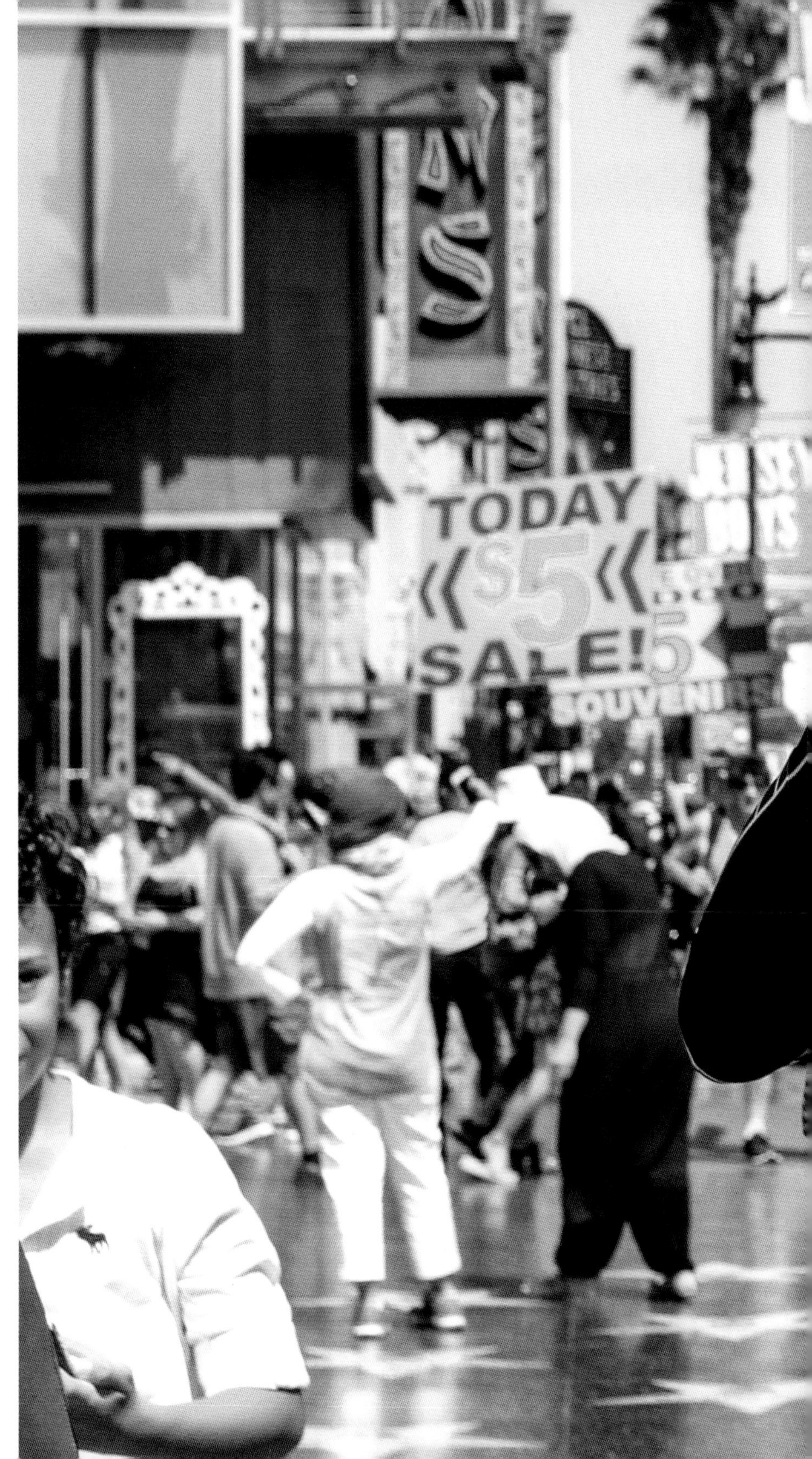

TODAY
$5
SALE!5
SOUVENIR

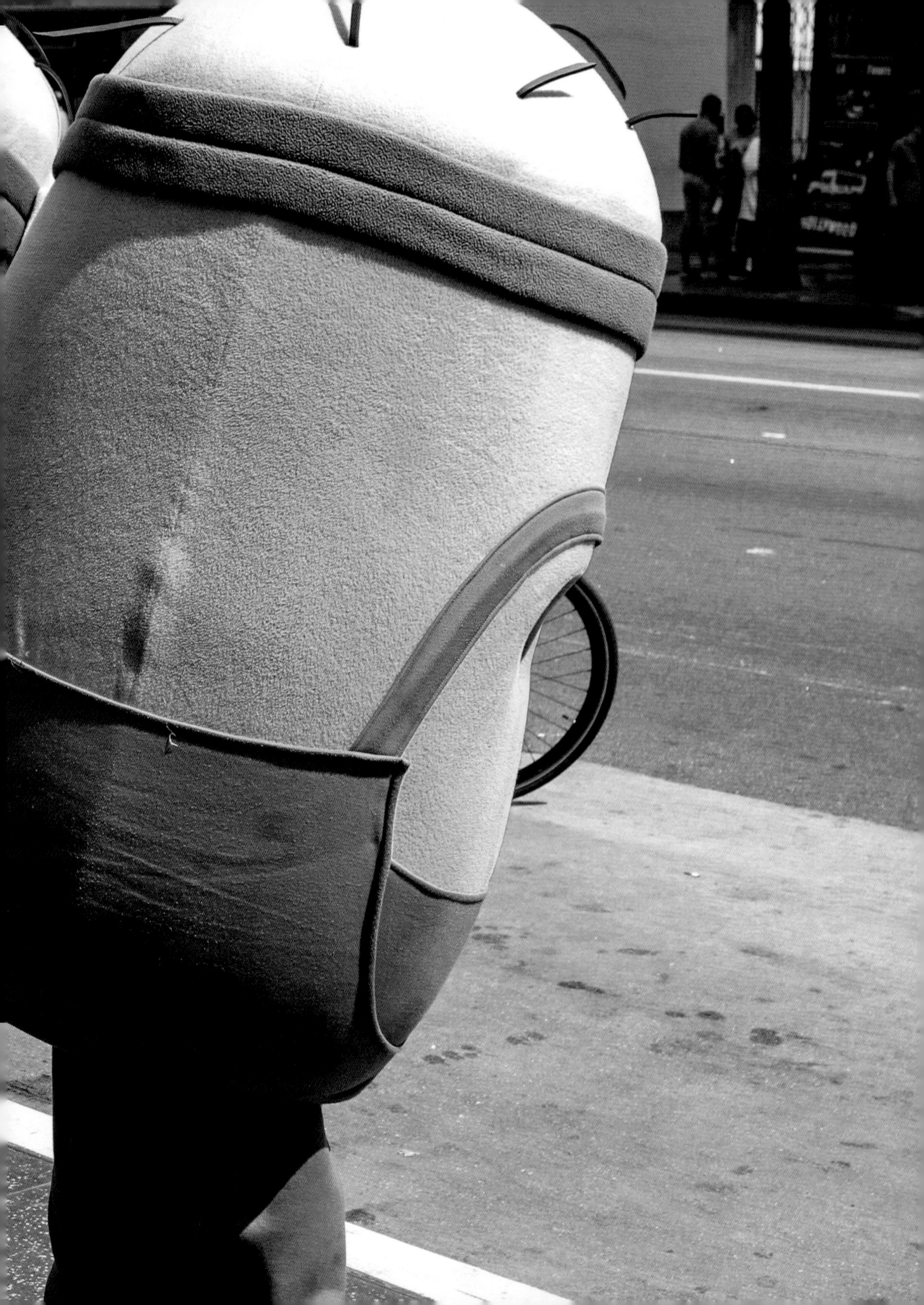

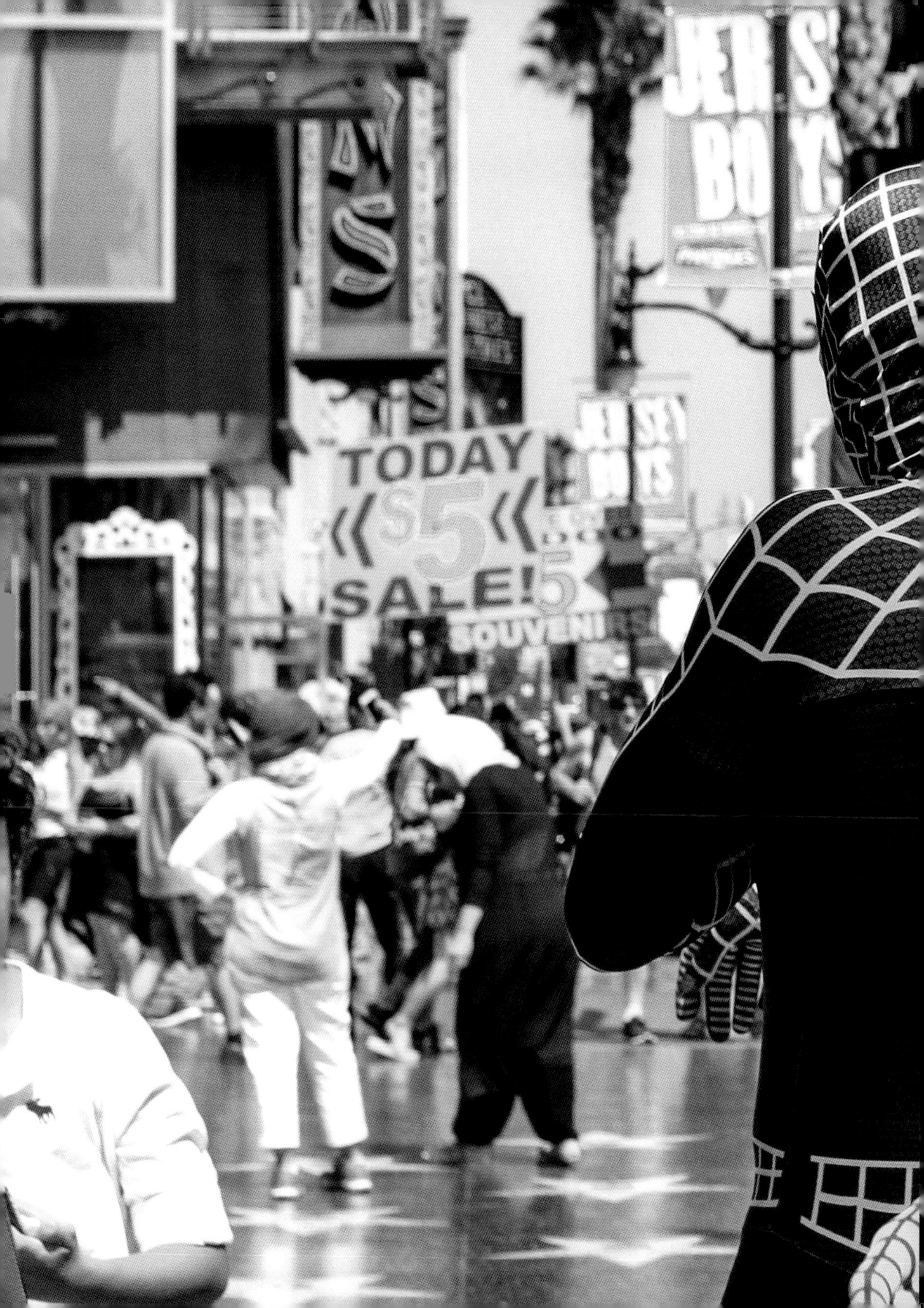
JER S'
BO Y
TODAY
$5
SALE!5
SOUVENI
JER SEY
BO S

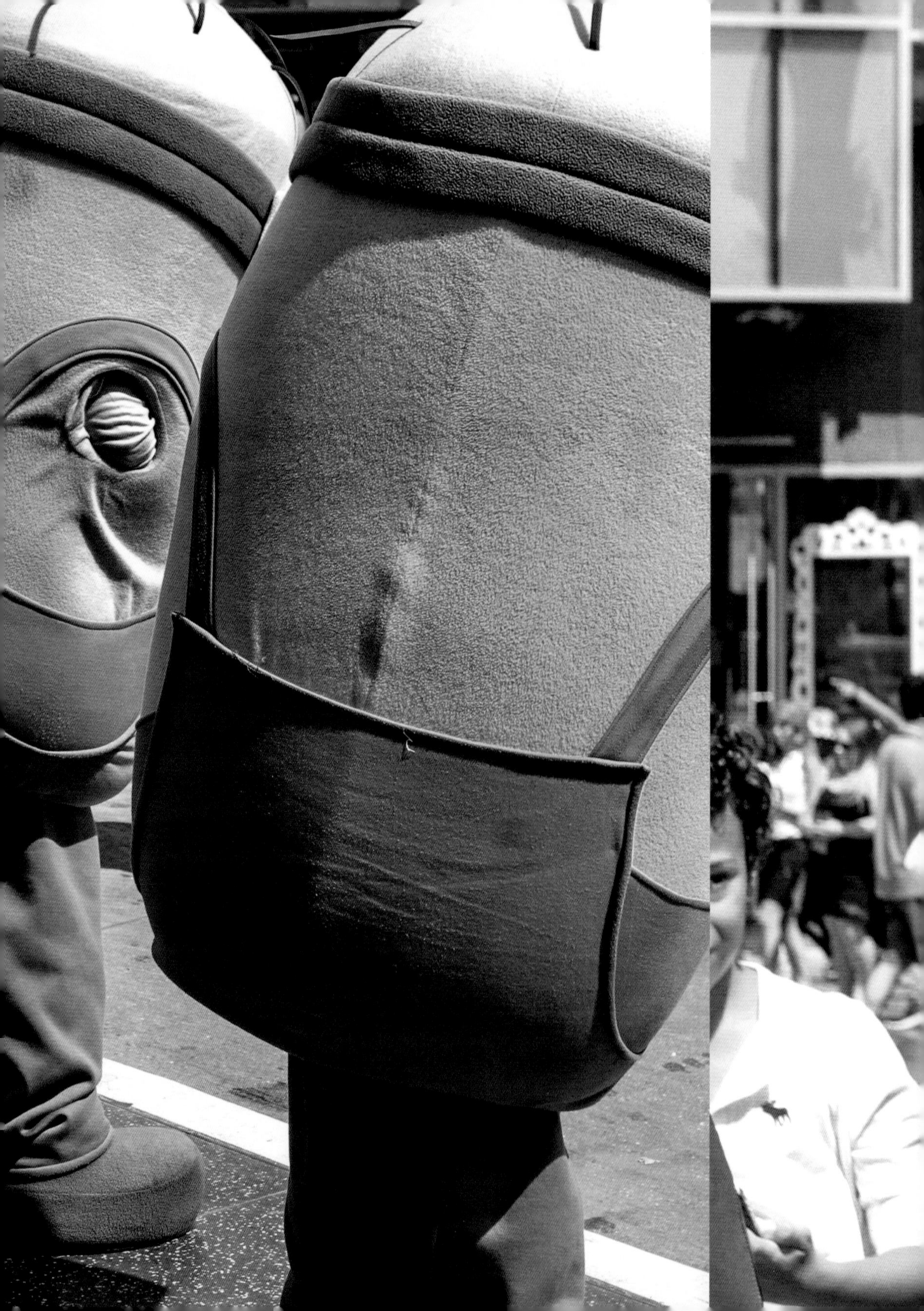

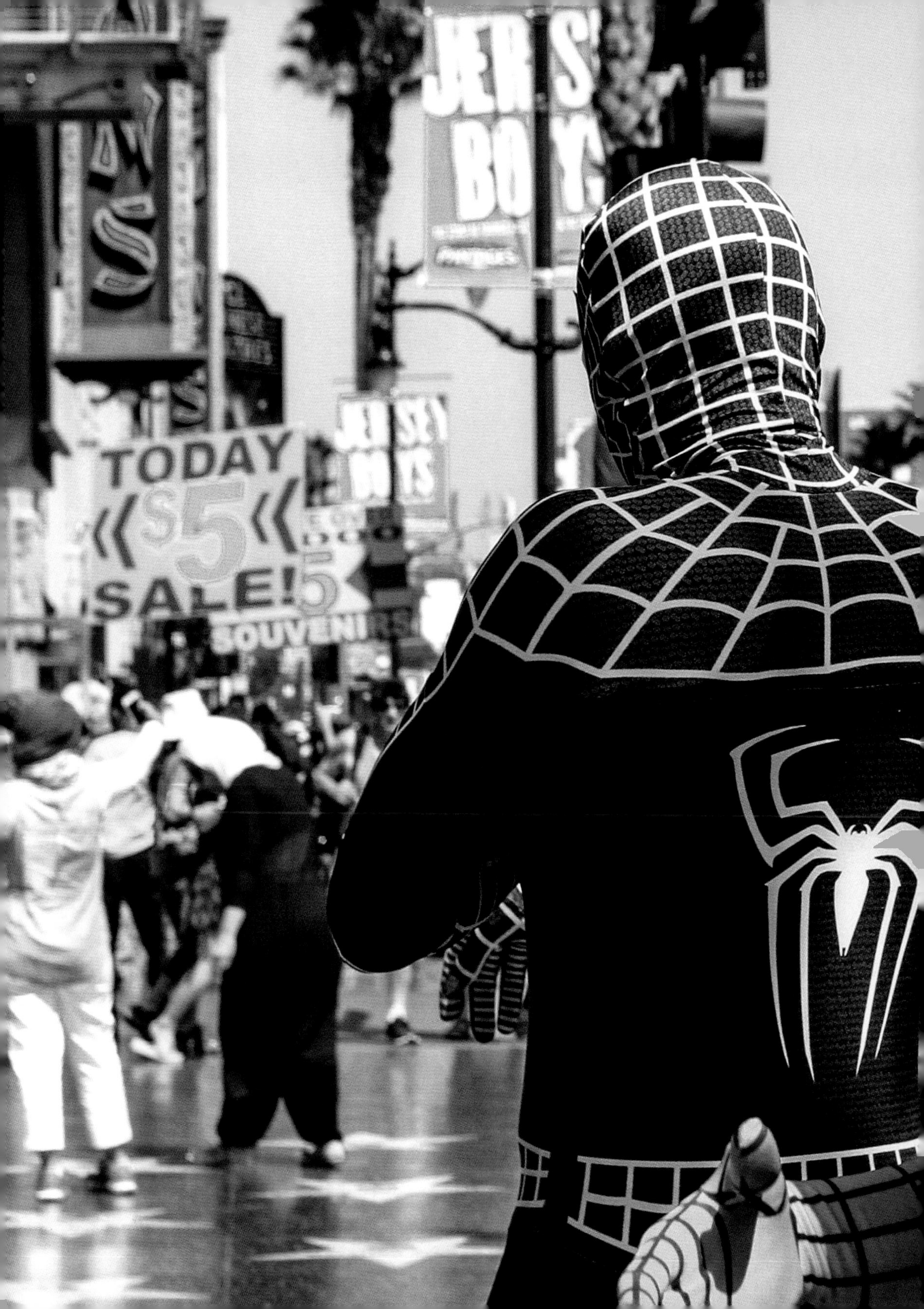

JERS'
BOYS
JERSEY
BOYS
TODAY
$5
SALE!5
SOUVENIRS

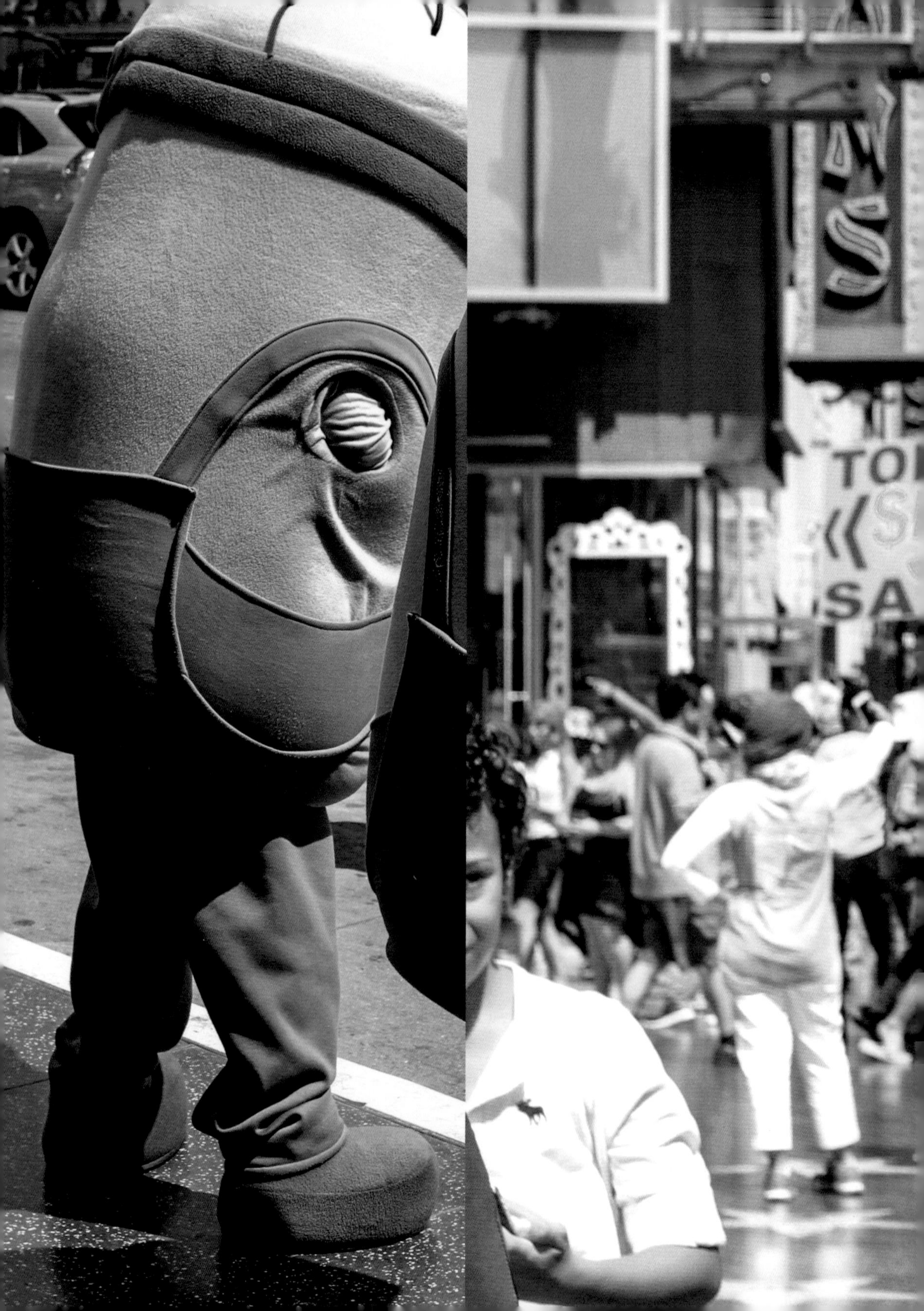

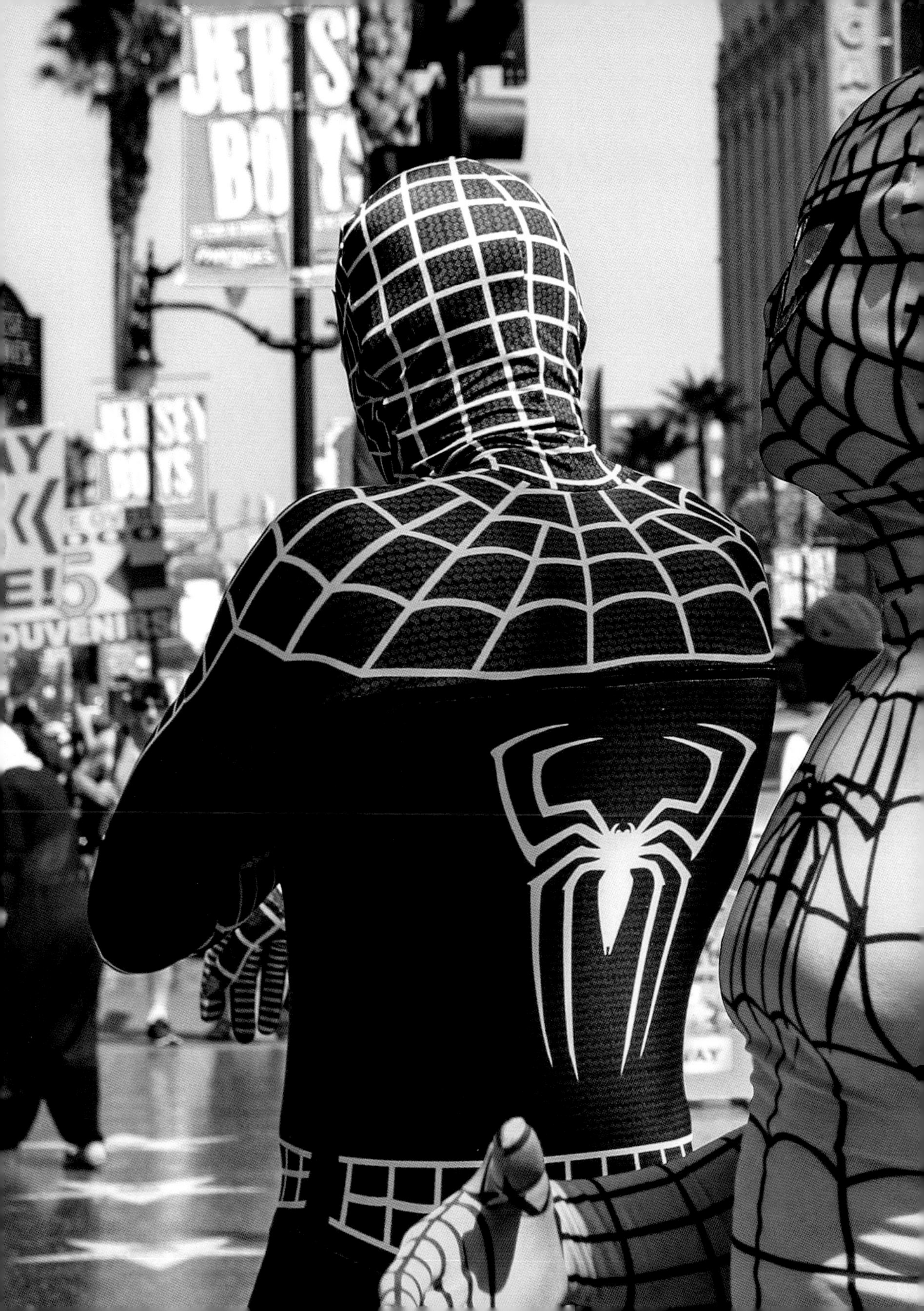
JER S'
BOY.
JERSEY
BOYS

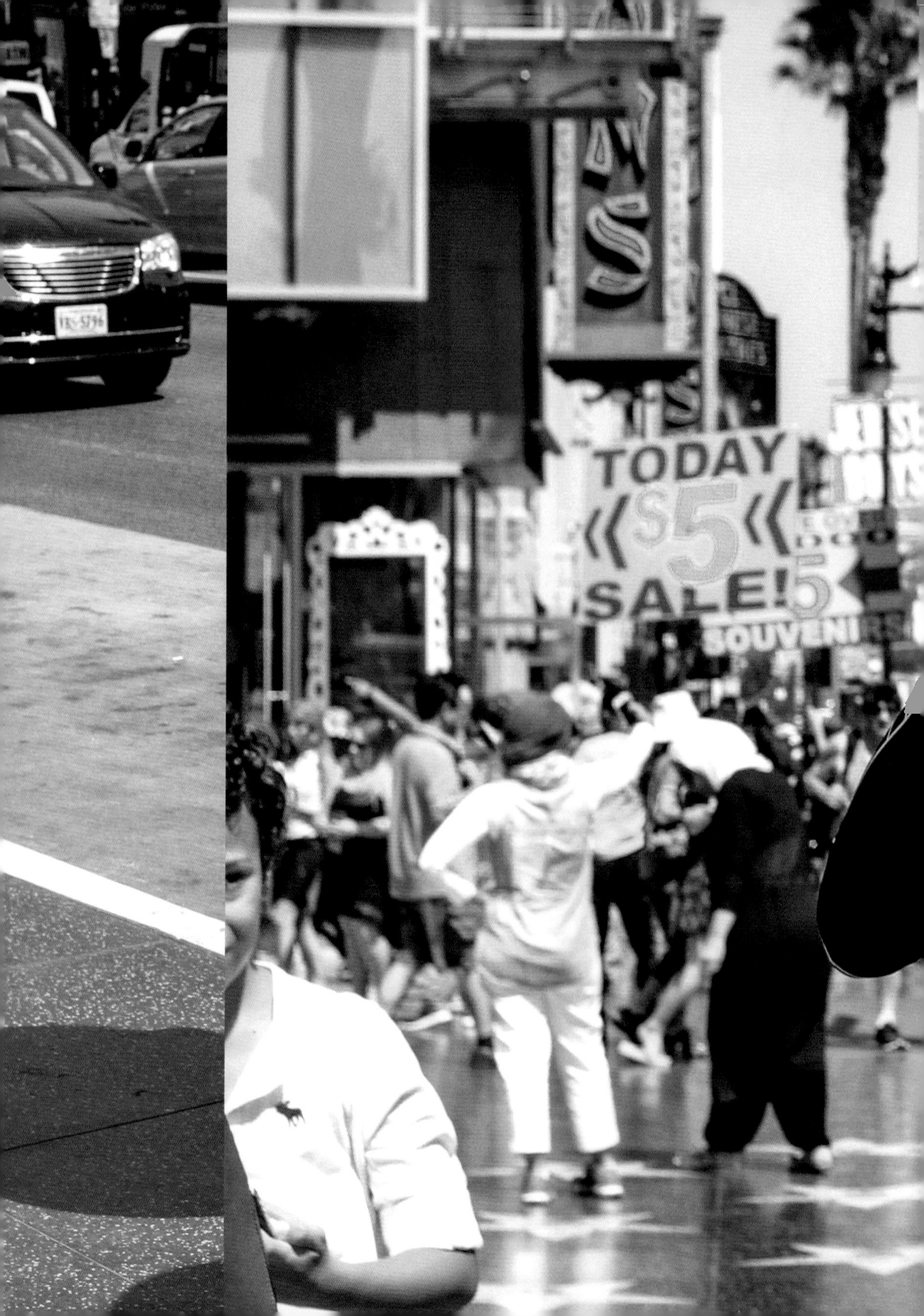

TODAY
$5
SALE!
SOUVENIR

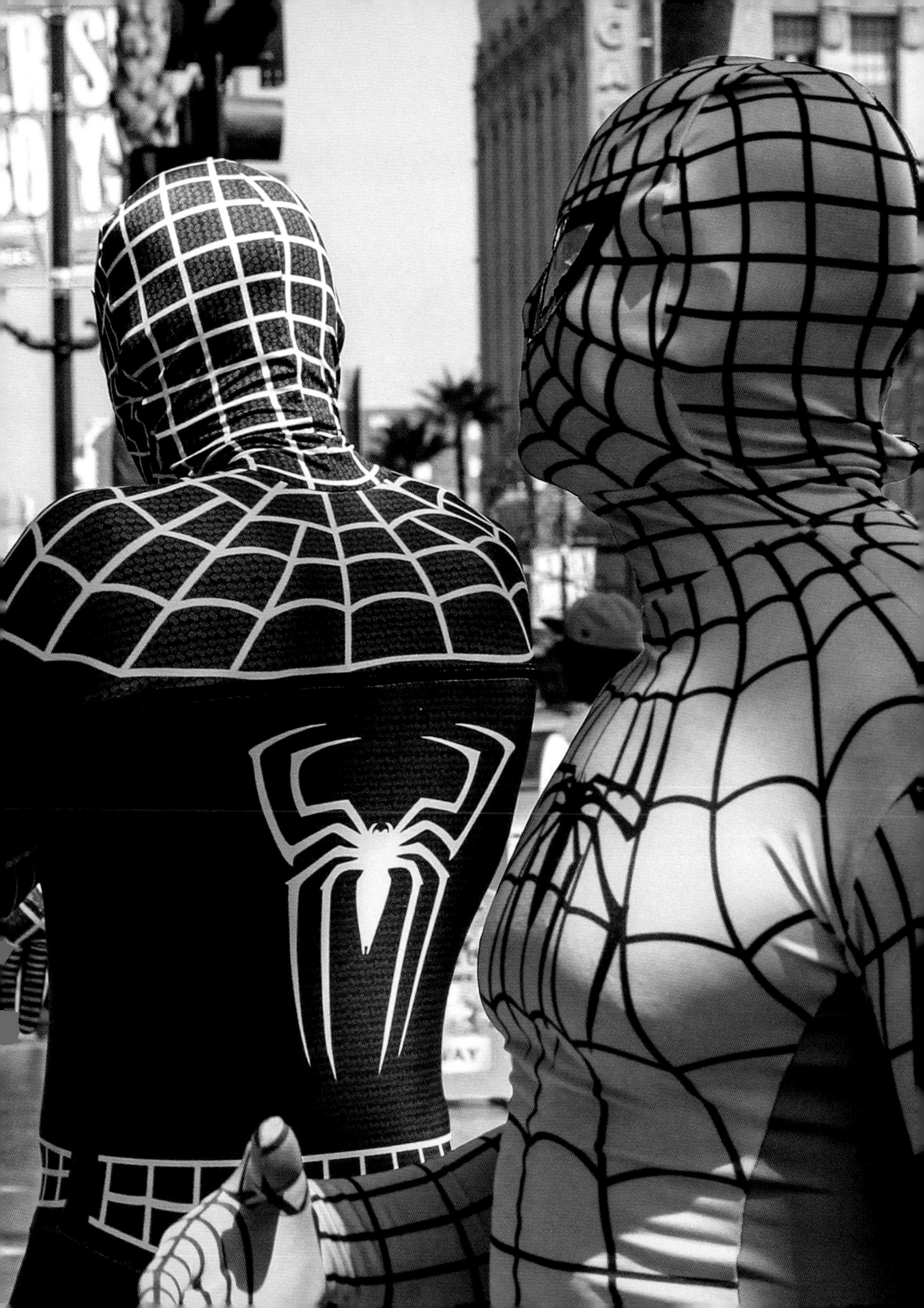

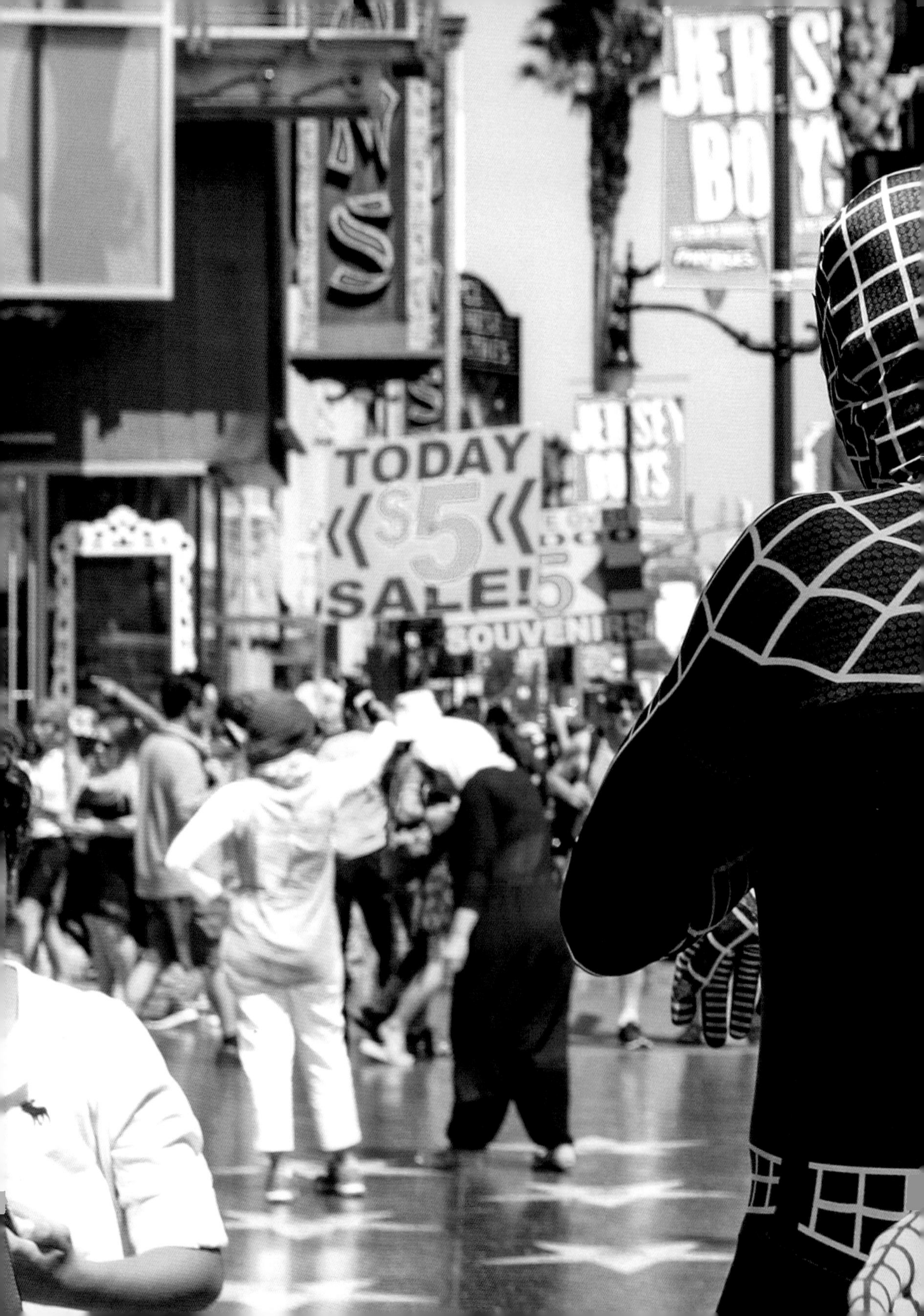

JER S'
BO Y
JERSEY BOYS
TODAY
$5
SALE! 5
SOUVENIRS

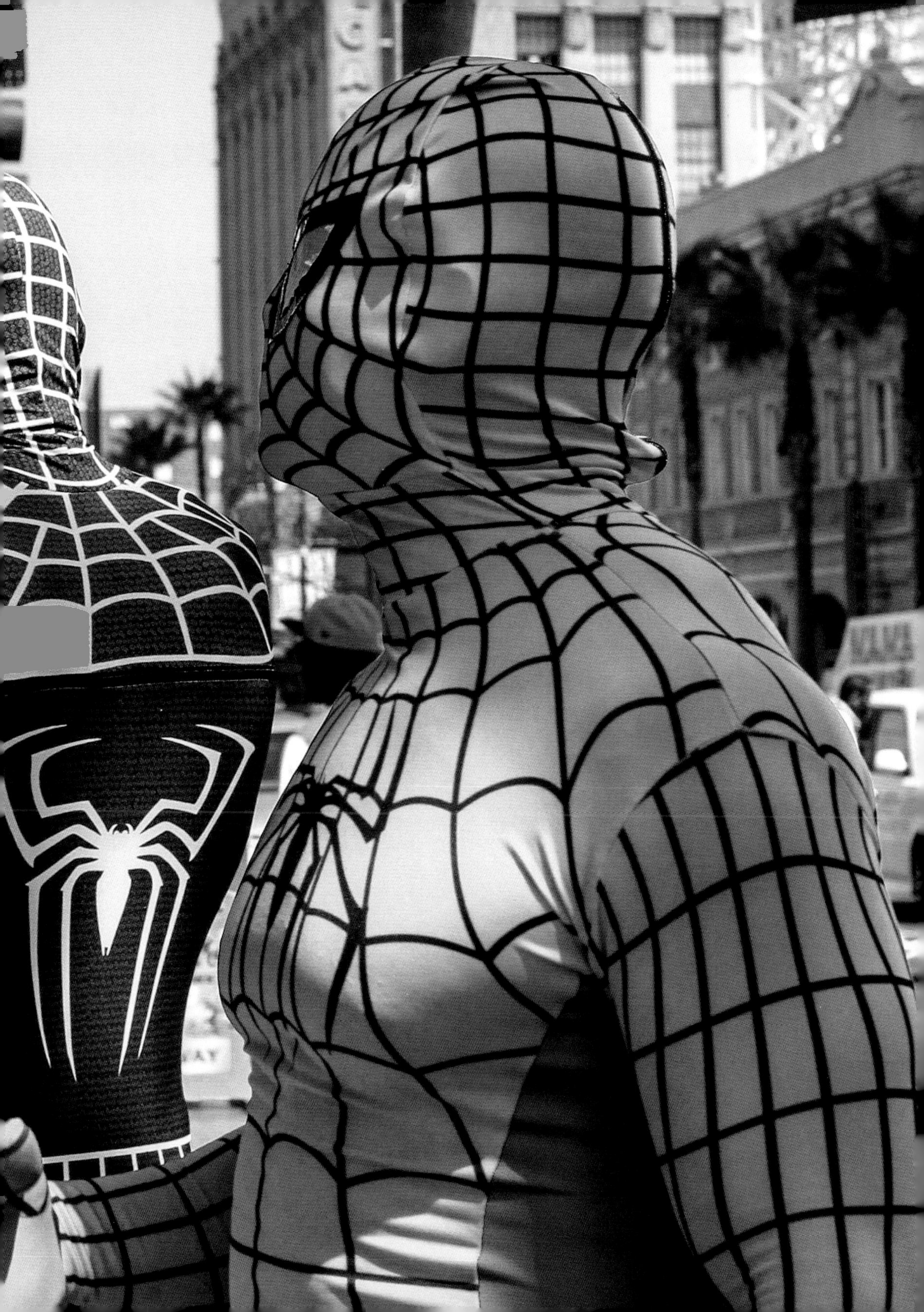

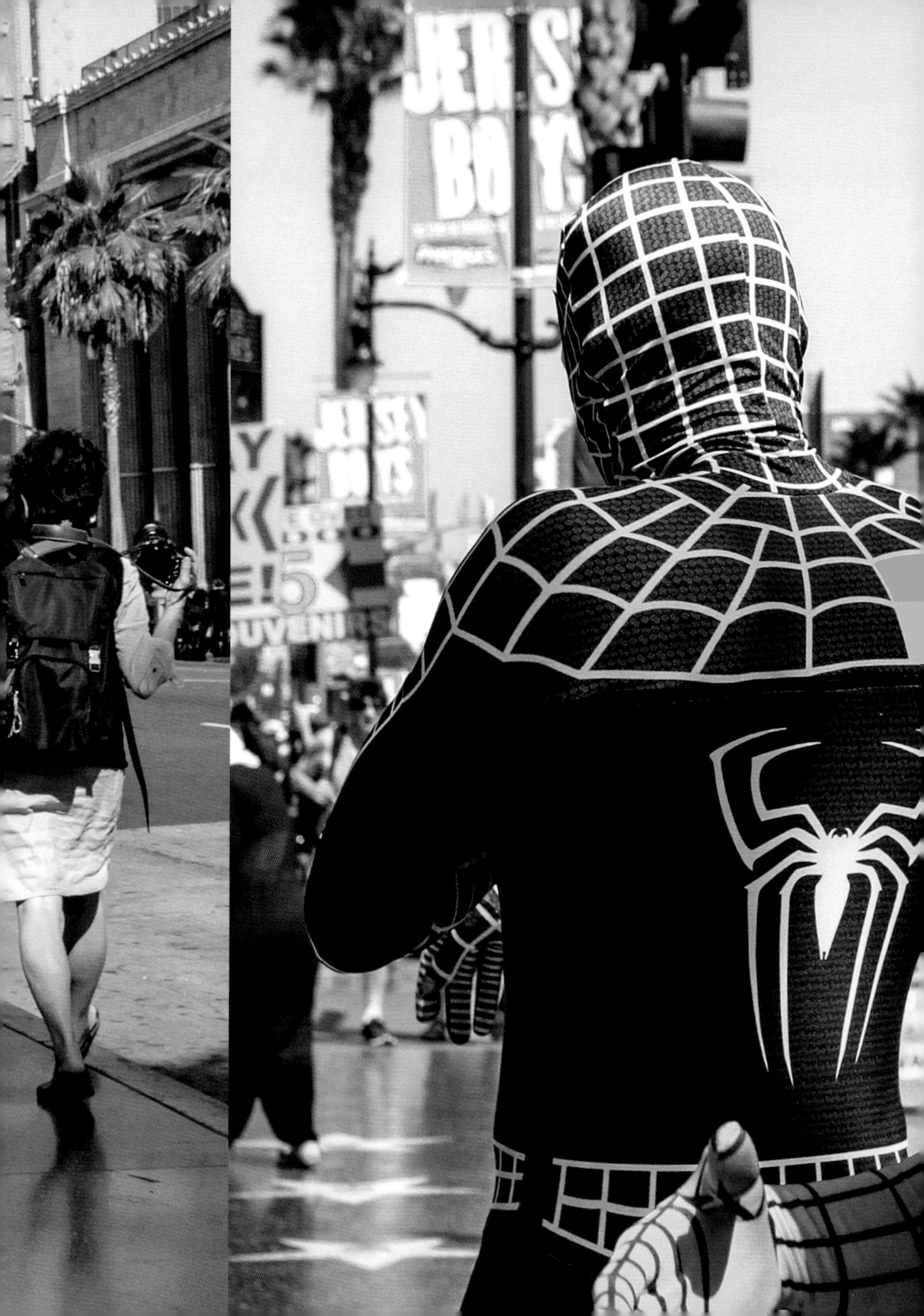

JER S'
BO Y.S
JERSEY
BOYS

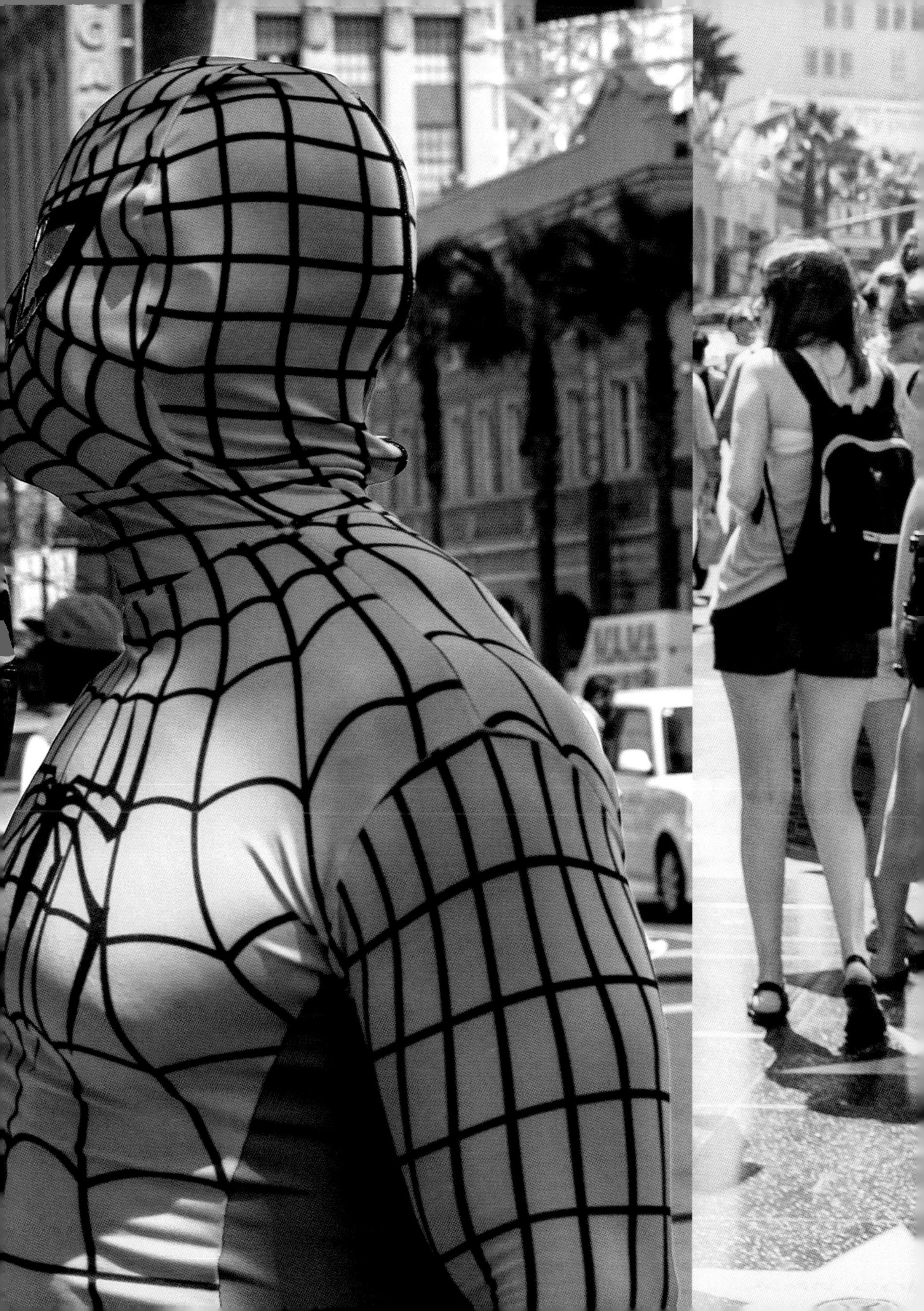

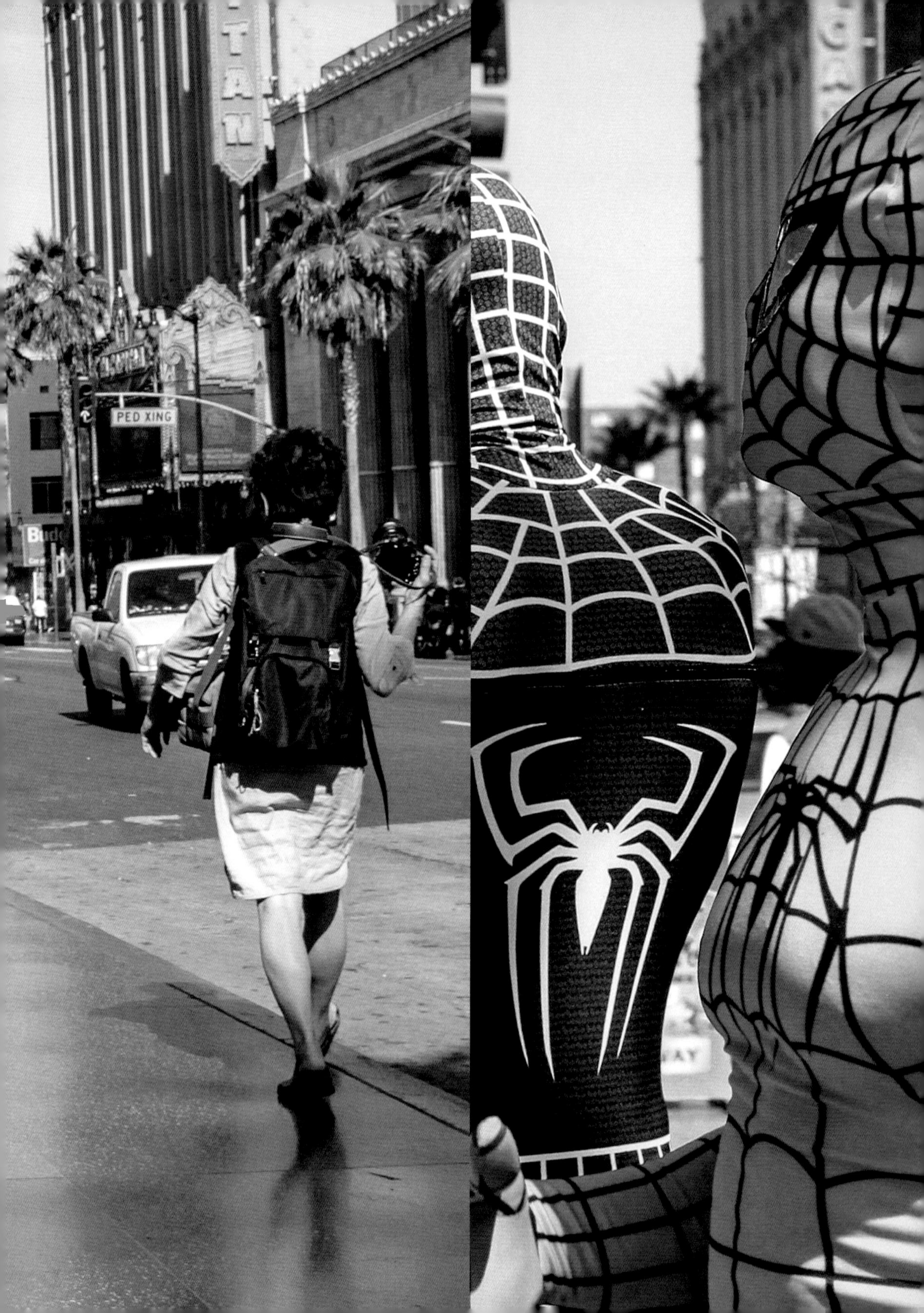
PED XING

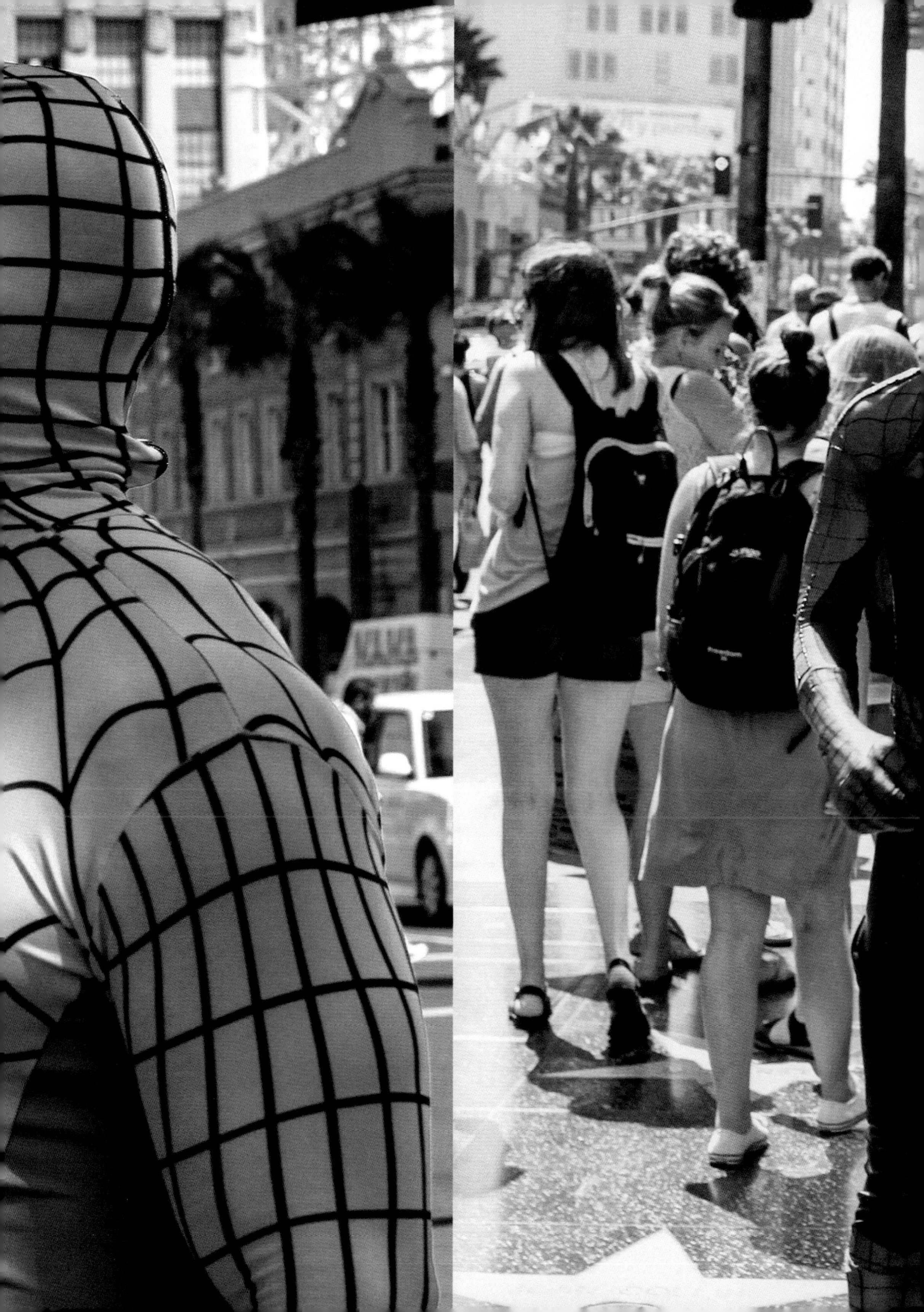

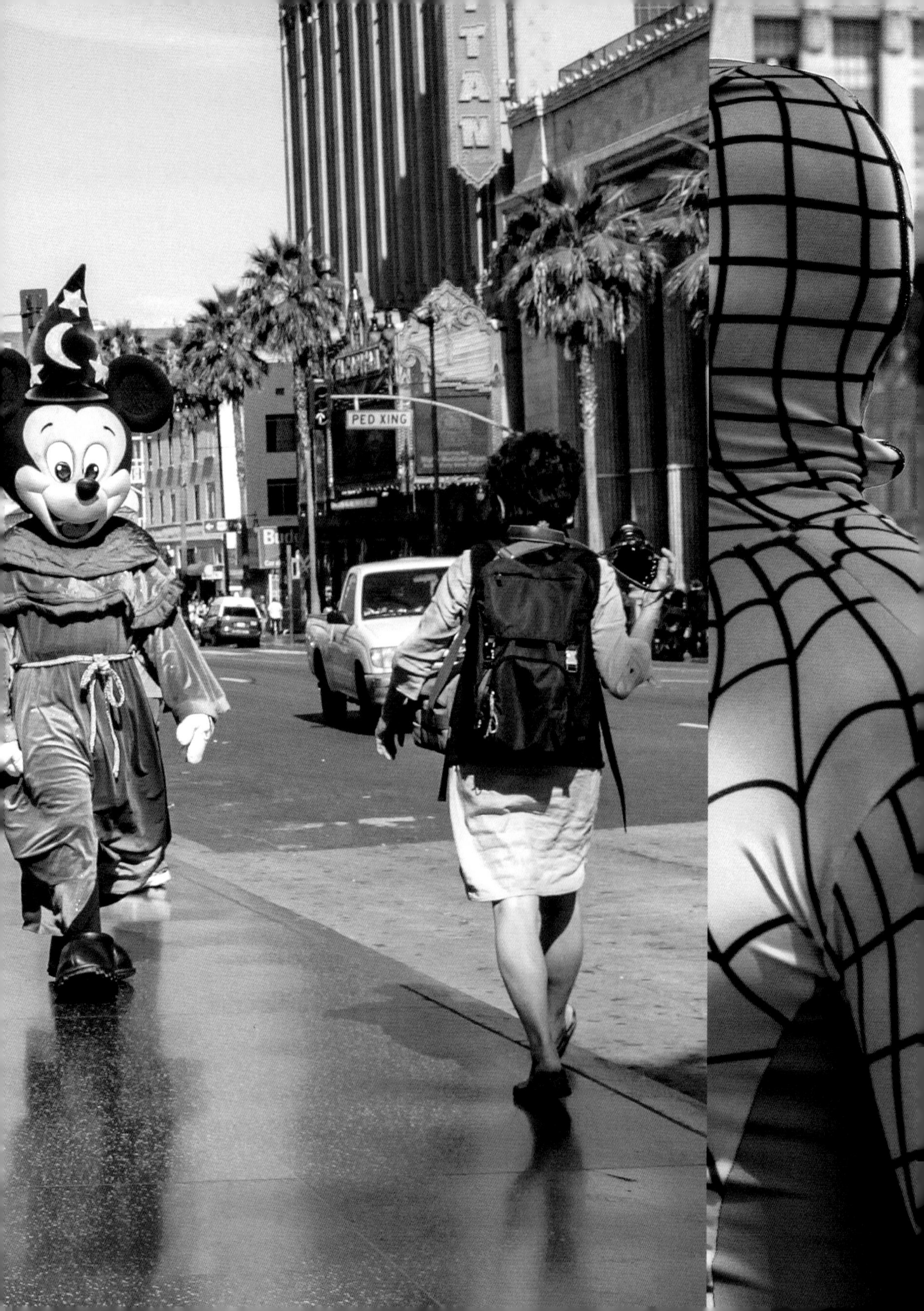

TAN
PED XING

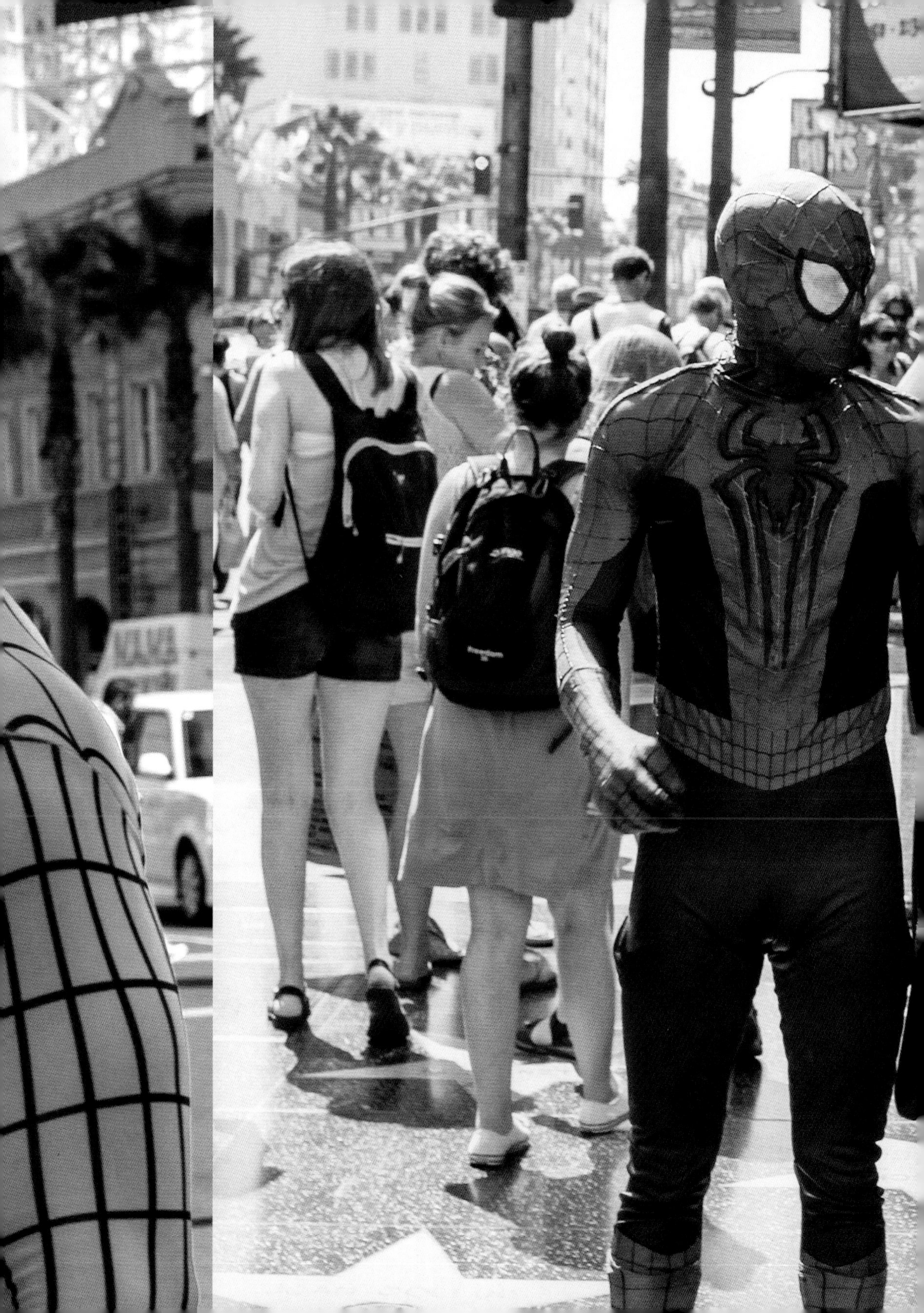

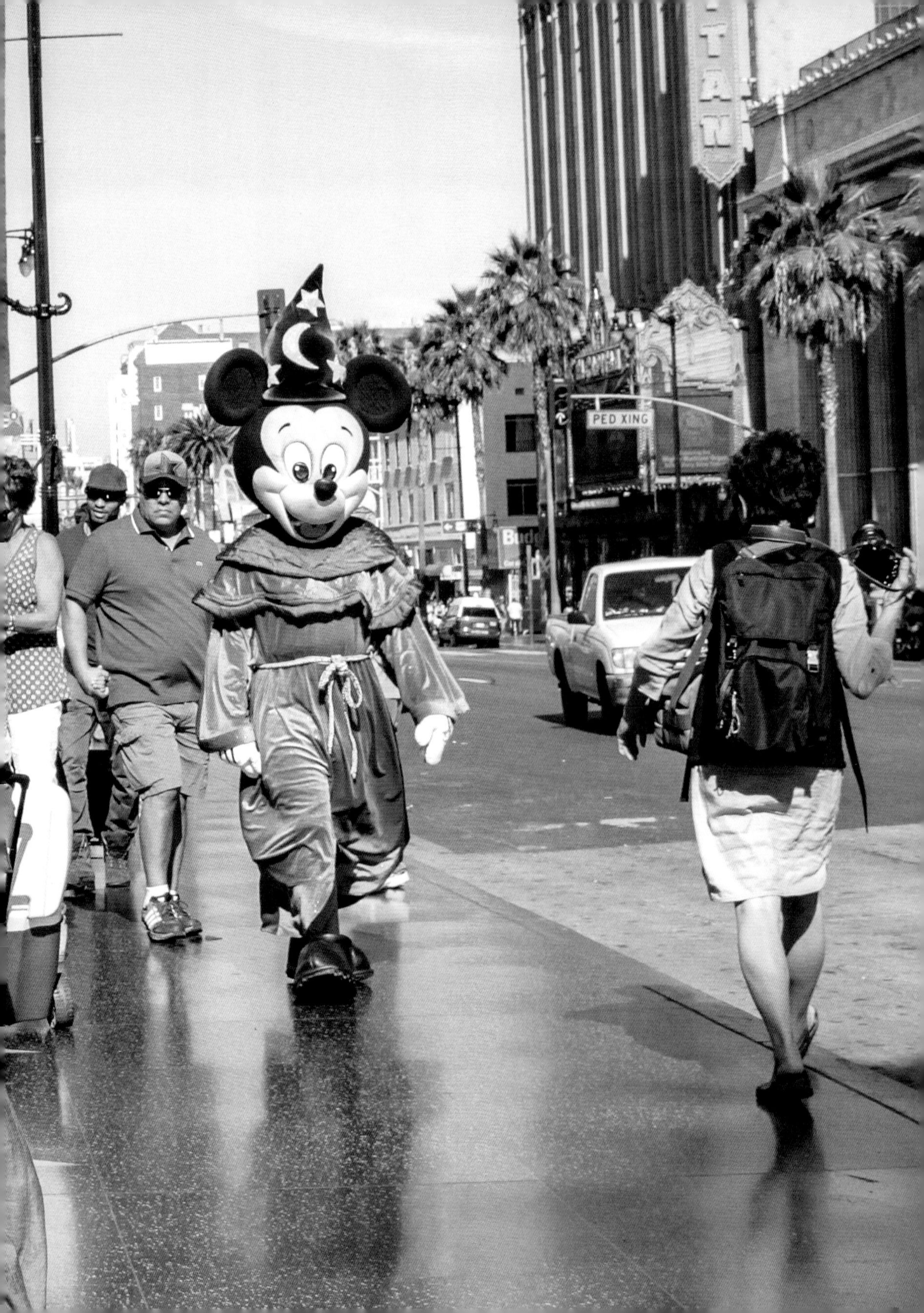
PED XING

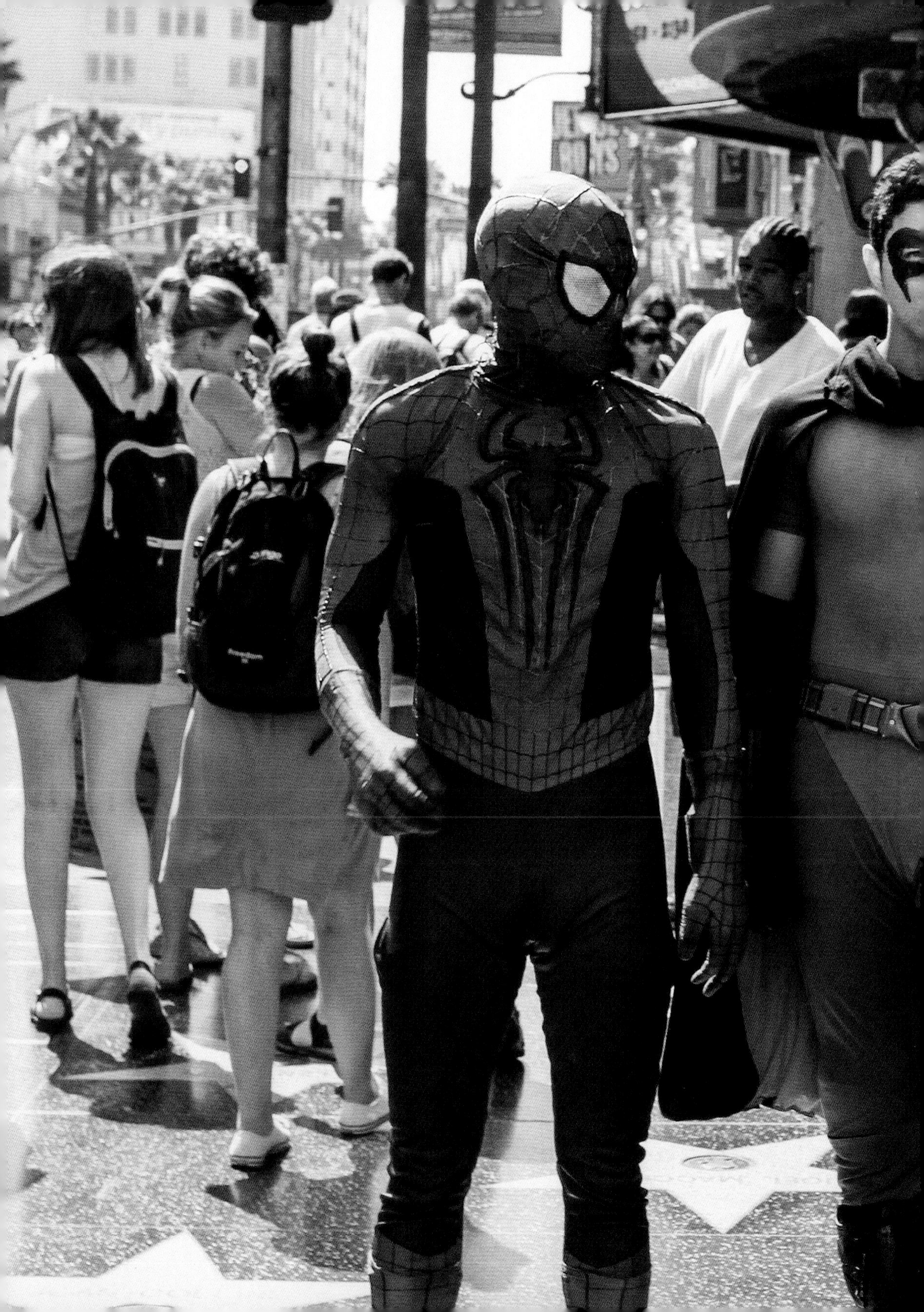

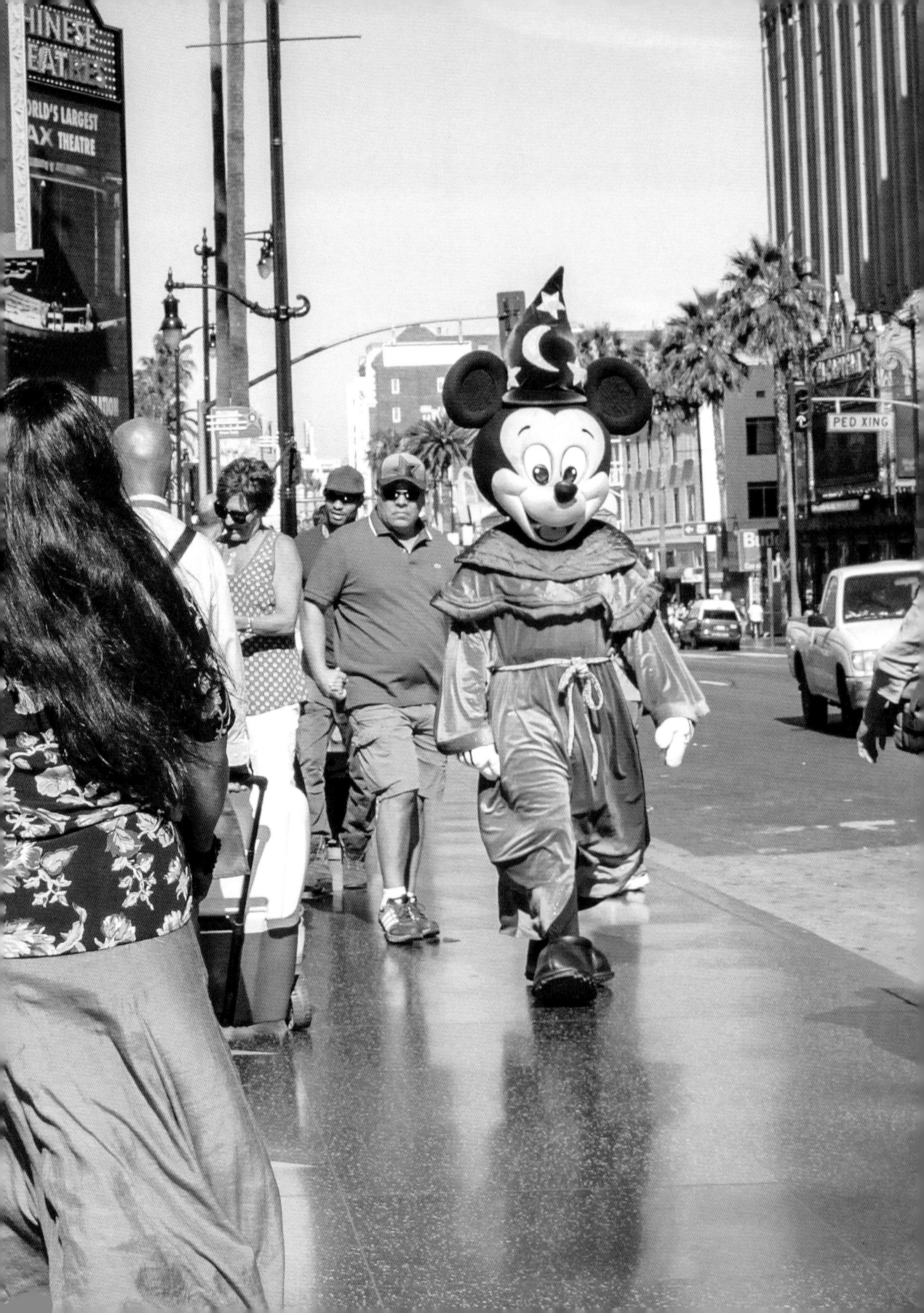
HINESE
EATRE
WORLD'S LARGEST
AX THEATRE
PED XING

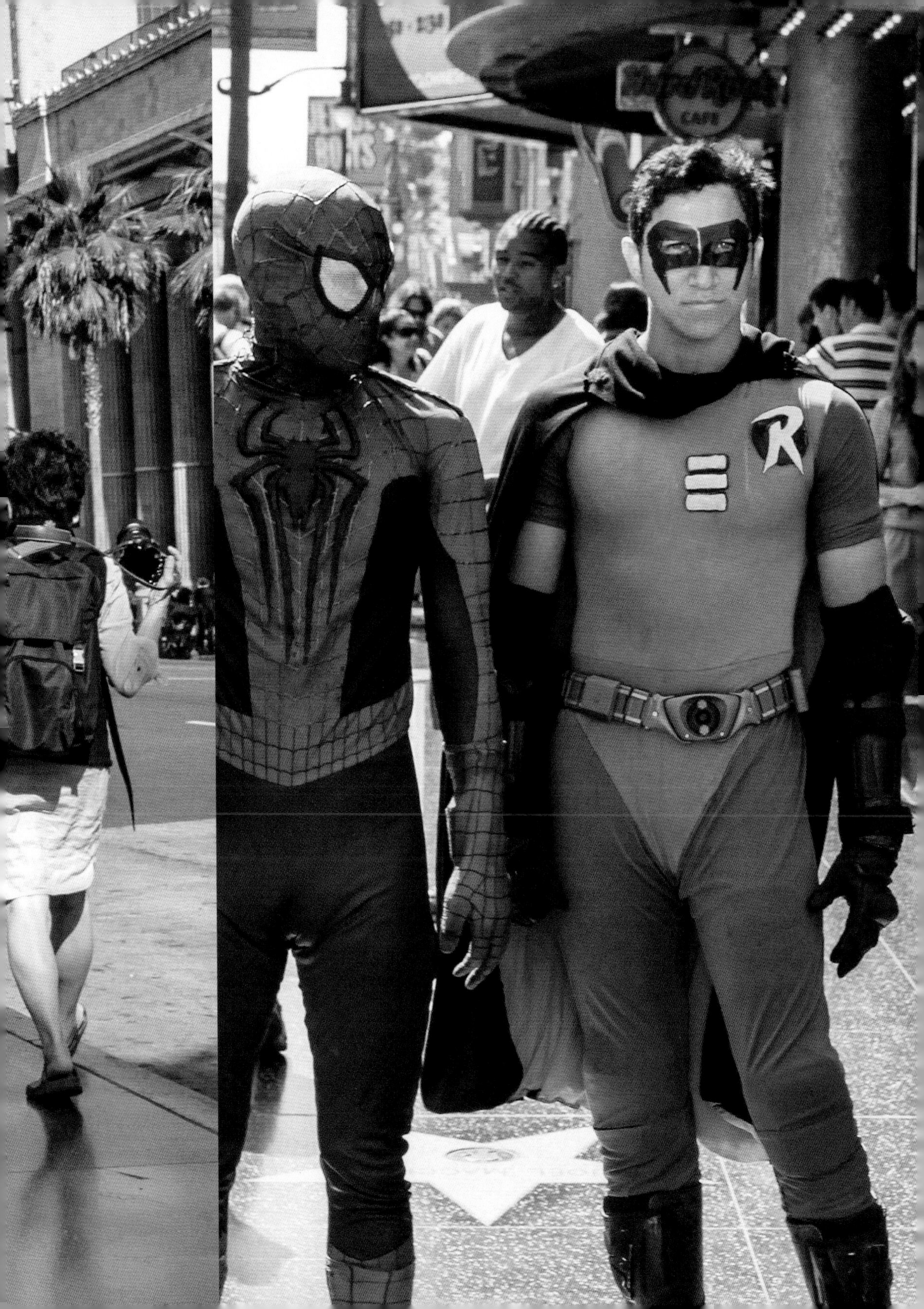

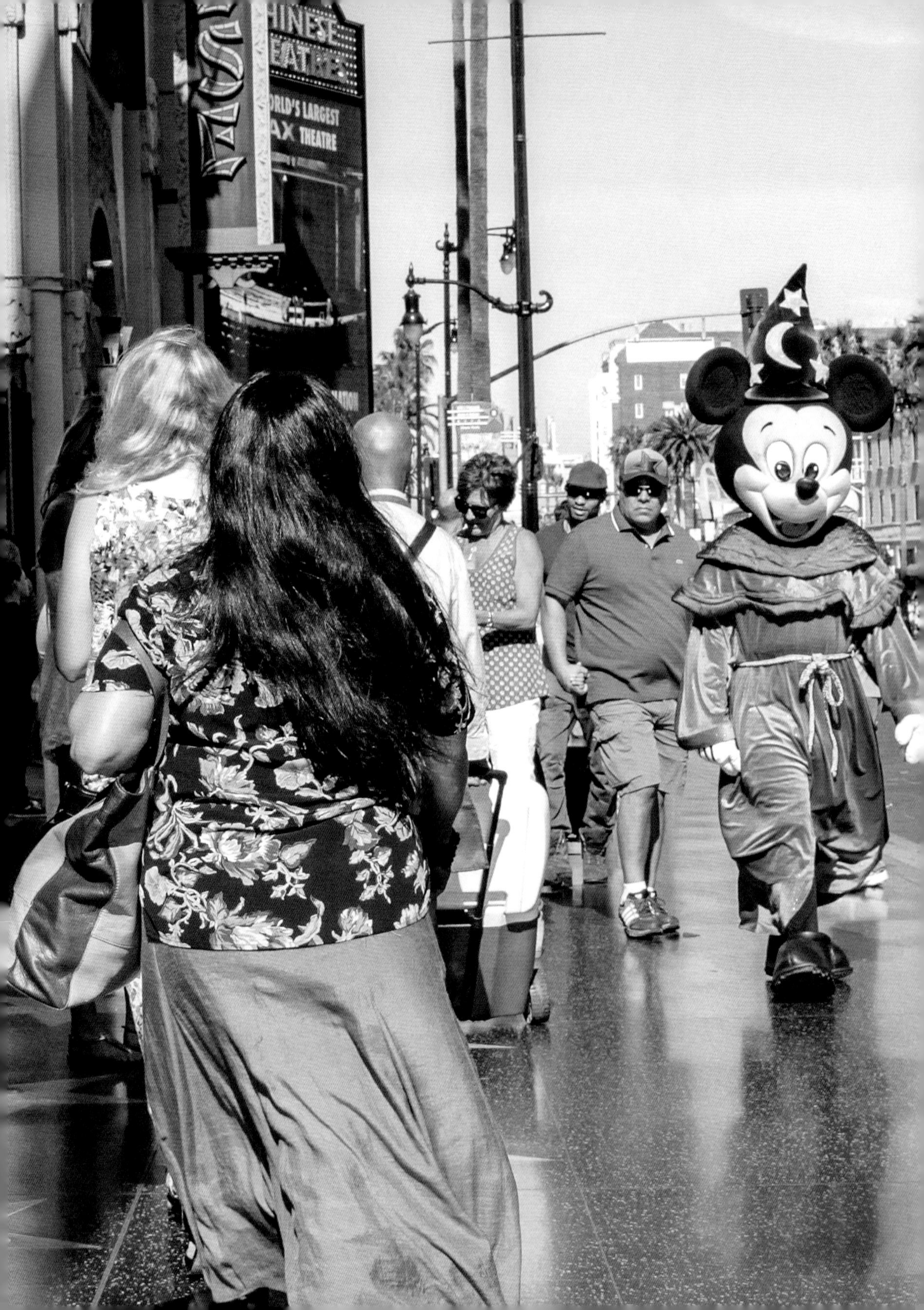

CHINESE
THEATRE
WORLD'S LARGEST
IMAX THEATRE

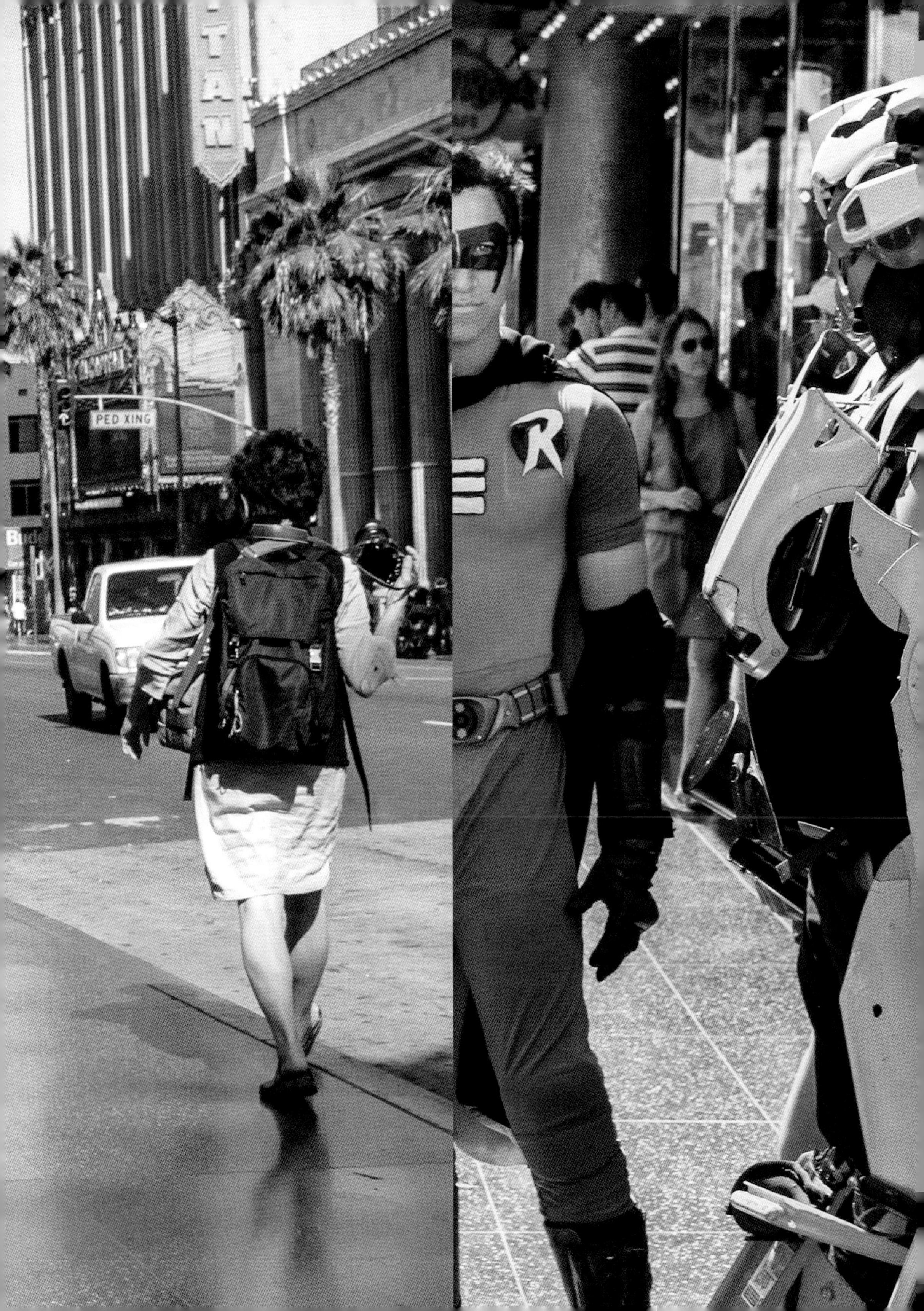

PED XING
R

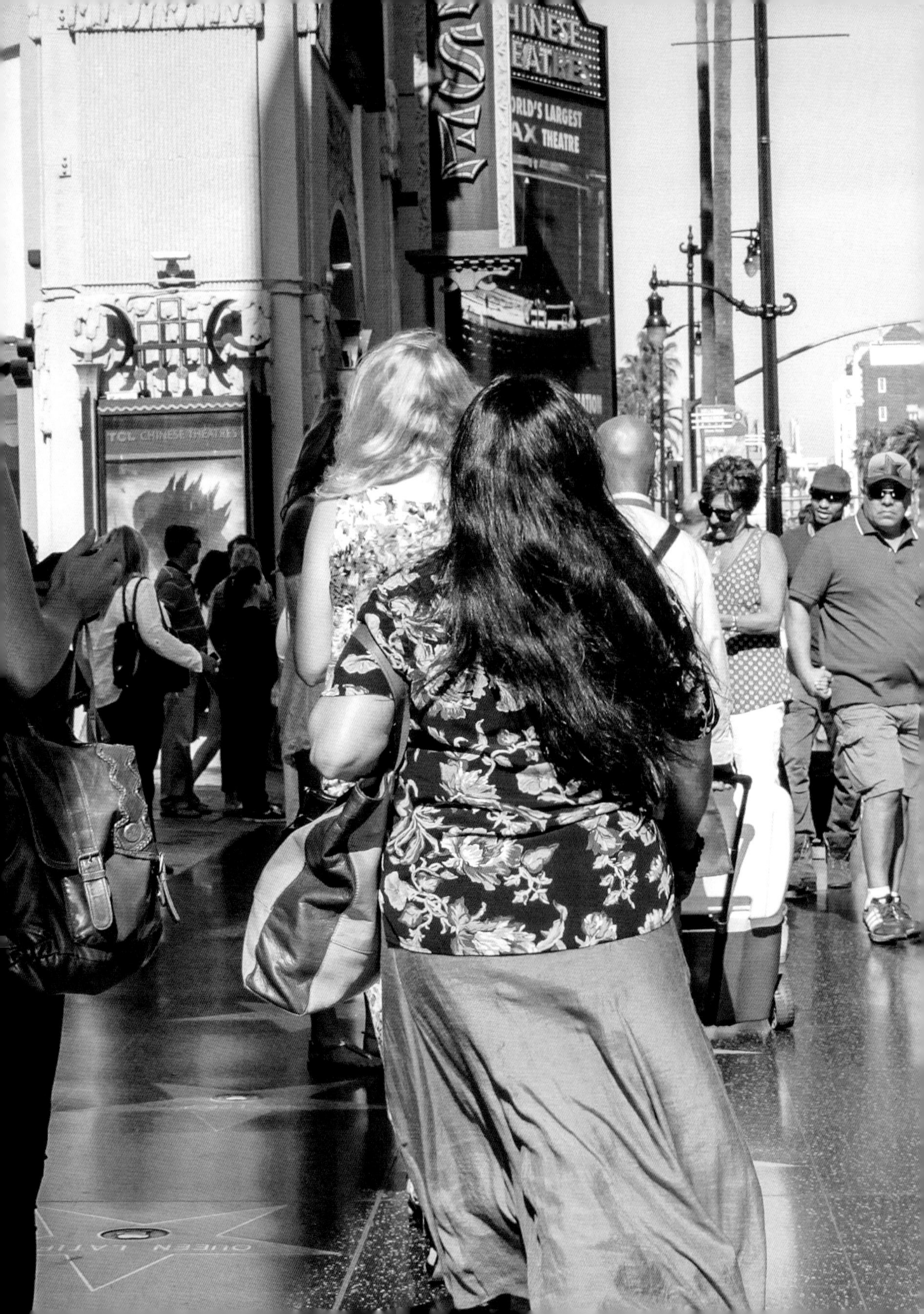
CHINESE
THEATRE
WORLD'S LARGEST
IMAX
THEATRE
TCL CHINESE THEATRES

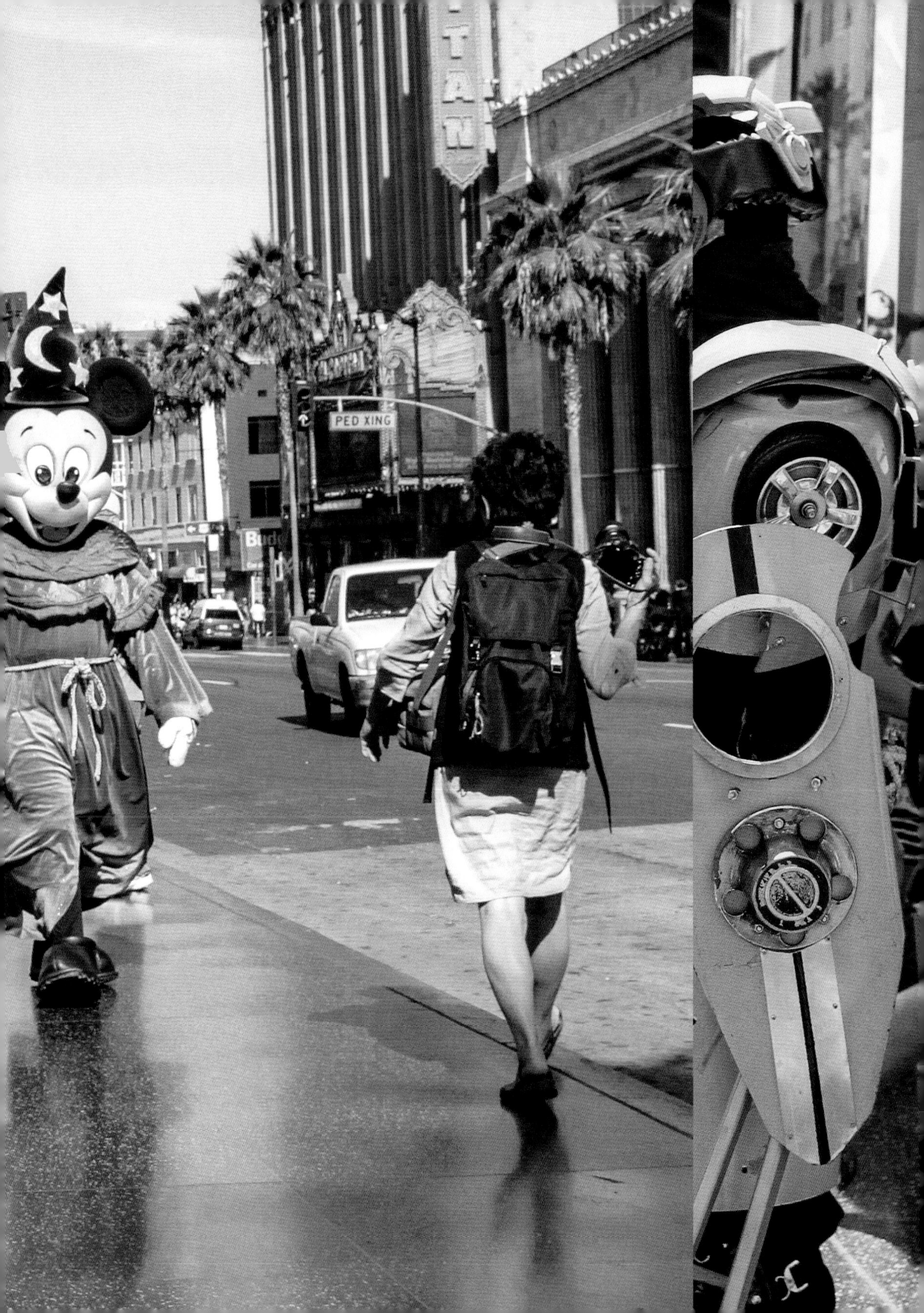

PED XING

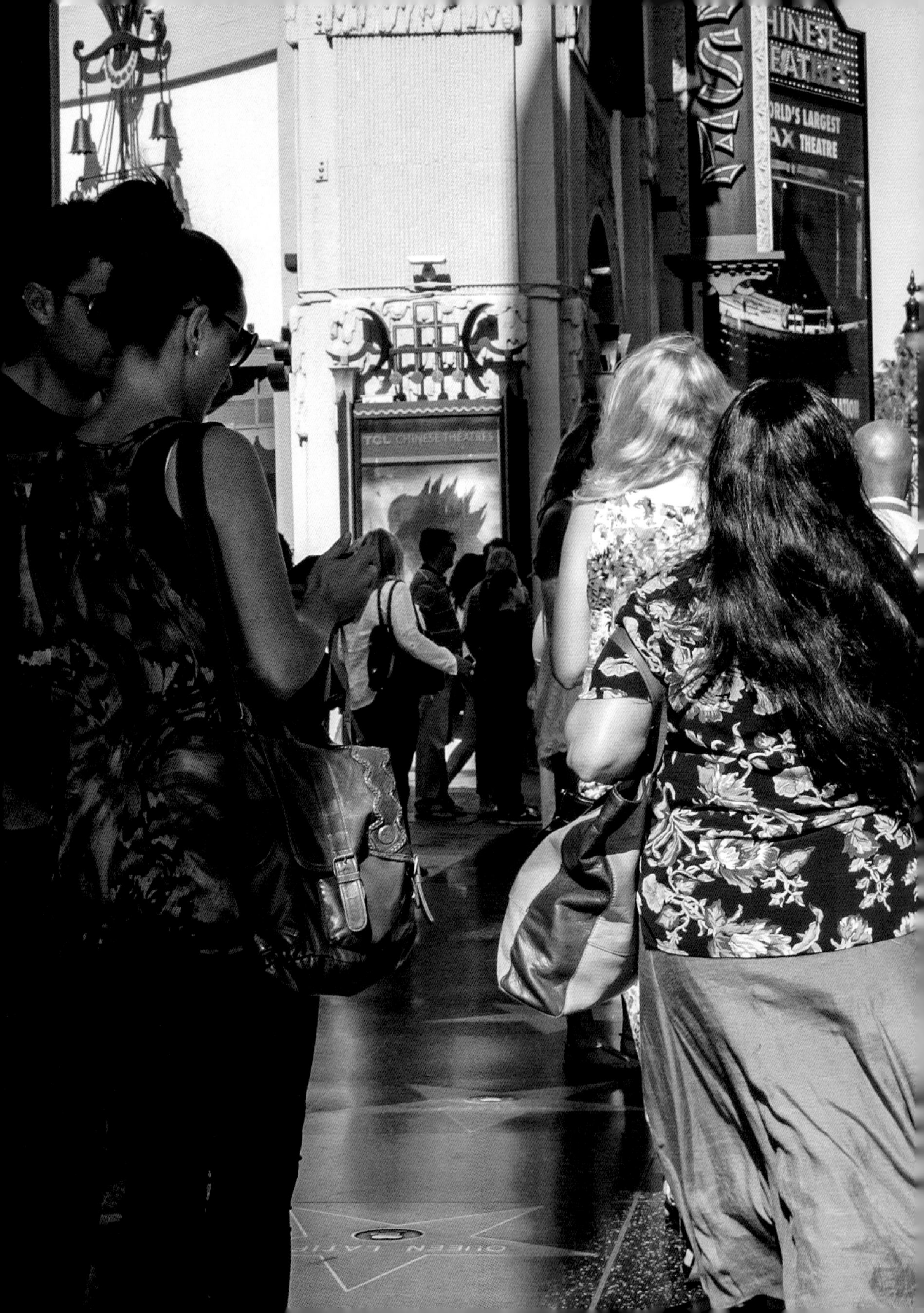

CHINESE
THEATRE
WORLD'S LARGEST
IMAX THEATRE
TCL CHINESE THEATRES

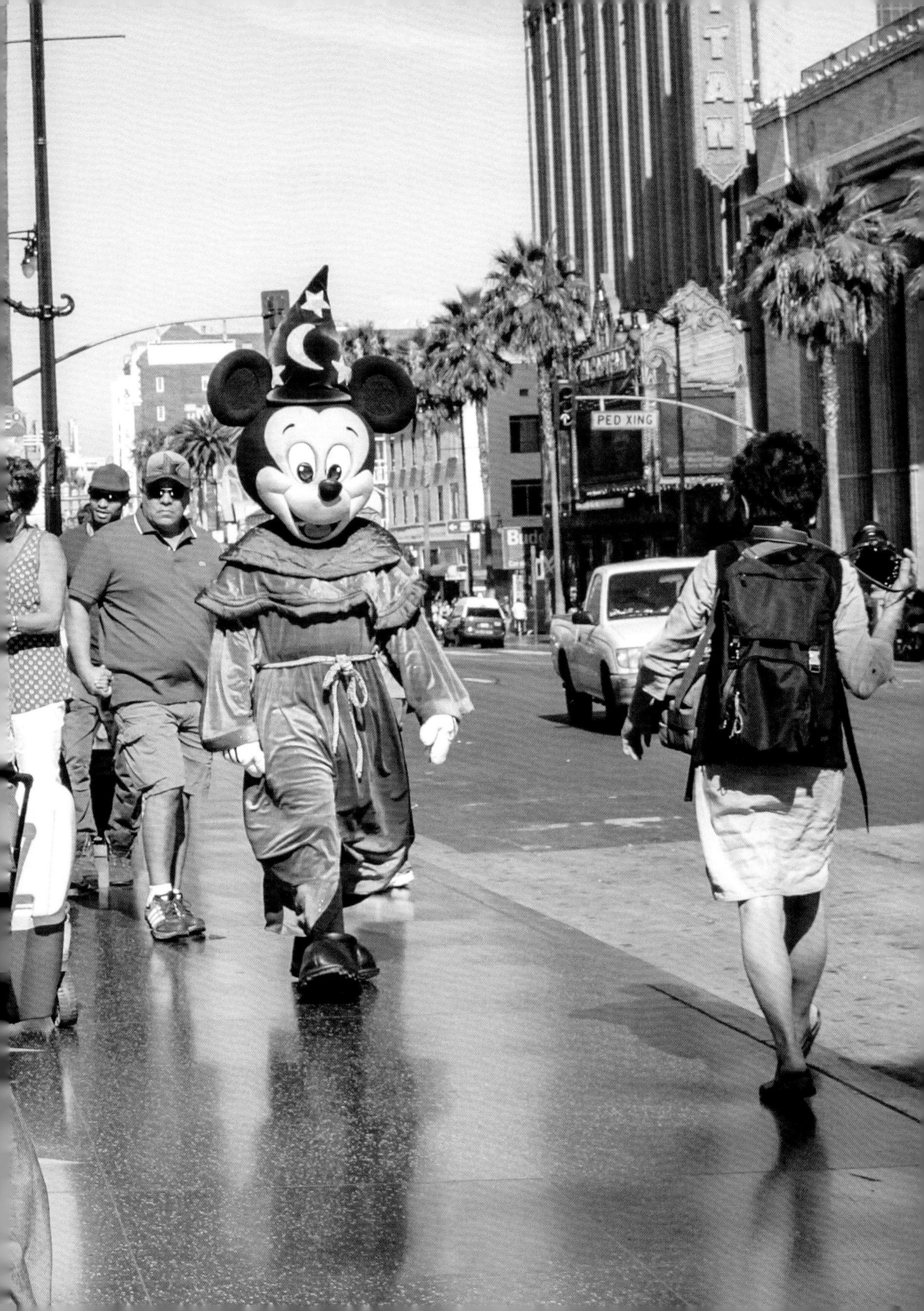
TAN
PED XING

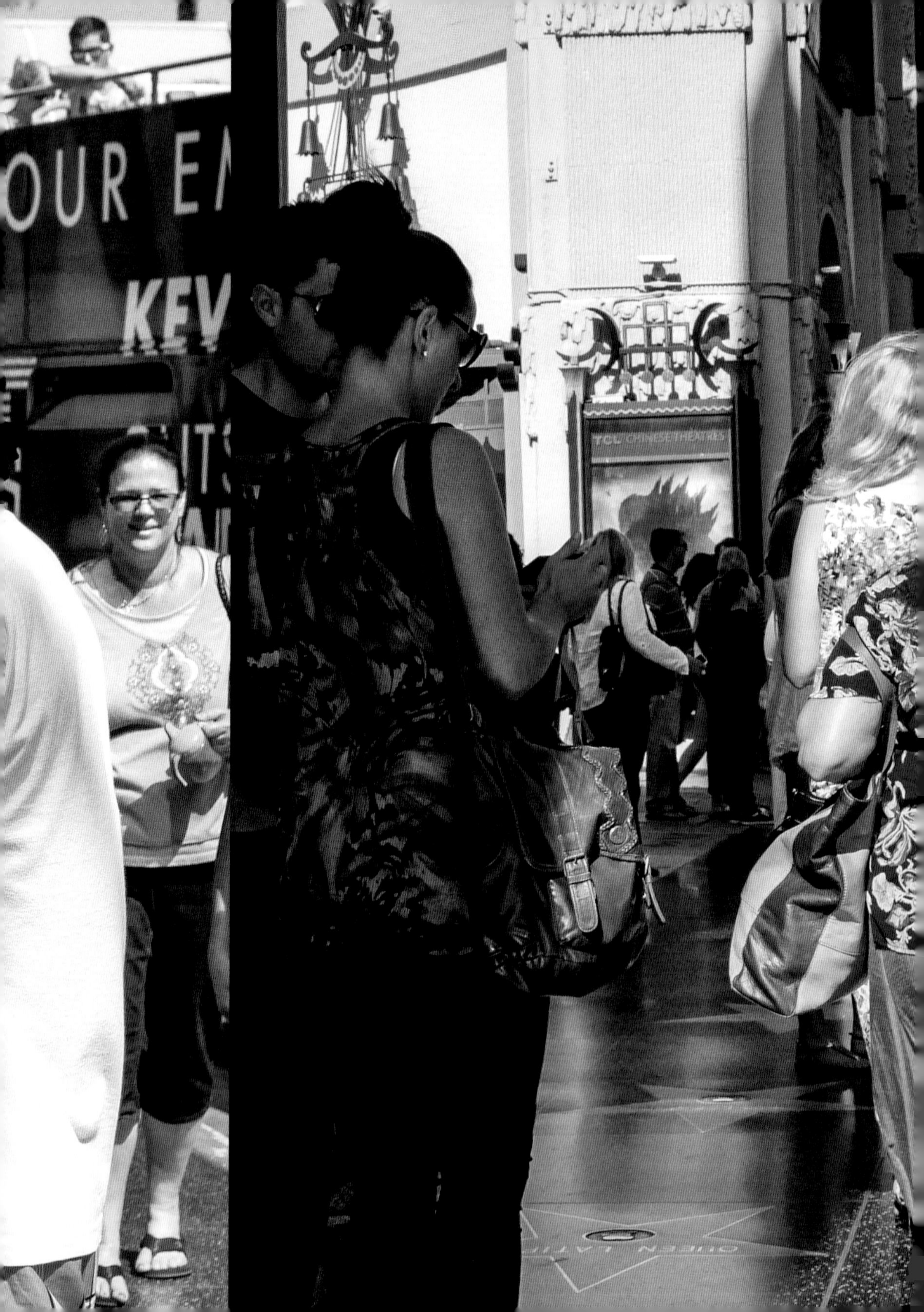
OUR EM
KEV
TCL CHINESE THEATRES

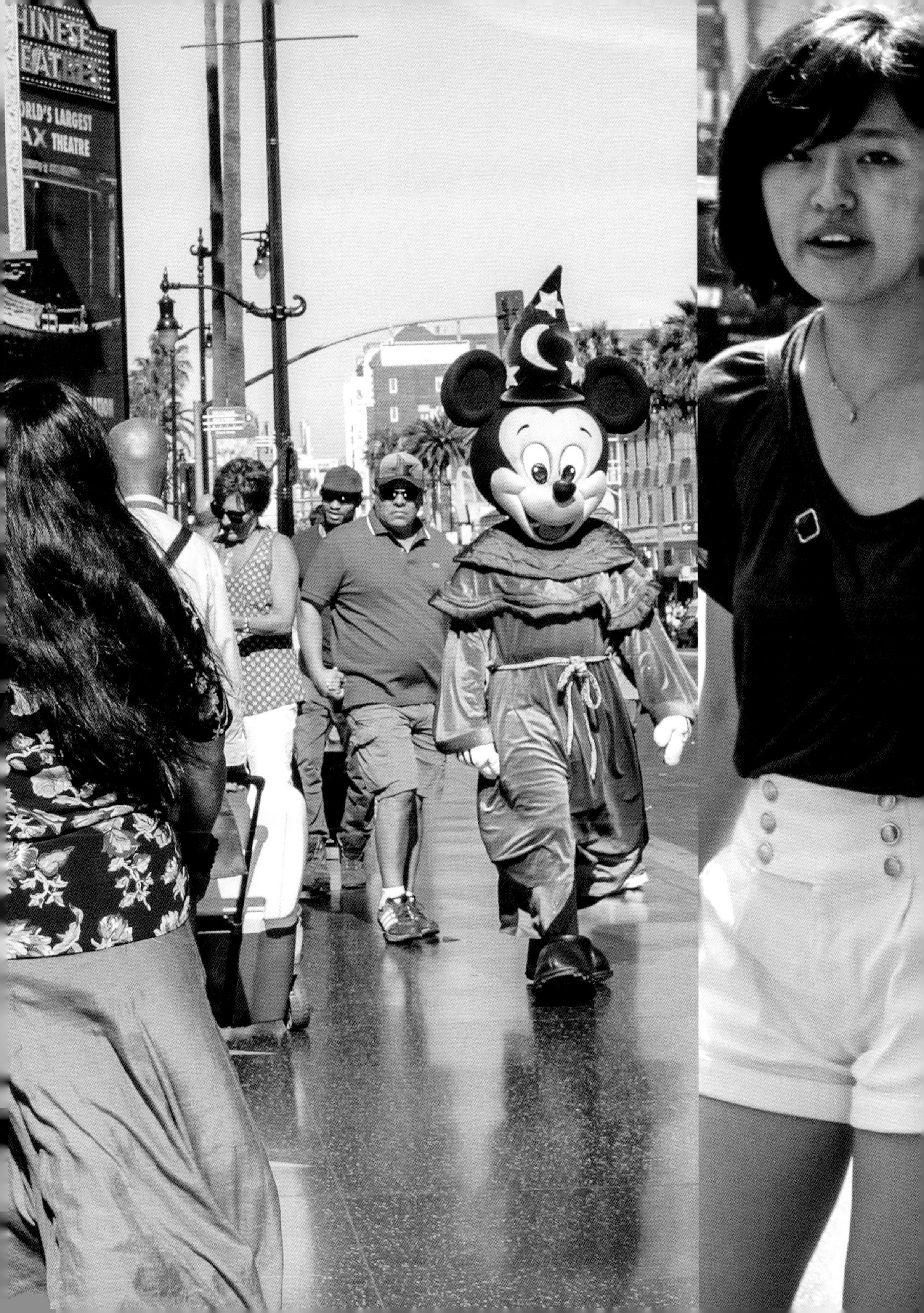

HINESE
EATRE
ORLD'S LARGEST
AX THEATRE

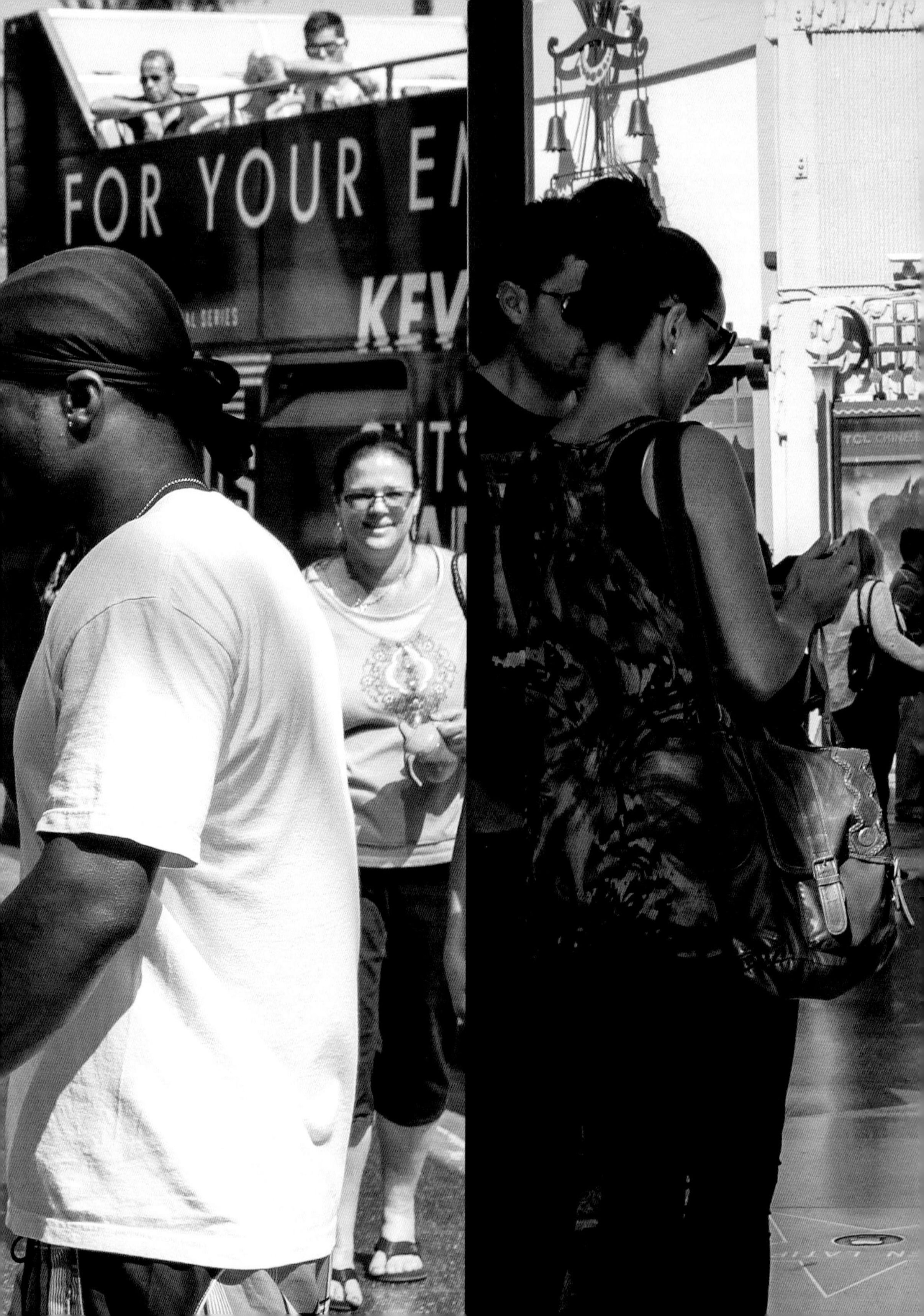

FOR YOUR E
KEV
TCL CHINESE

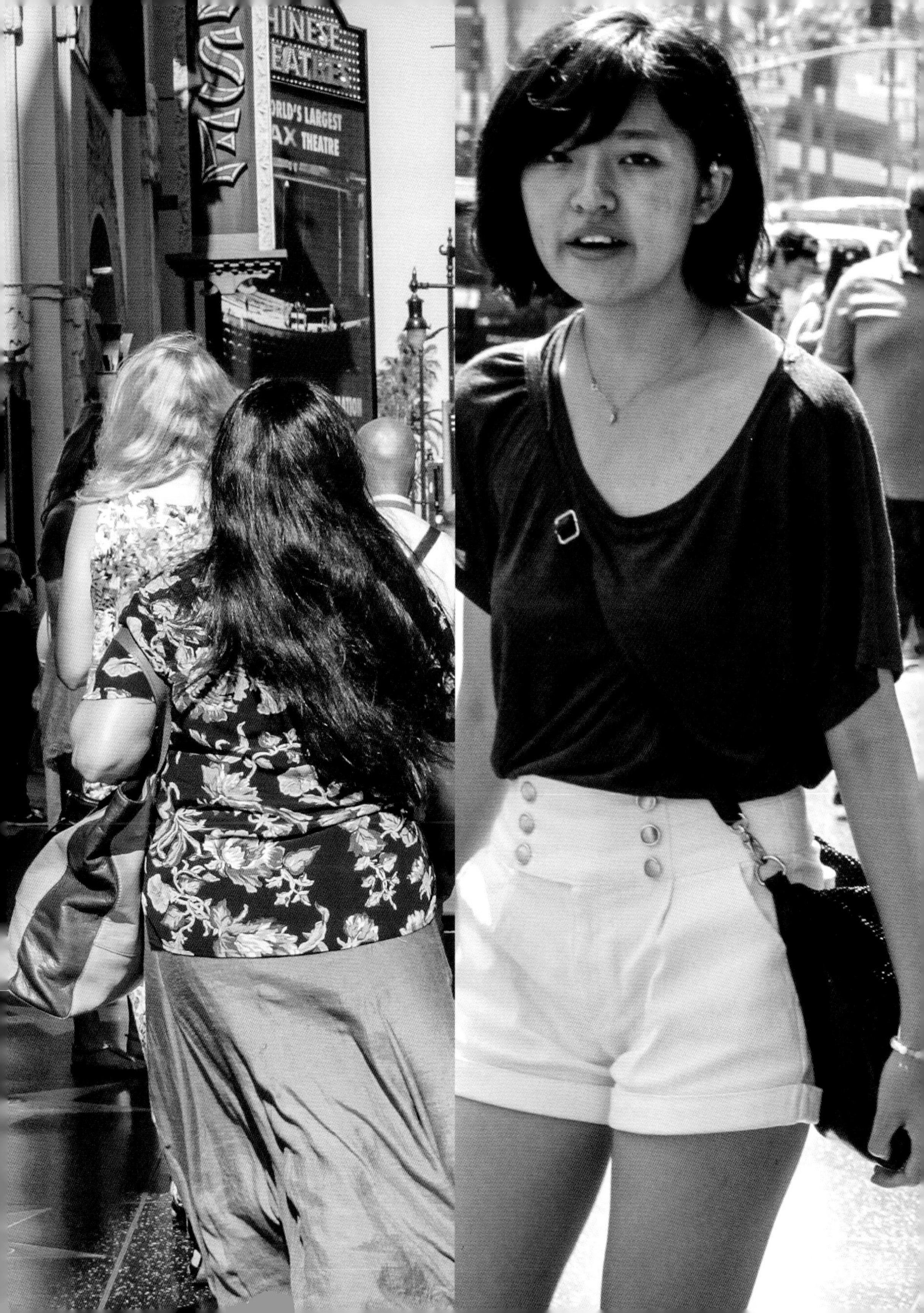

HINESE
HEAT
WORLD'S LARGEST
AX THEATRE

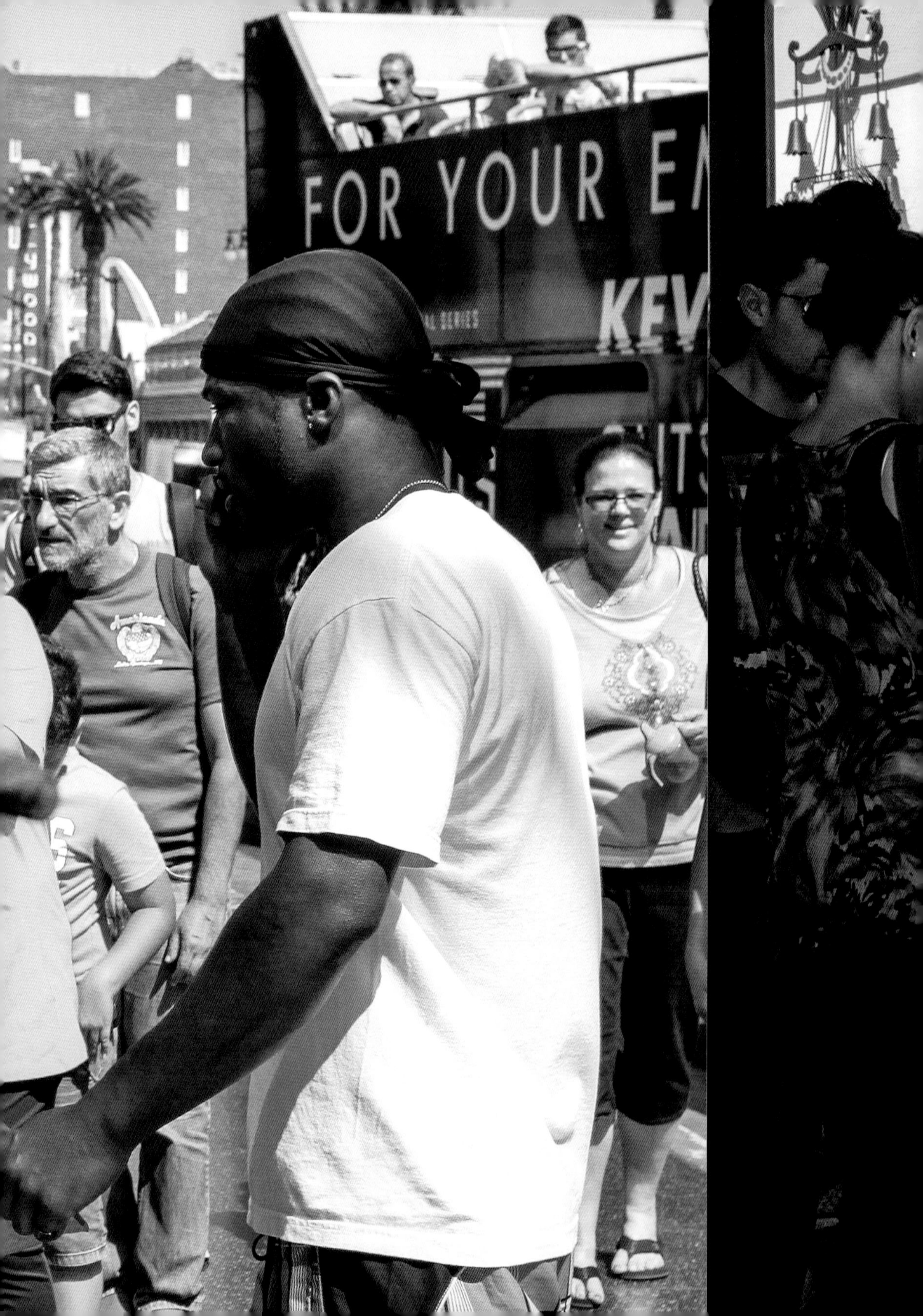

FOR YOUR E
KEV

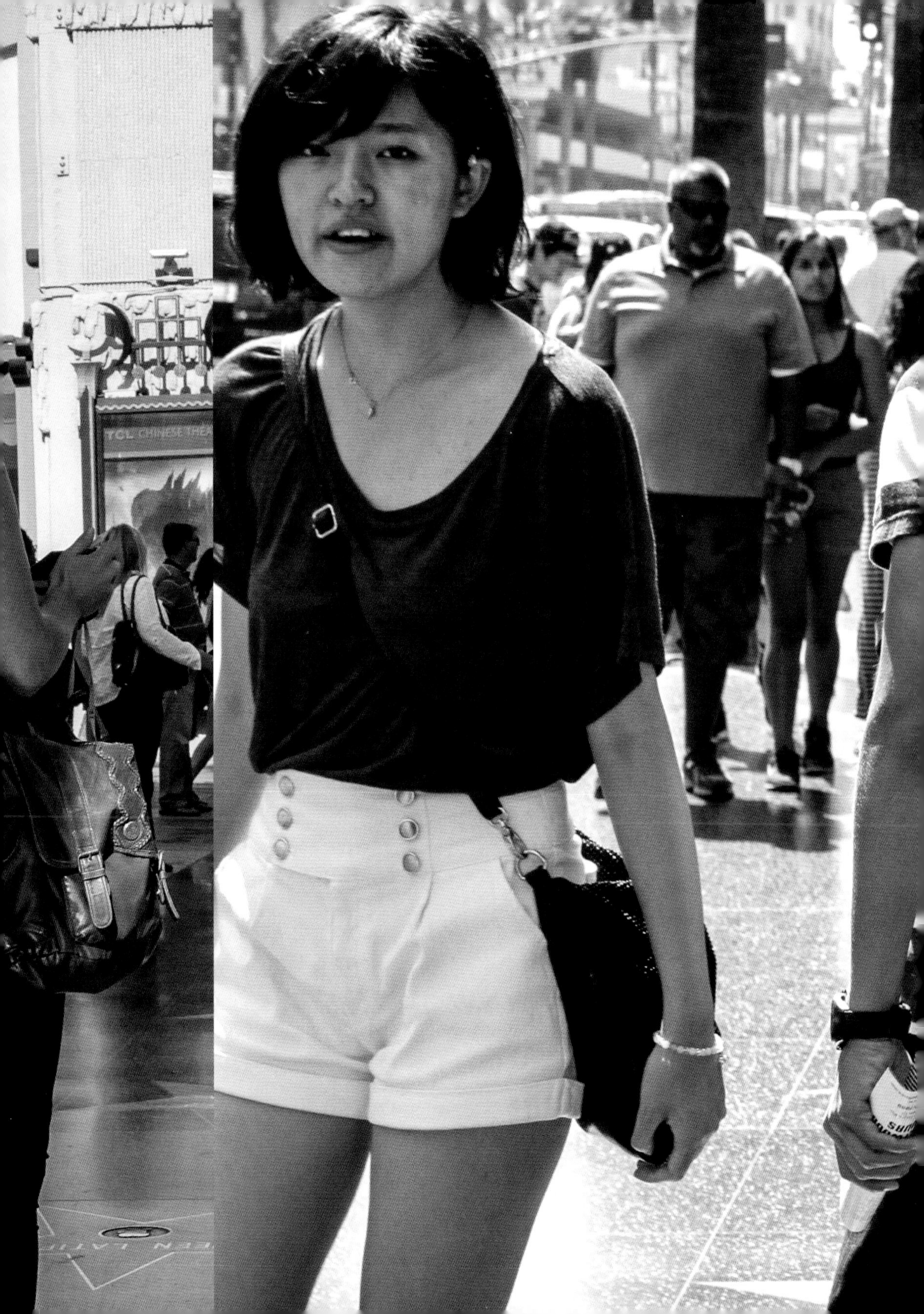

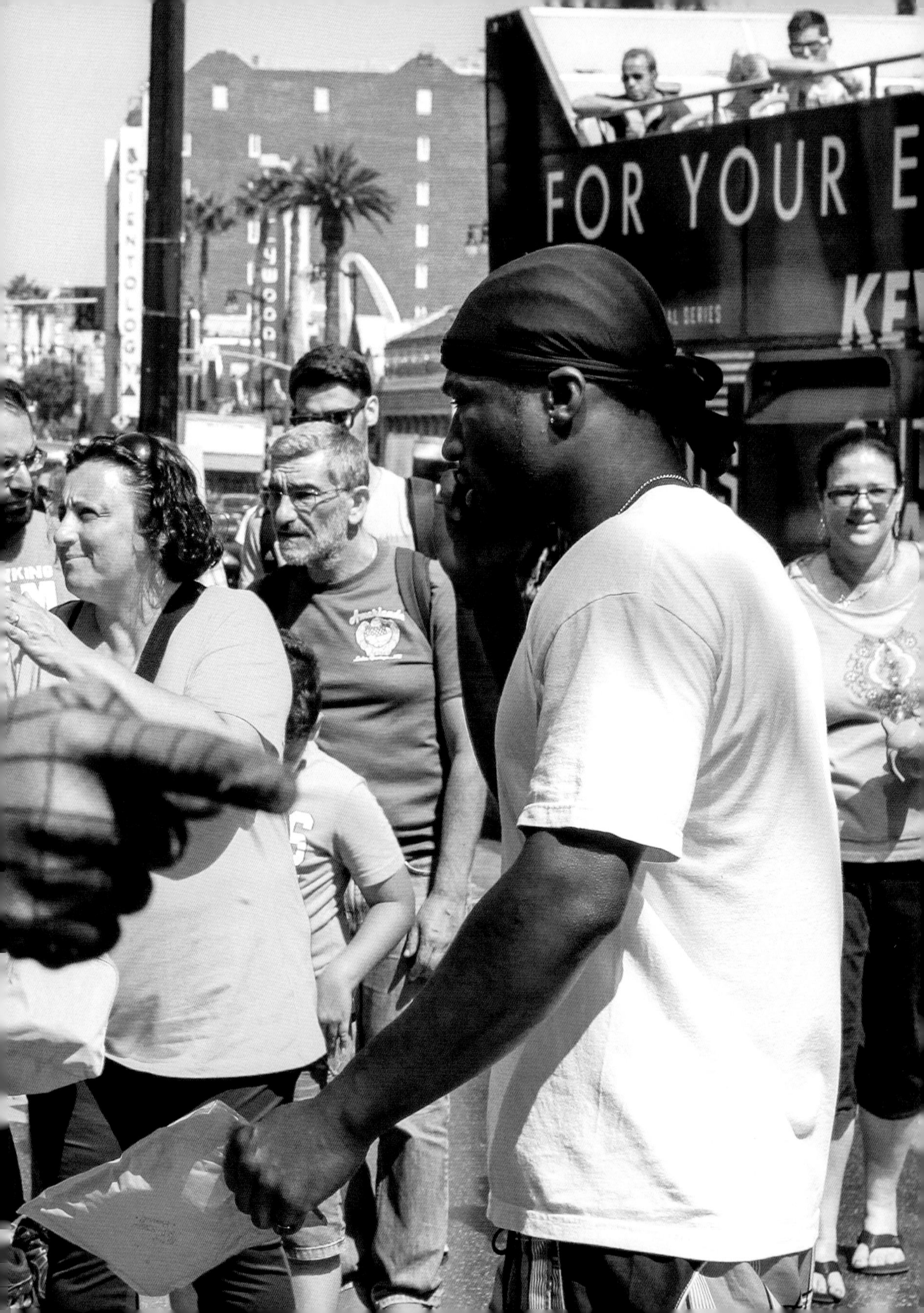

FOR YOUR E
KE

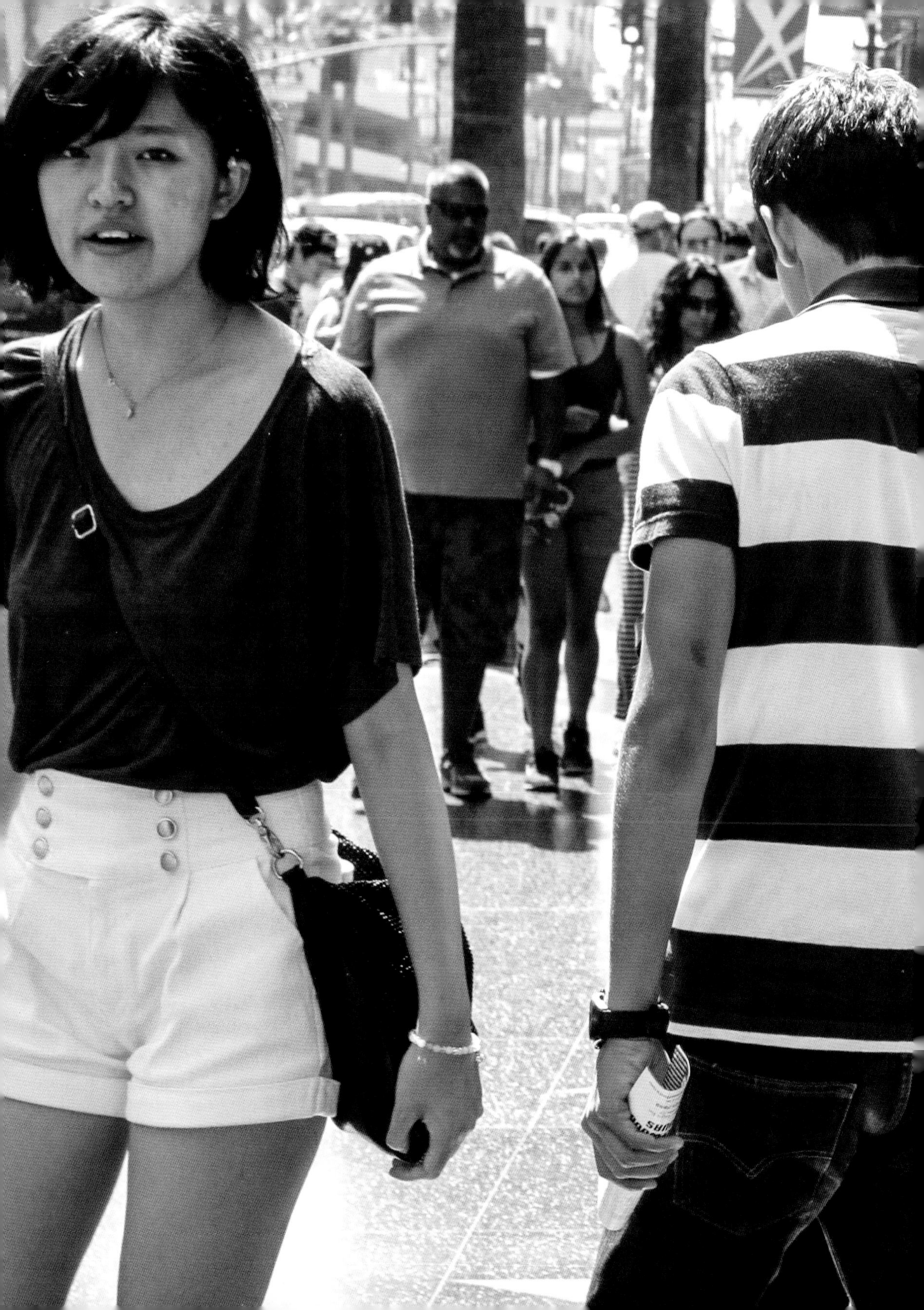

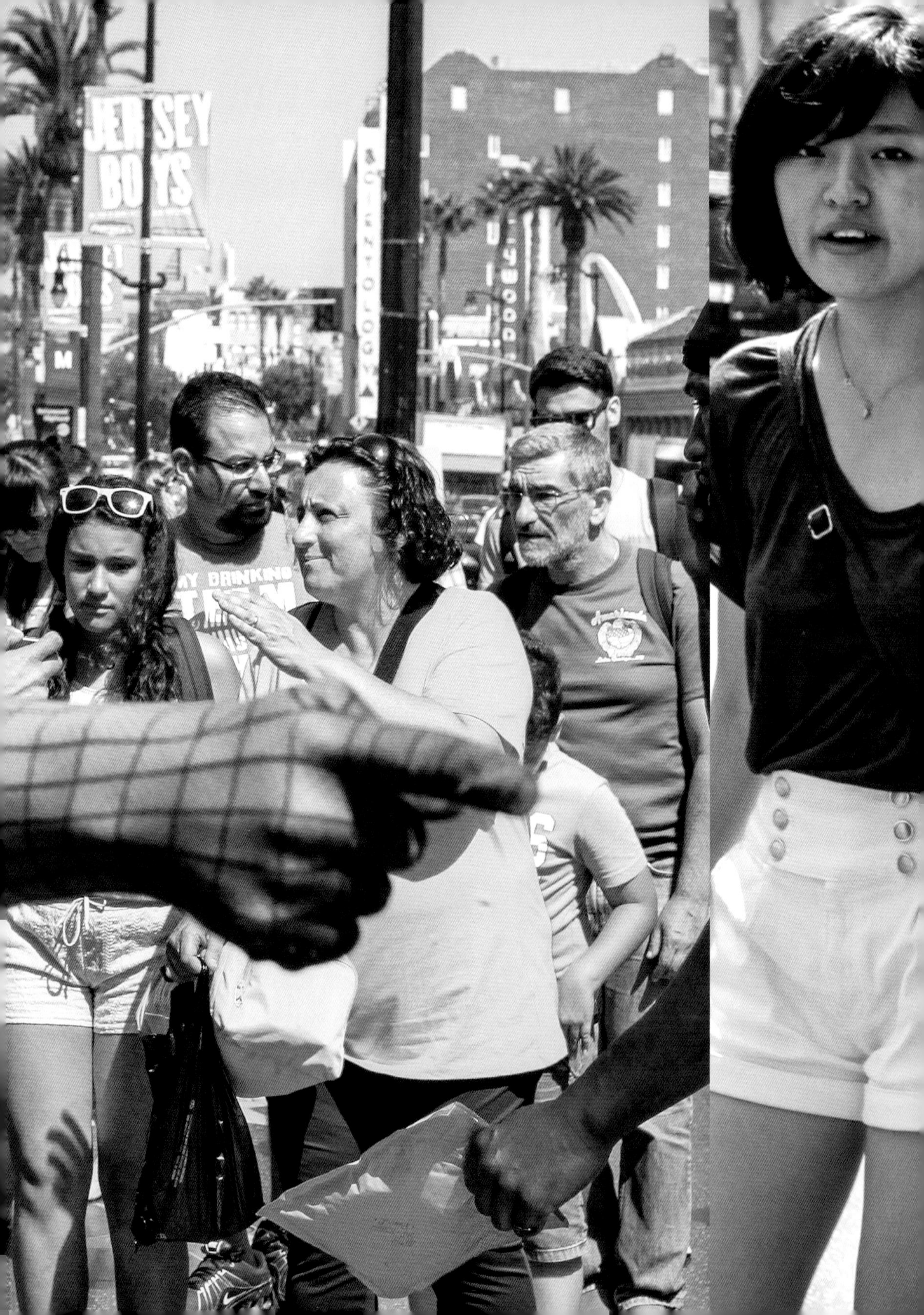
JER SEY
BO TS
SCIENTOLOGY
MY DRINKING
TEAM

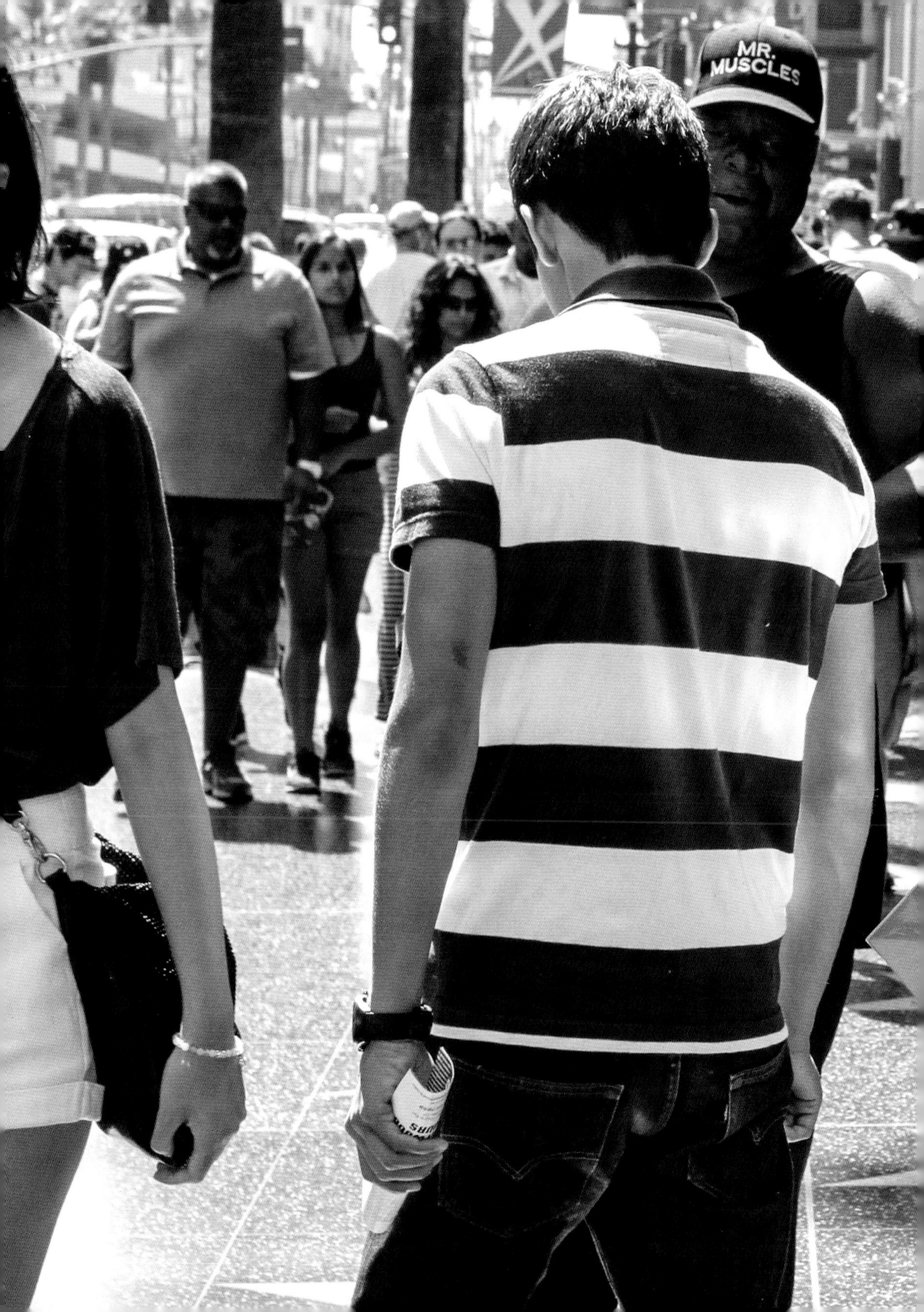

MR.
MUSCLES
MR.
MUSCLES

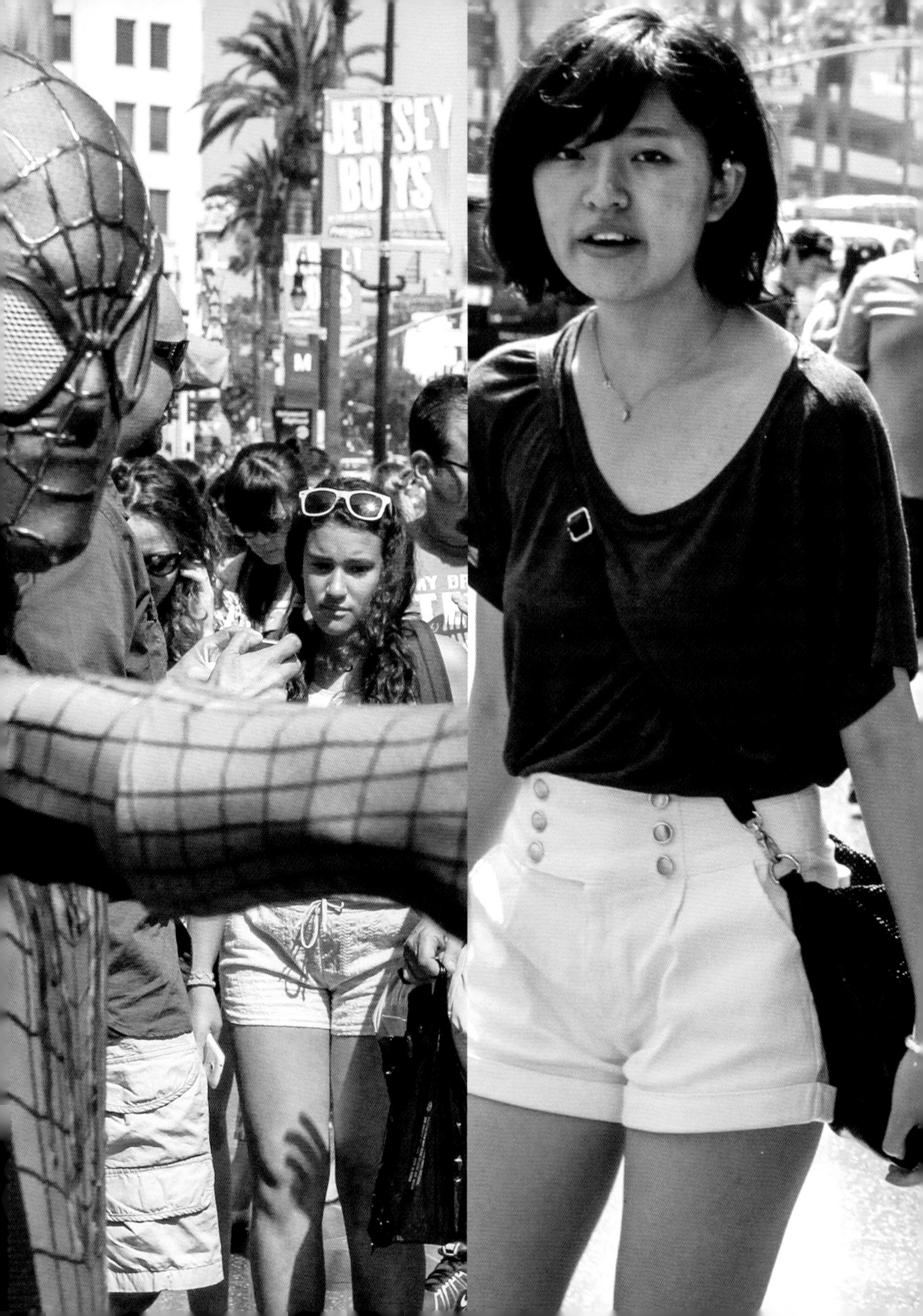

JERSEY
BOYS

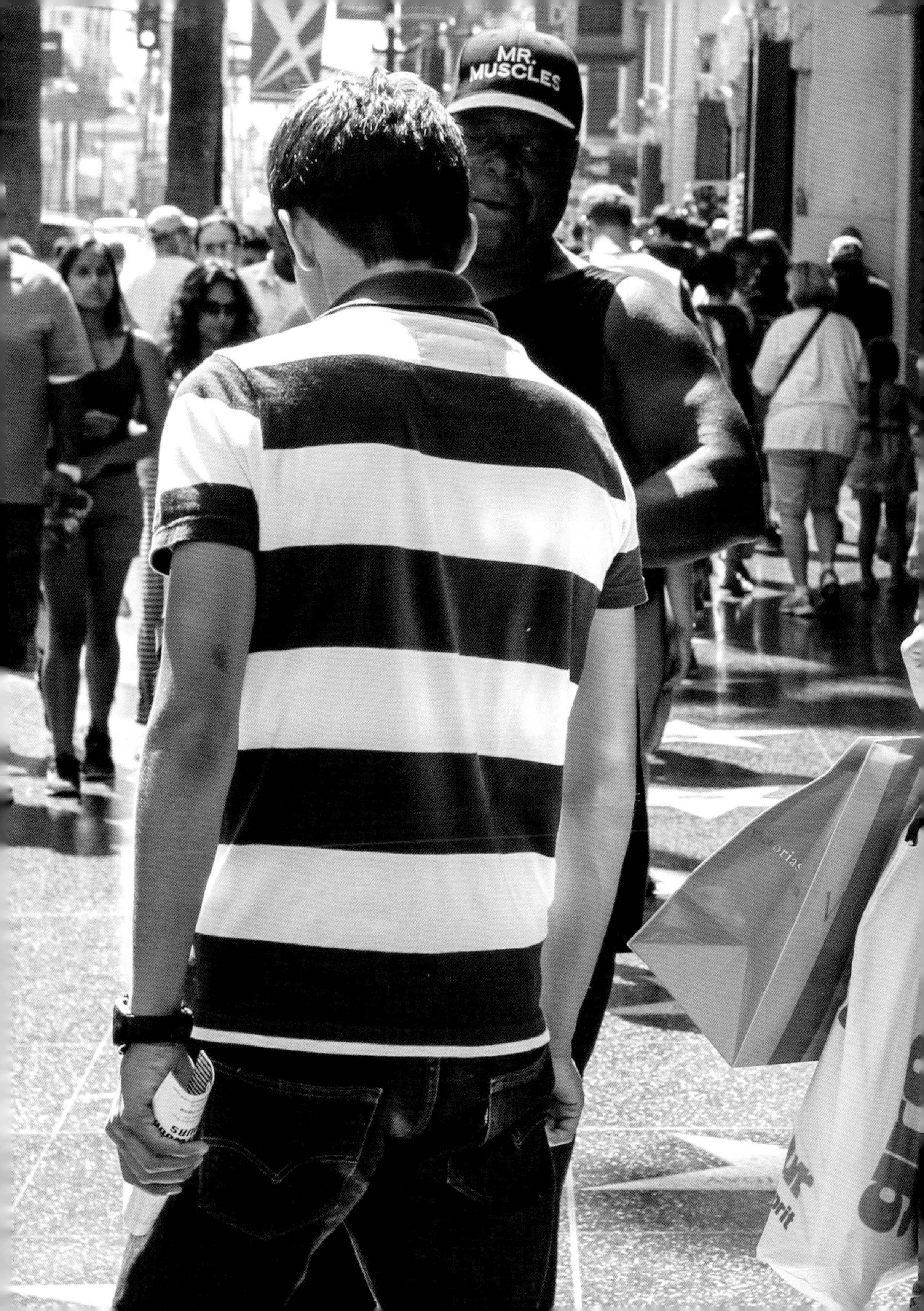

MR.
MUSCLES

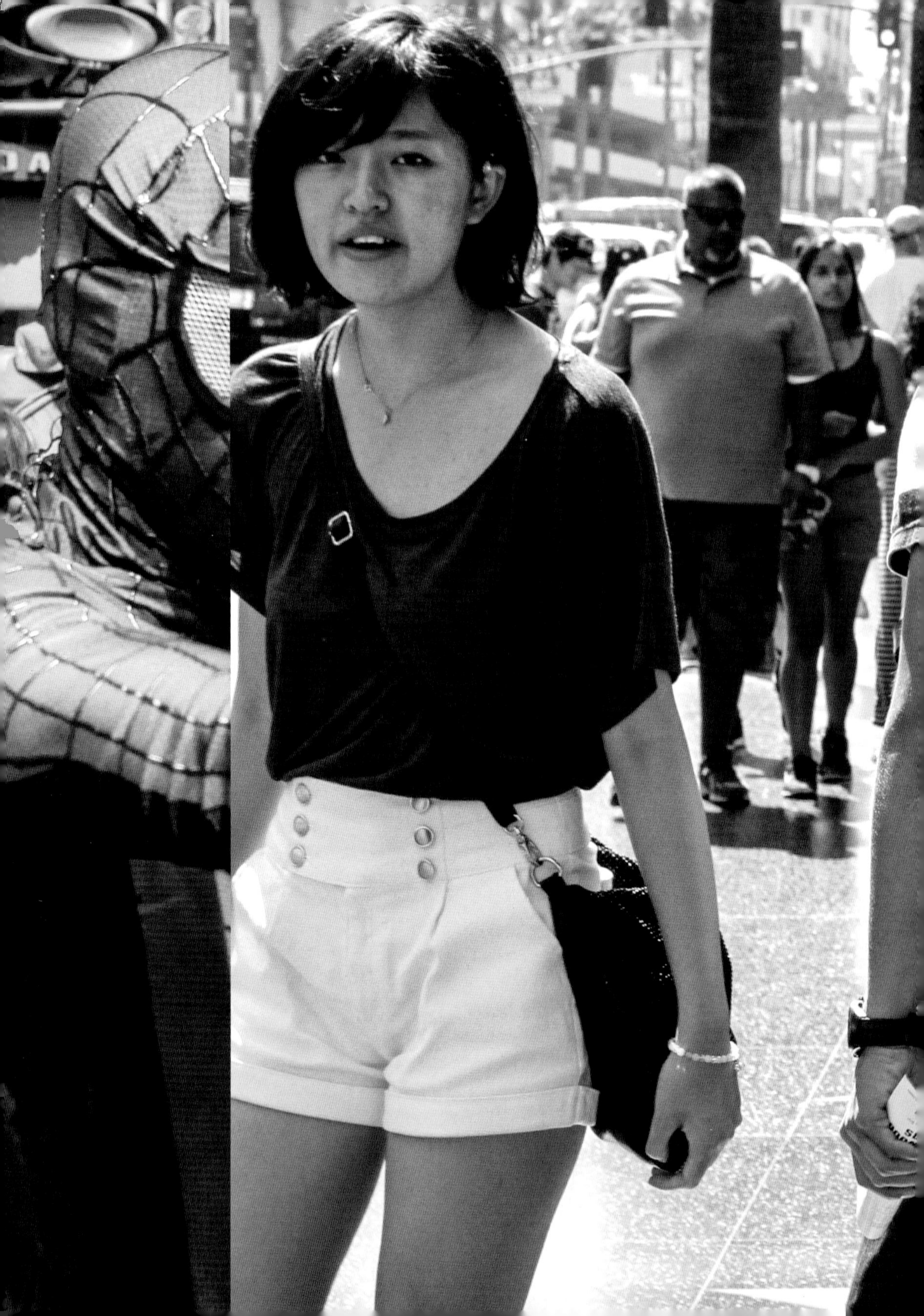

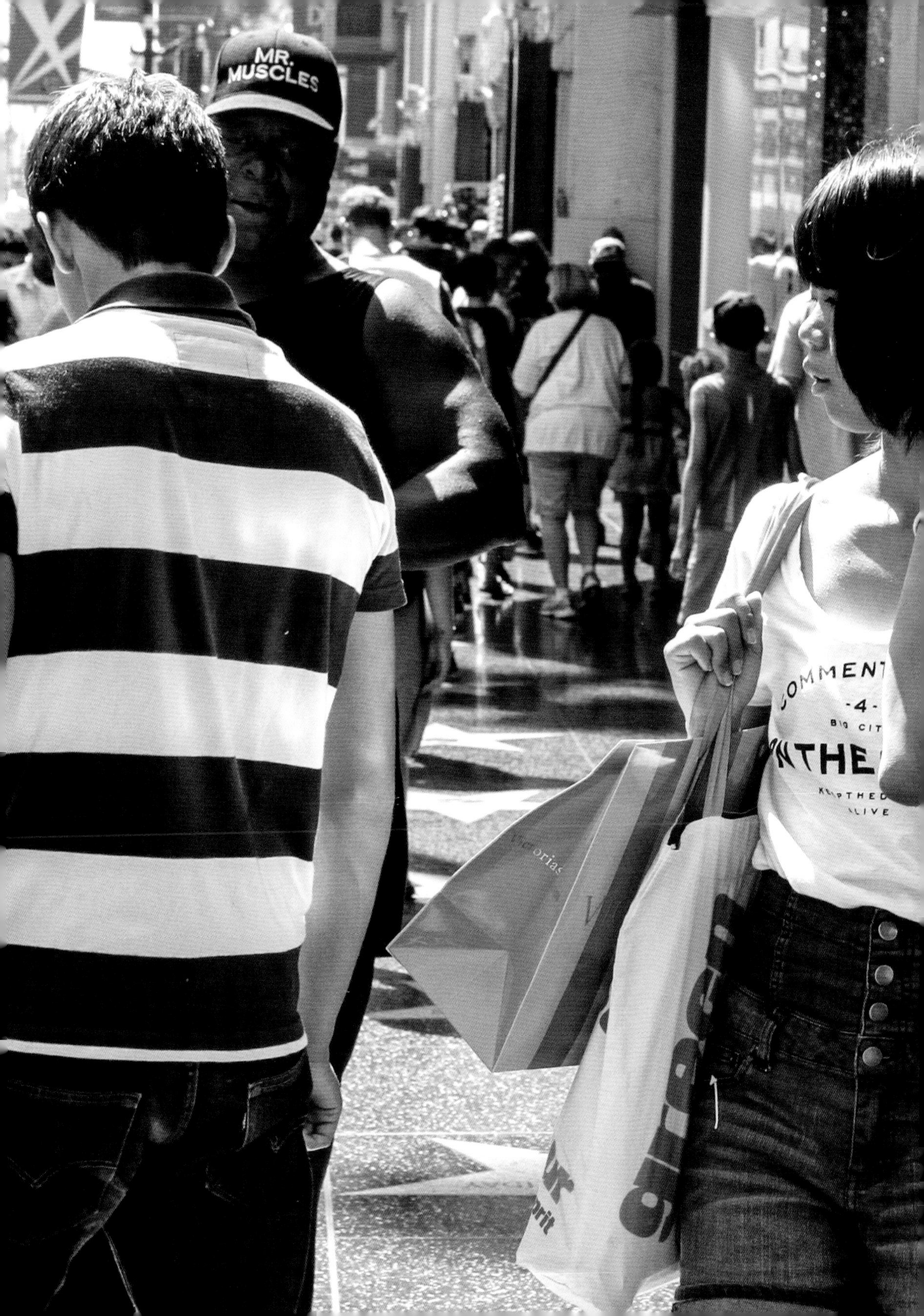

MR.
MUSCLES

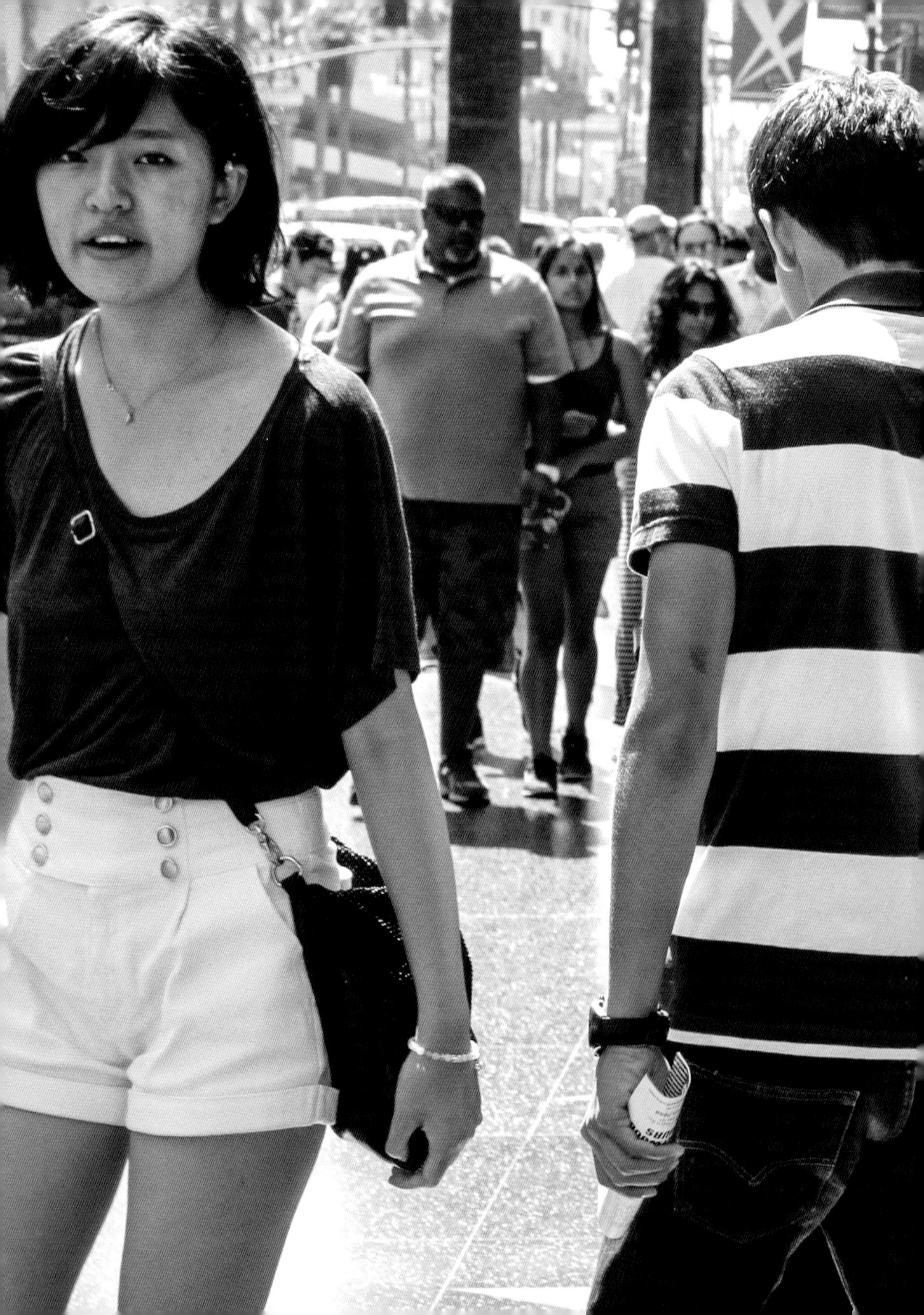

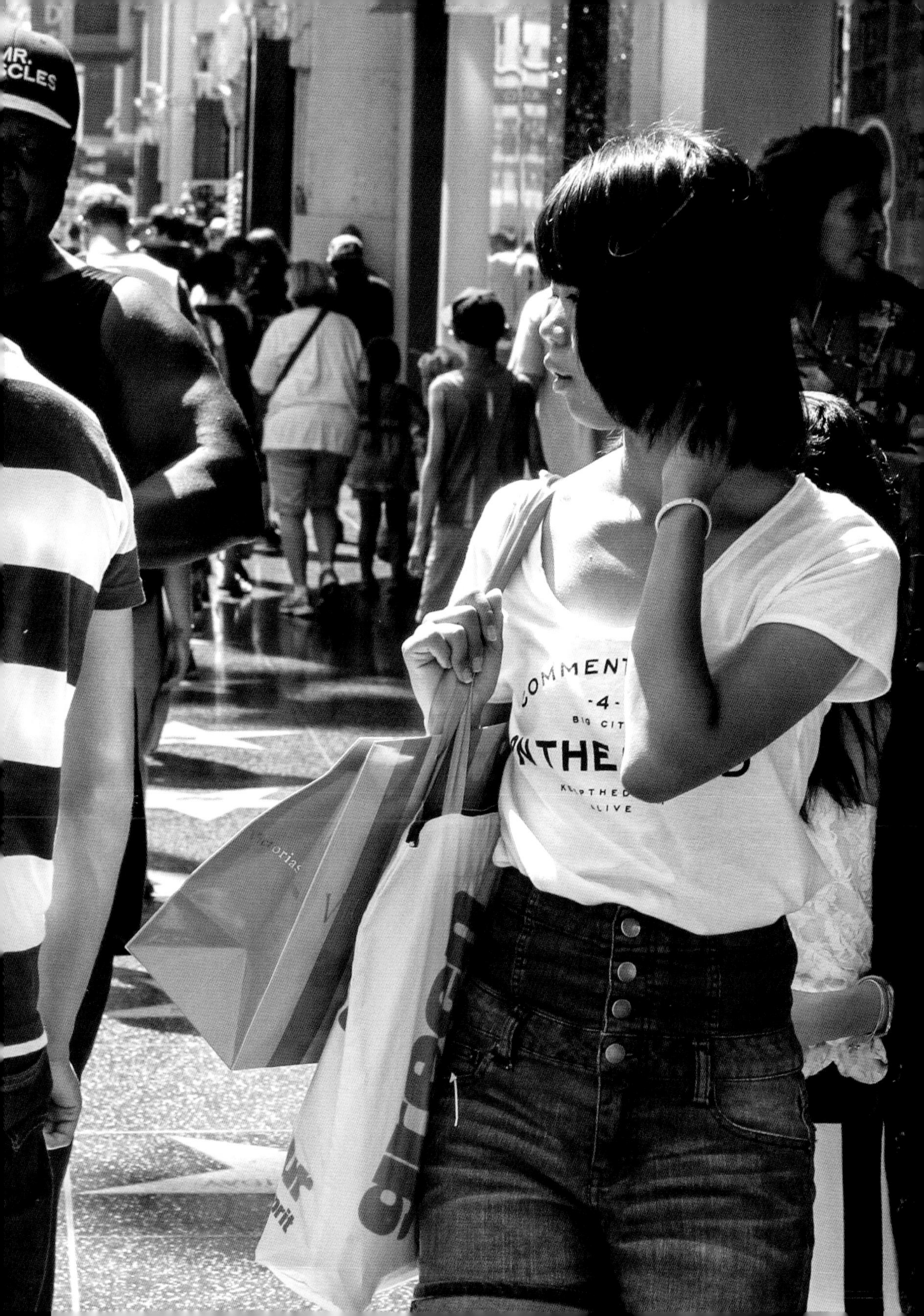

MR.
CLES
COMMENT
-4-
Big CIT
N THE
KEEP THE D
ALIVE

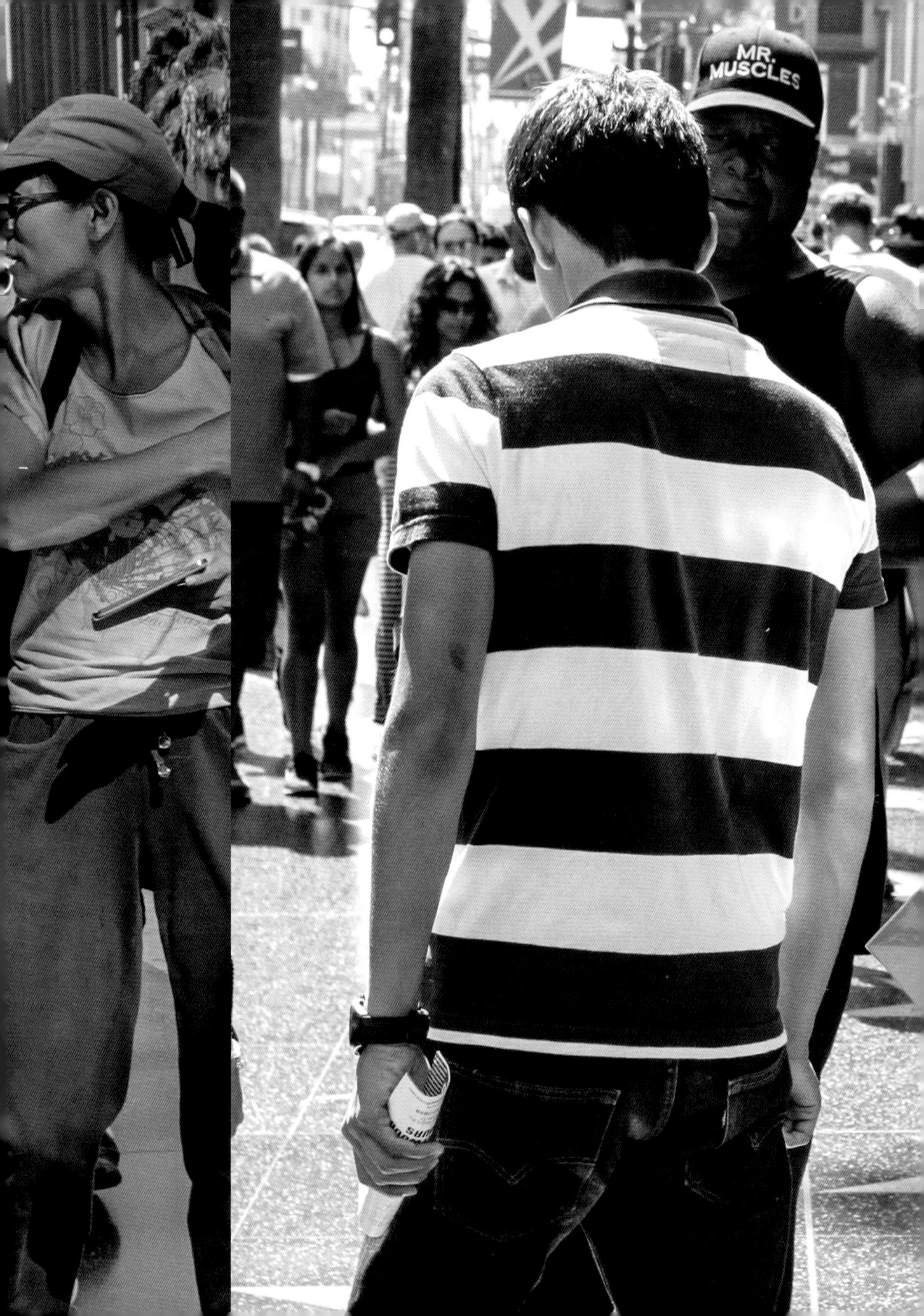

MR.
MUSCLES

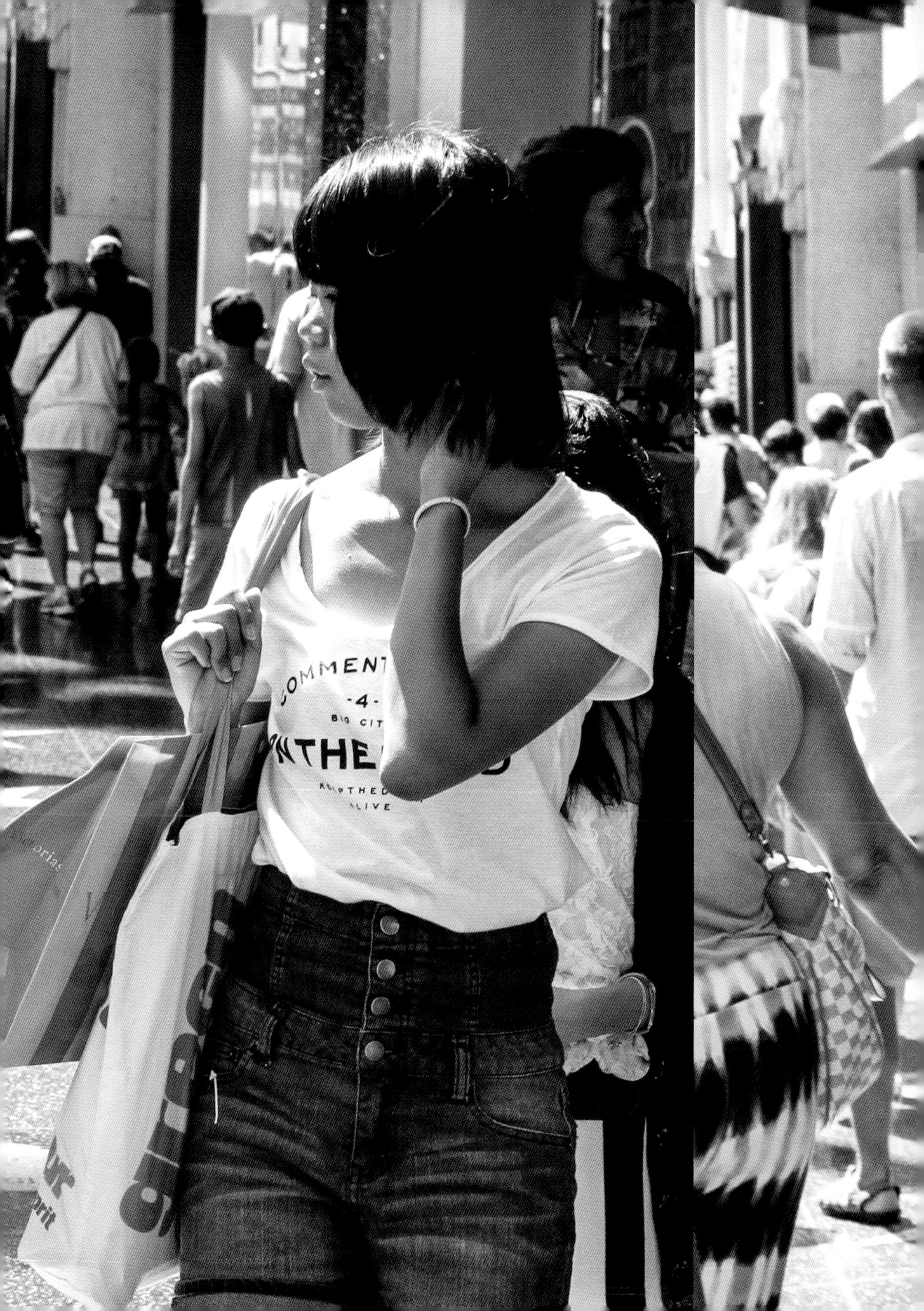

COMMENT
-4-
BiG CITY
N THE
KEEP THE
ALIVE

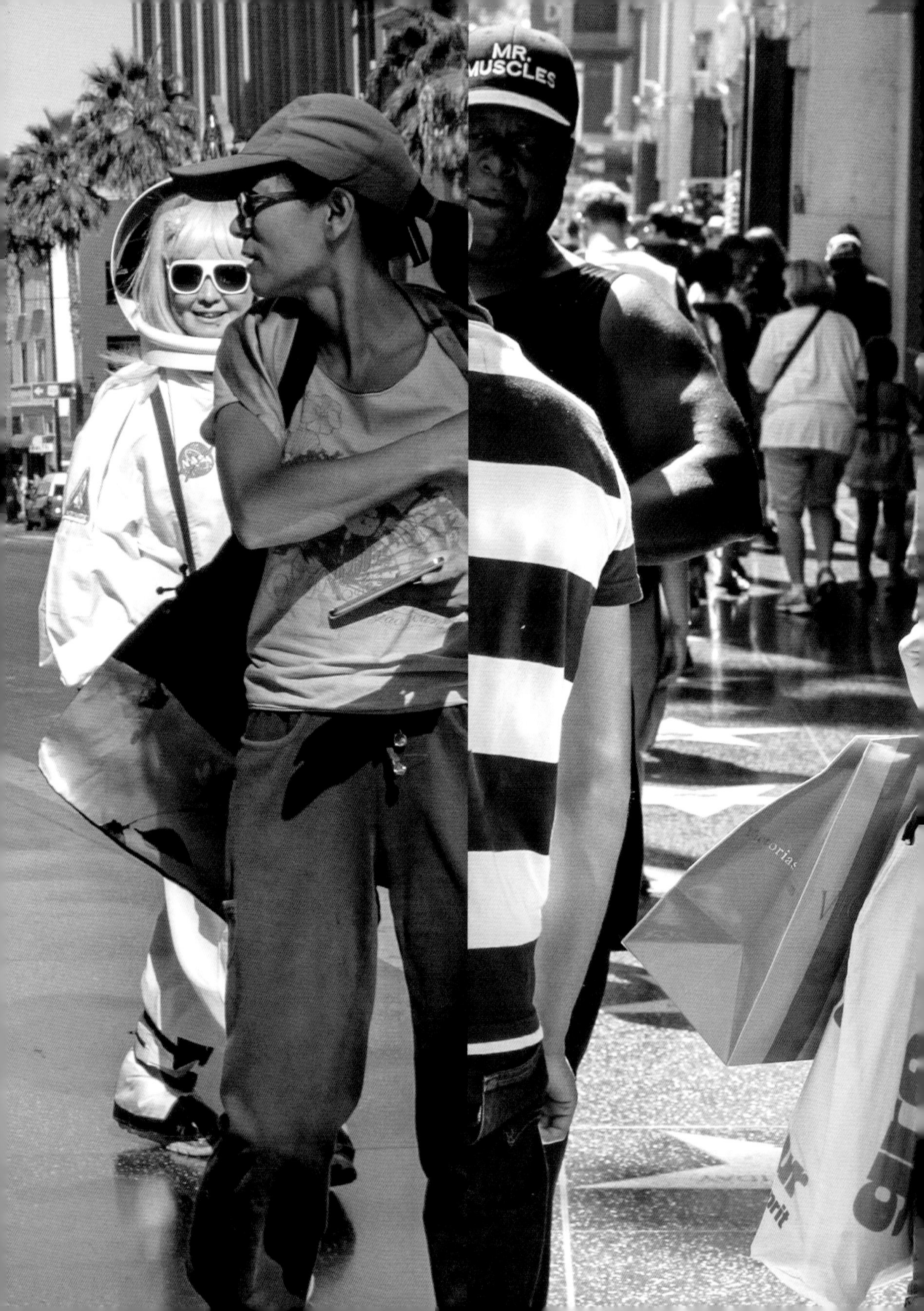

MR.
MUSCLES
MR.
MUSCLES

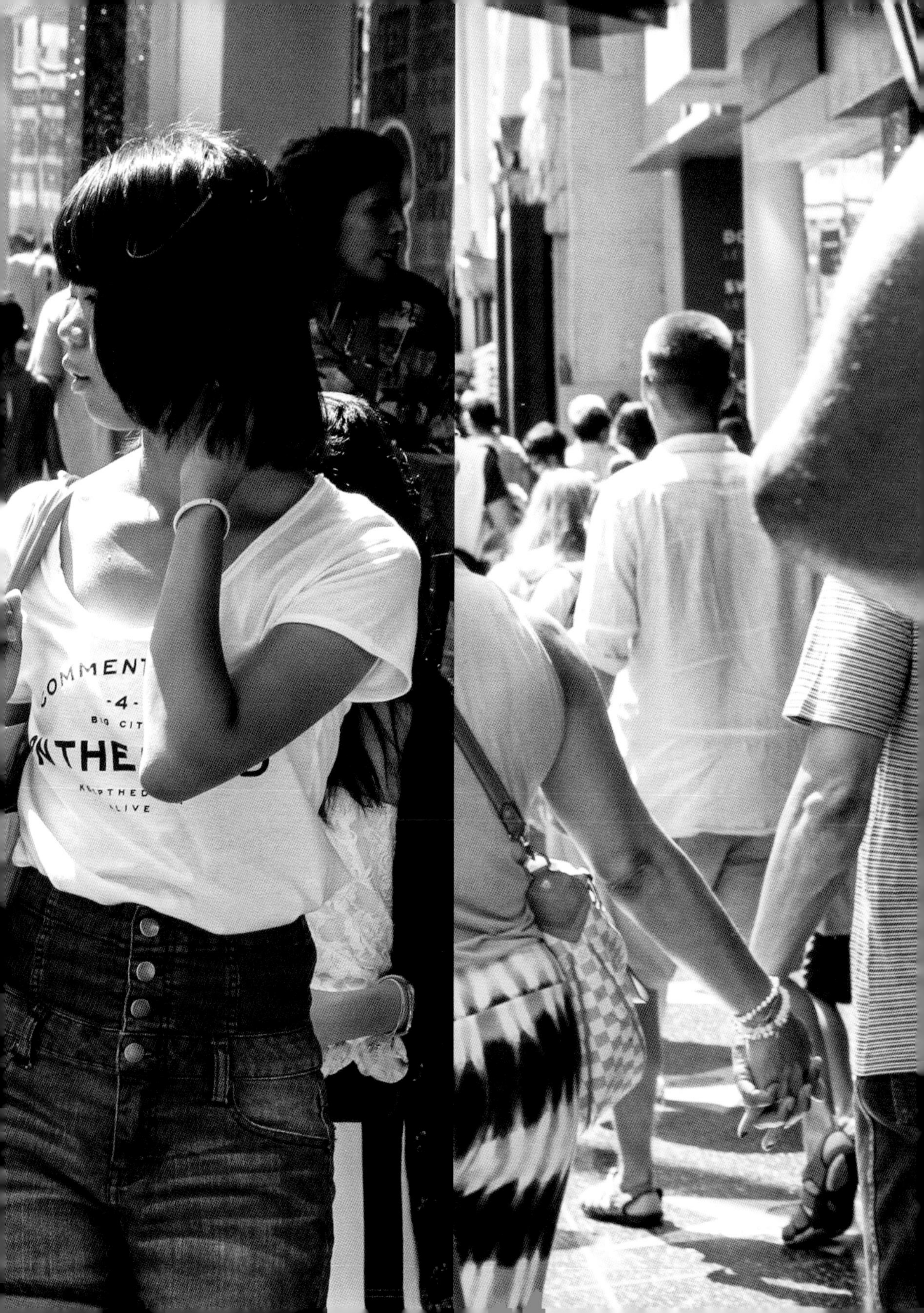

COMMENT
-4-
Big CIT
ON THE
KEEP THE
ALIVE

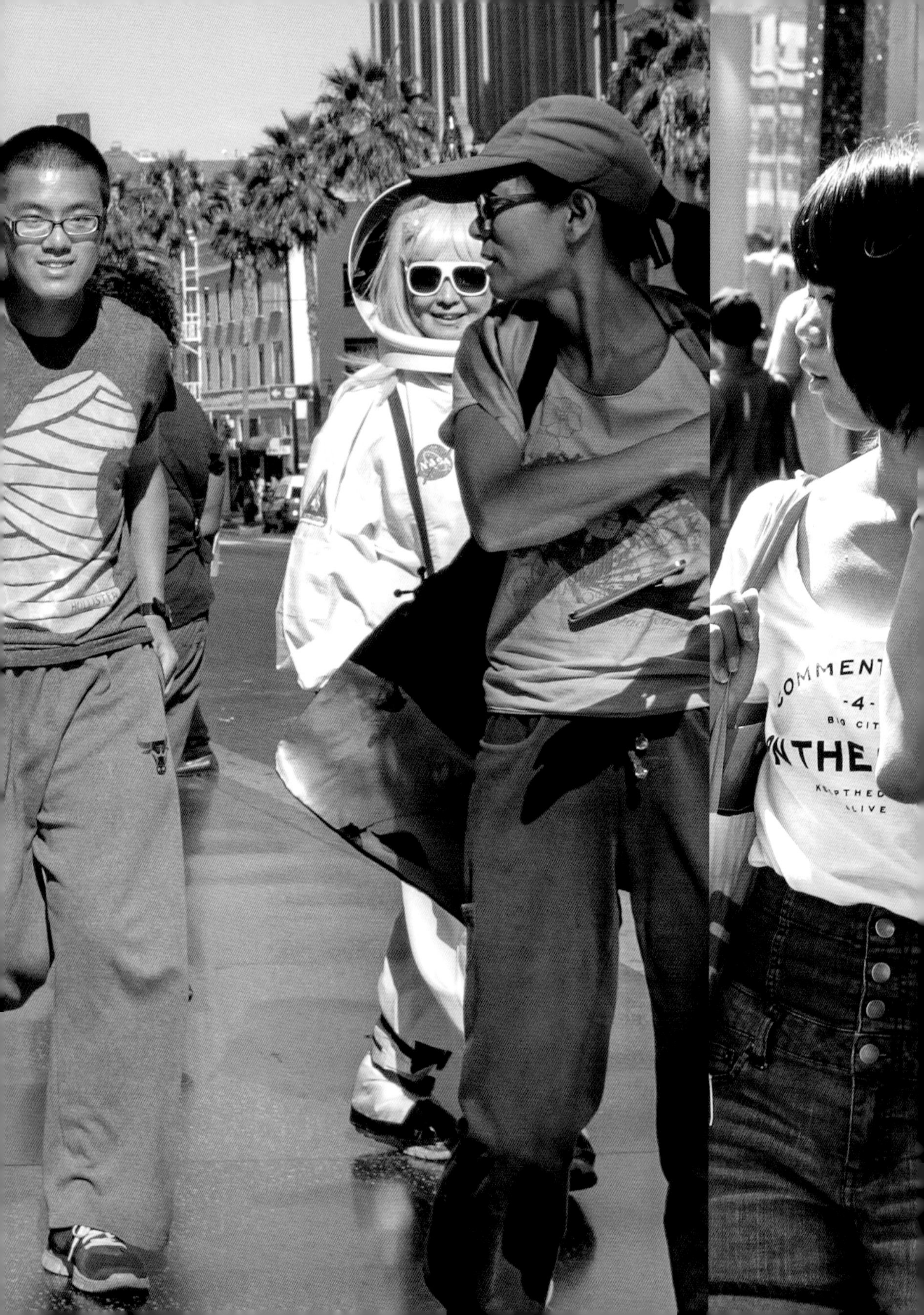

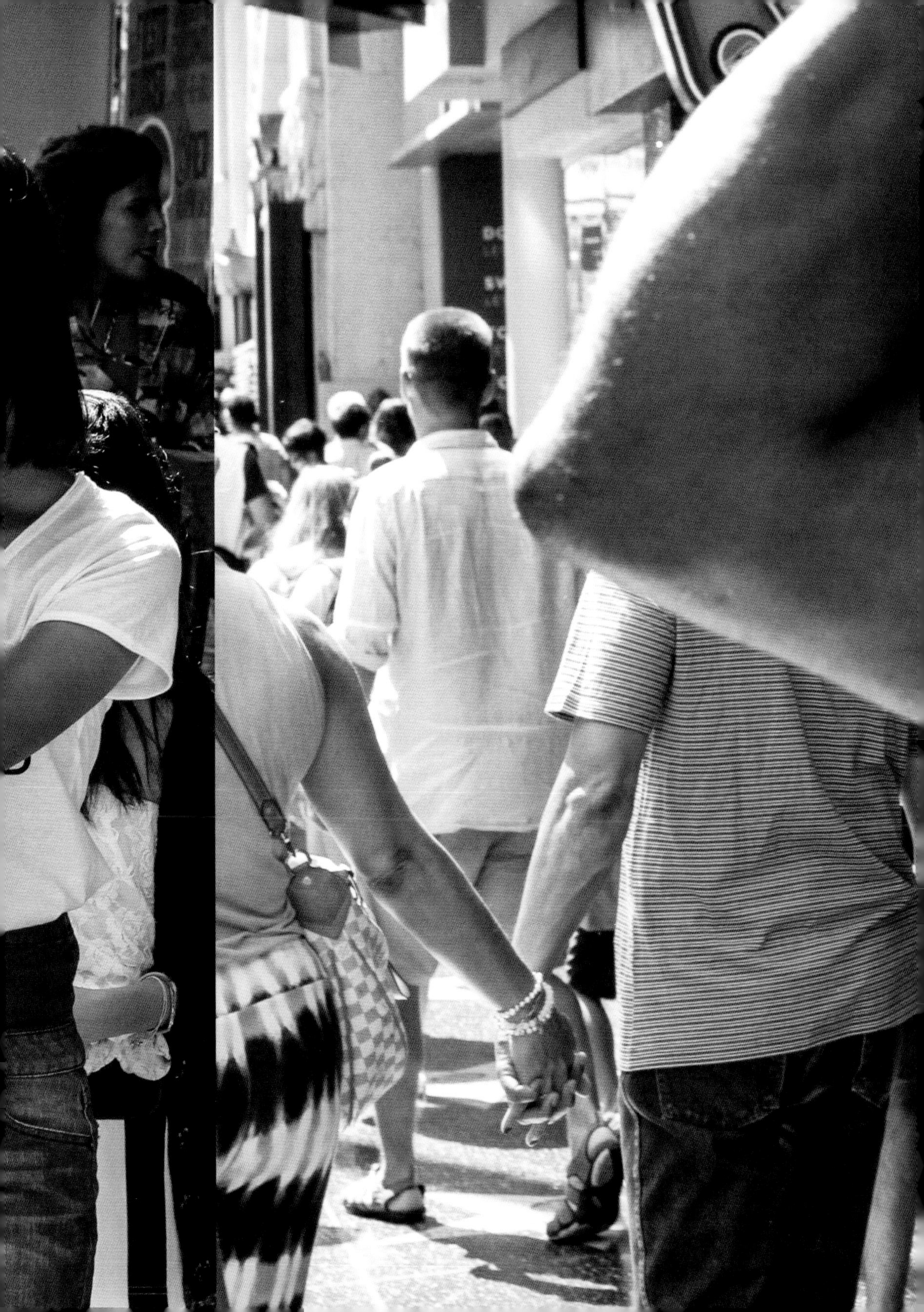

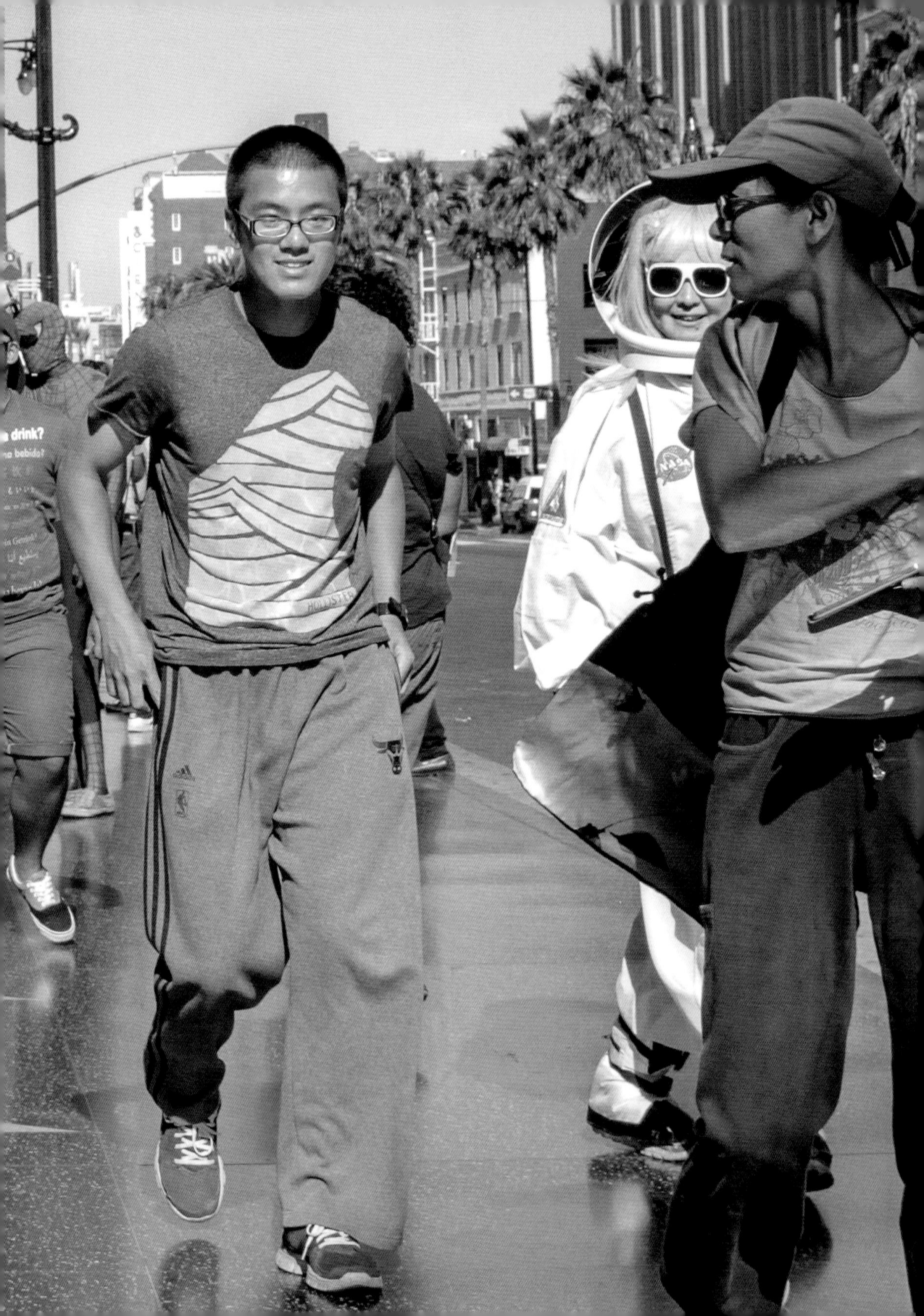

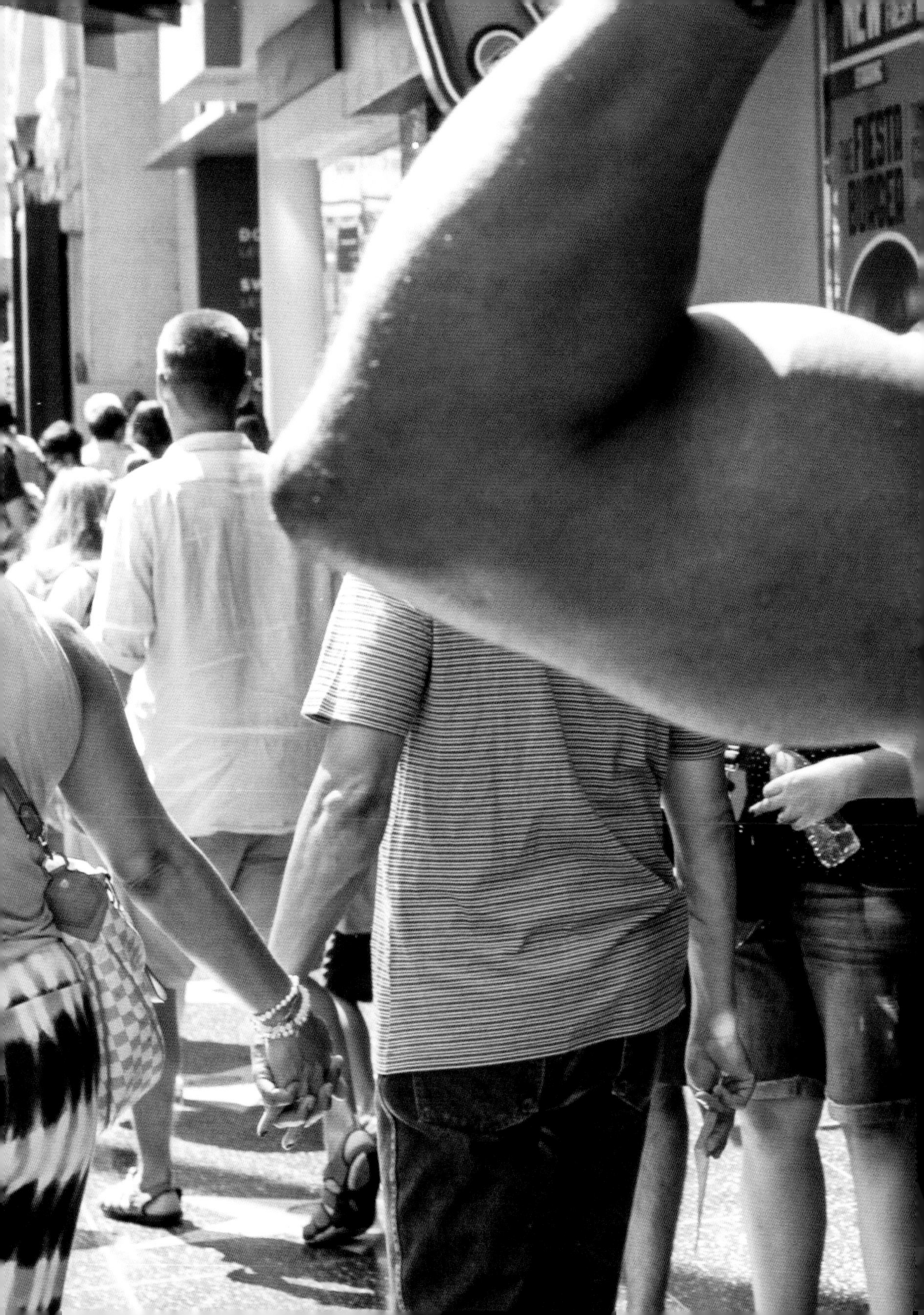

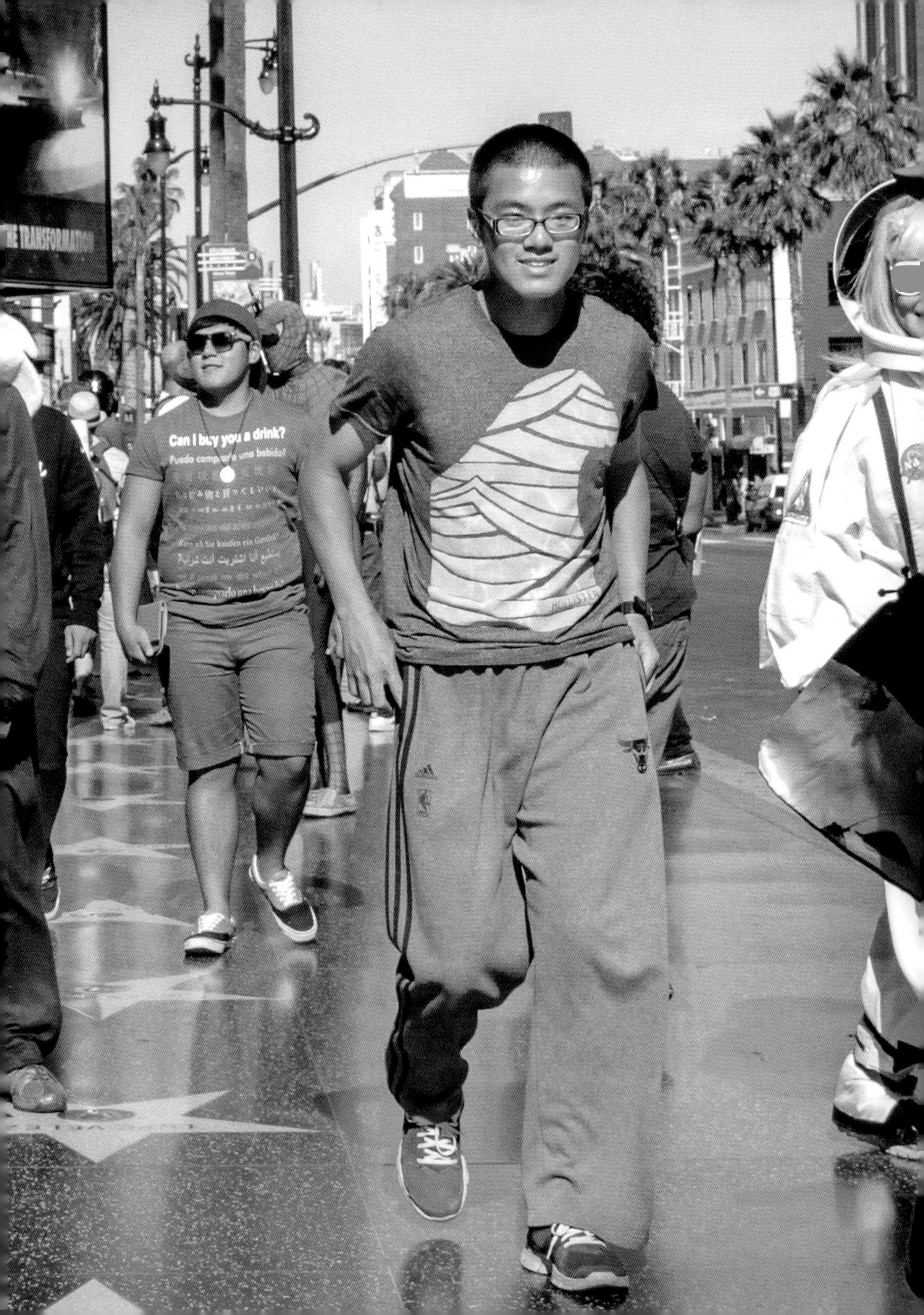
Can I buy you a drink?
Puedo comprarte una bebida?

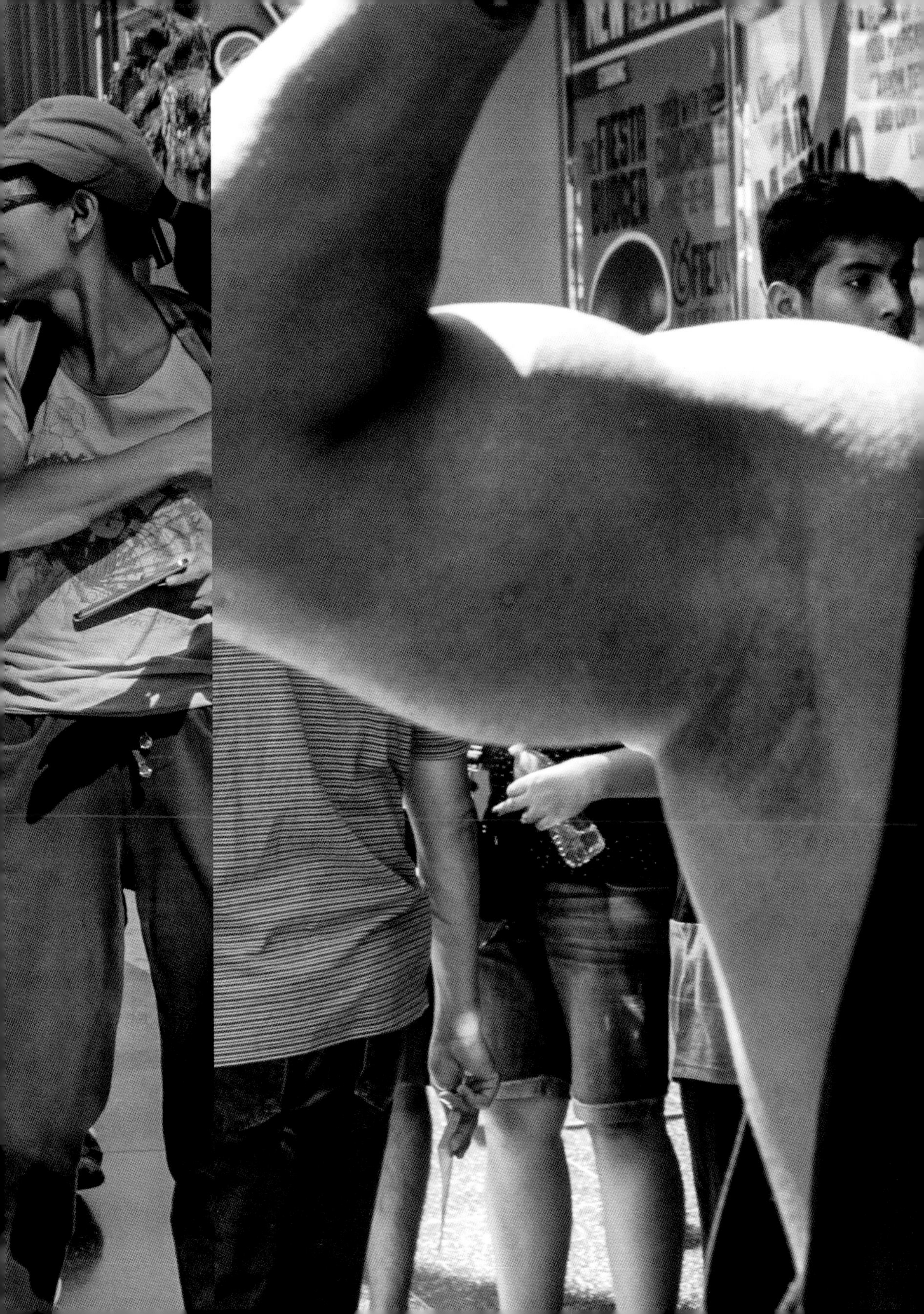

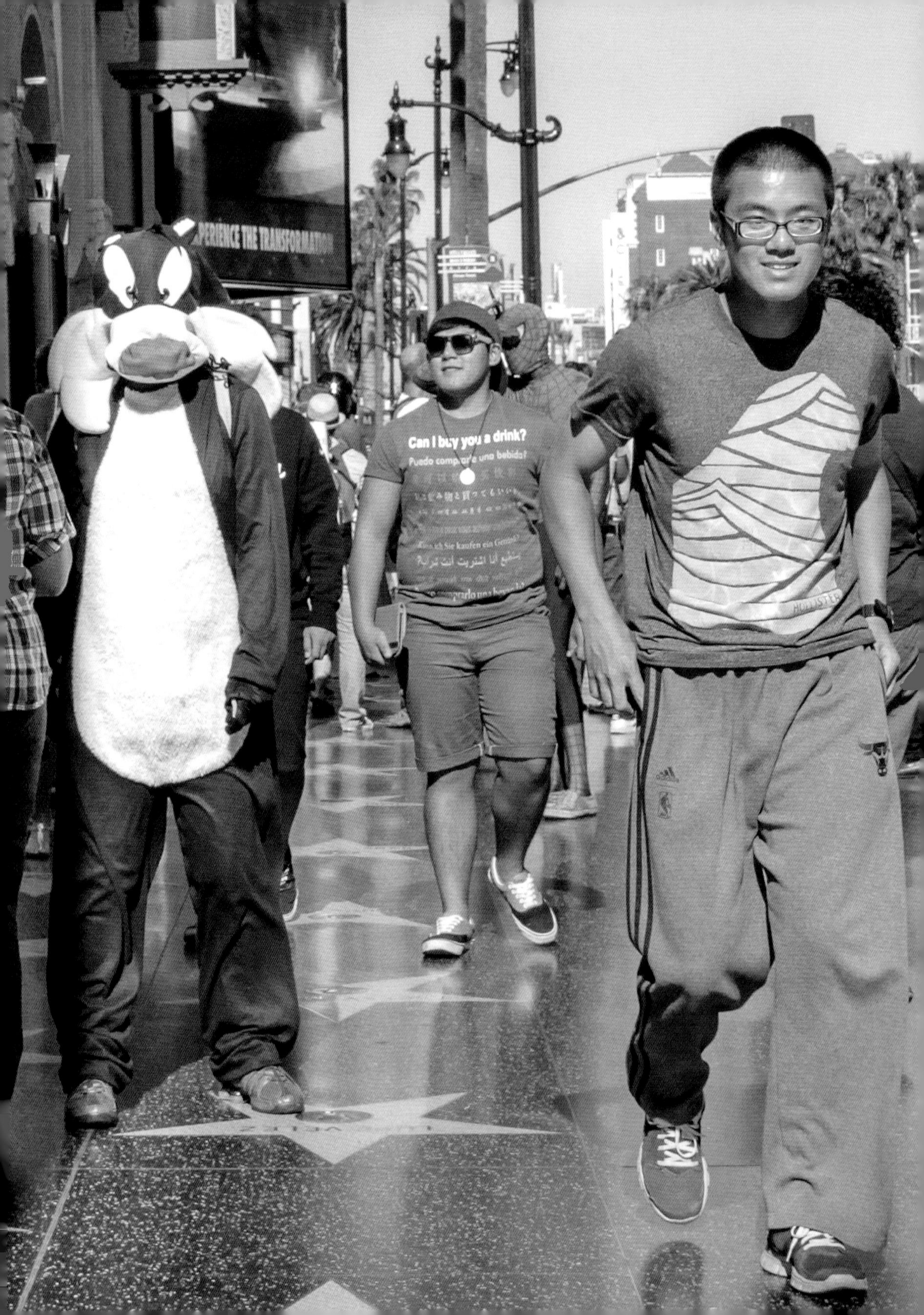

Can I buy you a drink?
Puedo comprarte una bebida?

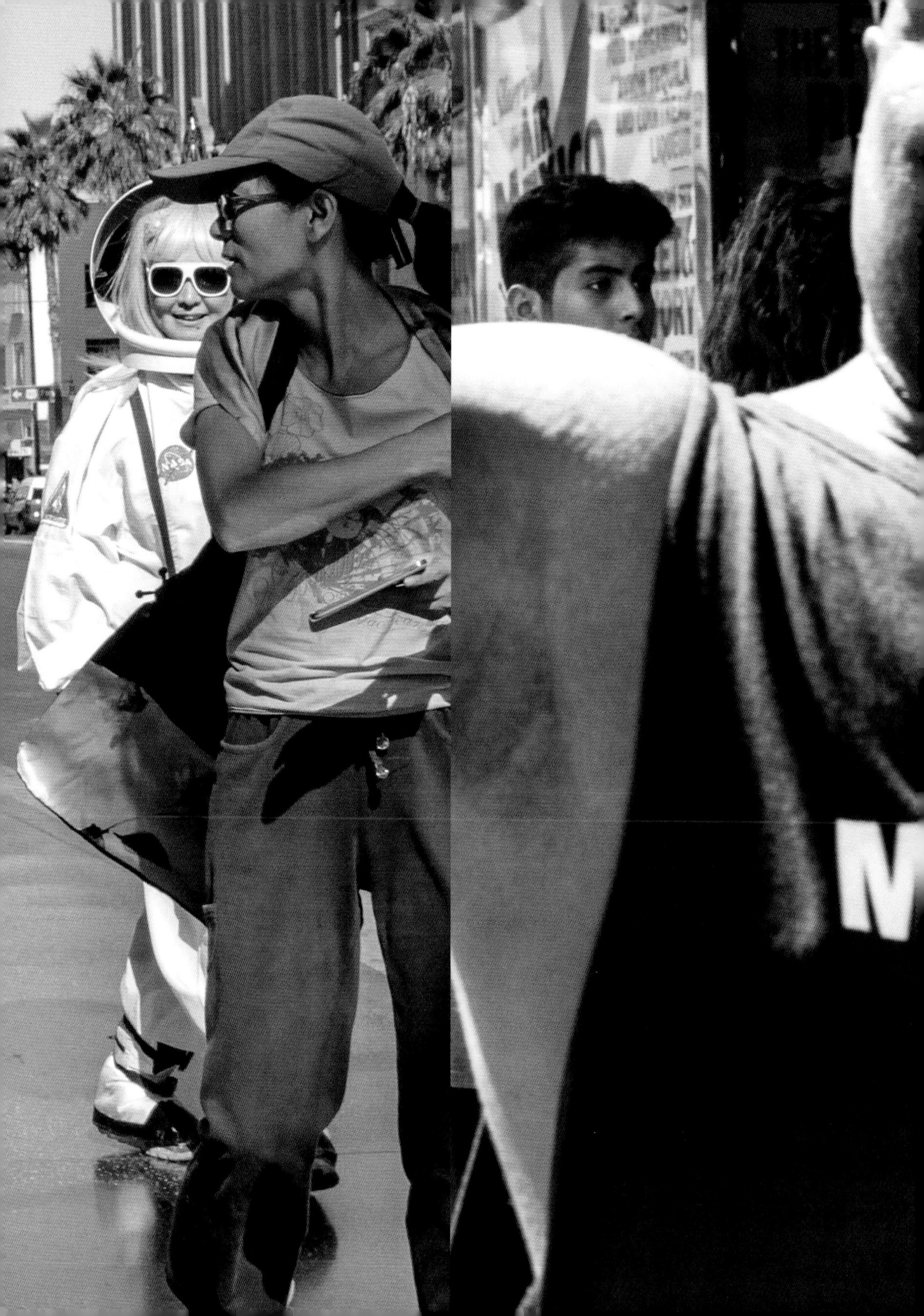

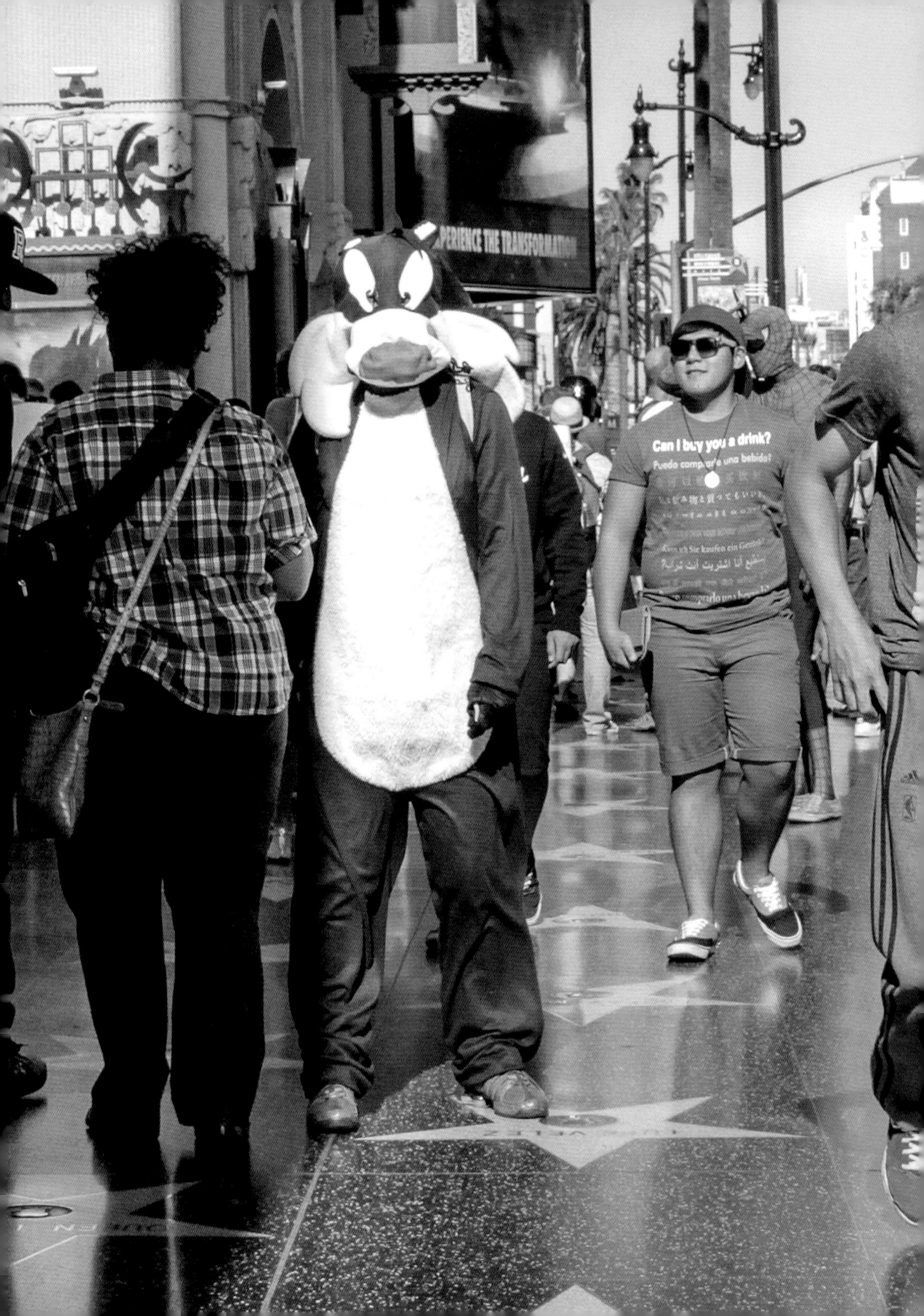

Can I buy you a drink?
Puedo comprarte una bebida?

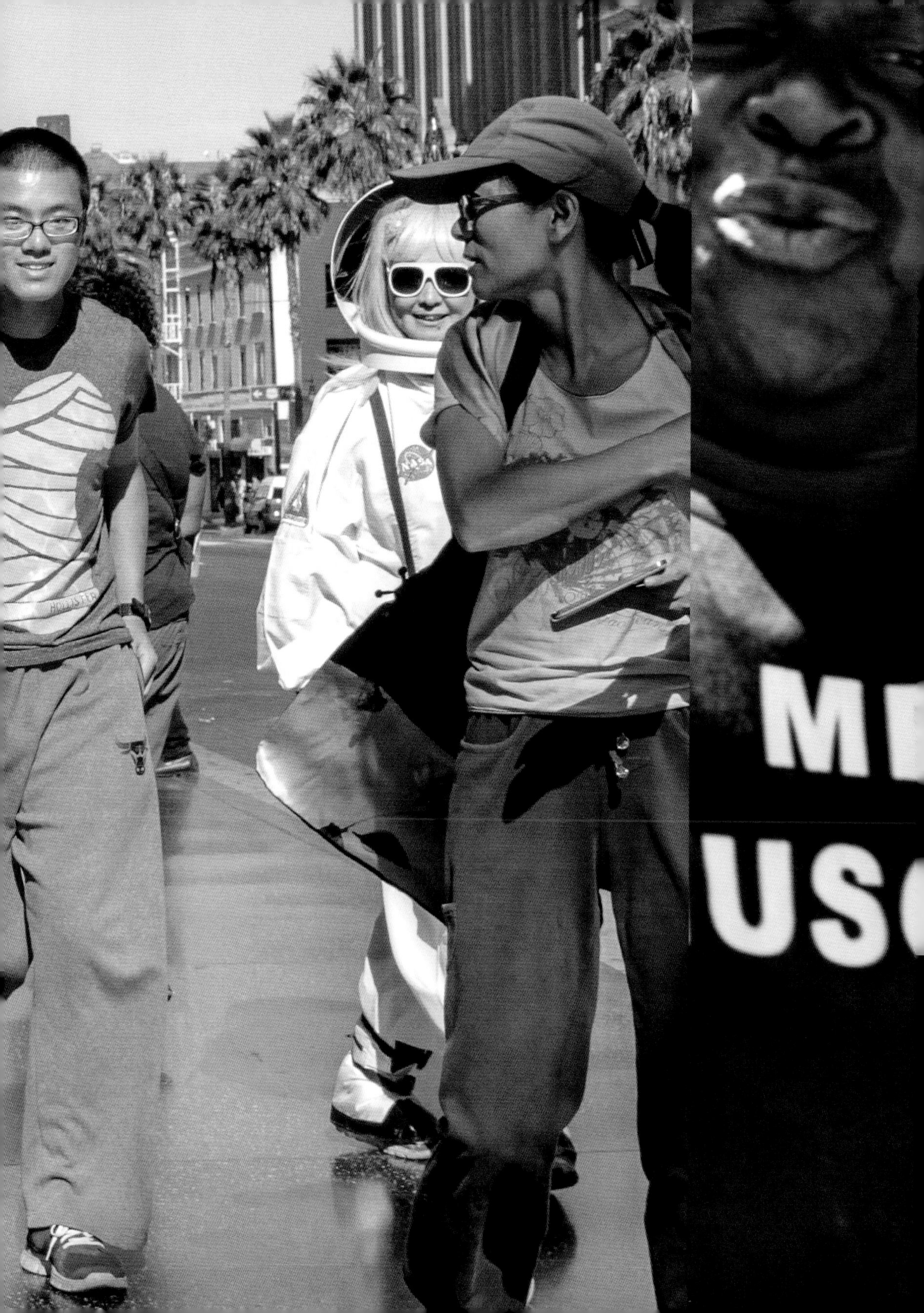

ME
USC

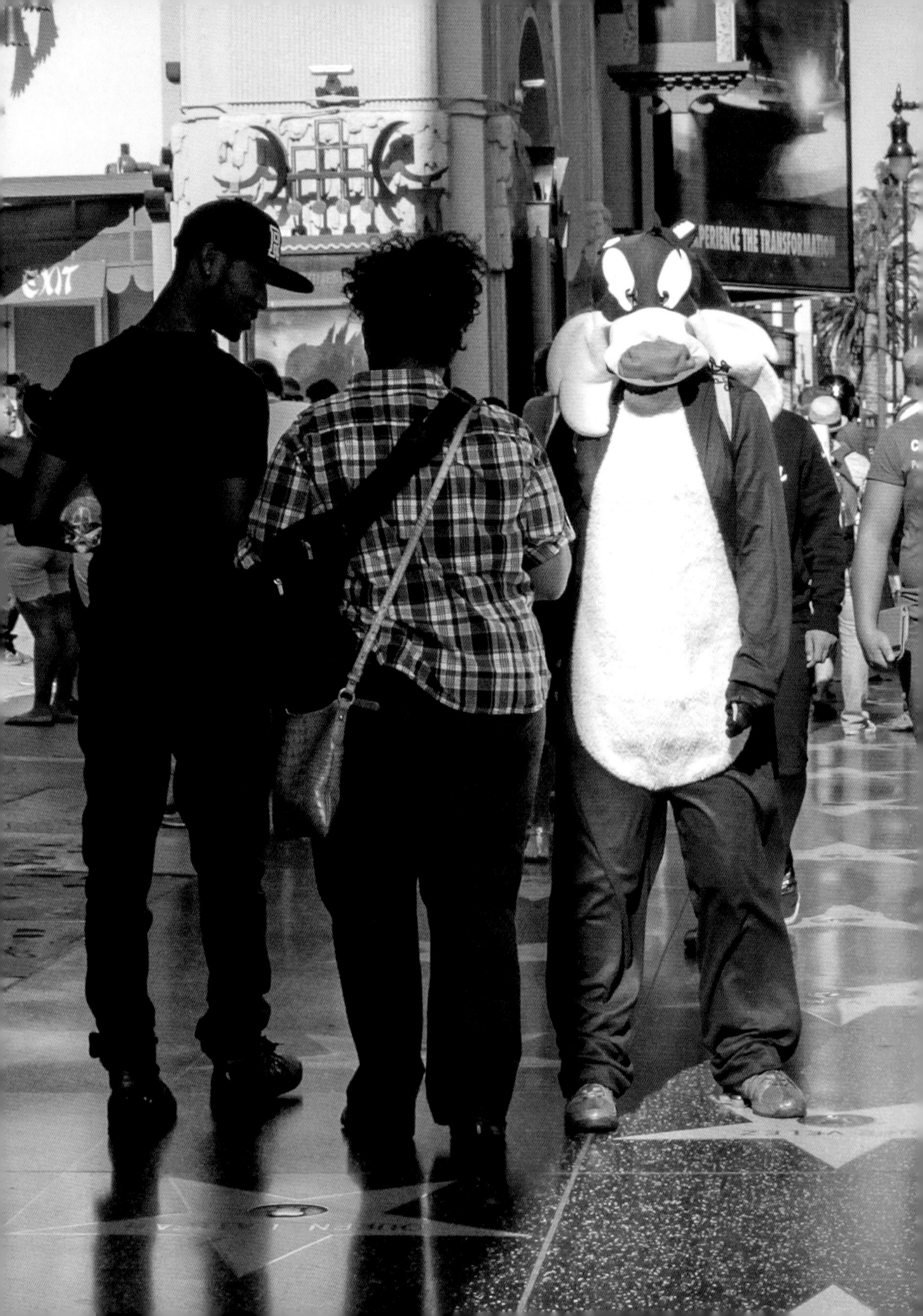

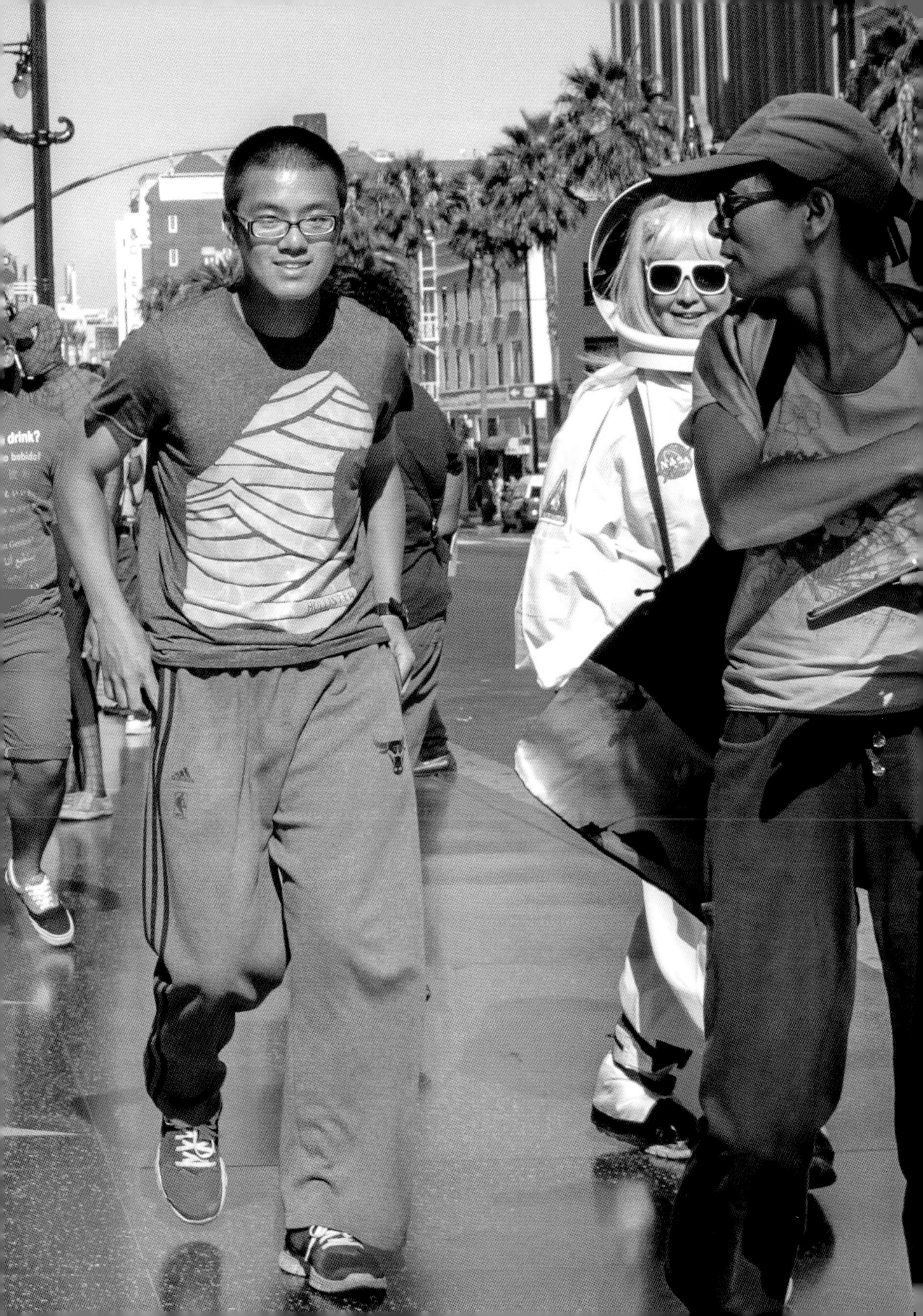

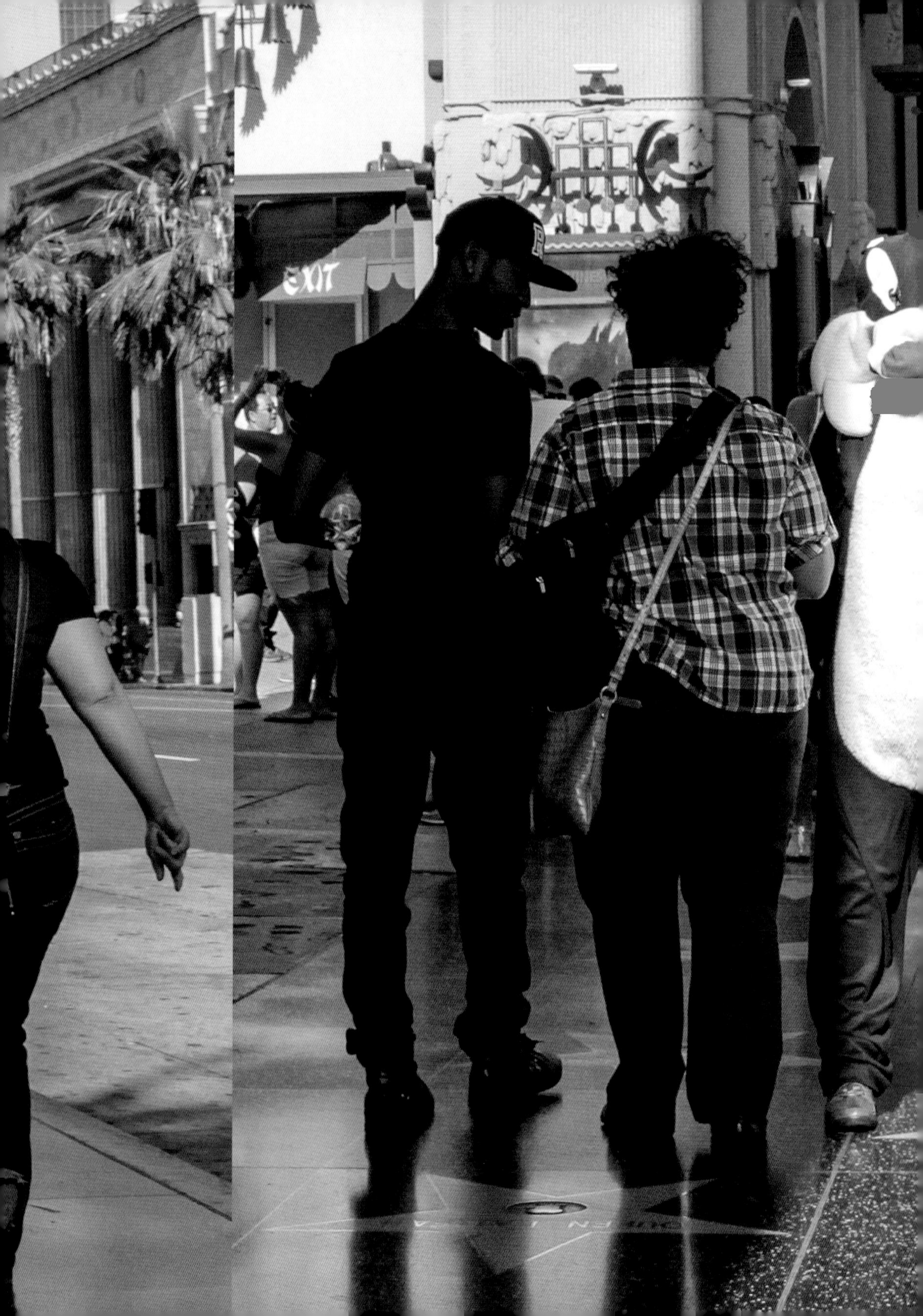

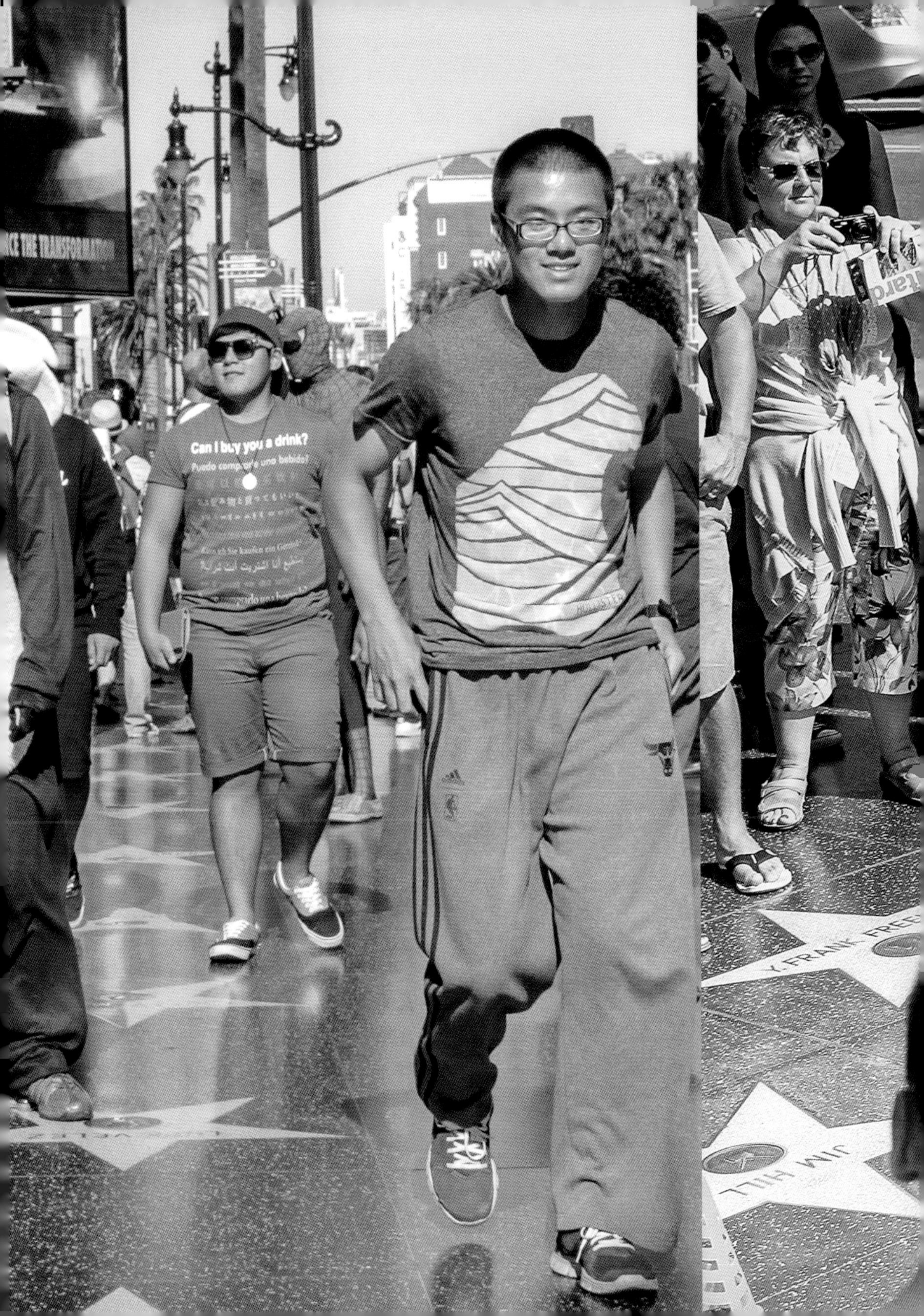

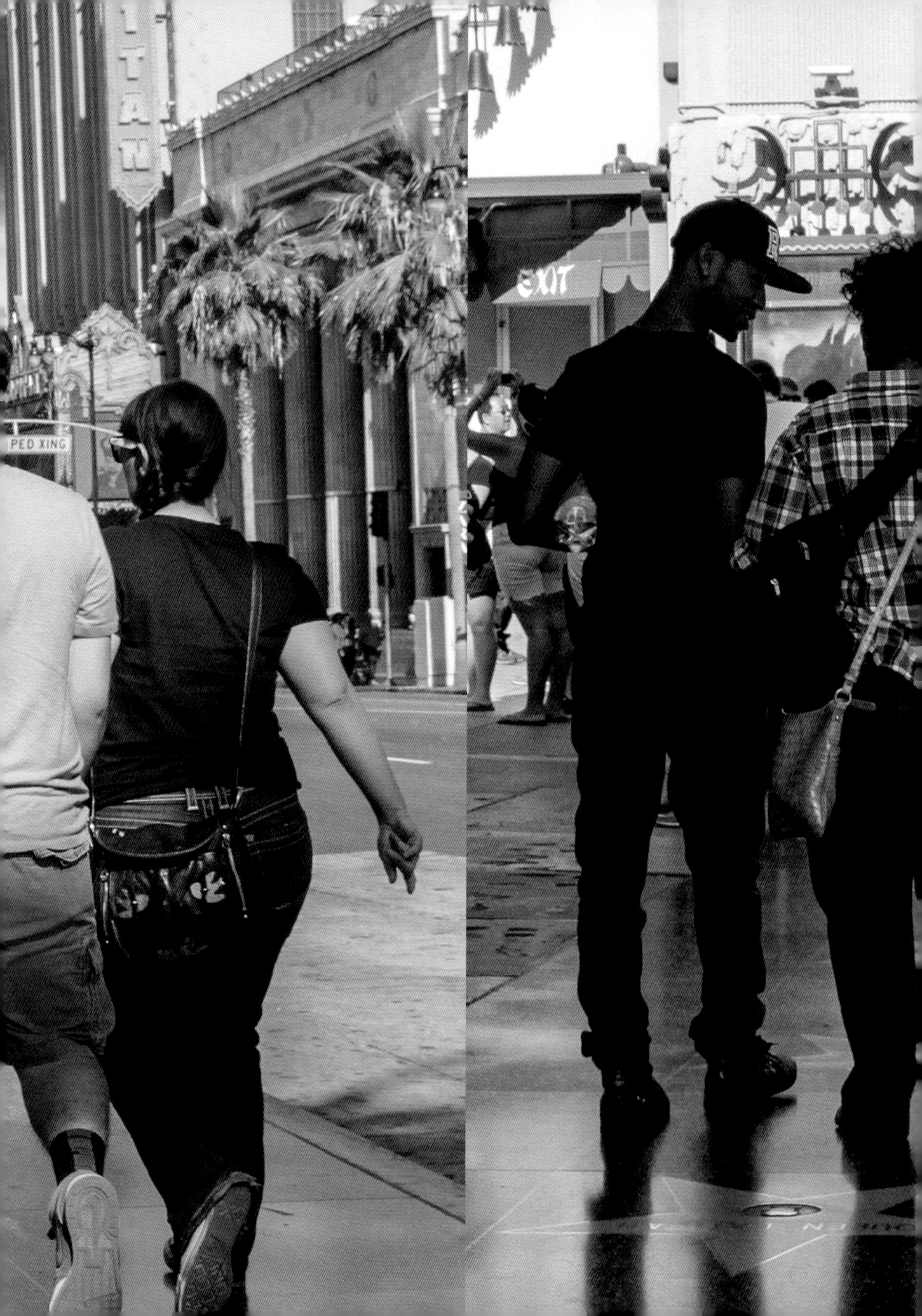

PED XING
EXIT

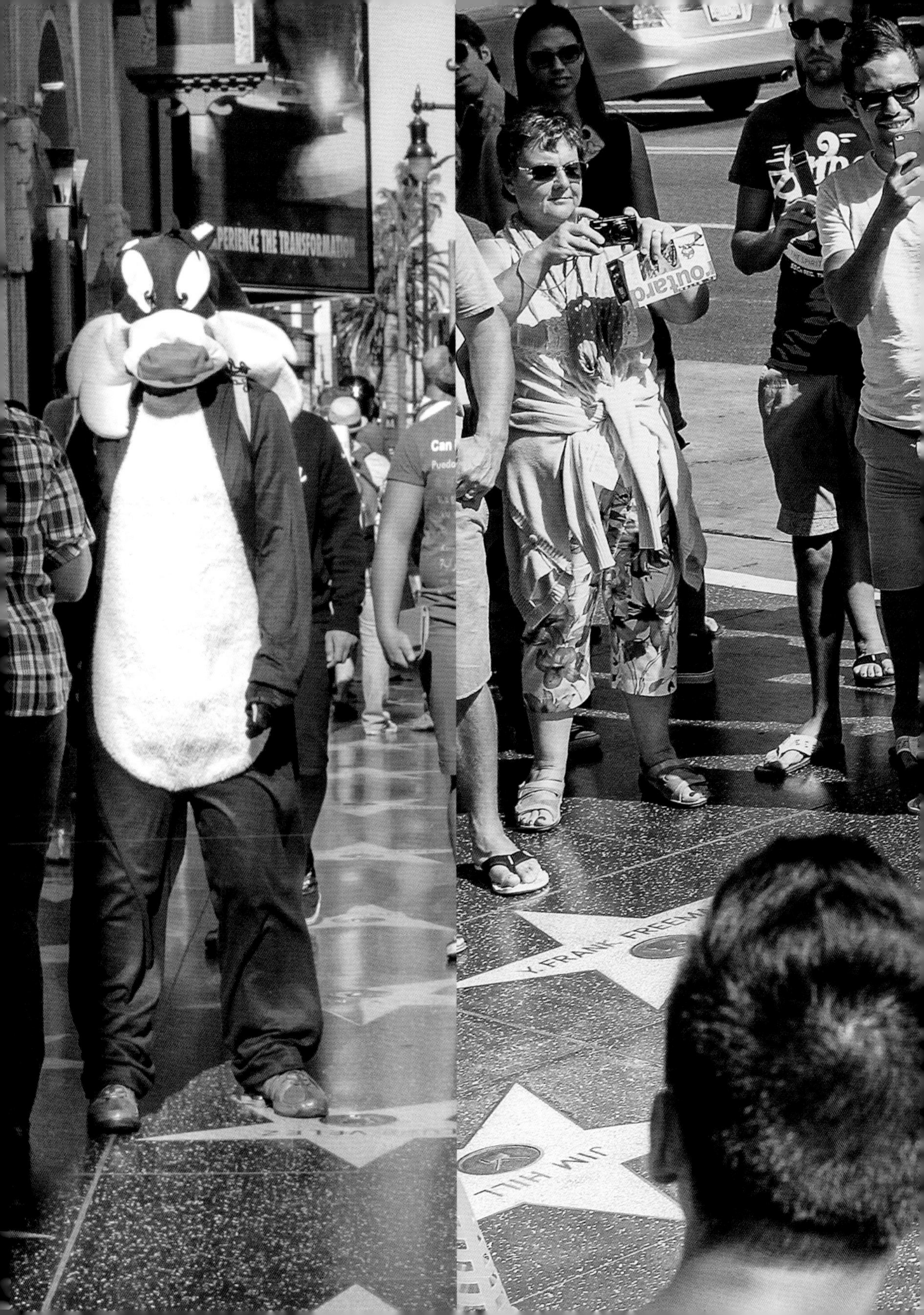

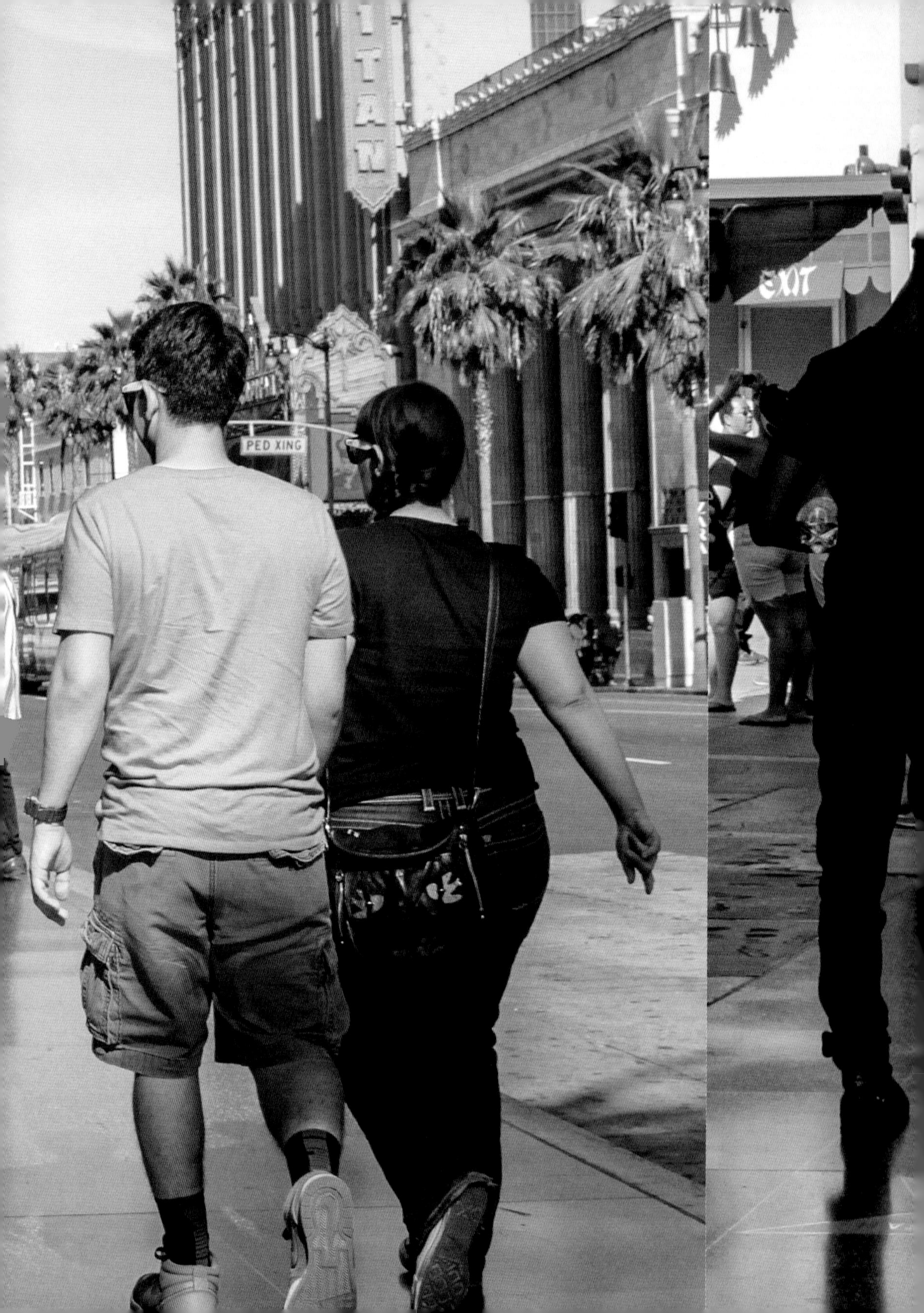
PED XING
EXIT

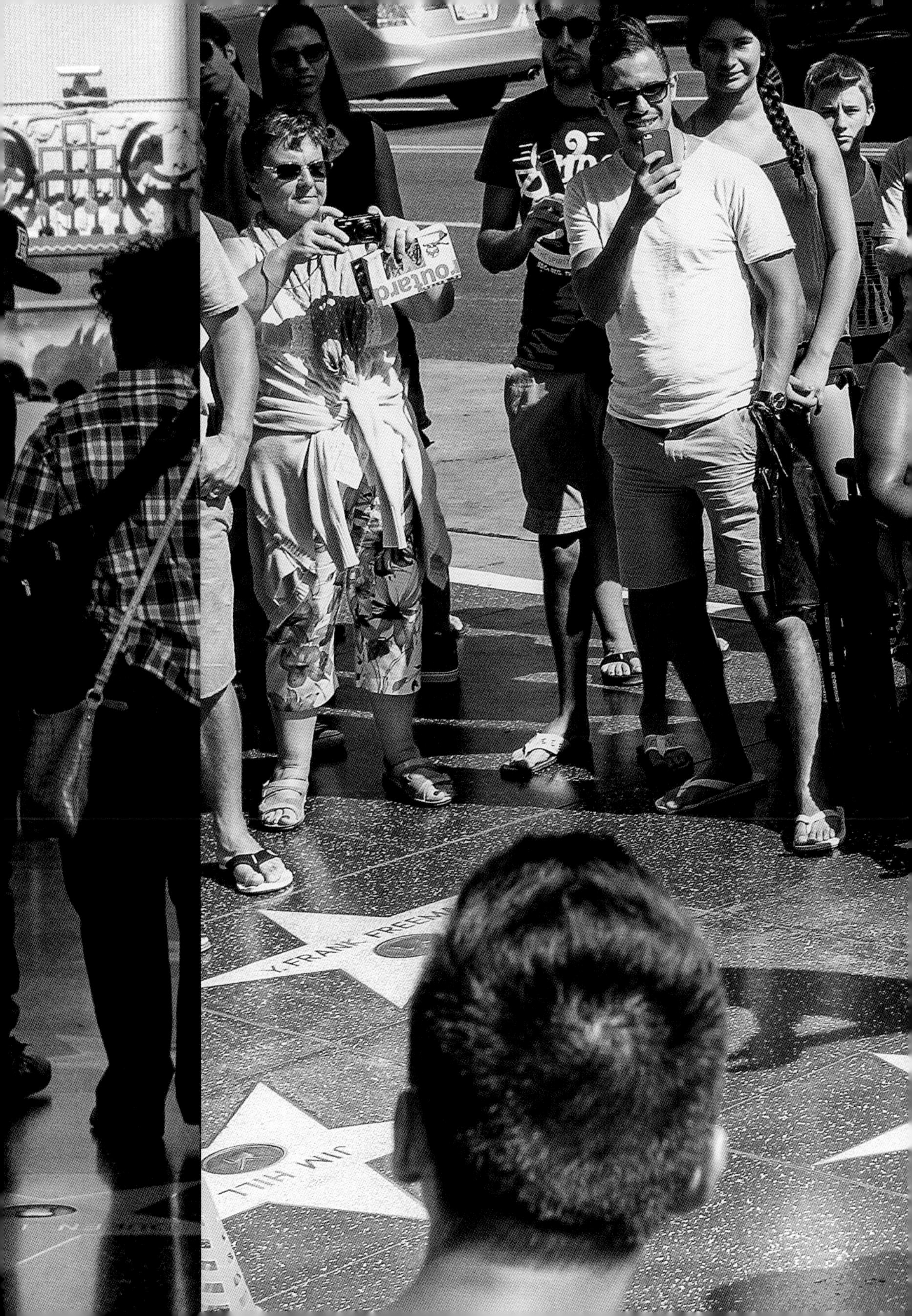

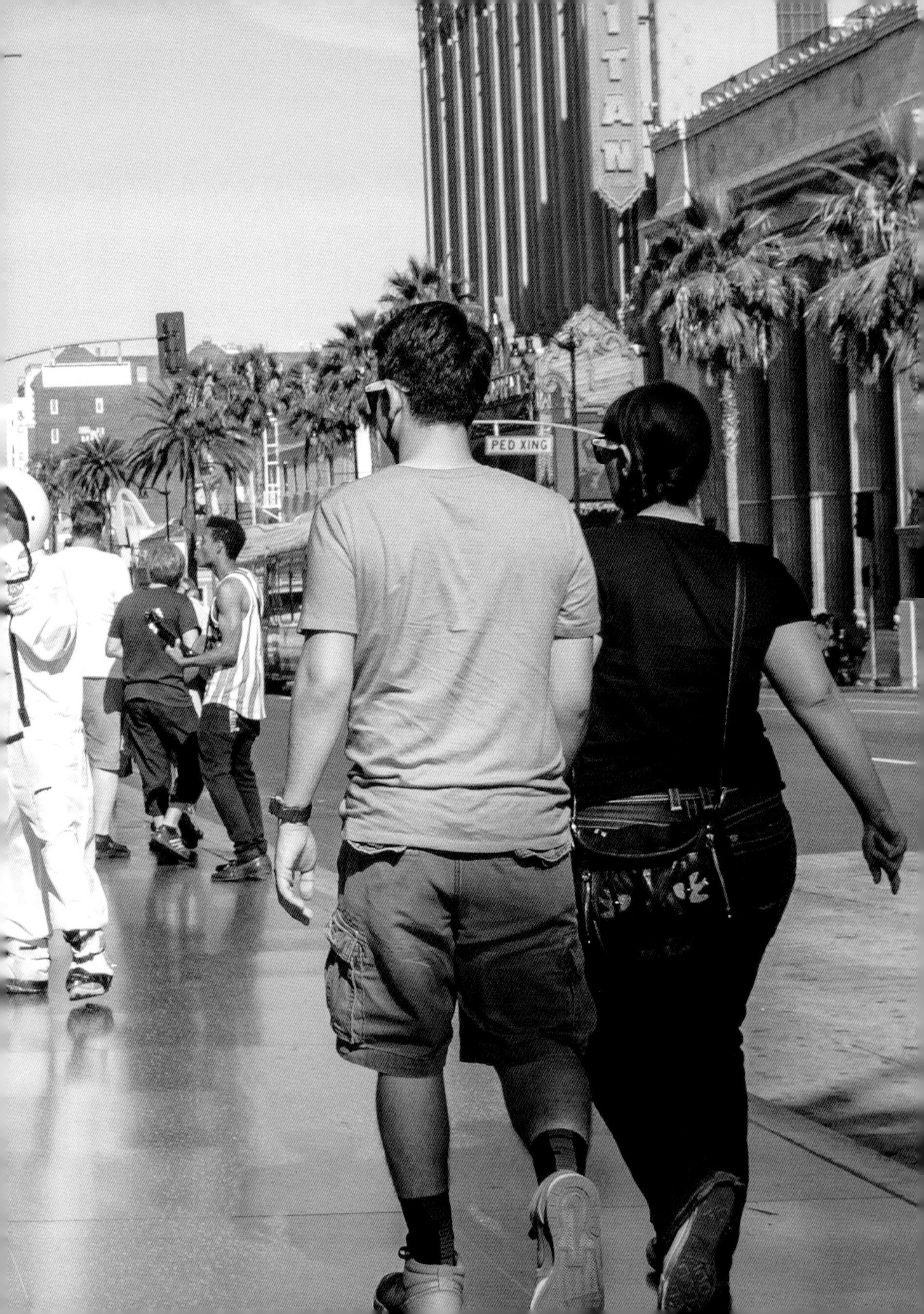

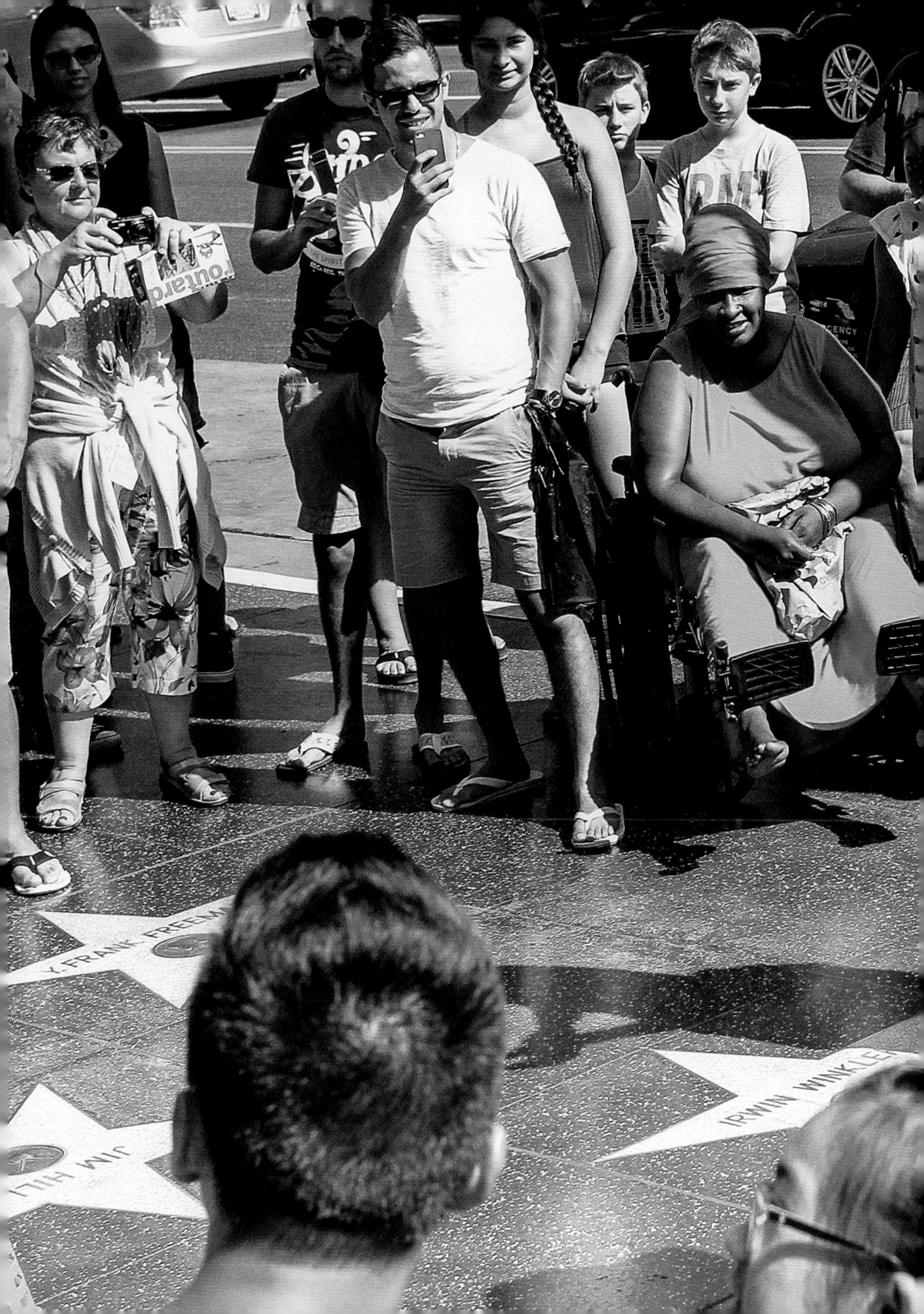
Y. FRANK FREEM
JIM HILL
IRWIN WINKLE

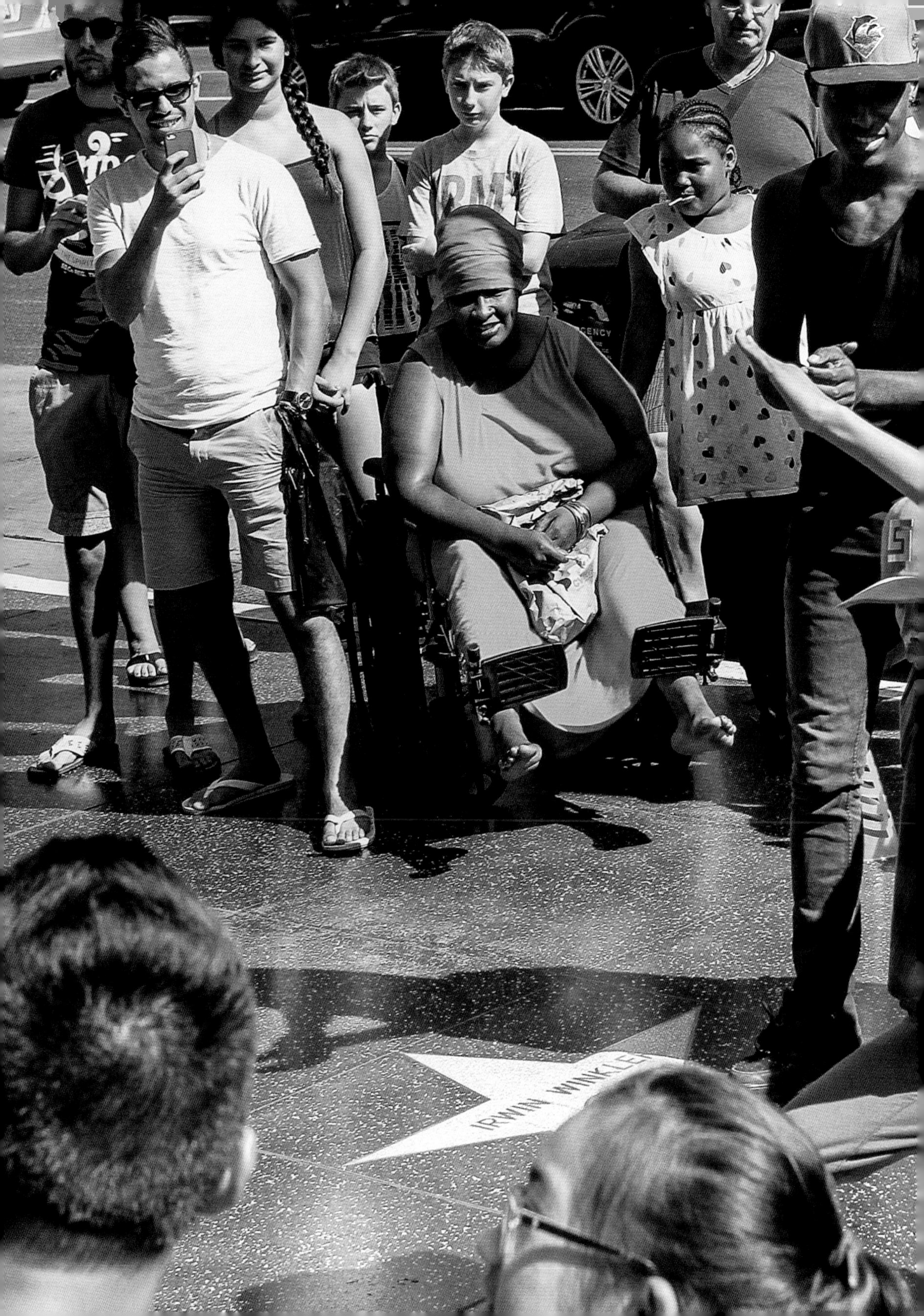

IRVIN WINKLER

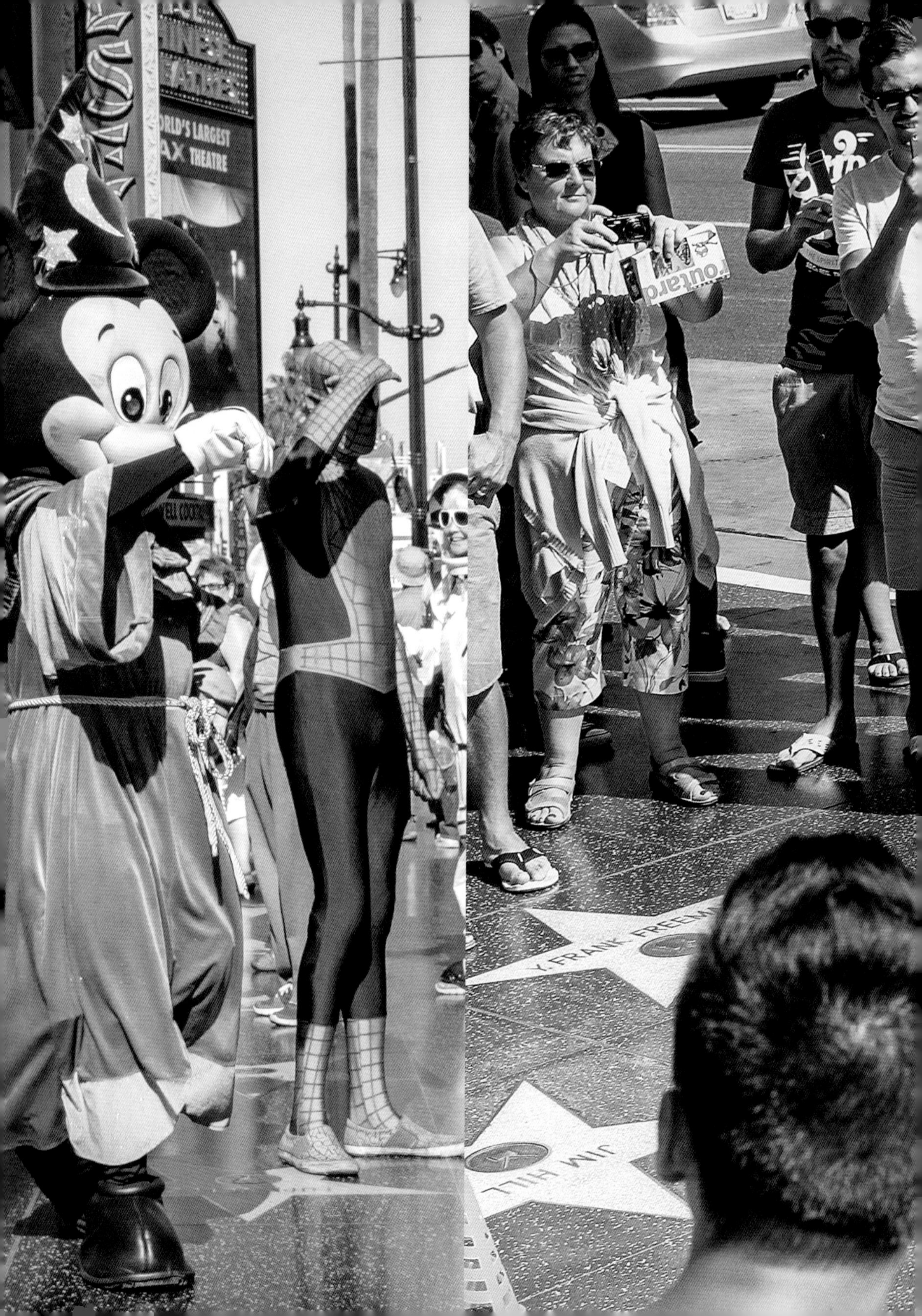

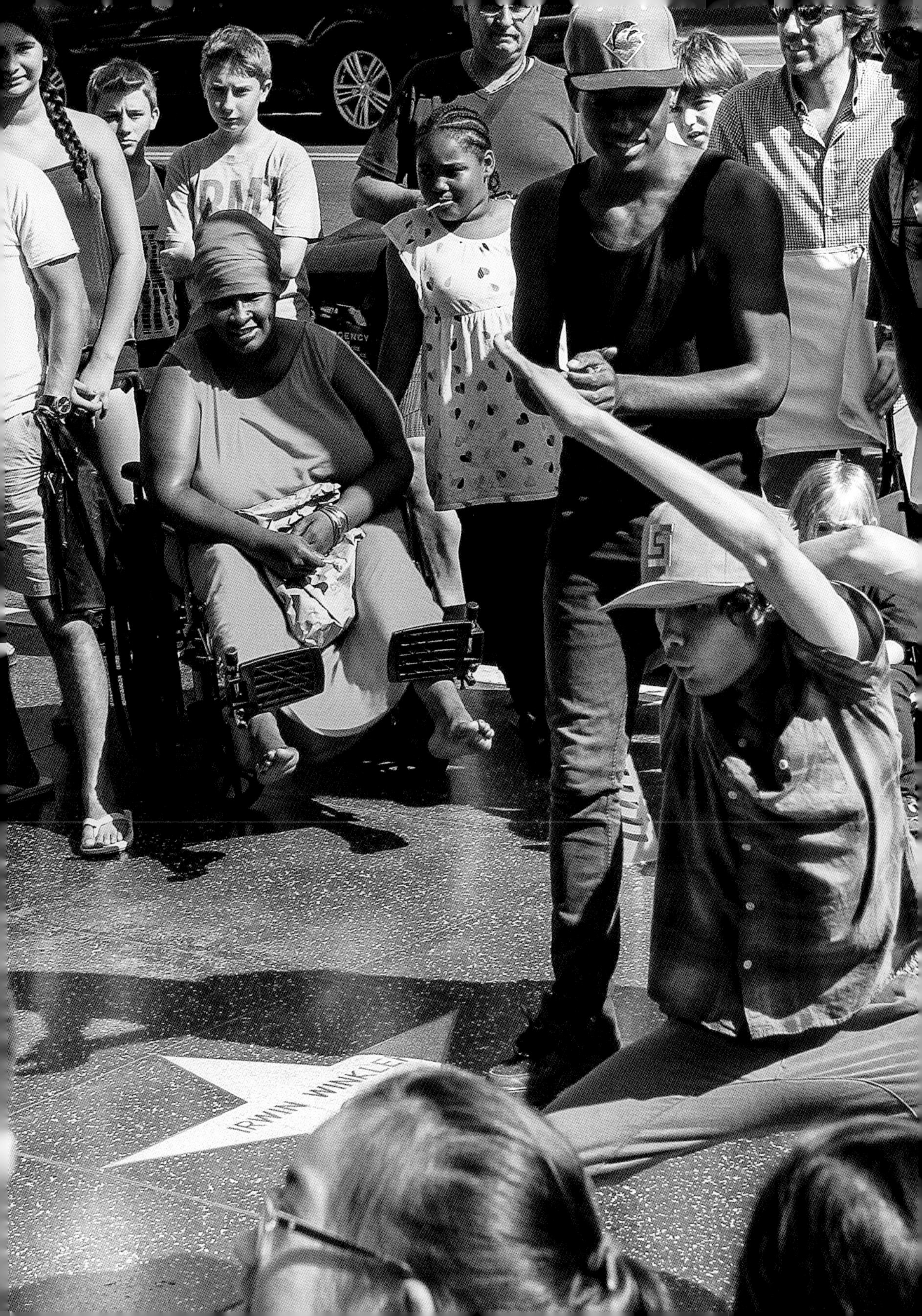
IRWIN WINKLER

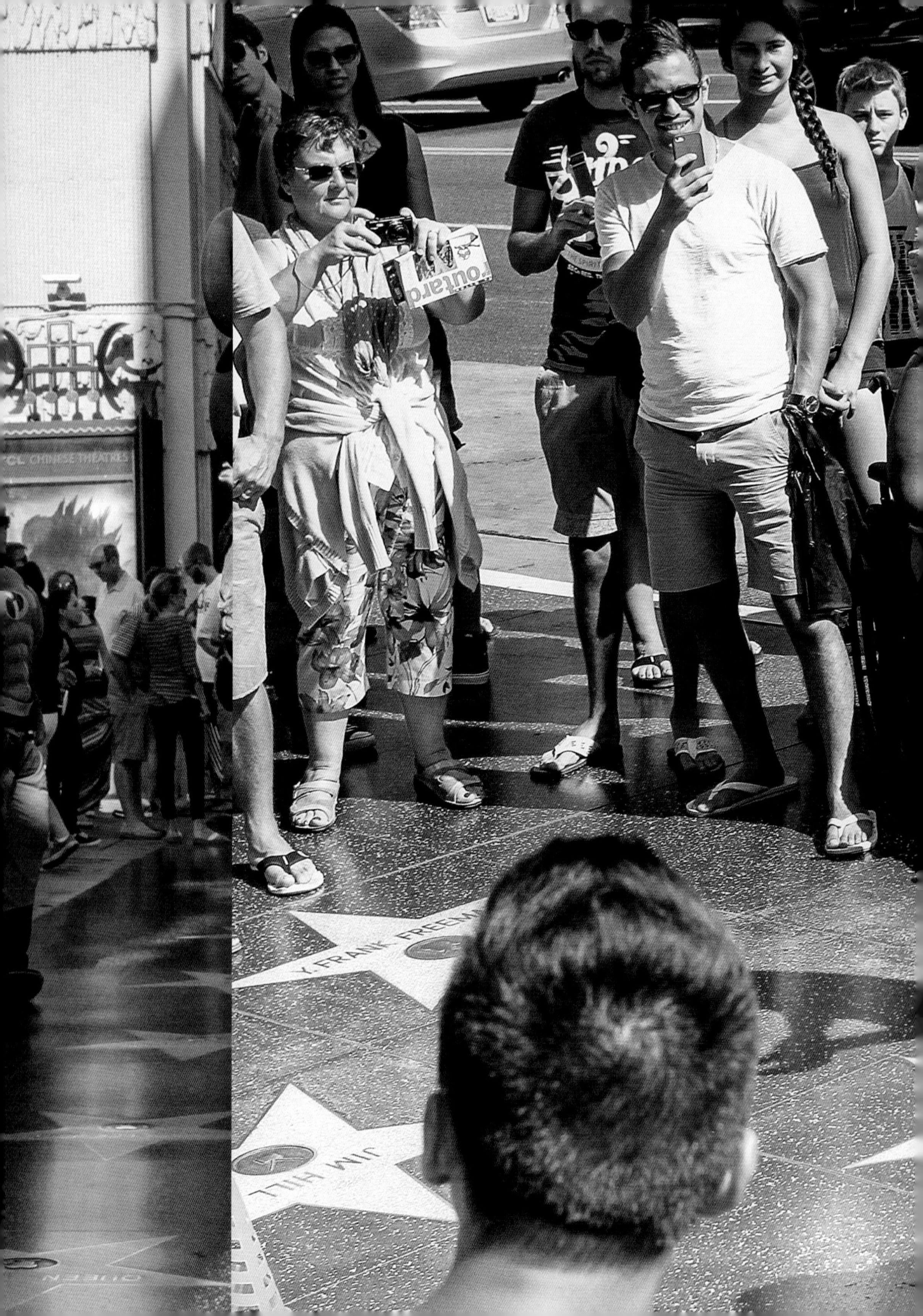

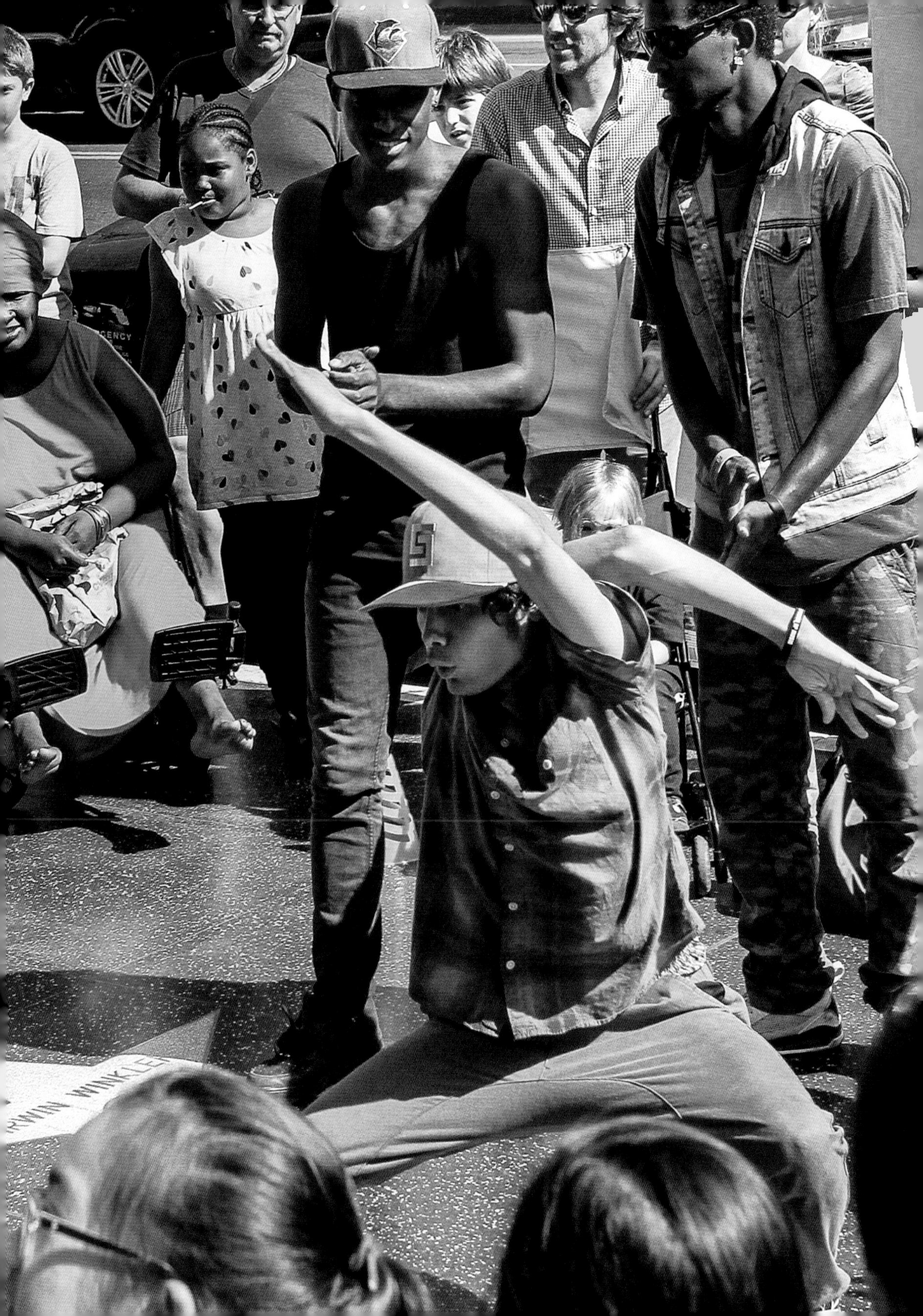

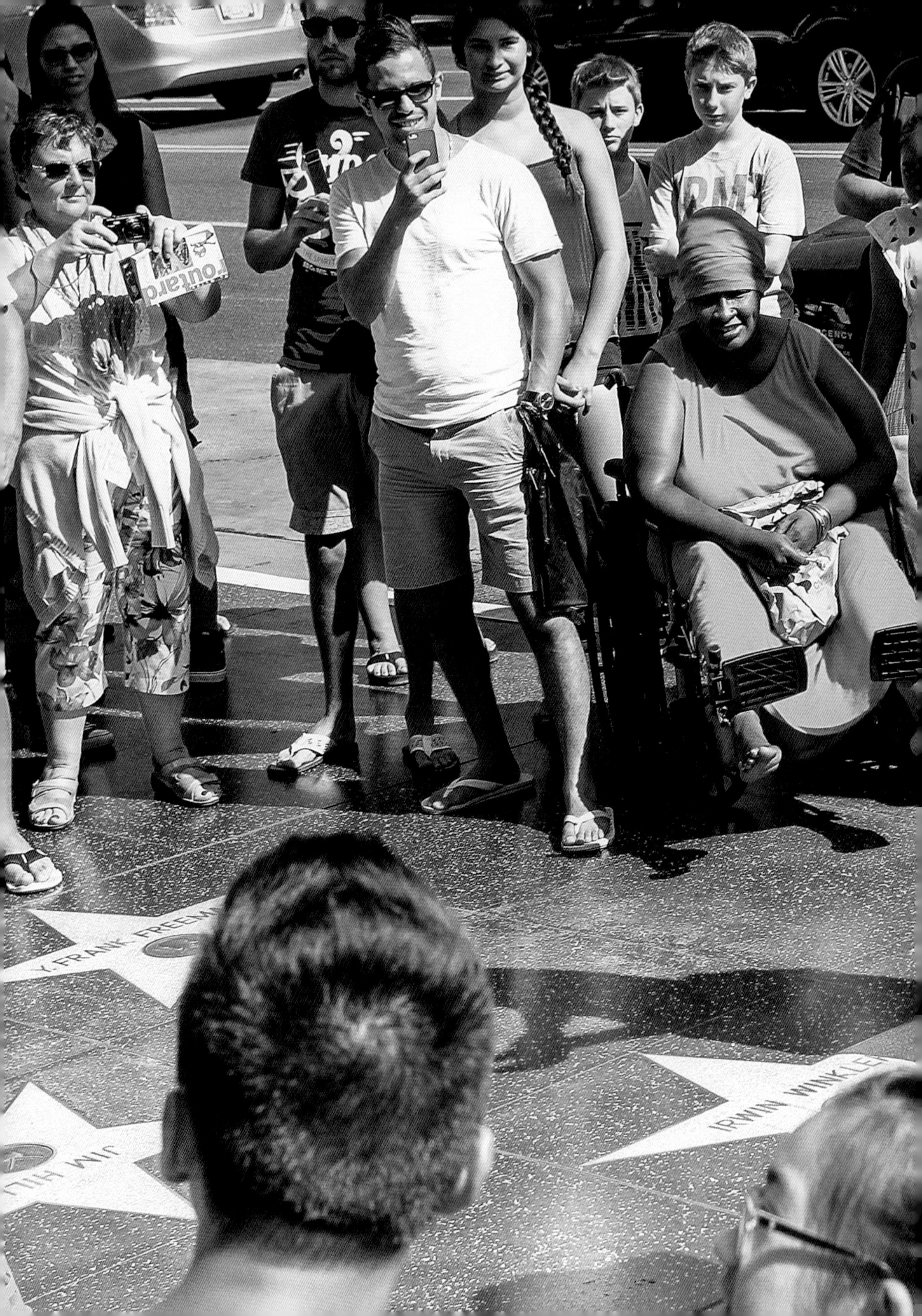
FRANK FREEM
IRWIN WINKLE
JIM HI

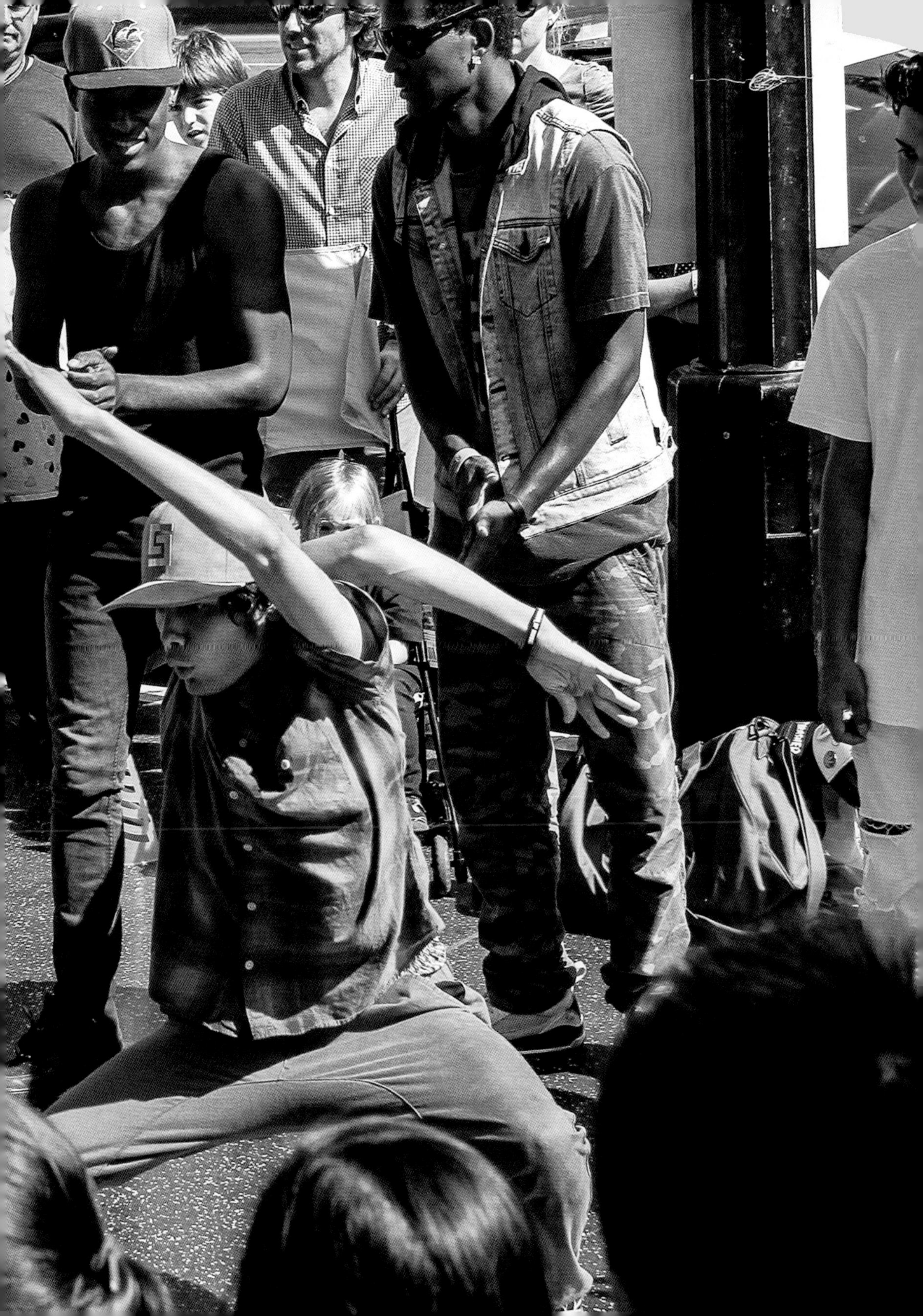

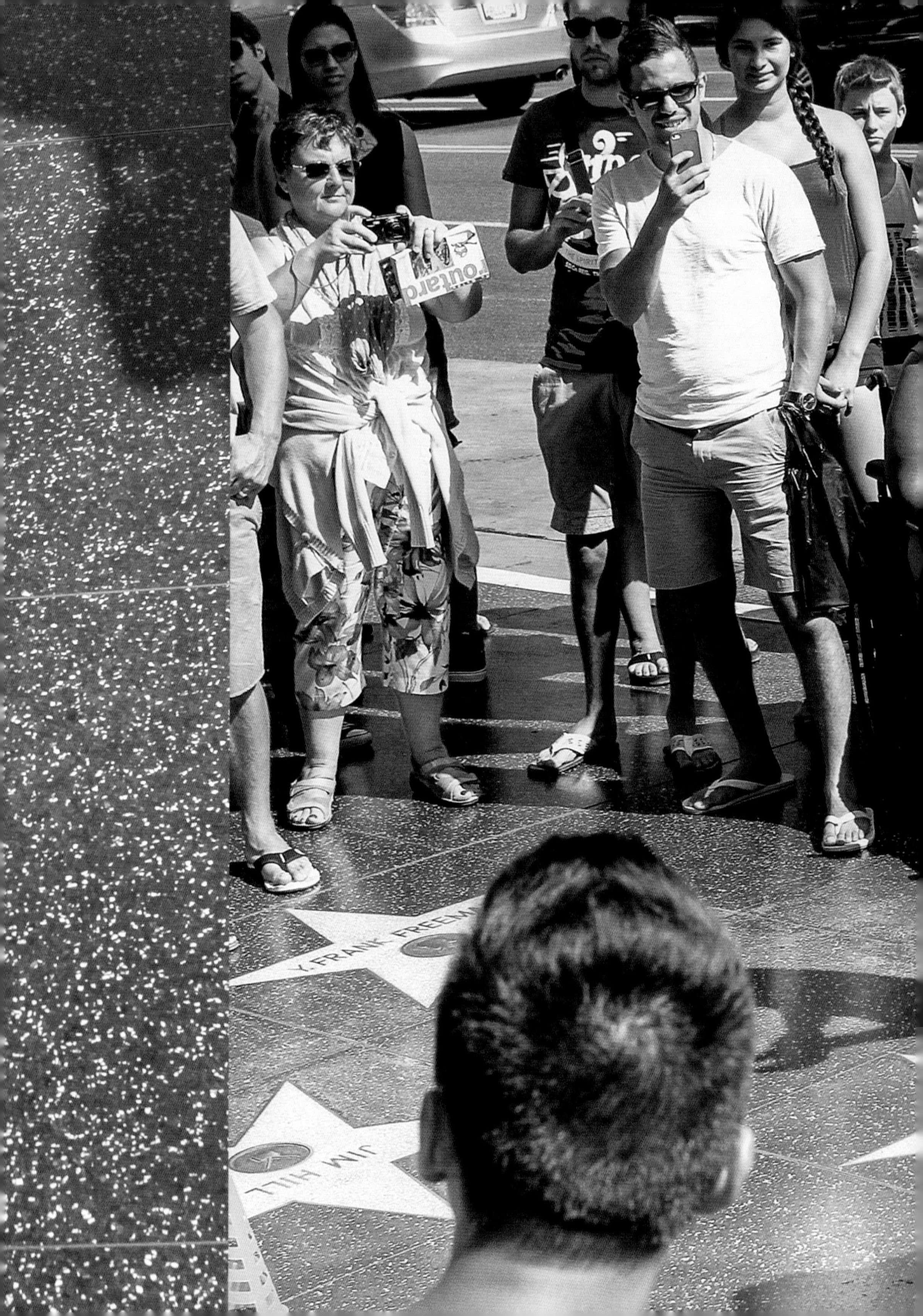

Y. FRANK FREEM
JIM HILL

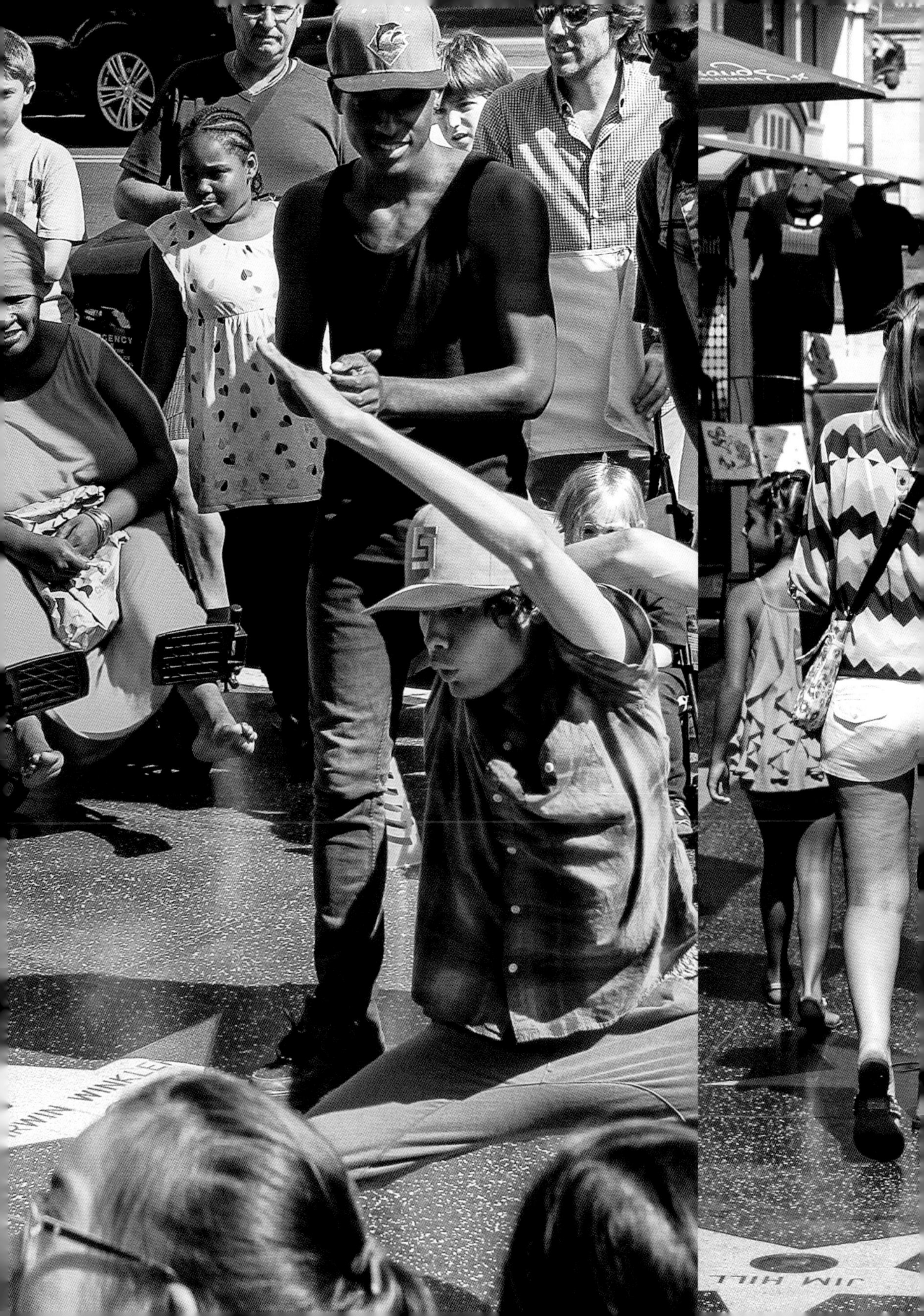

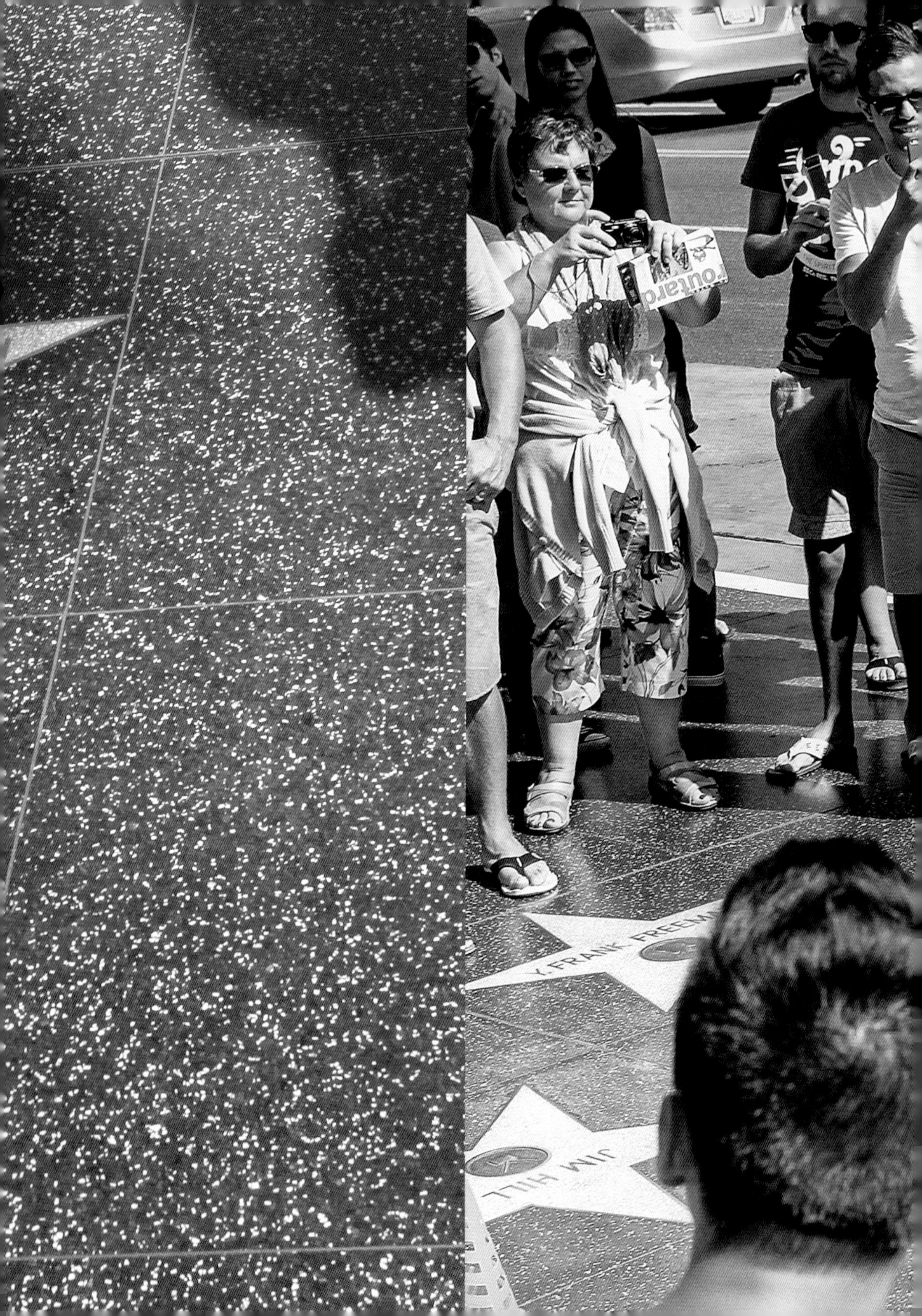

FRANK FREEMAN
JIM HILL

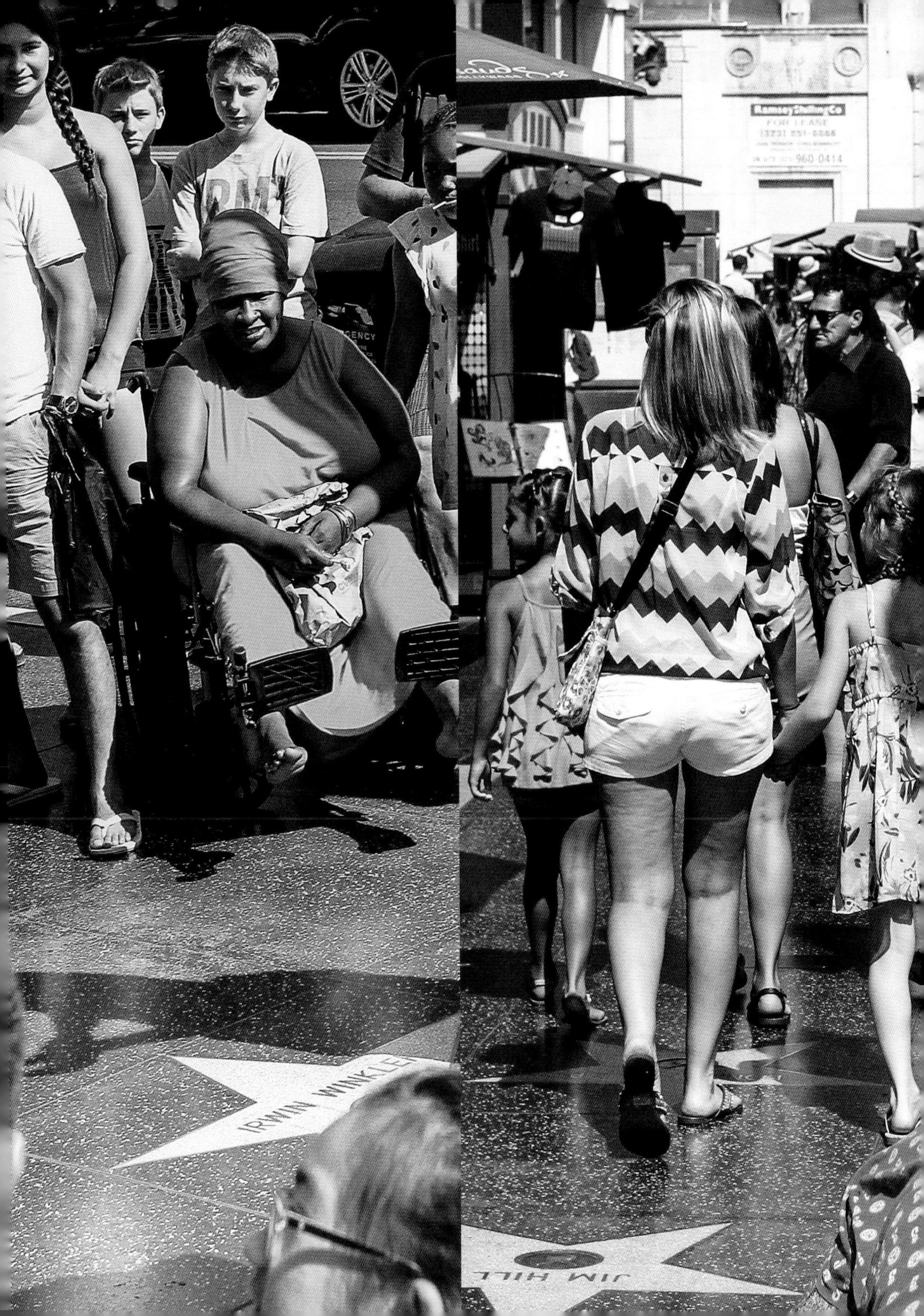

FOR LEASE
(323) 851-8686
960 0414
IRVIN WINKLER
JIM HILL

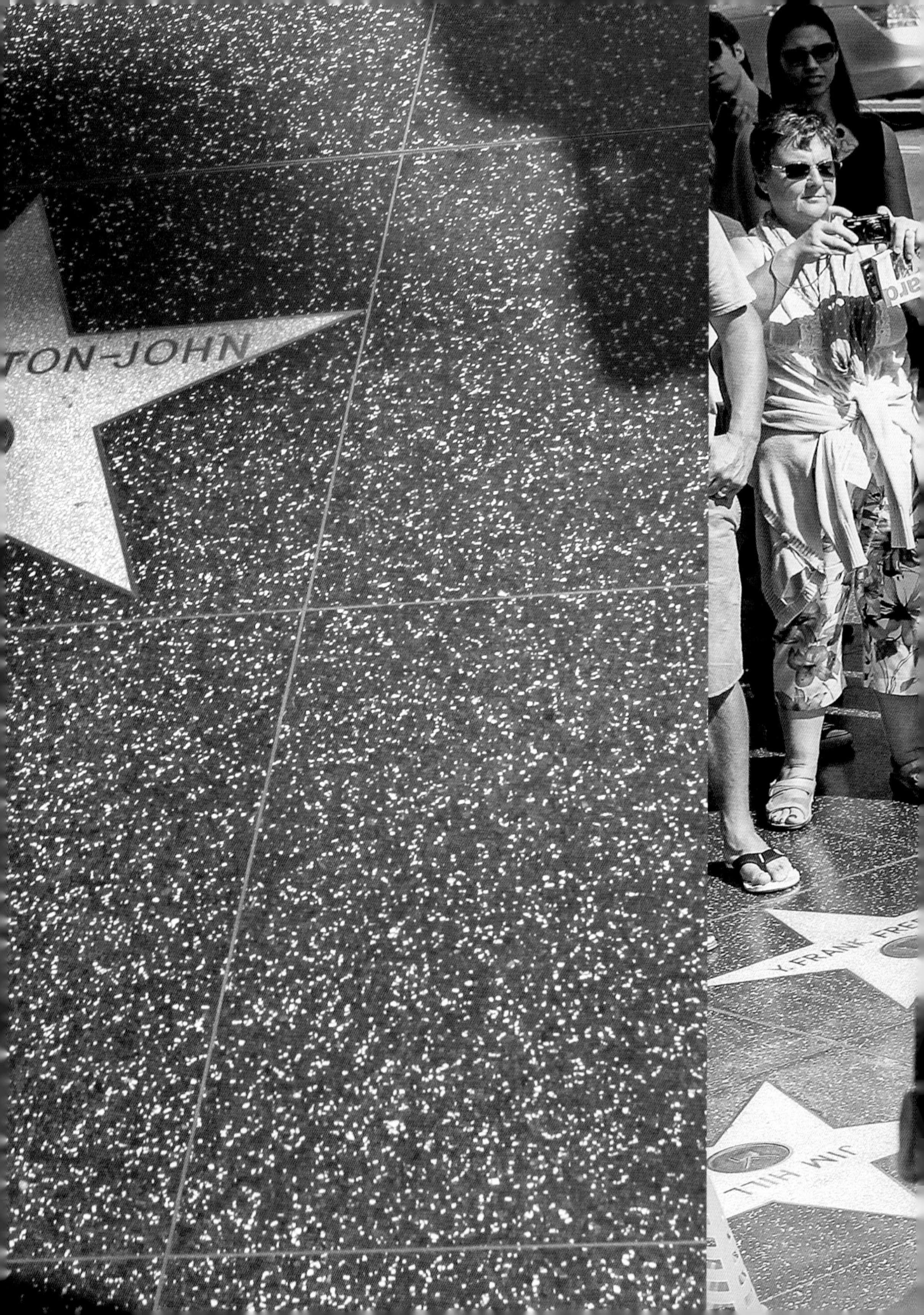

TON-JOHN
FRANK FRE
JIM HILL

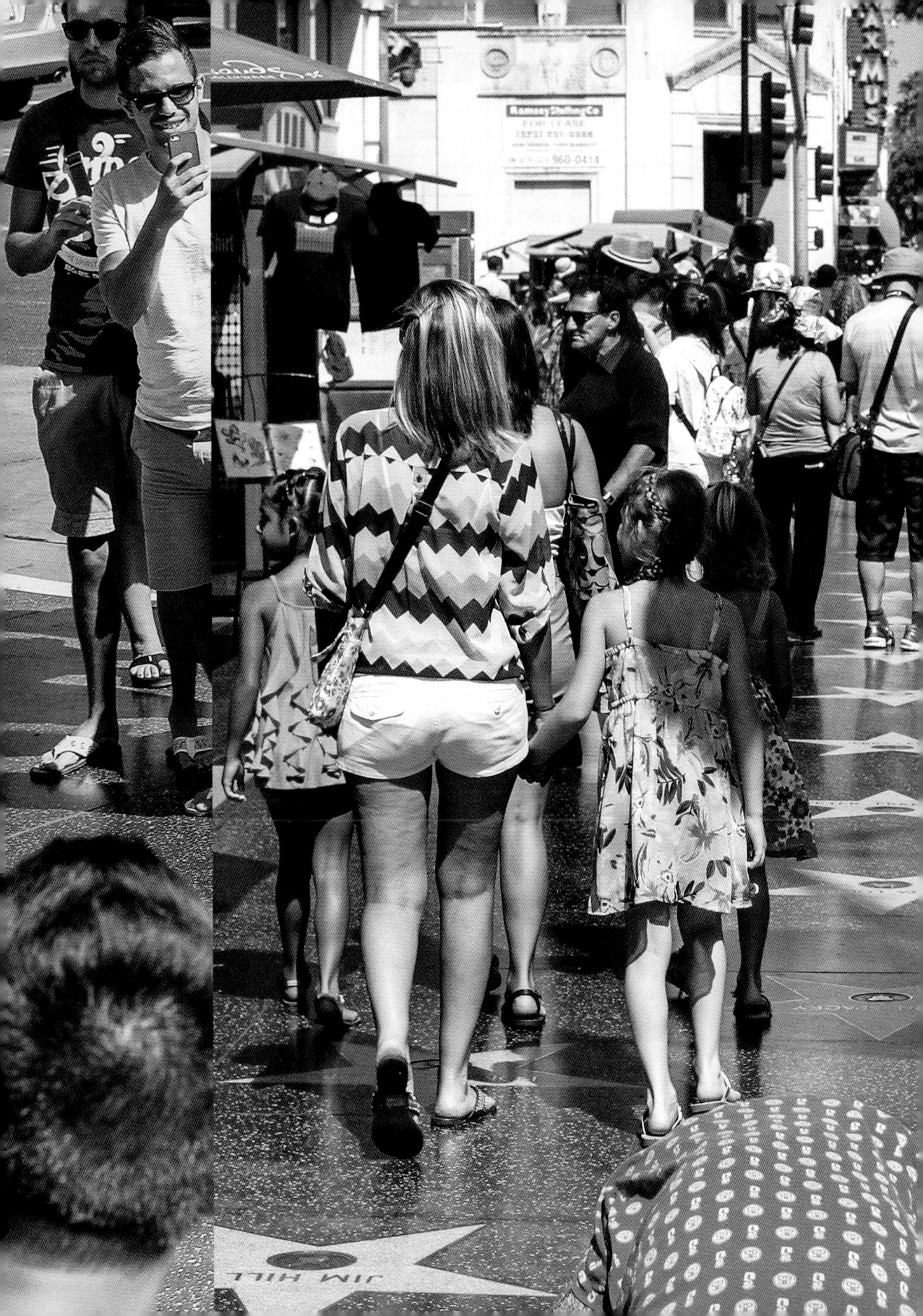

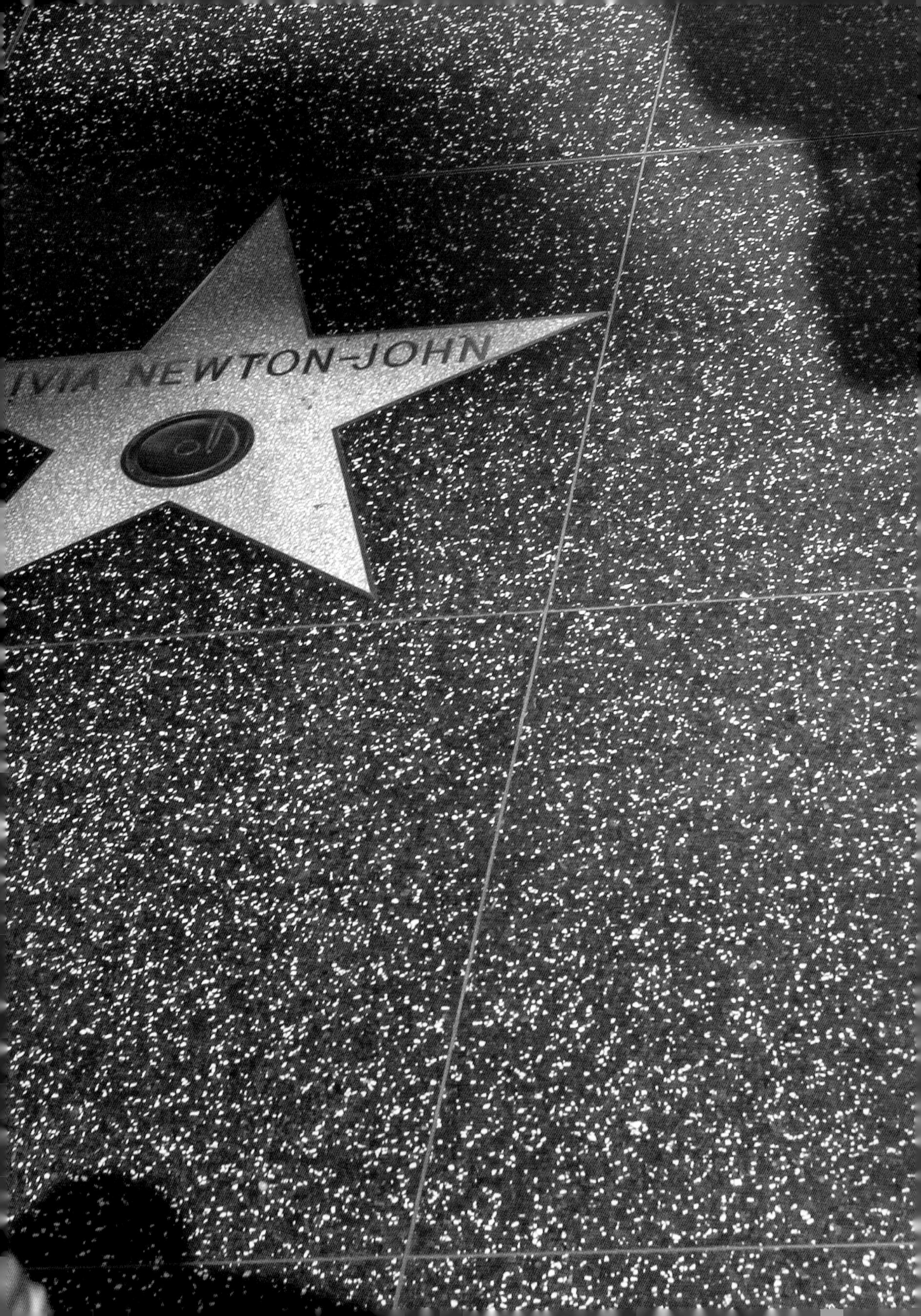

IVIA NEWTON-JOHN

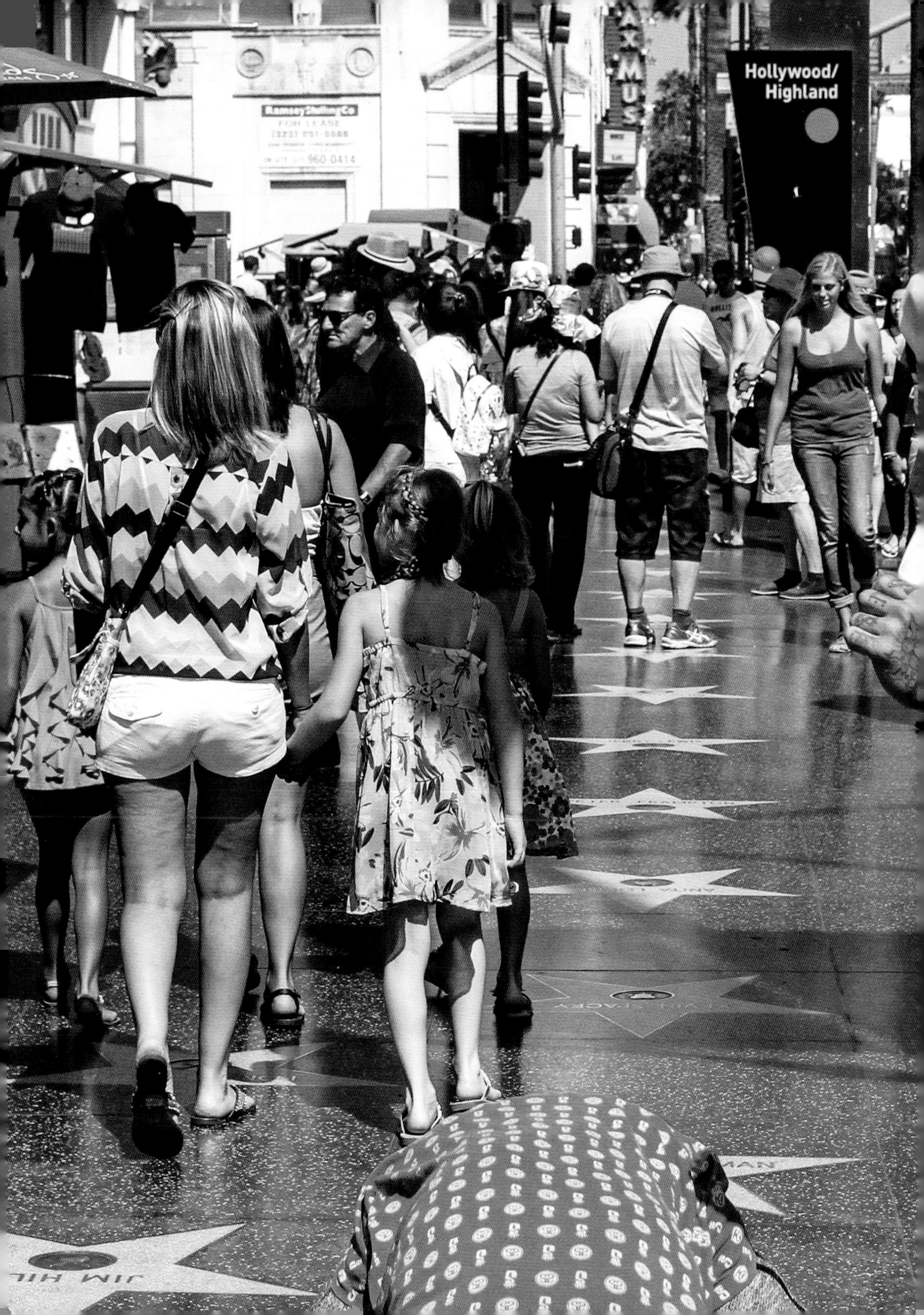

Hollywood/
Highland

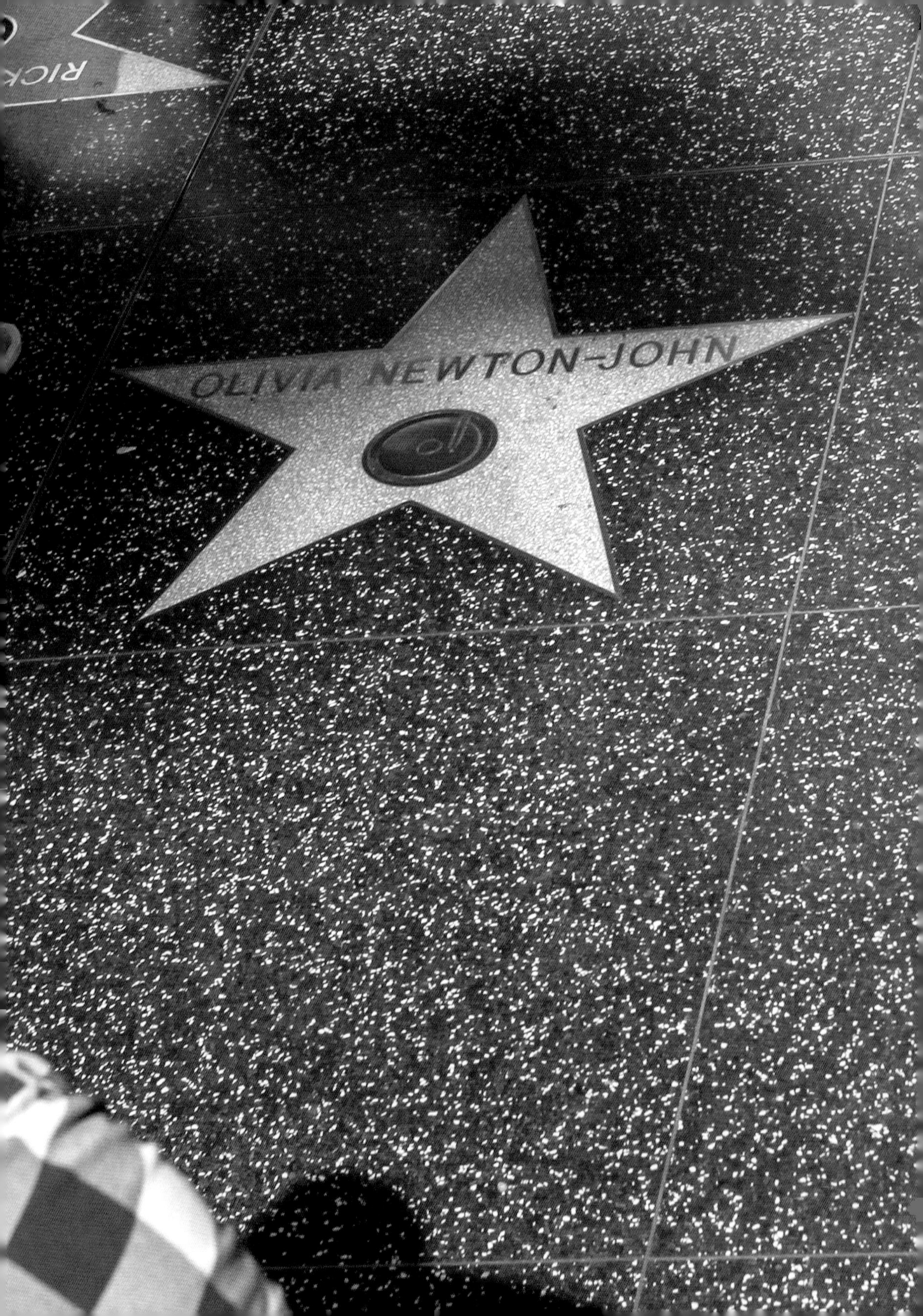
RIC
OLIVIA NEWTON-JOHN

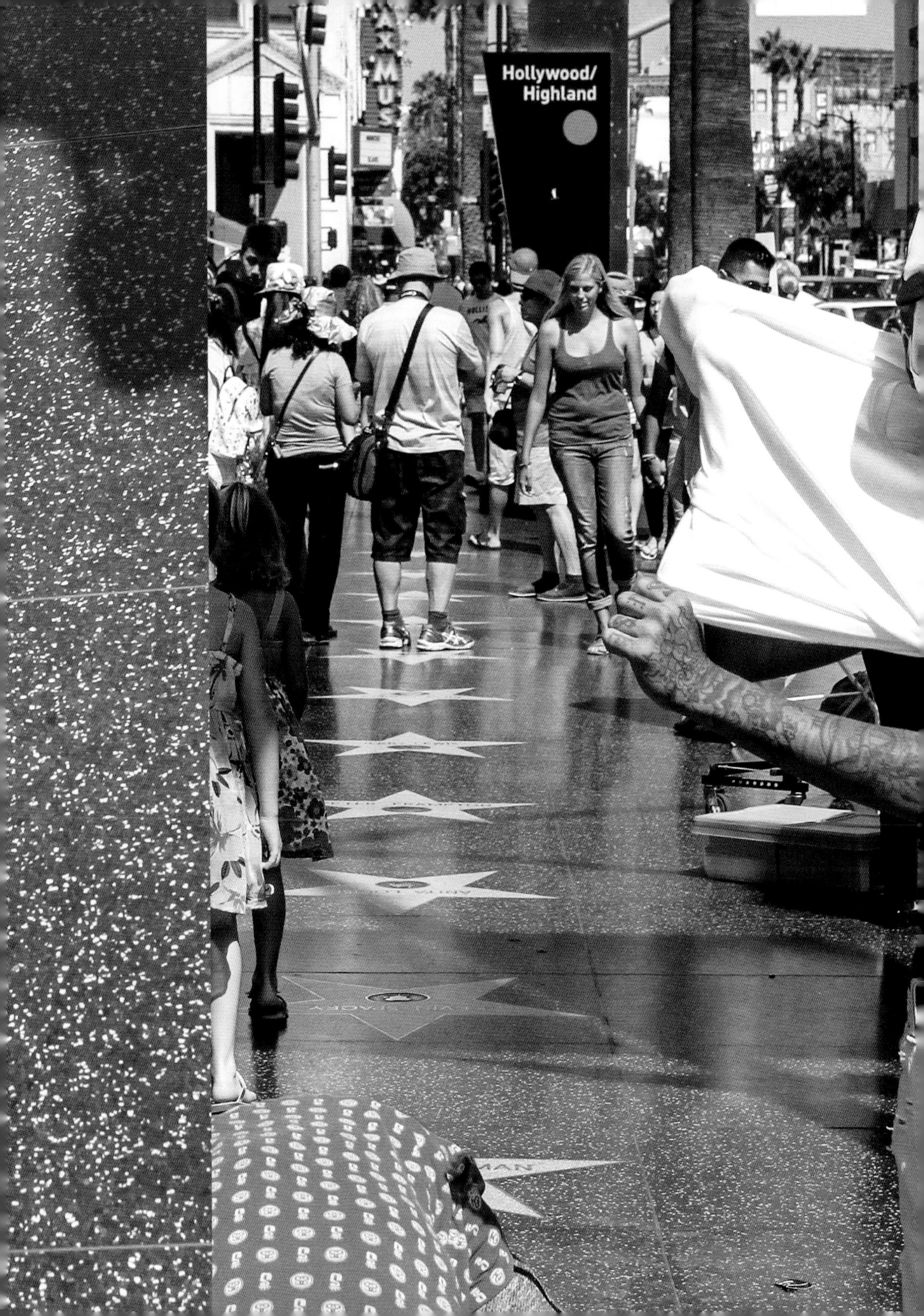

Hollywood/
Highland

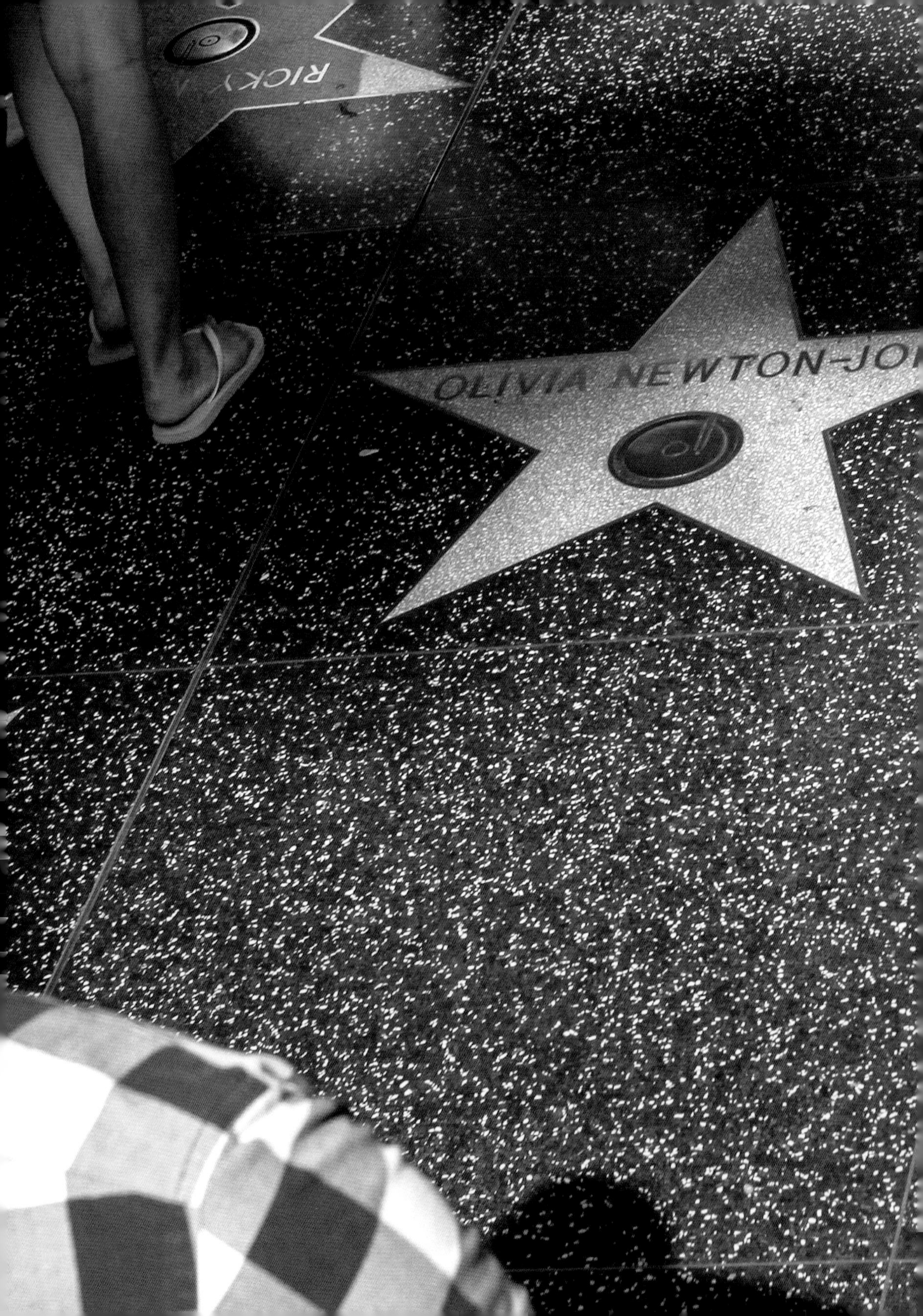
RICKY
OLIVIA NEWTON-JO

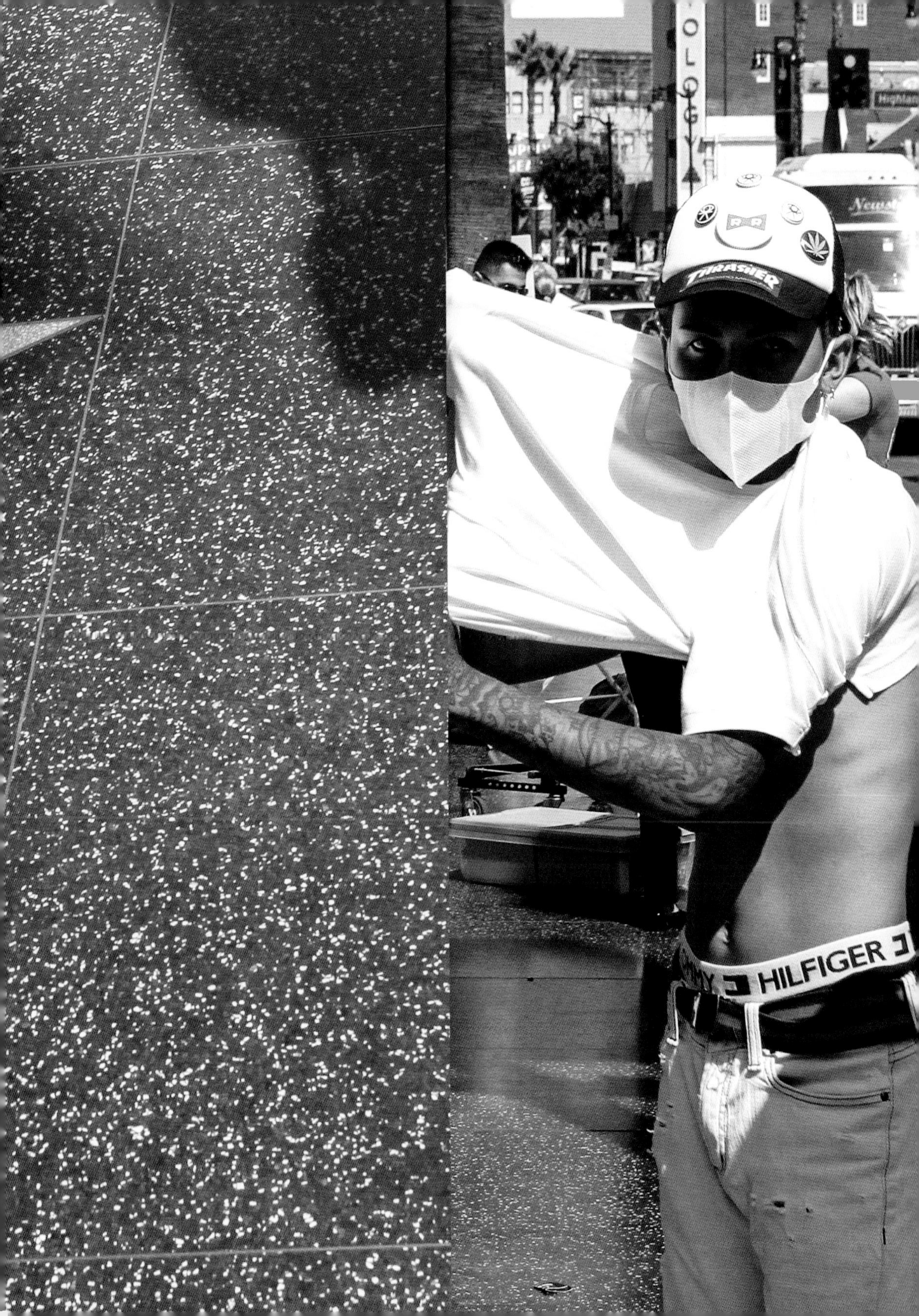
THRASHER
HILFIGER

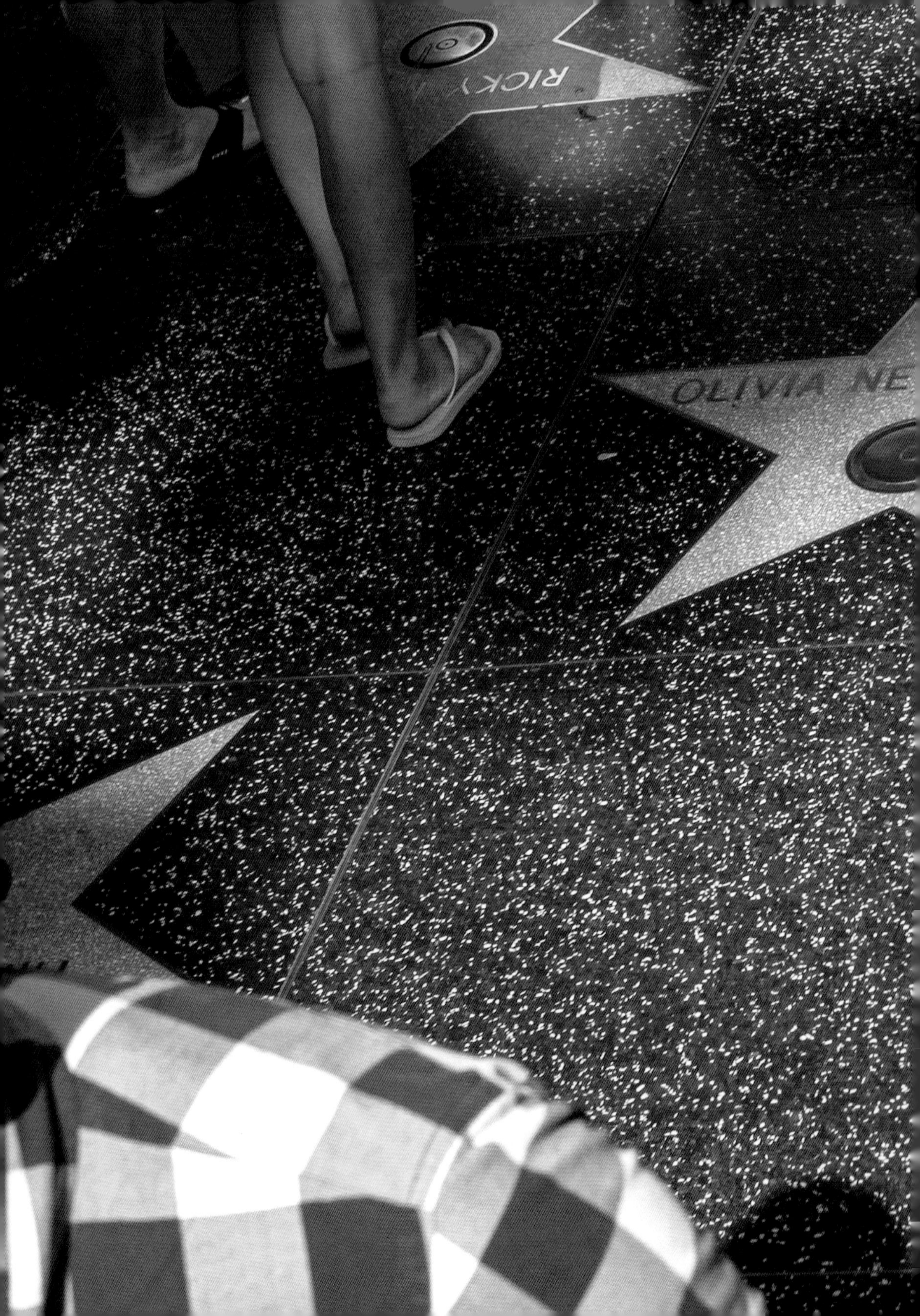

RICKY
OLIVIA NE

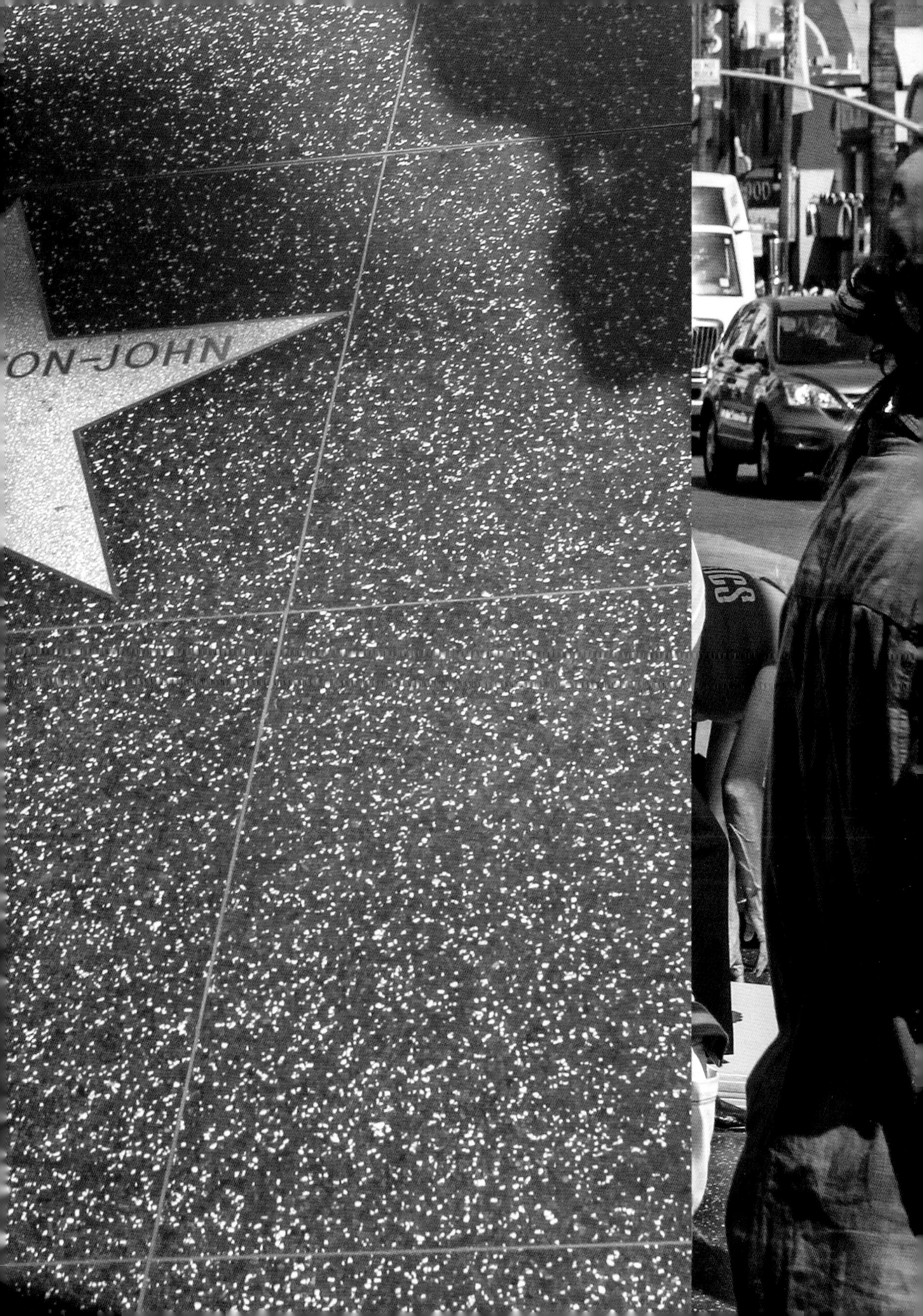

ON-JOHN

RICKY

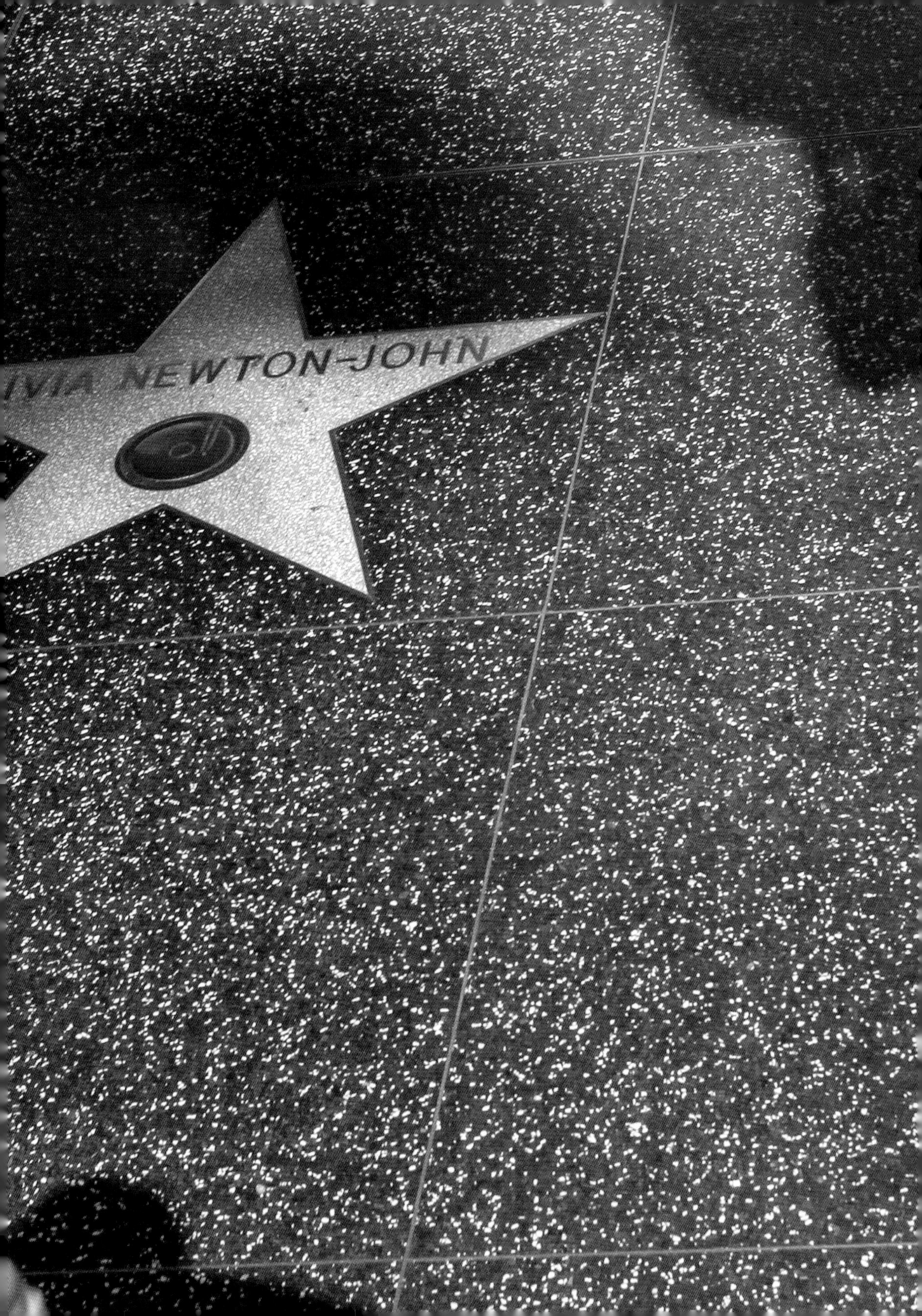

...IVIA NEWTON-JOHN

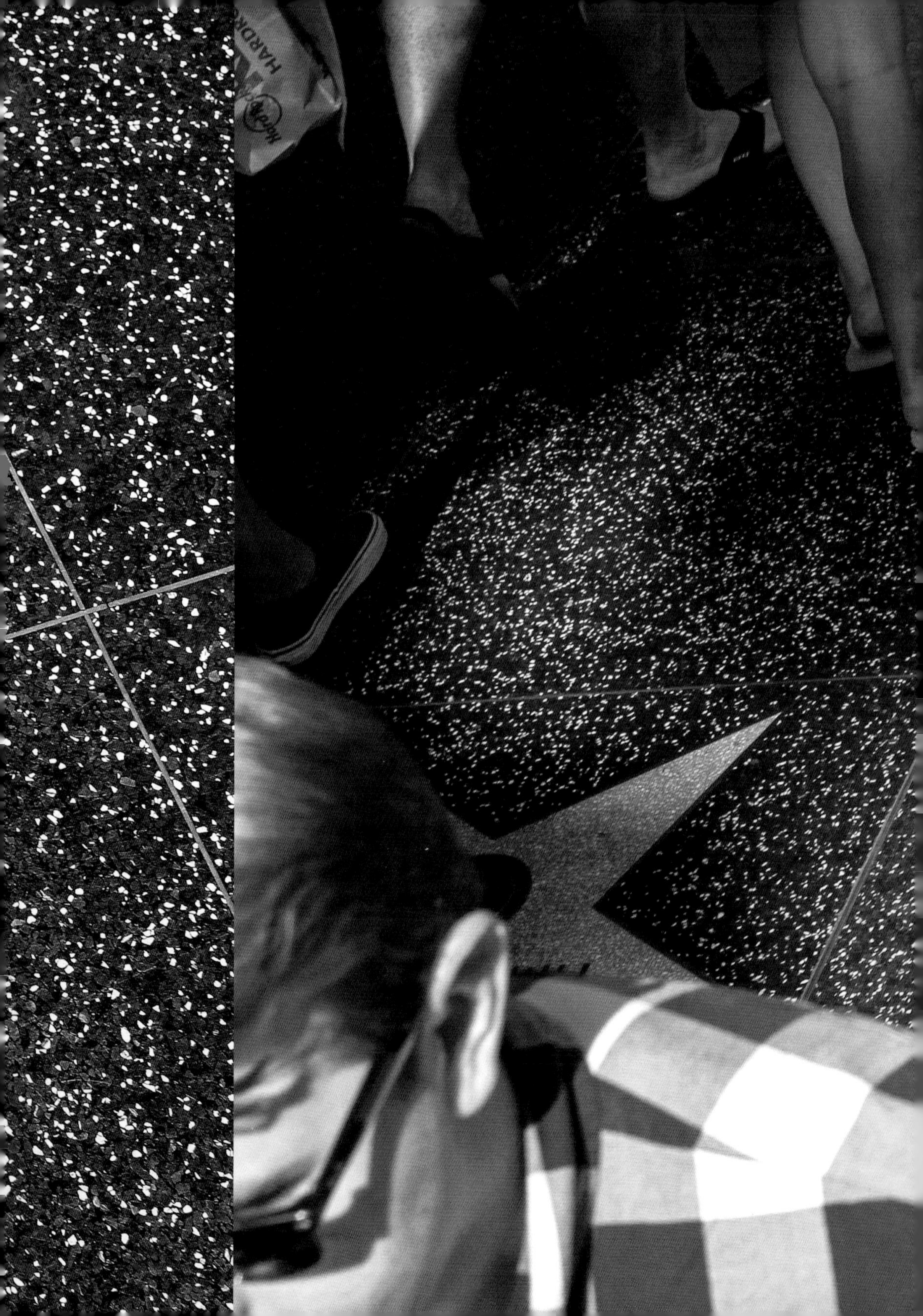

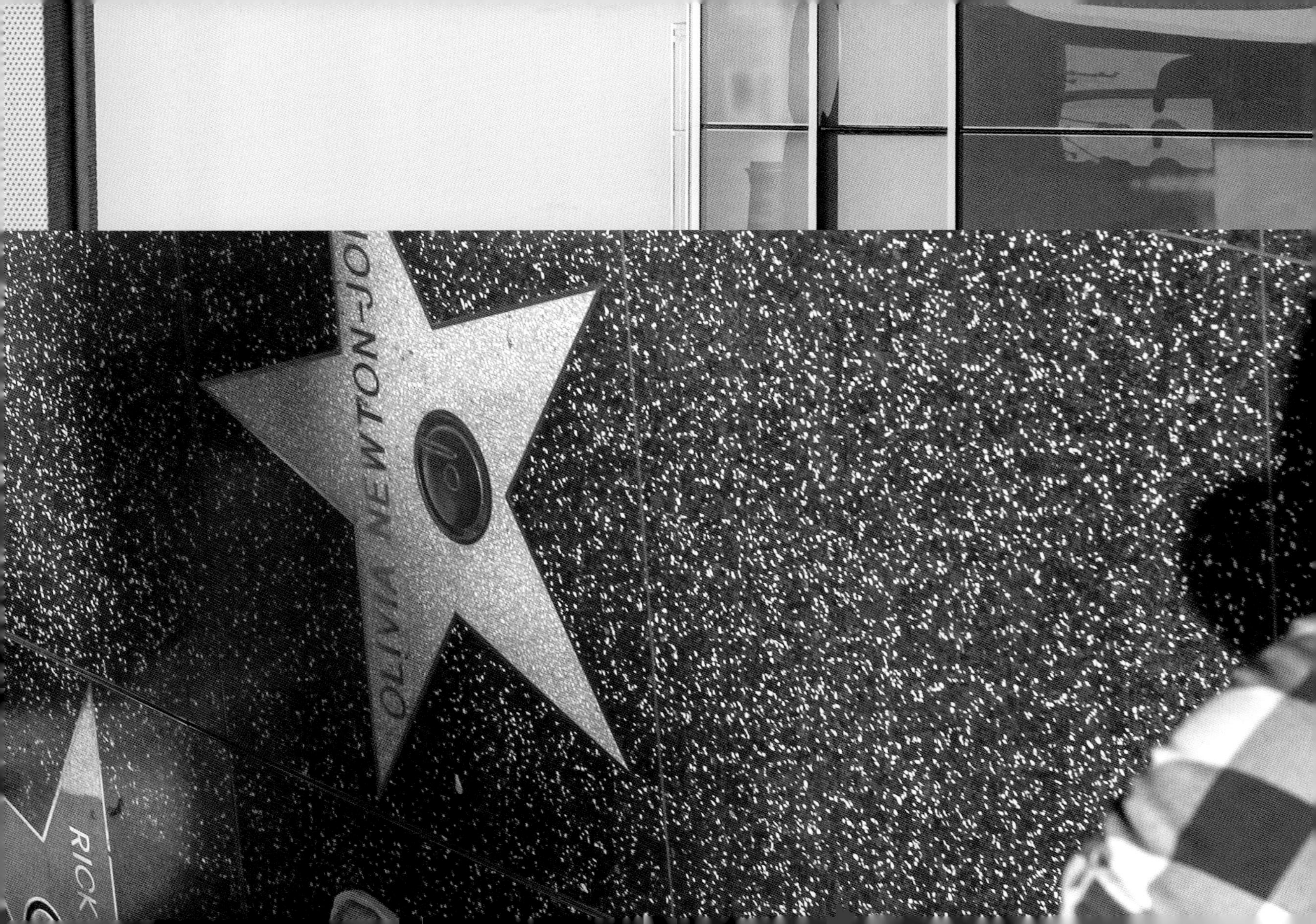

OLIVIA NEWTON-JO
RICK

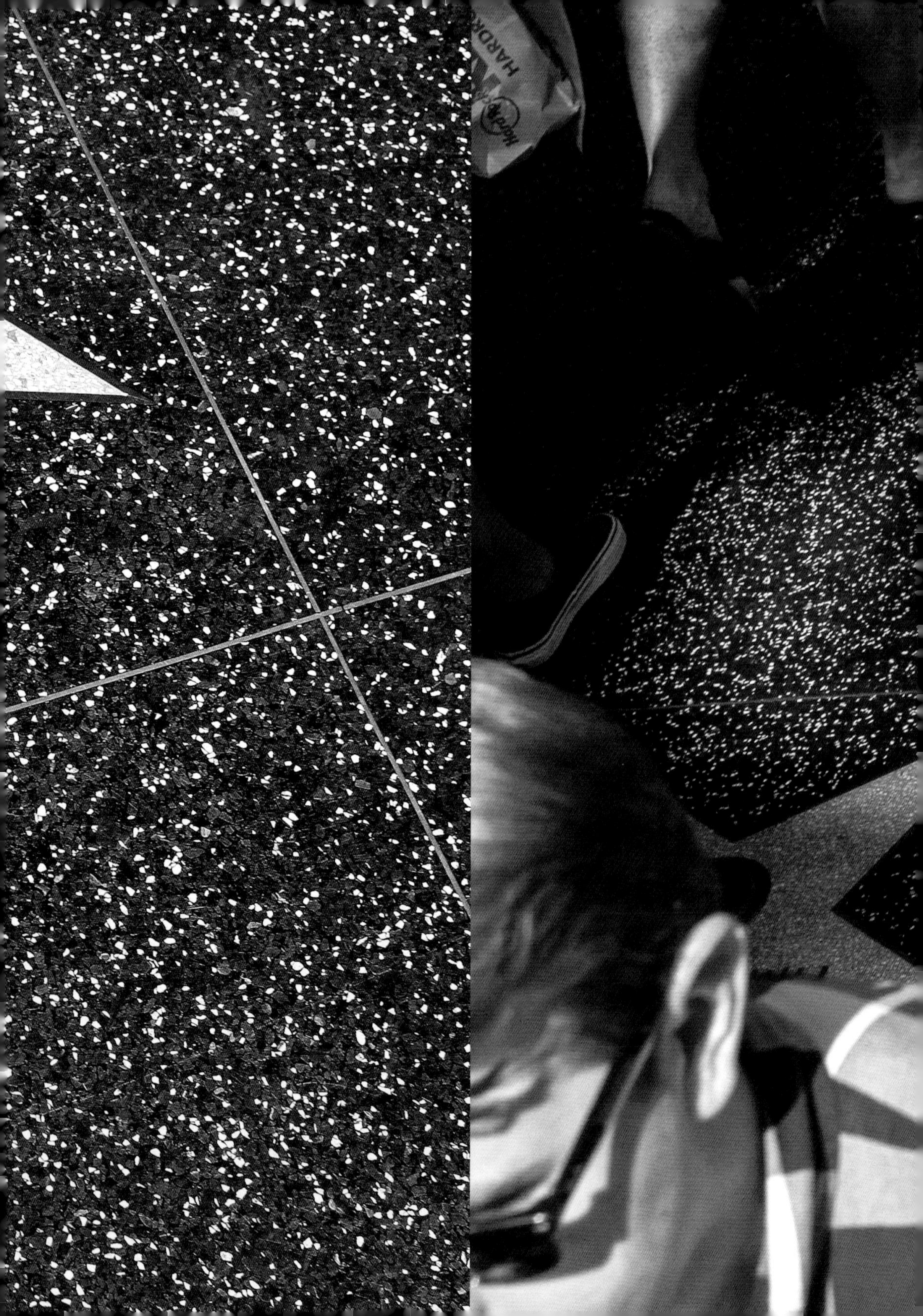

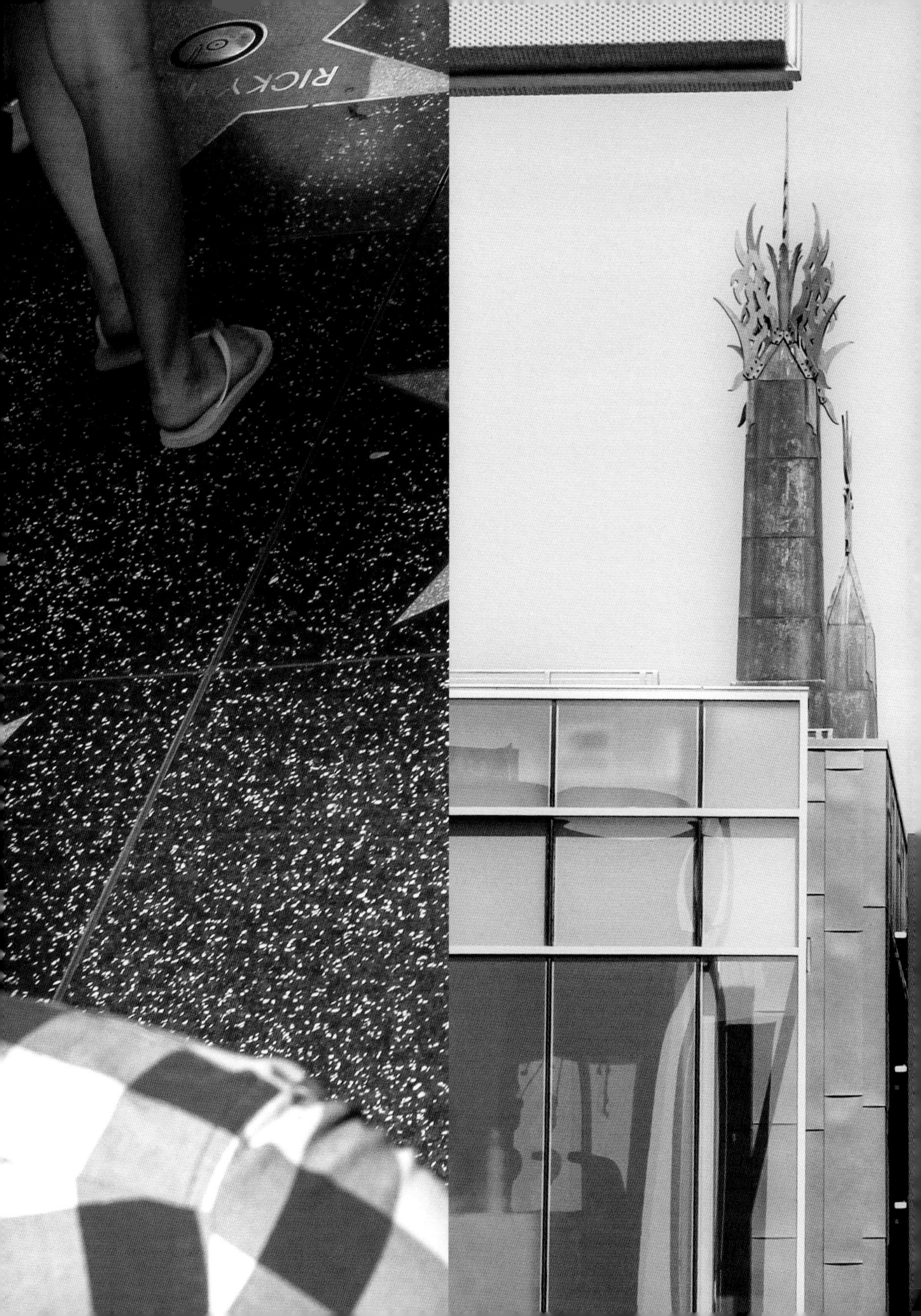

RICK

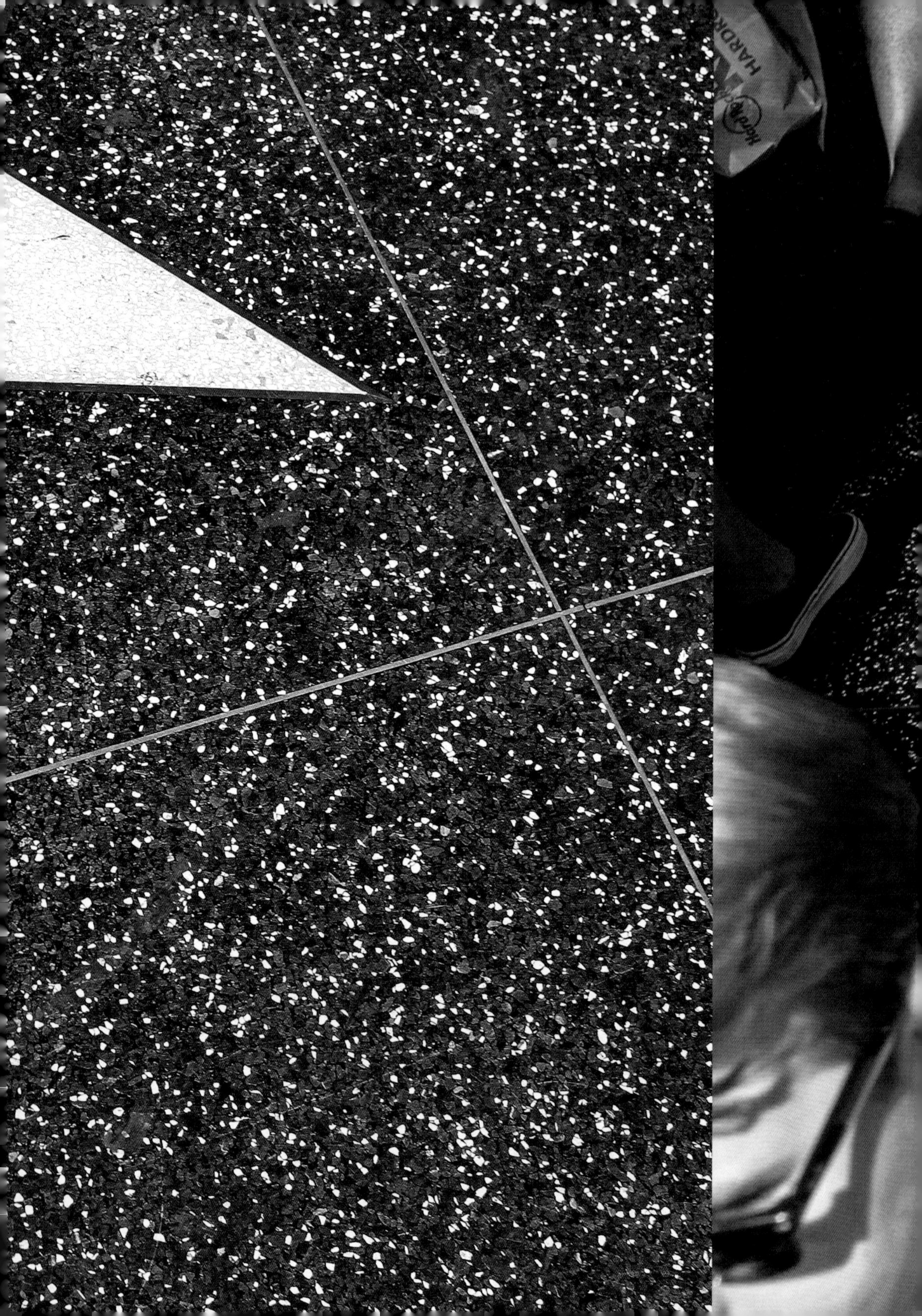

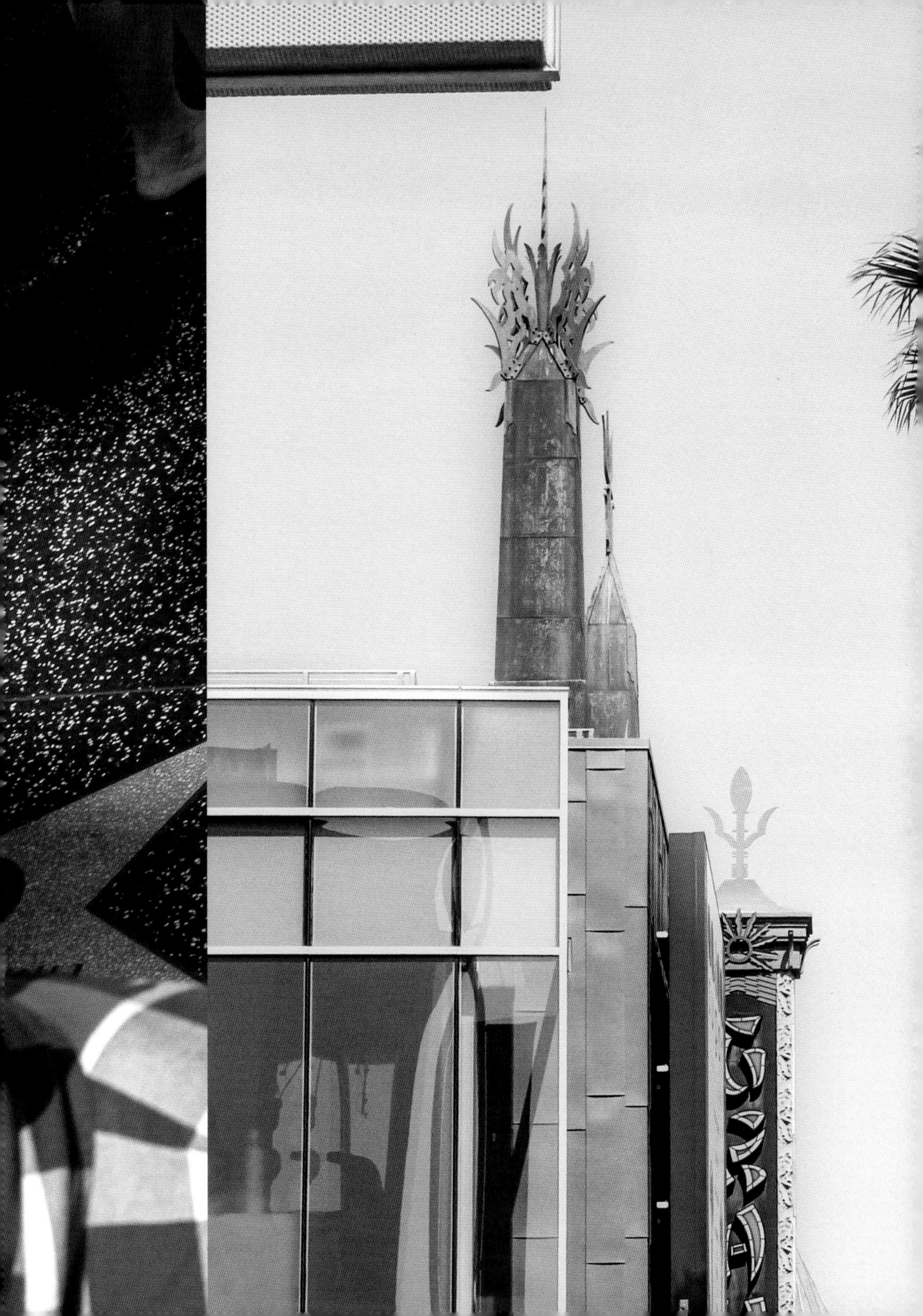

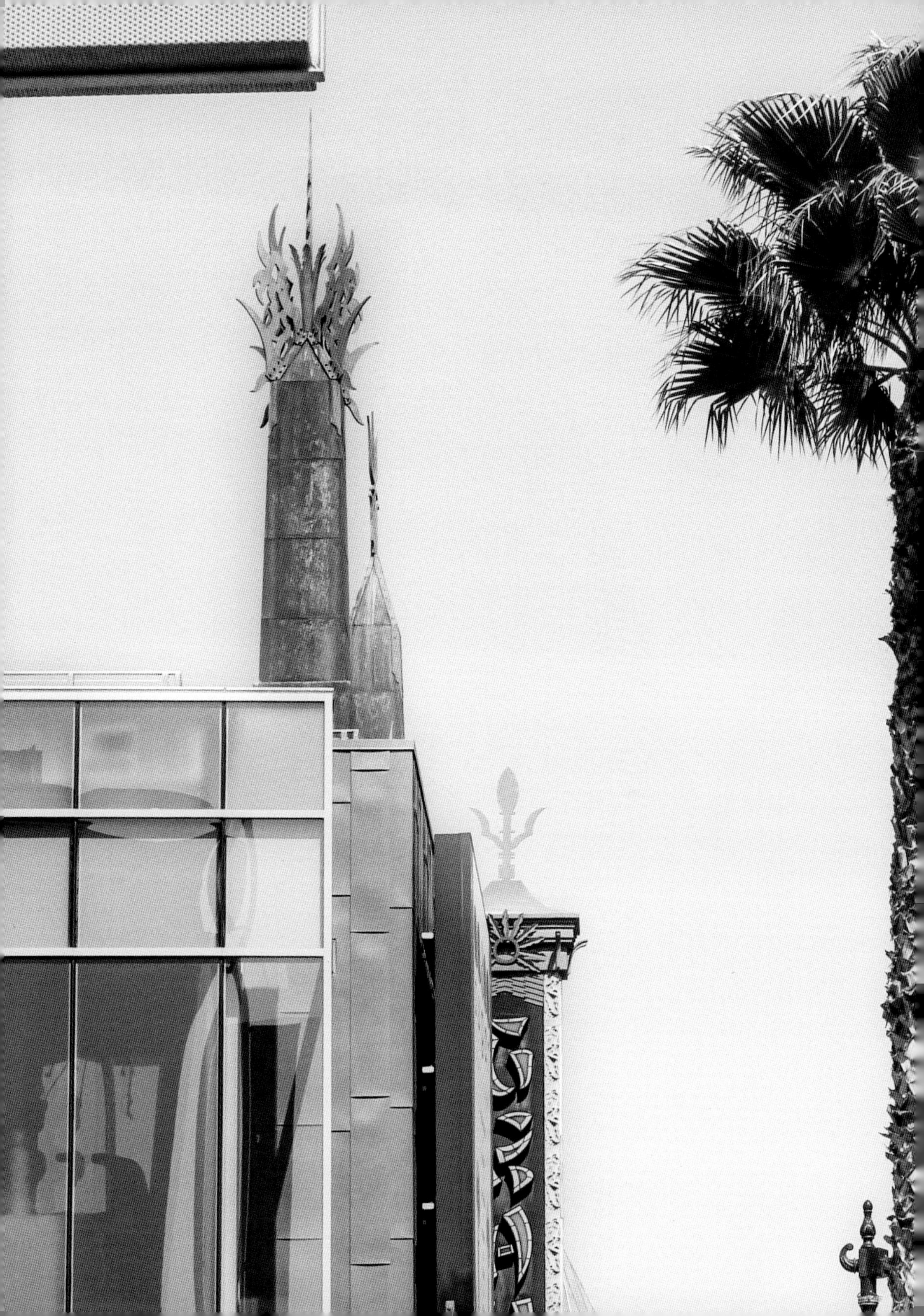

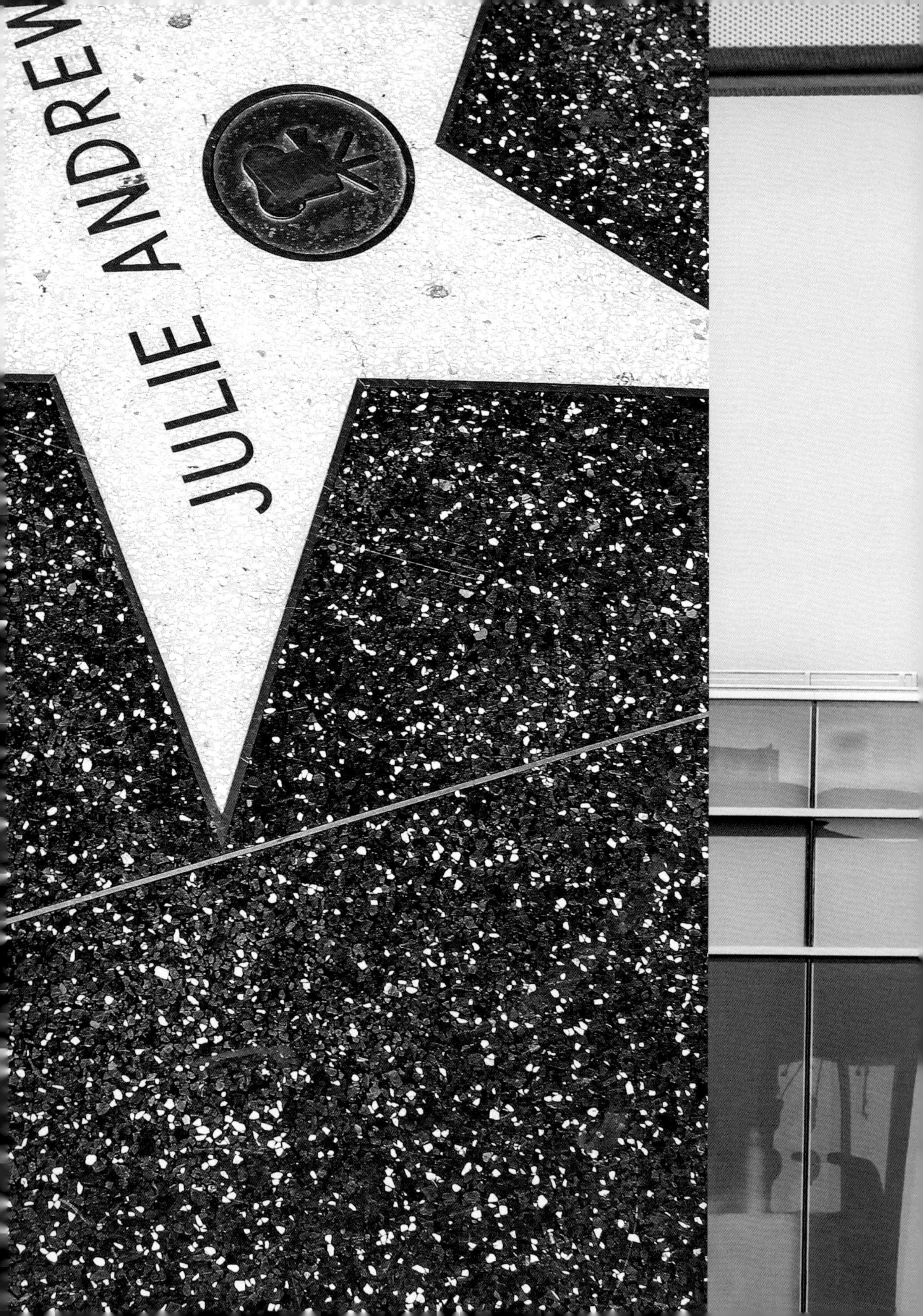

JULIE ANDREWS

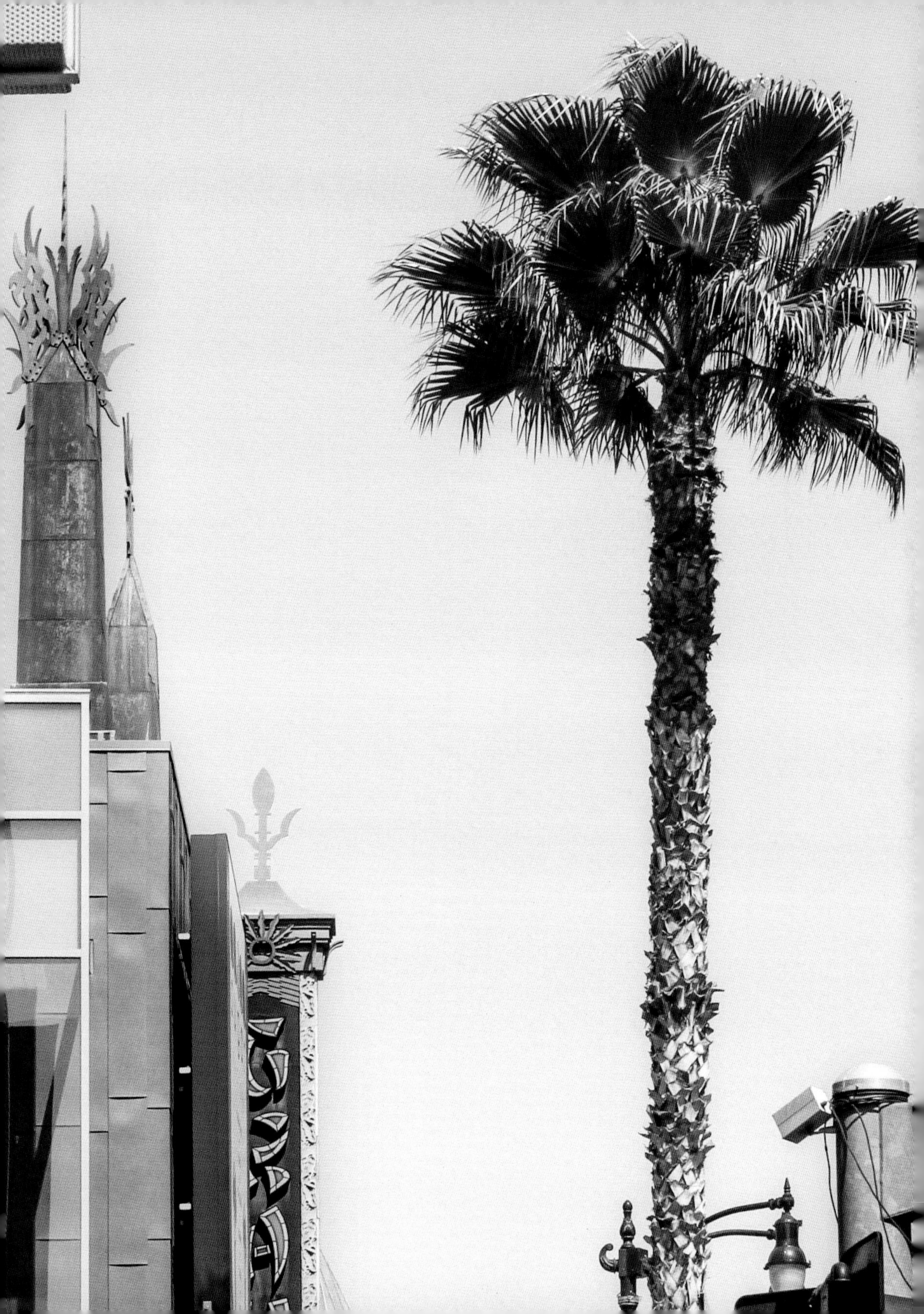

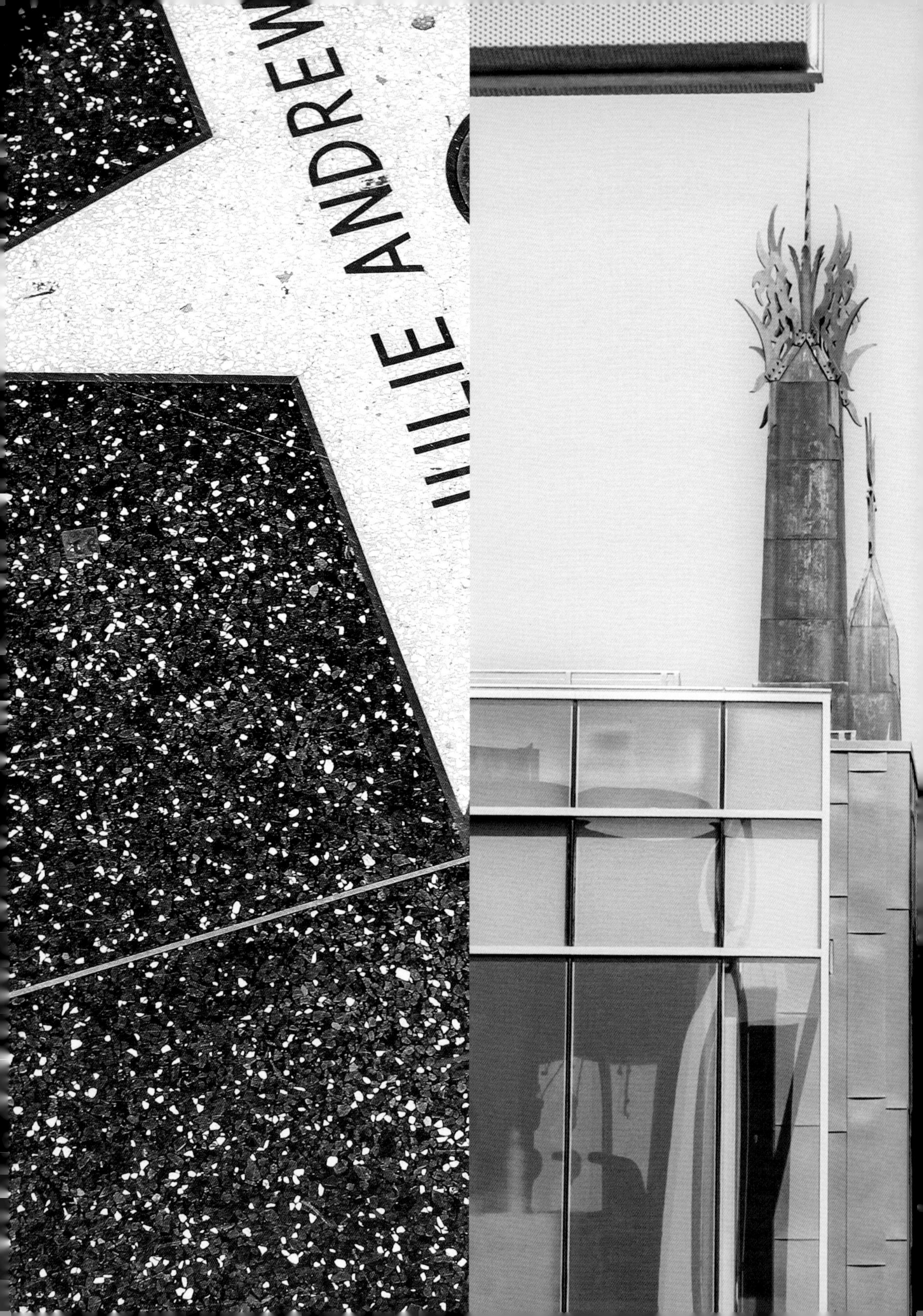
ILLIE ANDREW

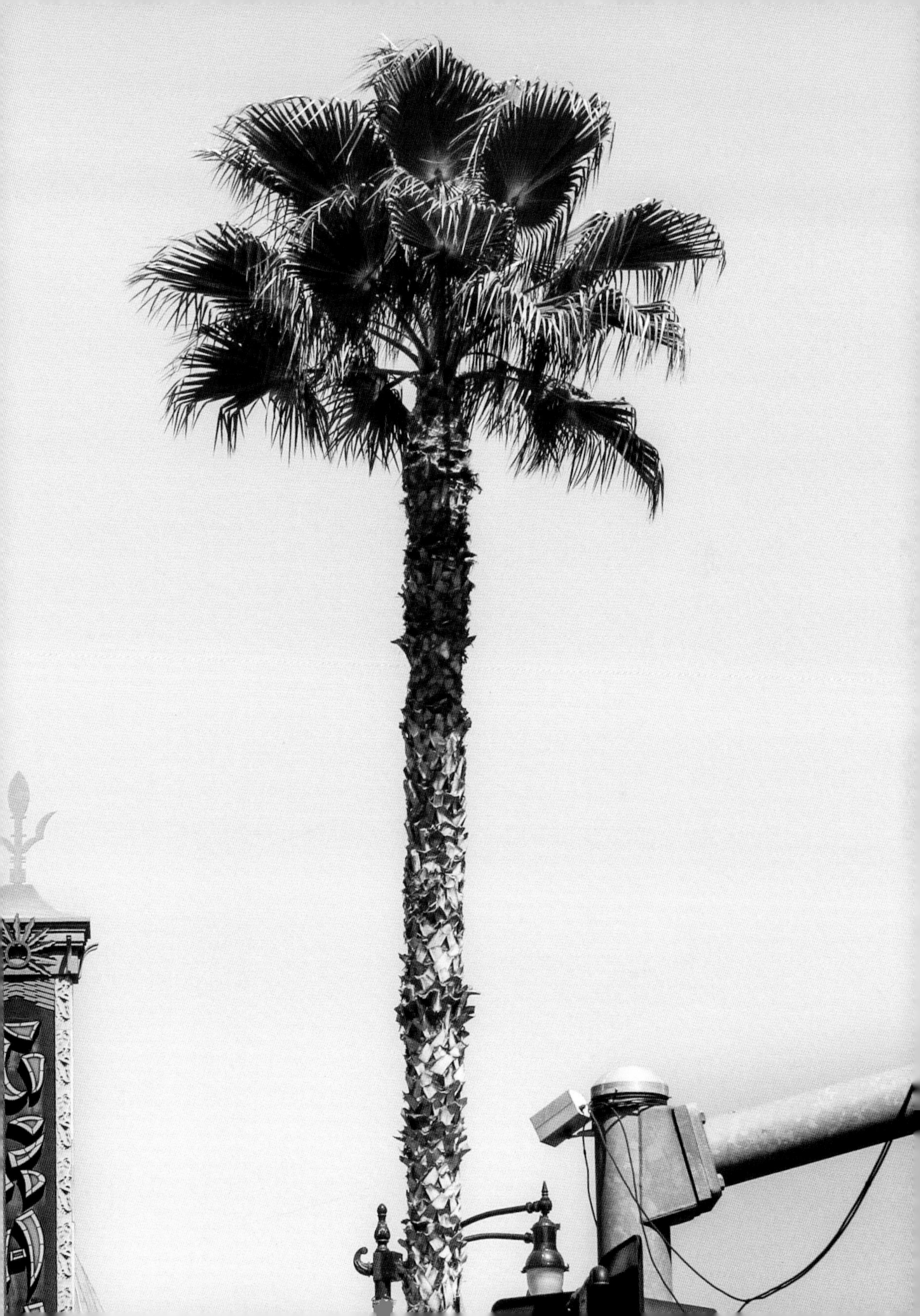

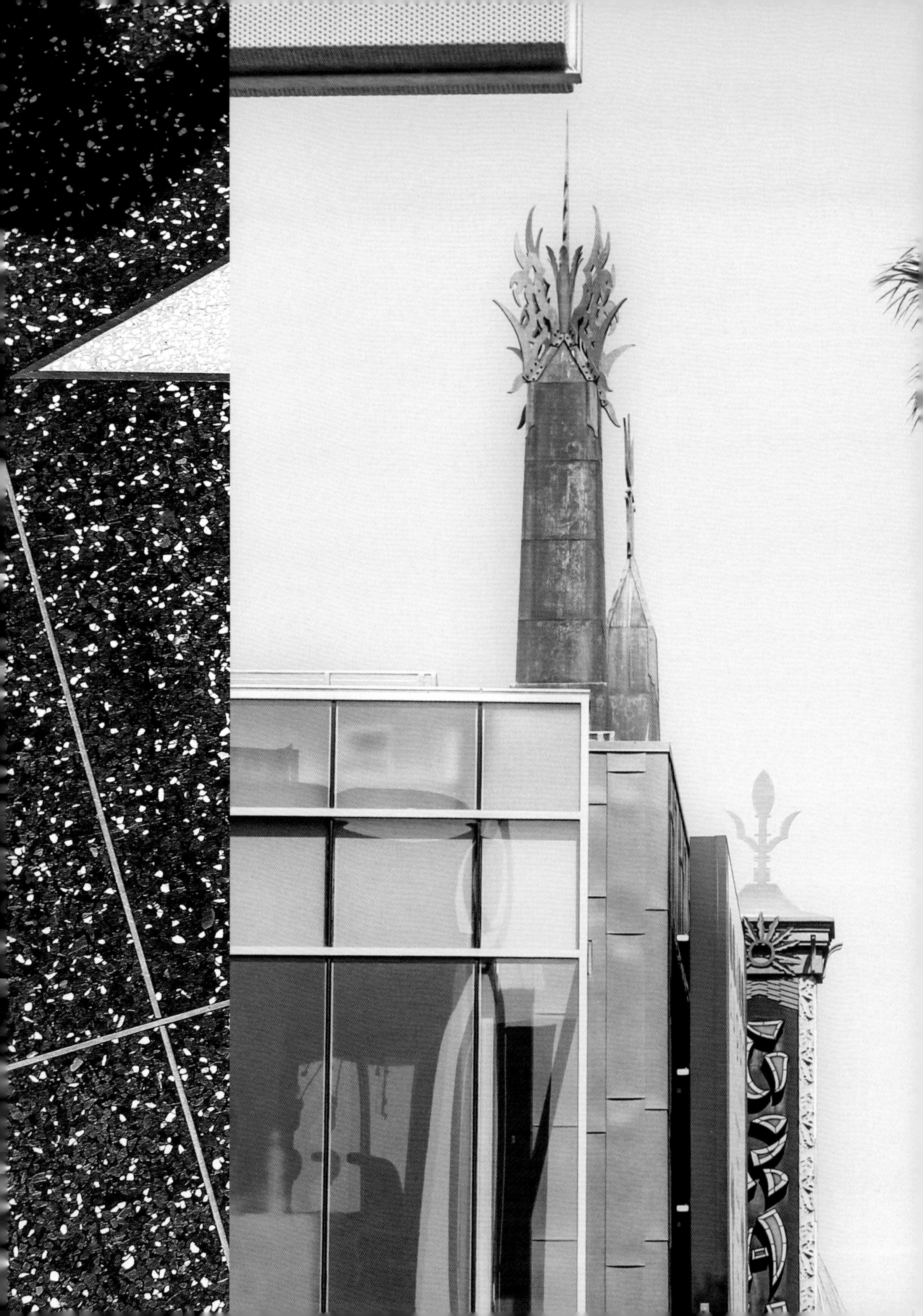

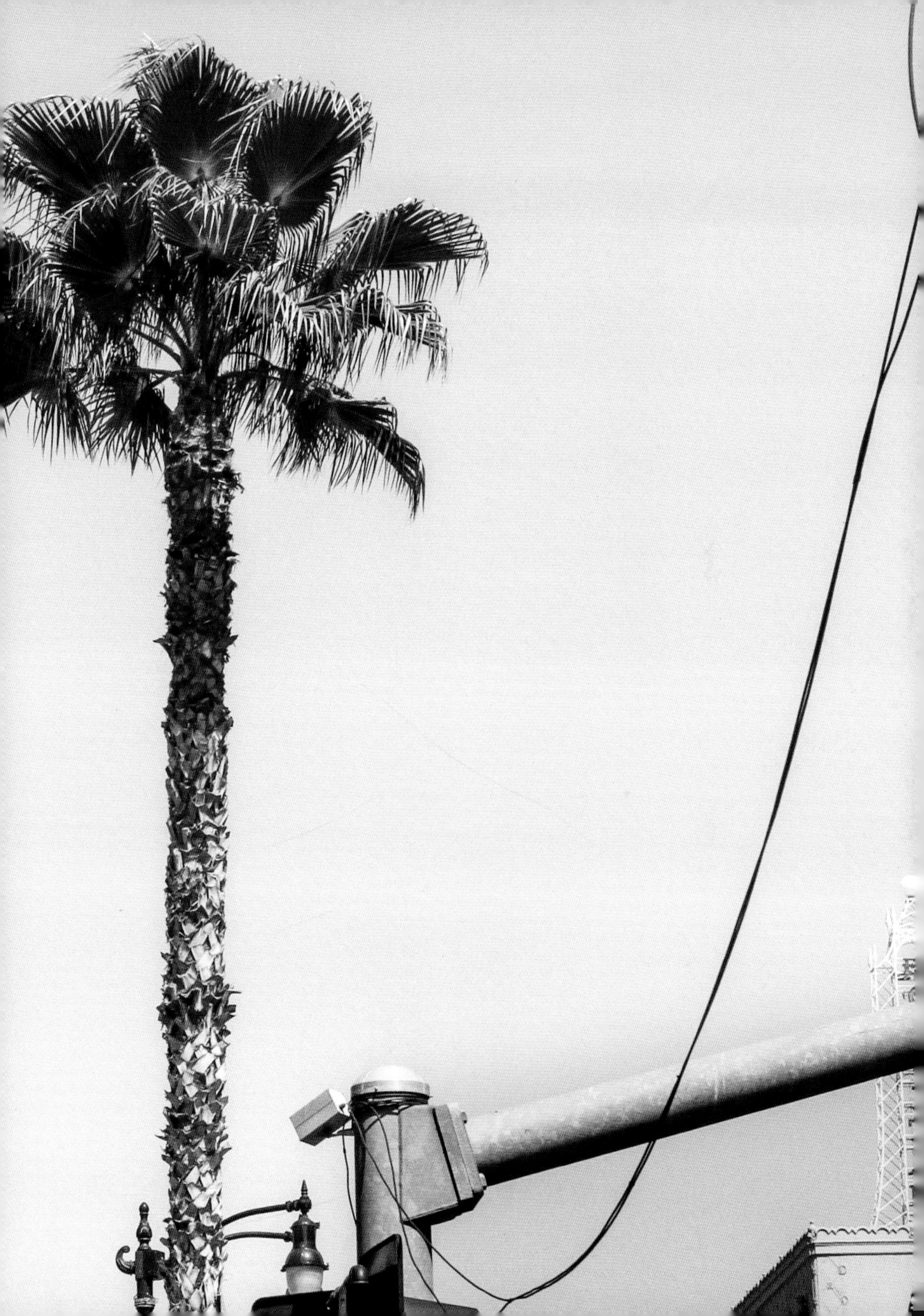

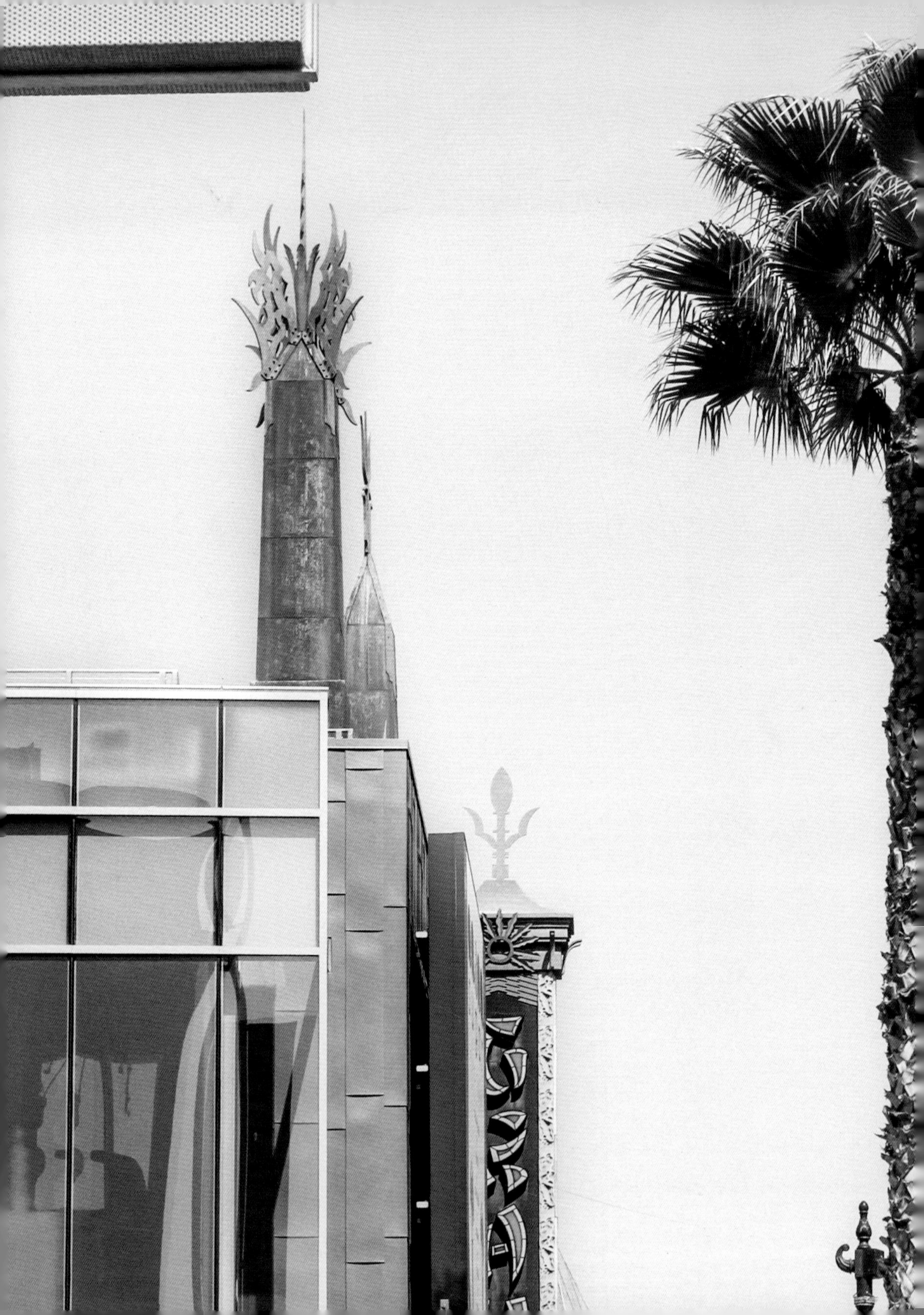

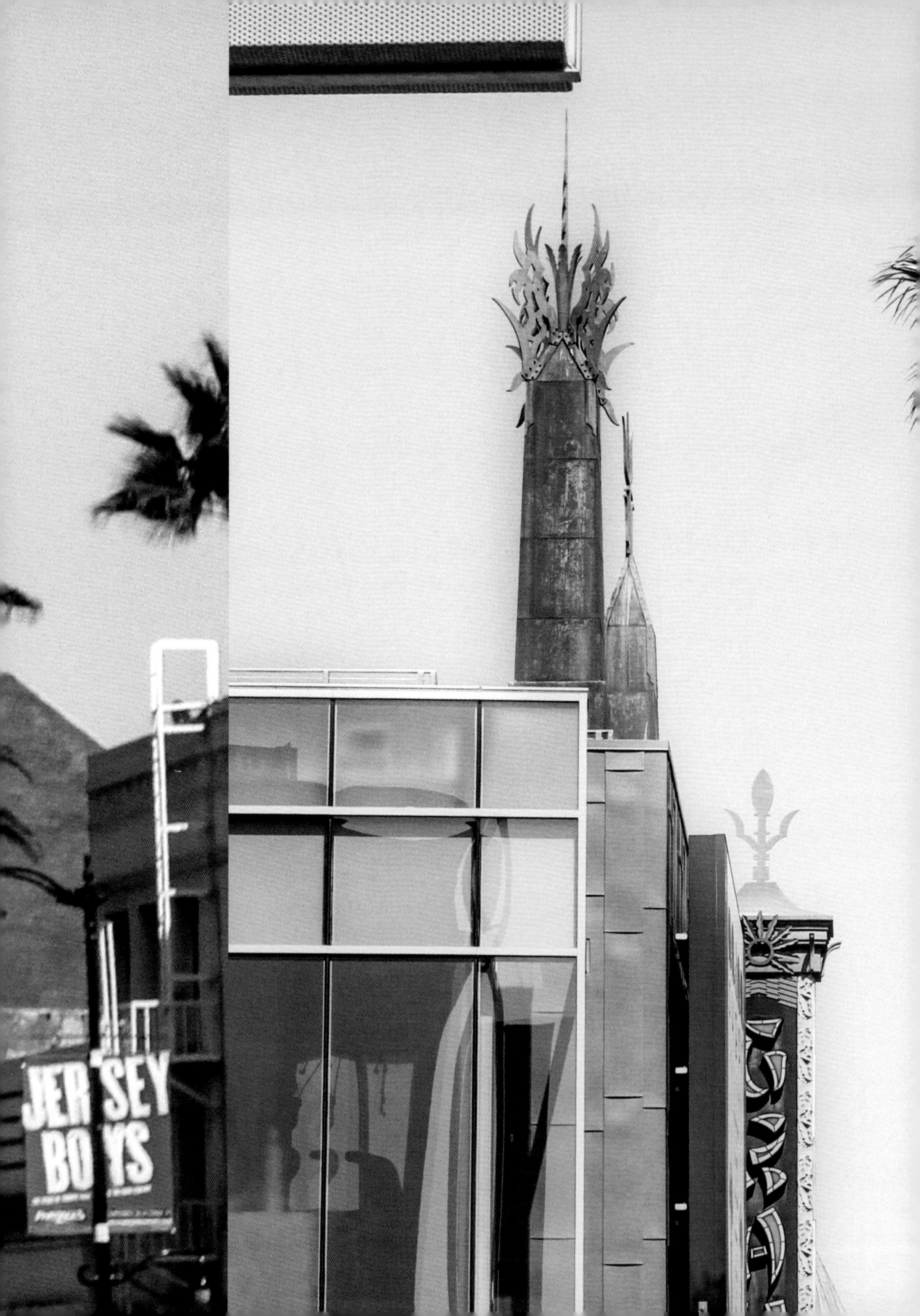
JER SEY
BO YS

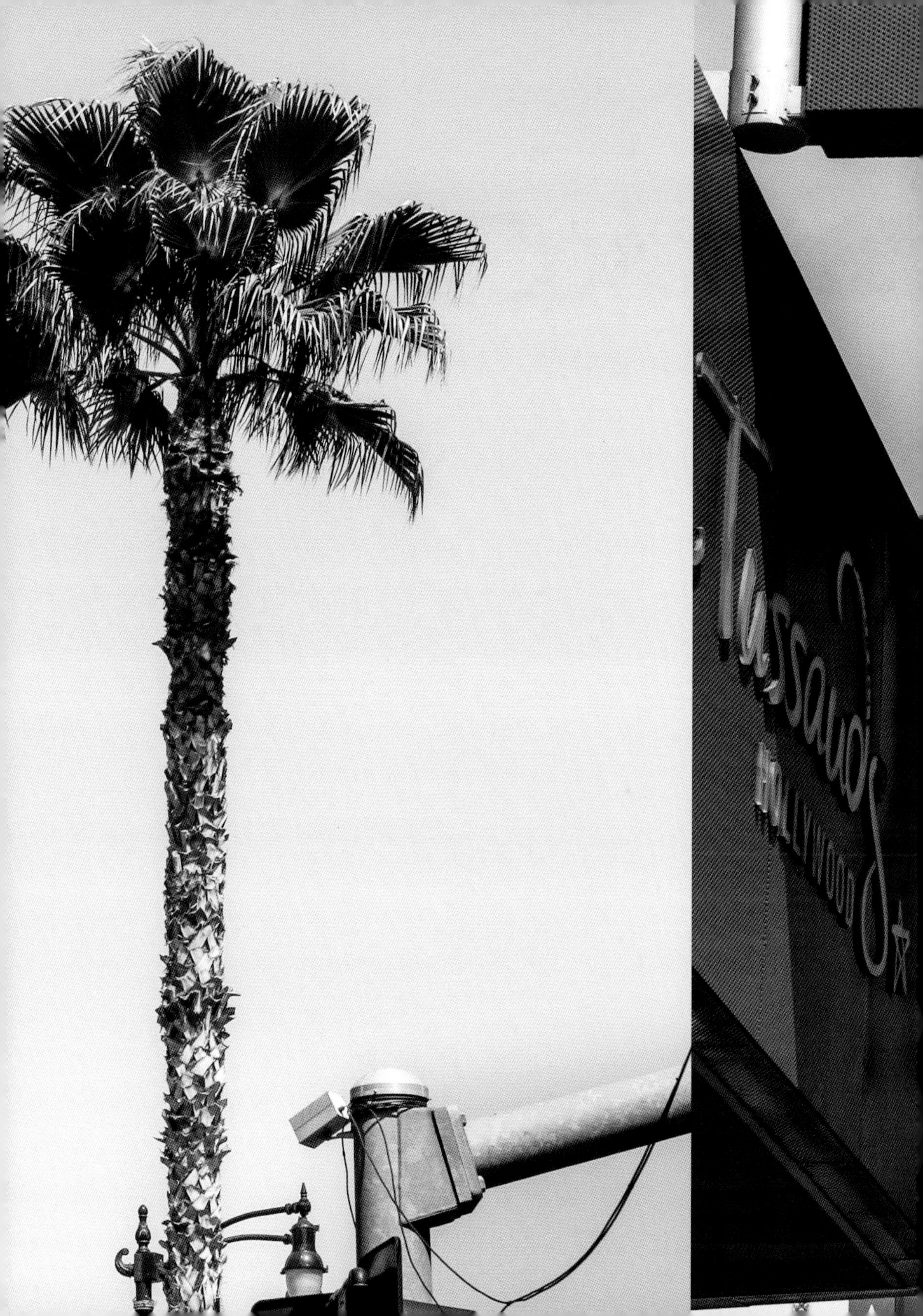

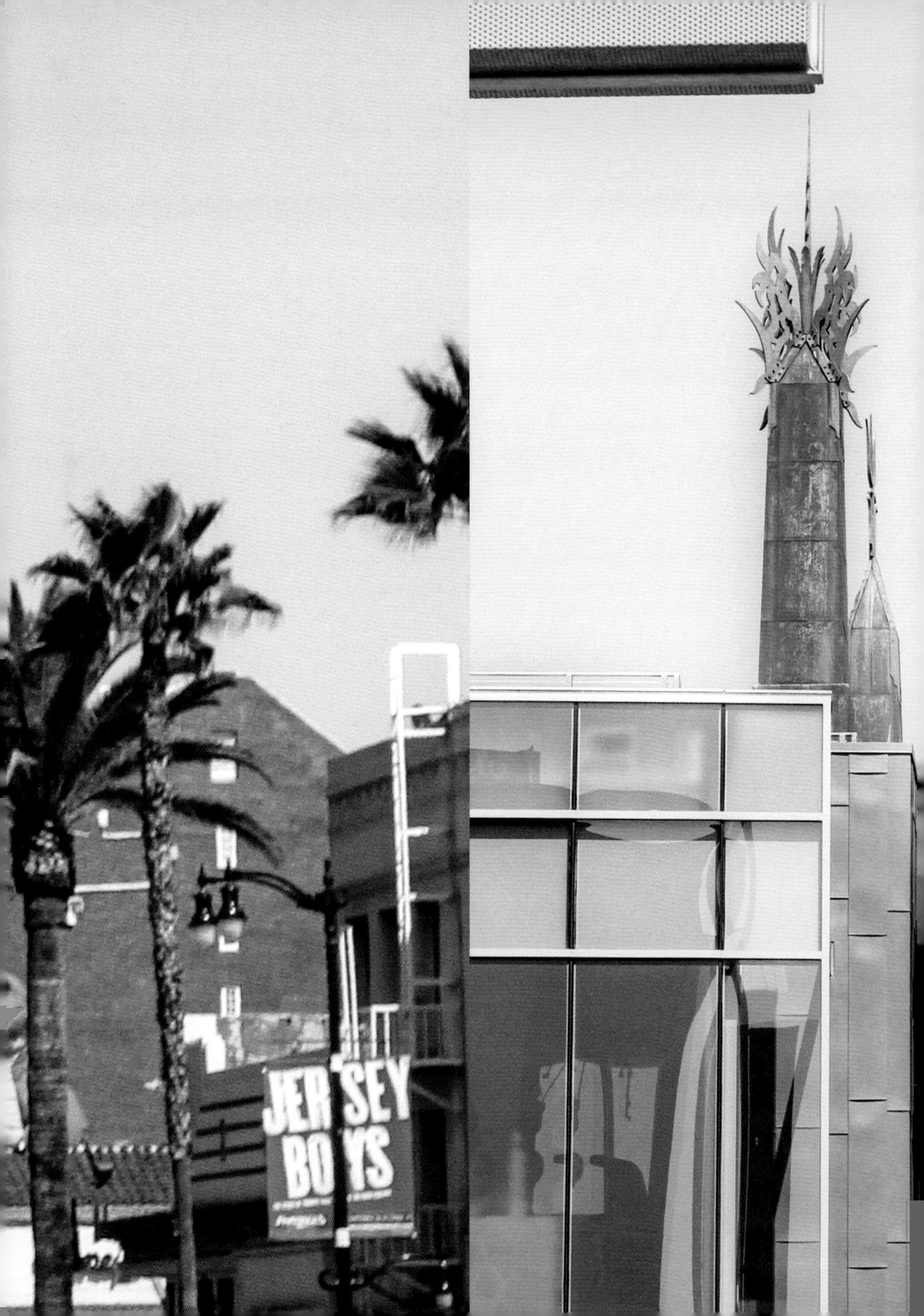

JER SEY
BO YS

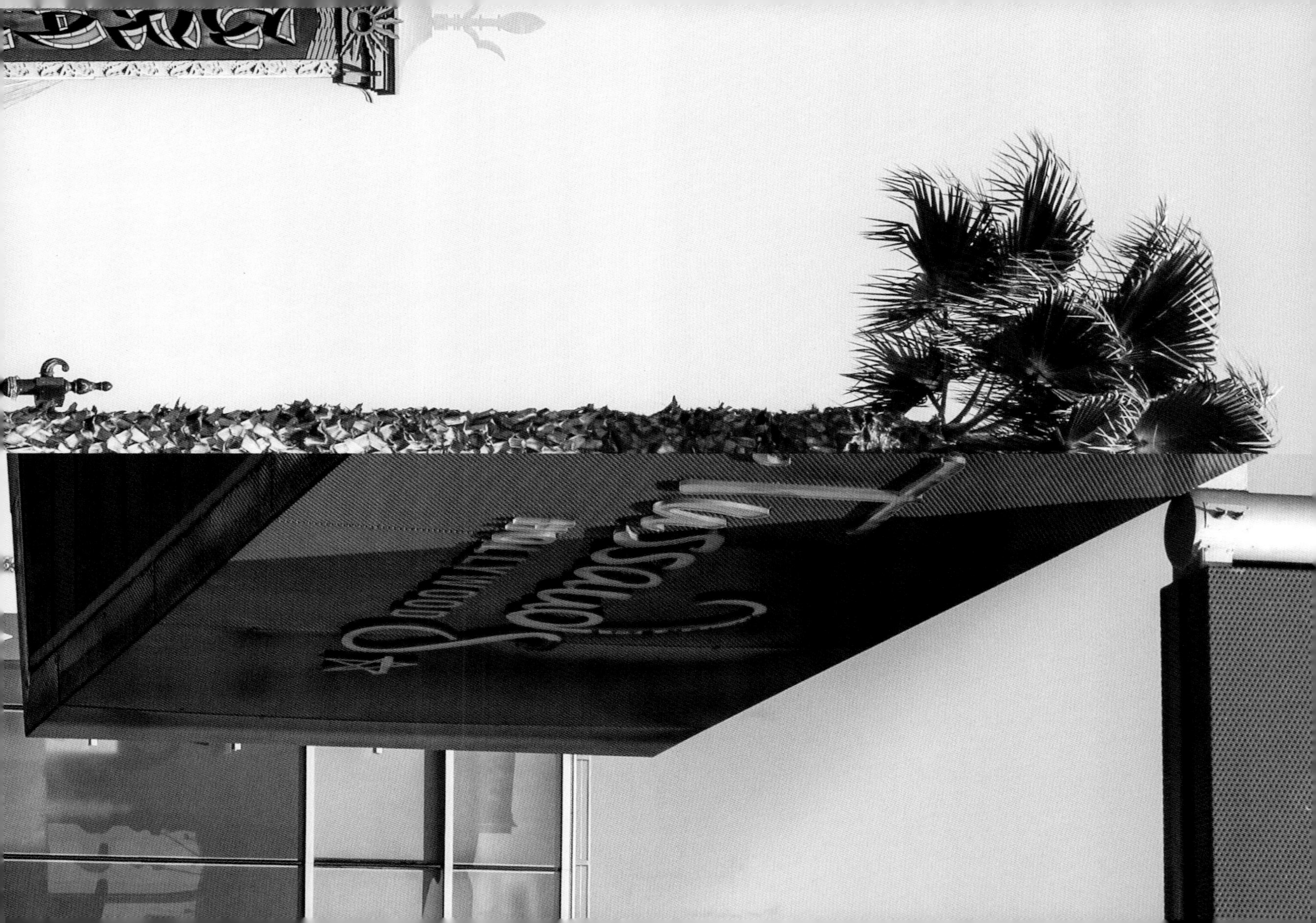

Tussauds
HOLLYWOOD

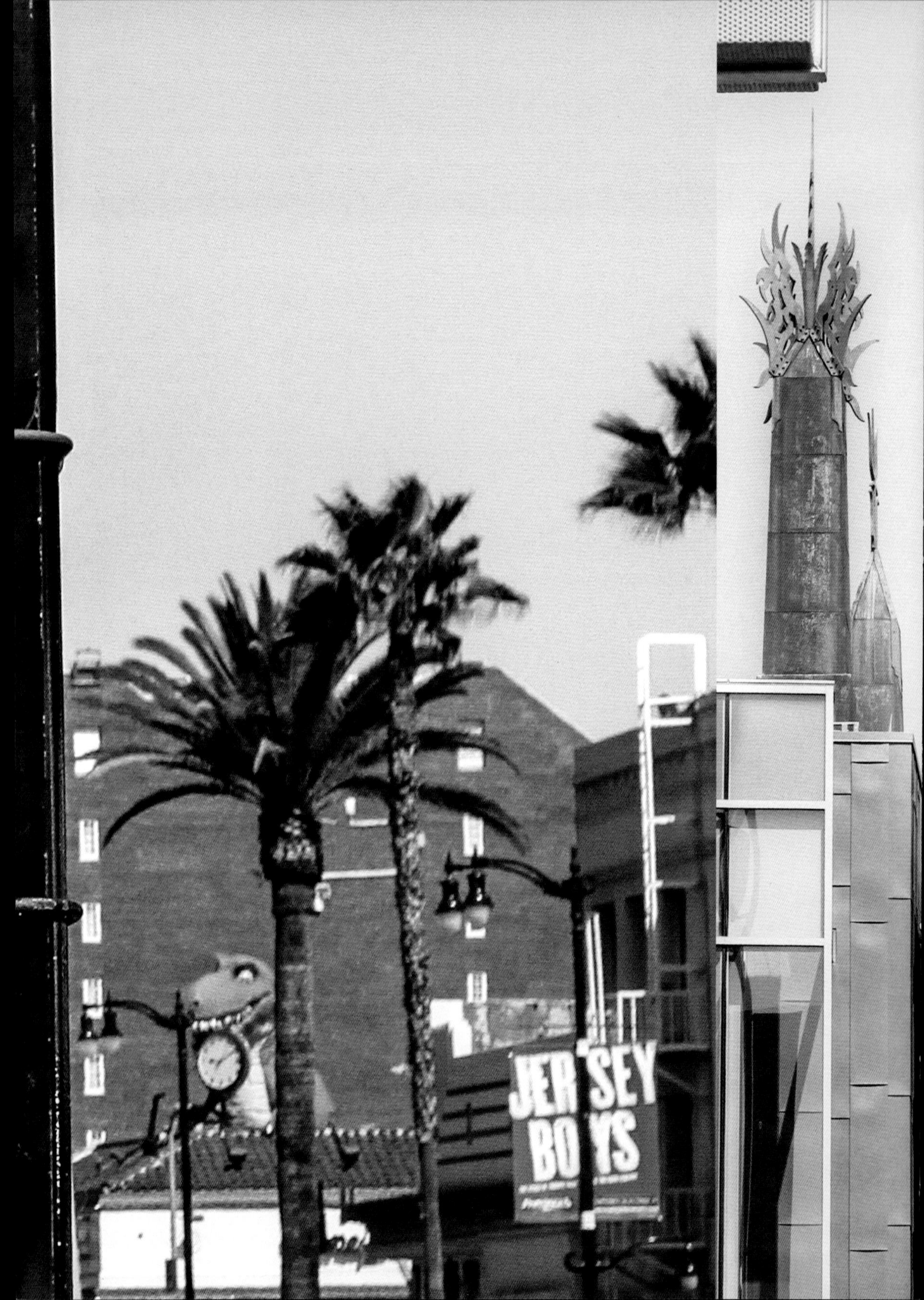

JER SEY
BO YS

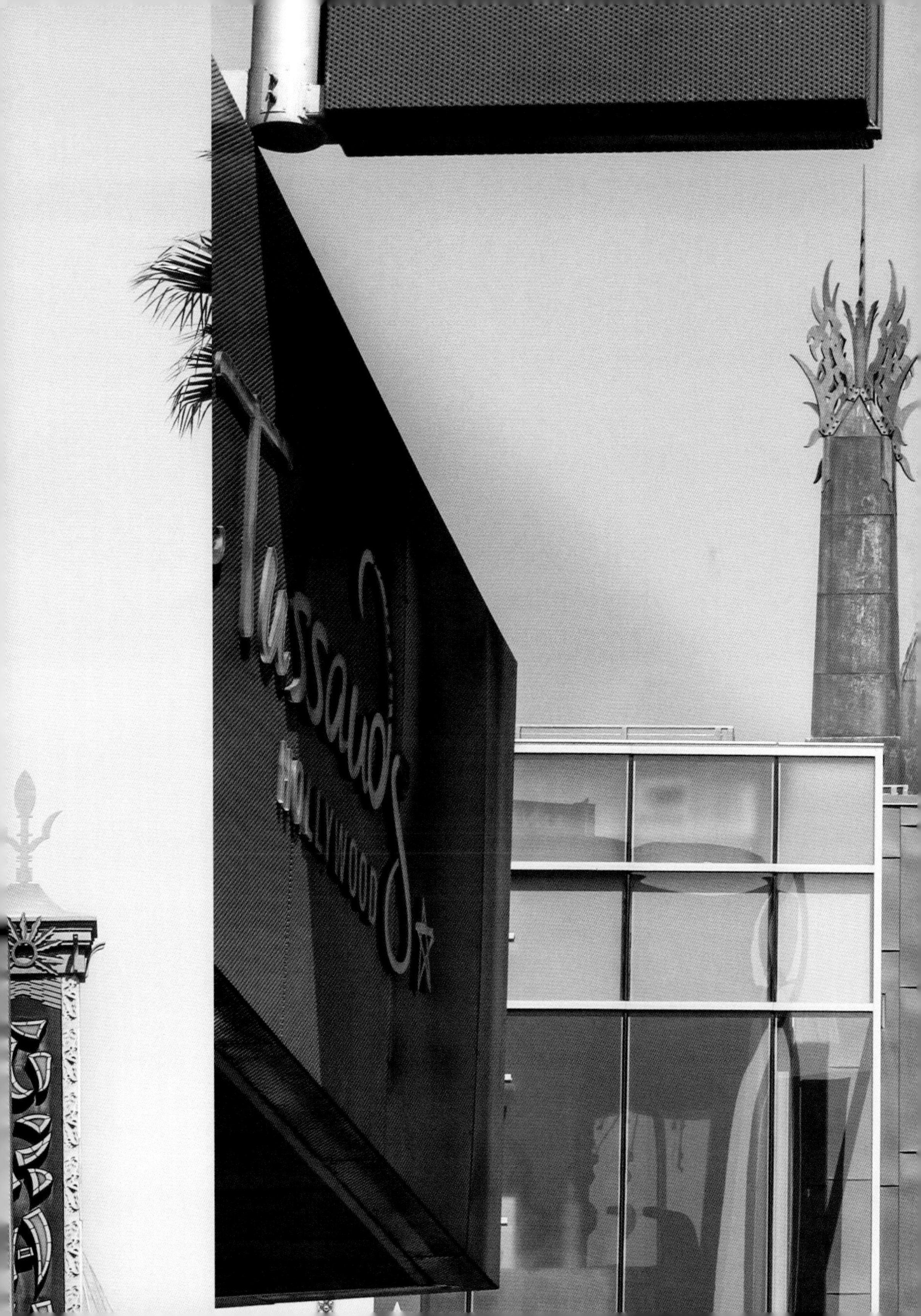
Tussauds
HOLLYWOOD

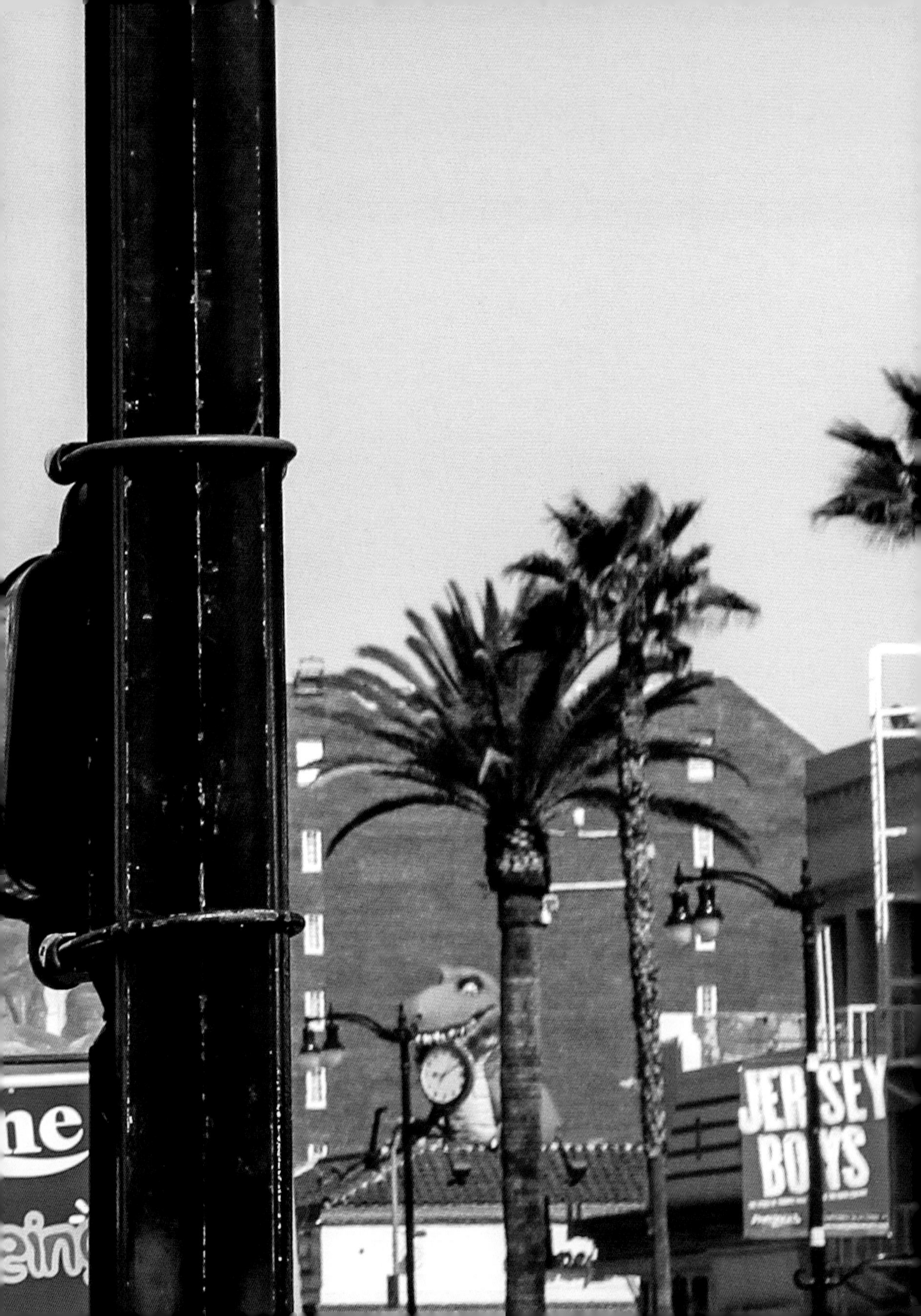
ne
JER SEY
BOYS

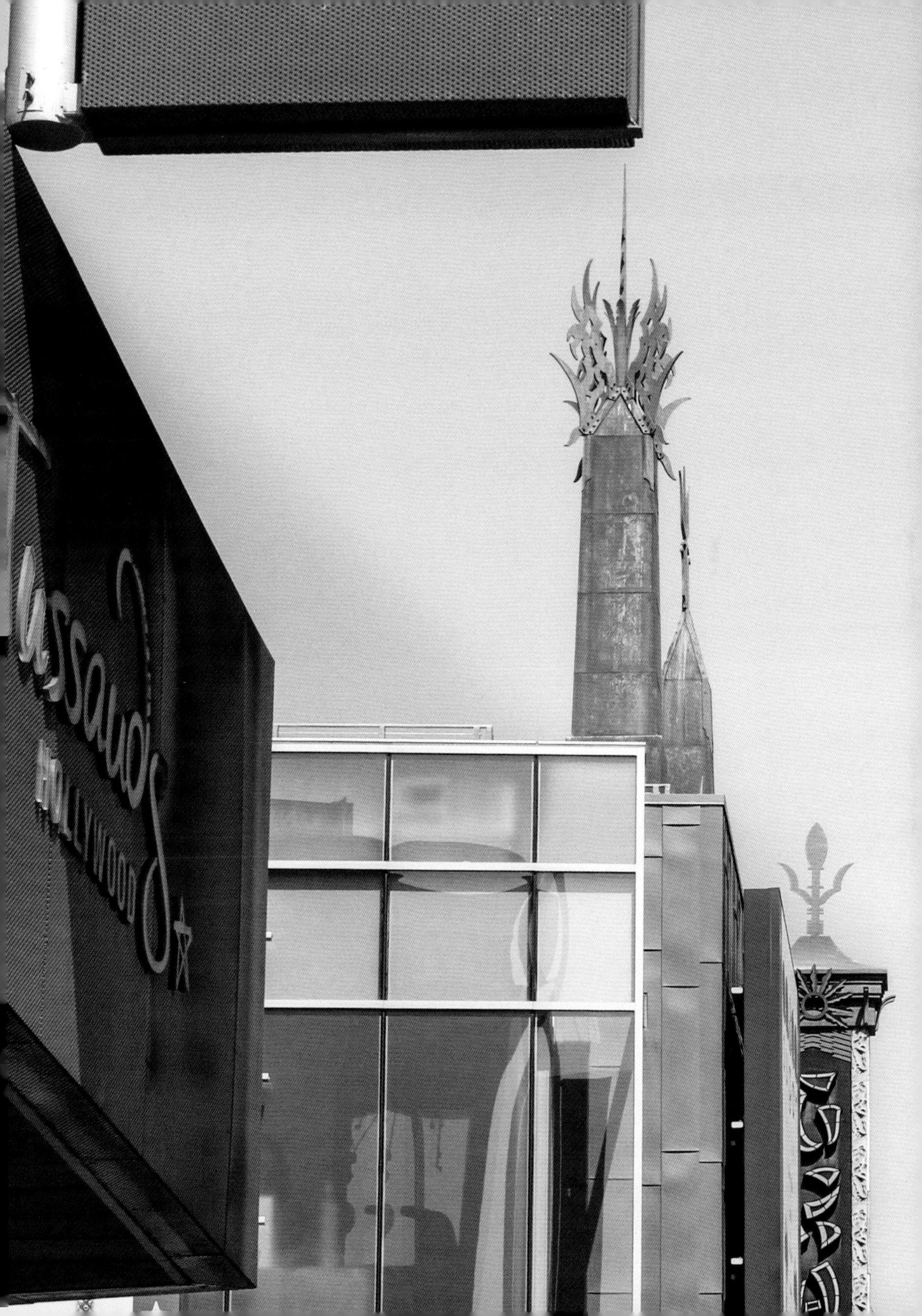

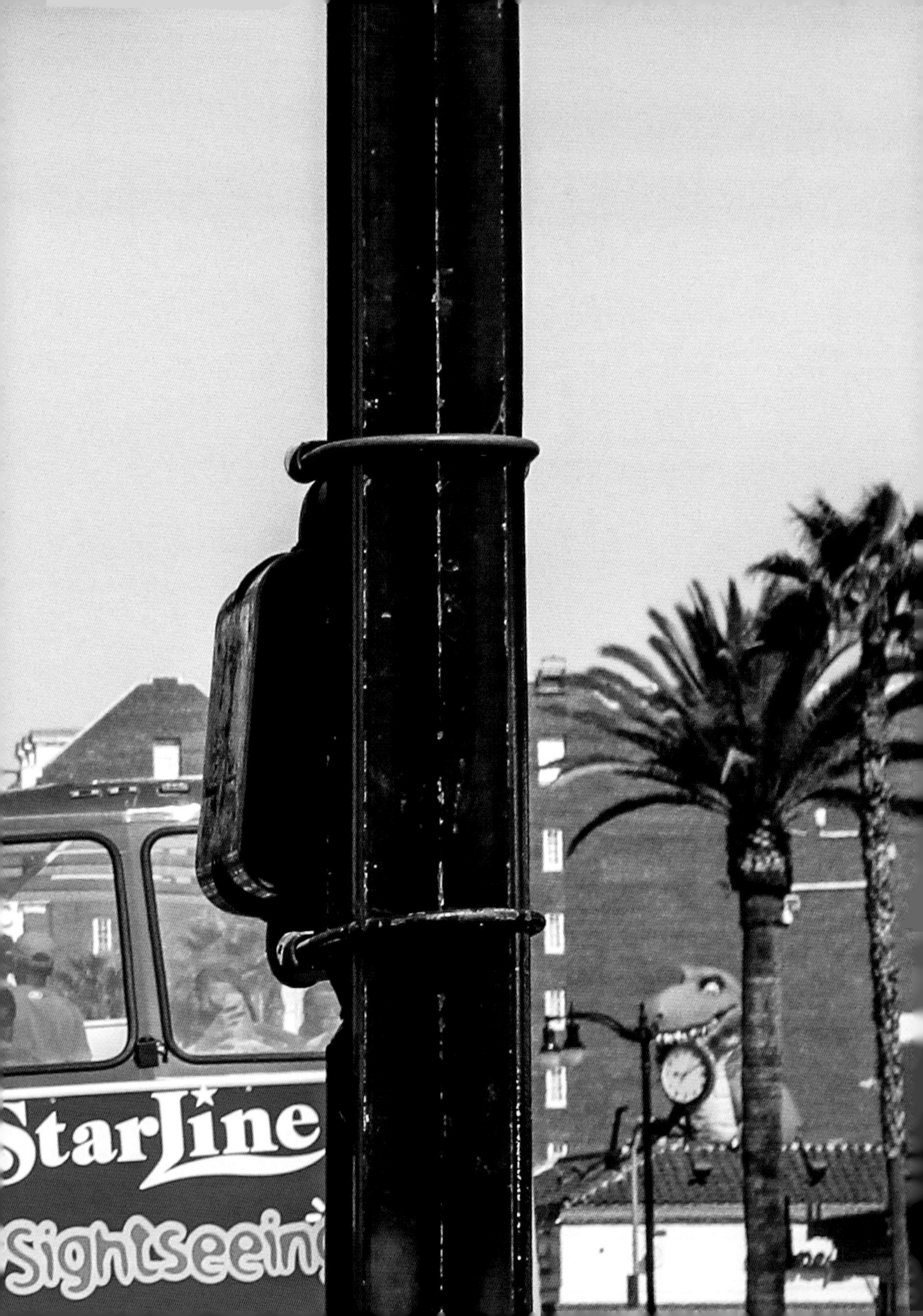

StarLine
Sightseein'

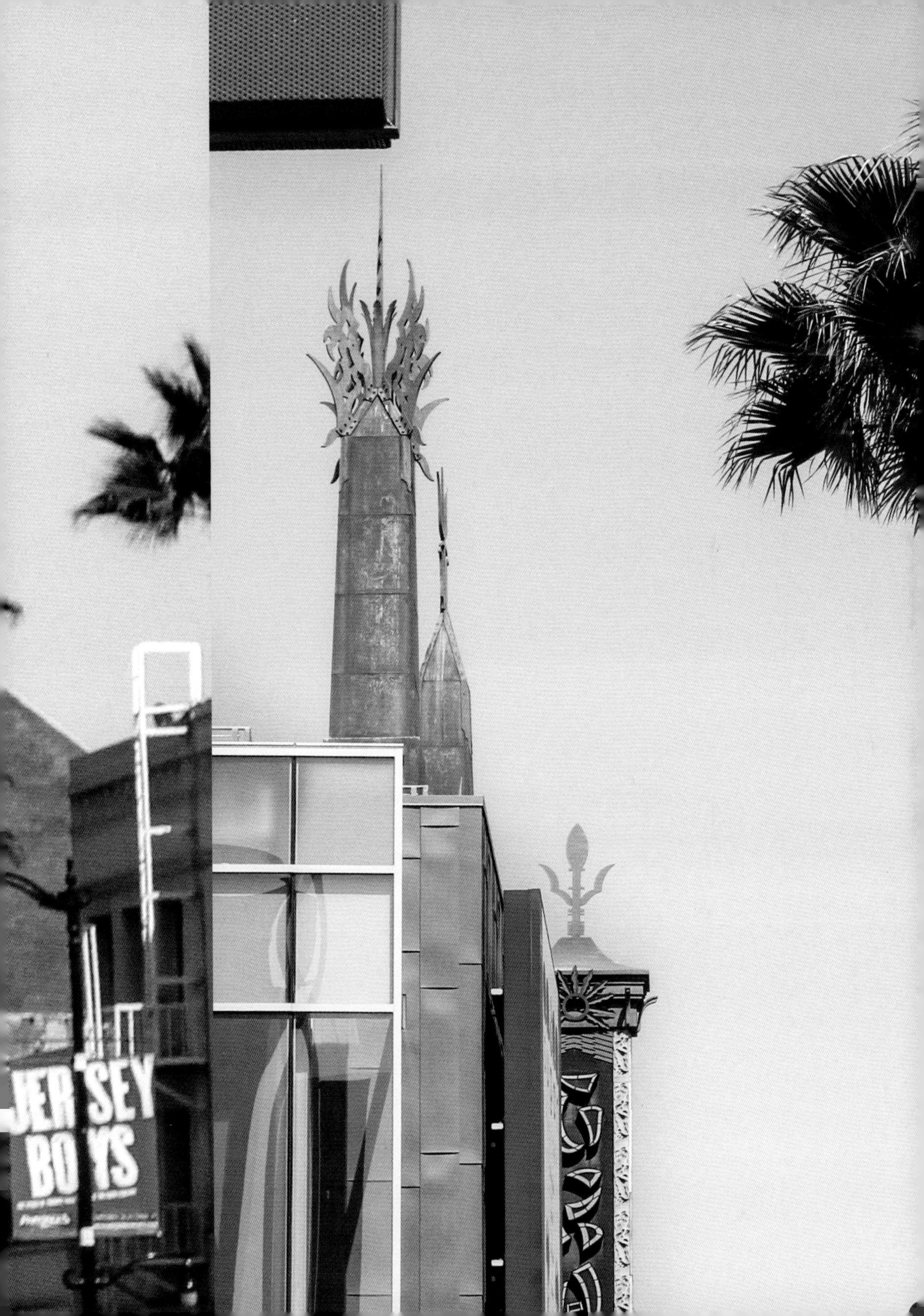
JER SEY
BO YS

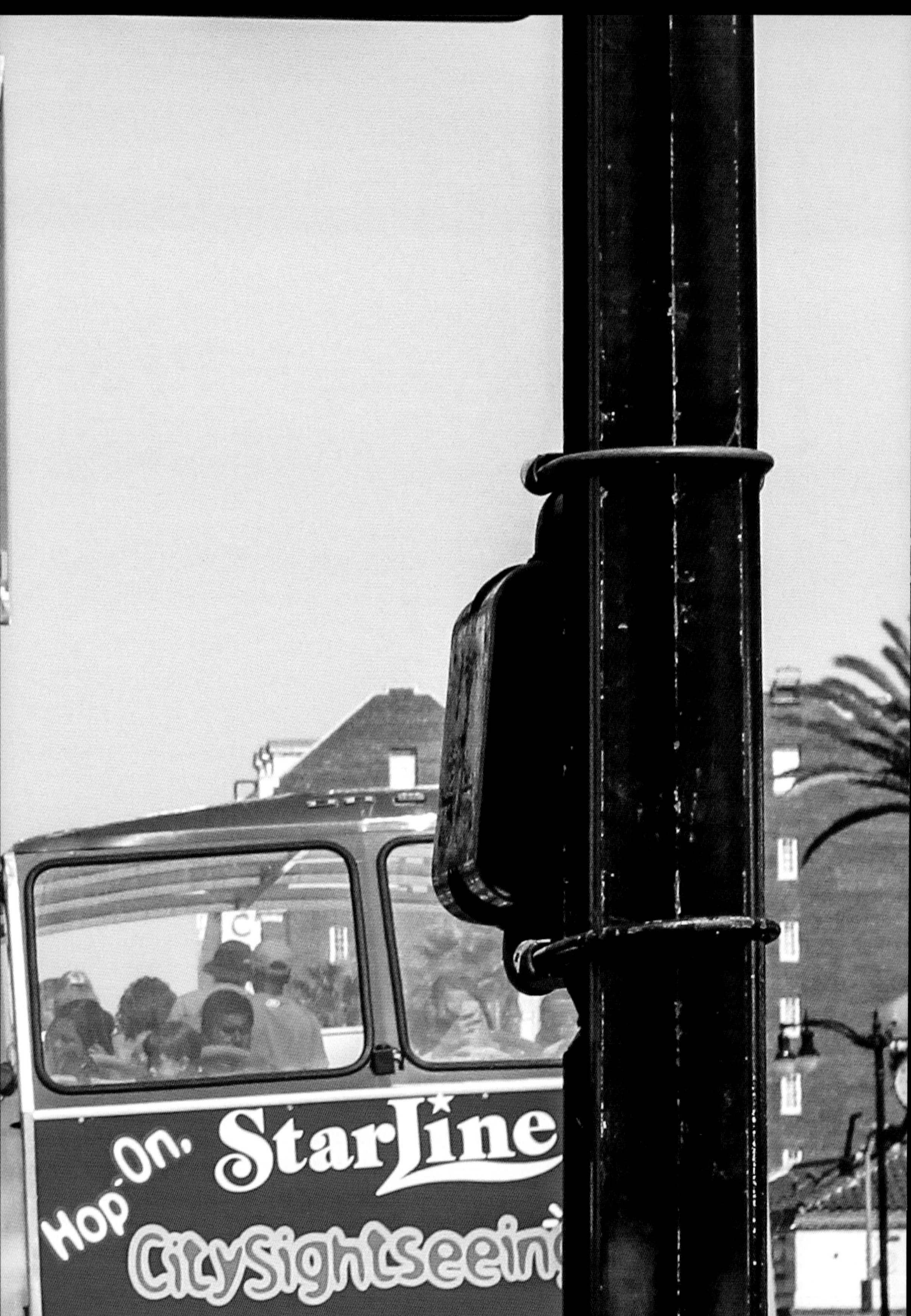

Hop-On. StarLine
CitySightseeing

JERSEY
BOYS

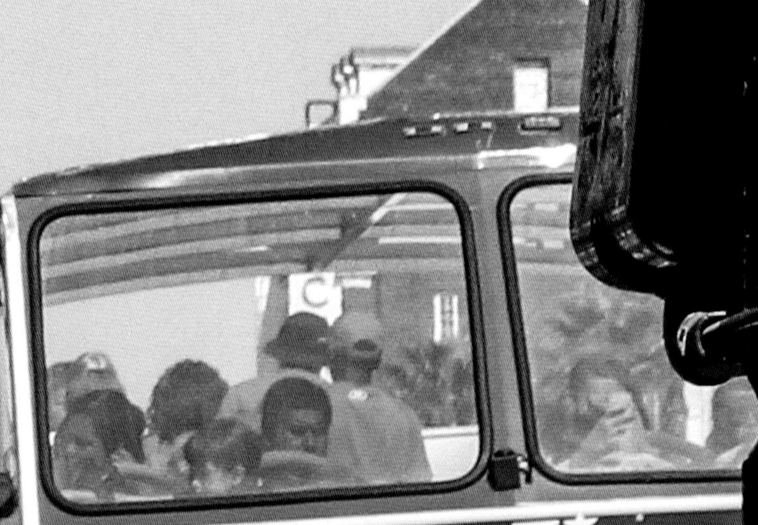
SEY
YS
& THE FOUR SEASONS
SEPTEMBER 30-OCTOBER 19
HOLLYWOODPANTAGES.COM
Hop-On StarLine
CitySightseein

JER SEY
BO YS

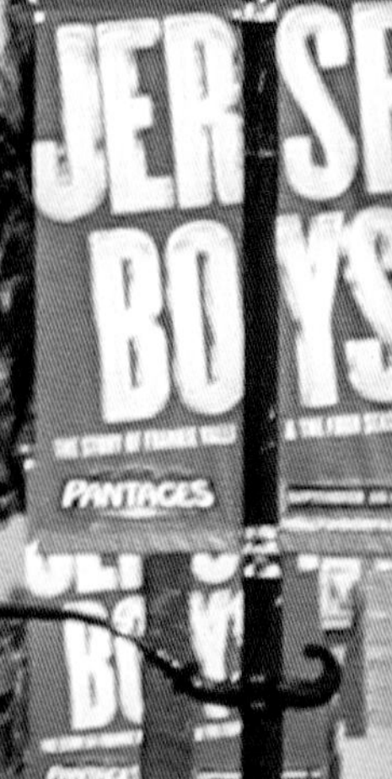

JER SEY
BO YS
THE STORY OF FRANKIE VALLI
& THE FOUR SEASONS
PANTAGES
SEPTEMBER 30-OCTOBER 19
HOLLYWOODPANTAGES.COM

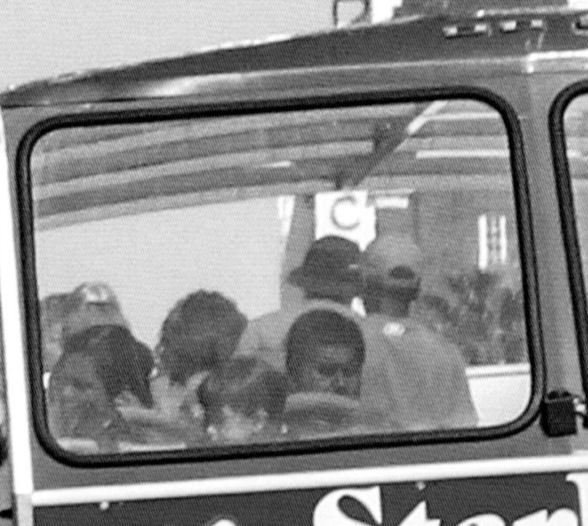

Hop-On. Star
CitySights

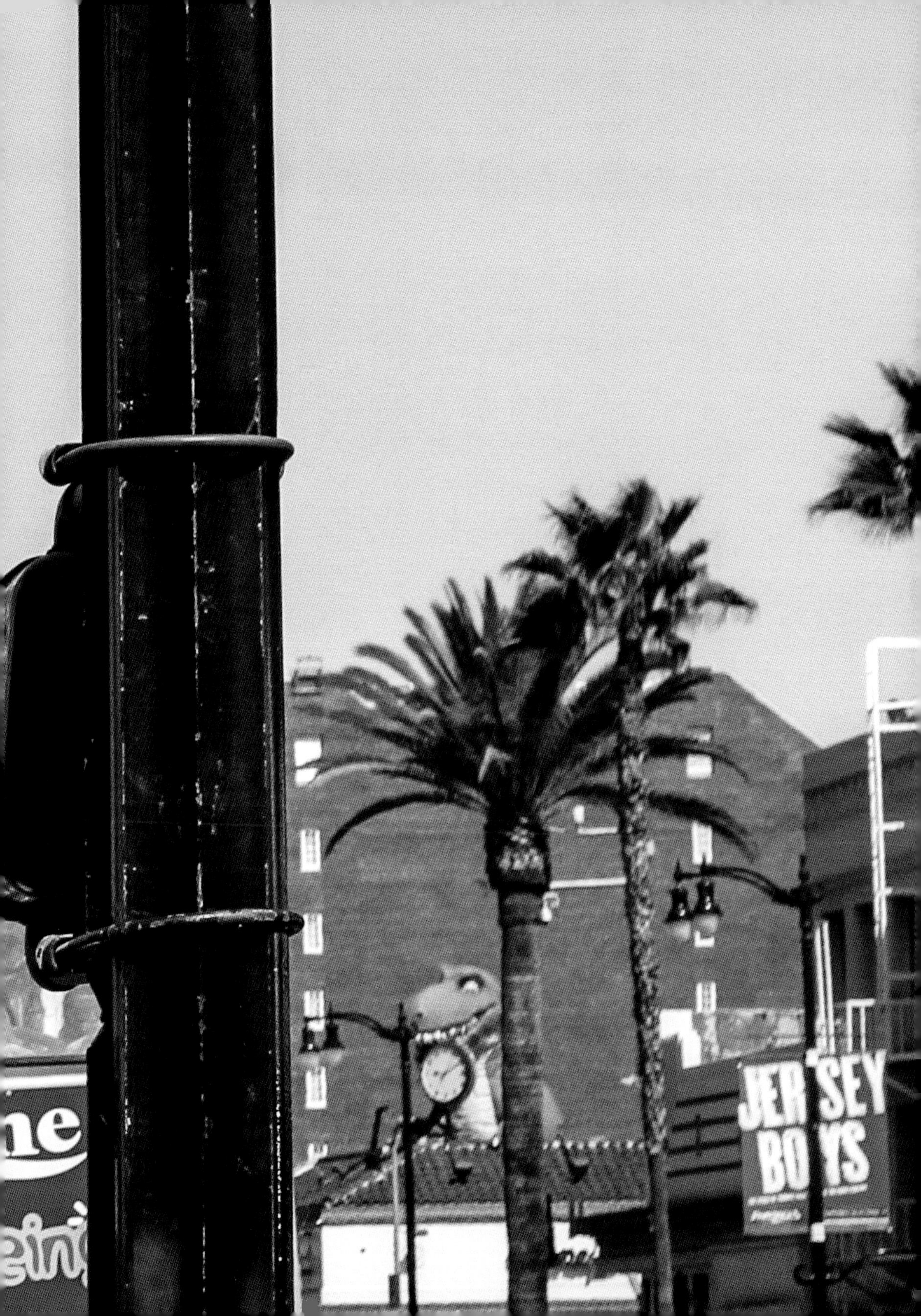
JER SEY
BO YS

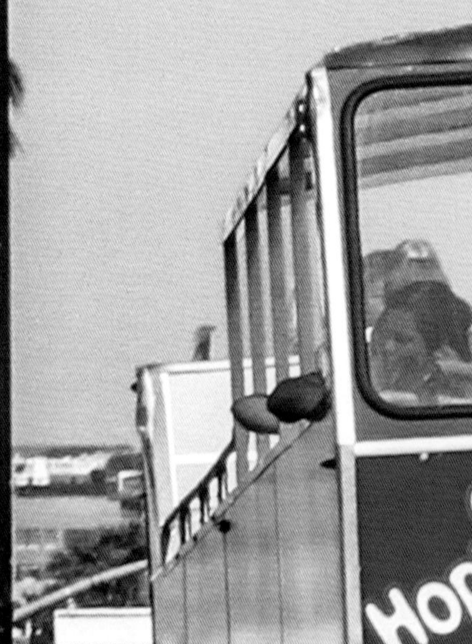

JER SEY
BO YS
THE STORY OF FRANKIE VALLI
& THE FOUR SEASONS
PANTAGES
SEPTEMBER 30–OCTOBER 19
HOLLYWOODPANTAGES.COM
JER SE
BO YS
THE STORY OF FRANKIE VALLI
& THE FOUR SEAS
PANTAGES
Hop-O

StarIine
Sightseeing

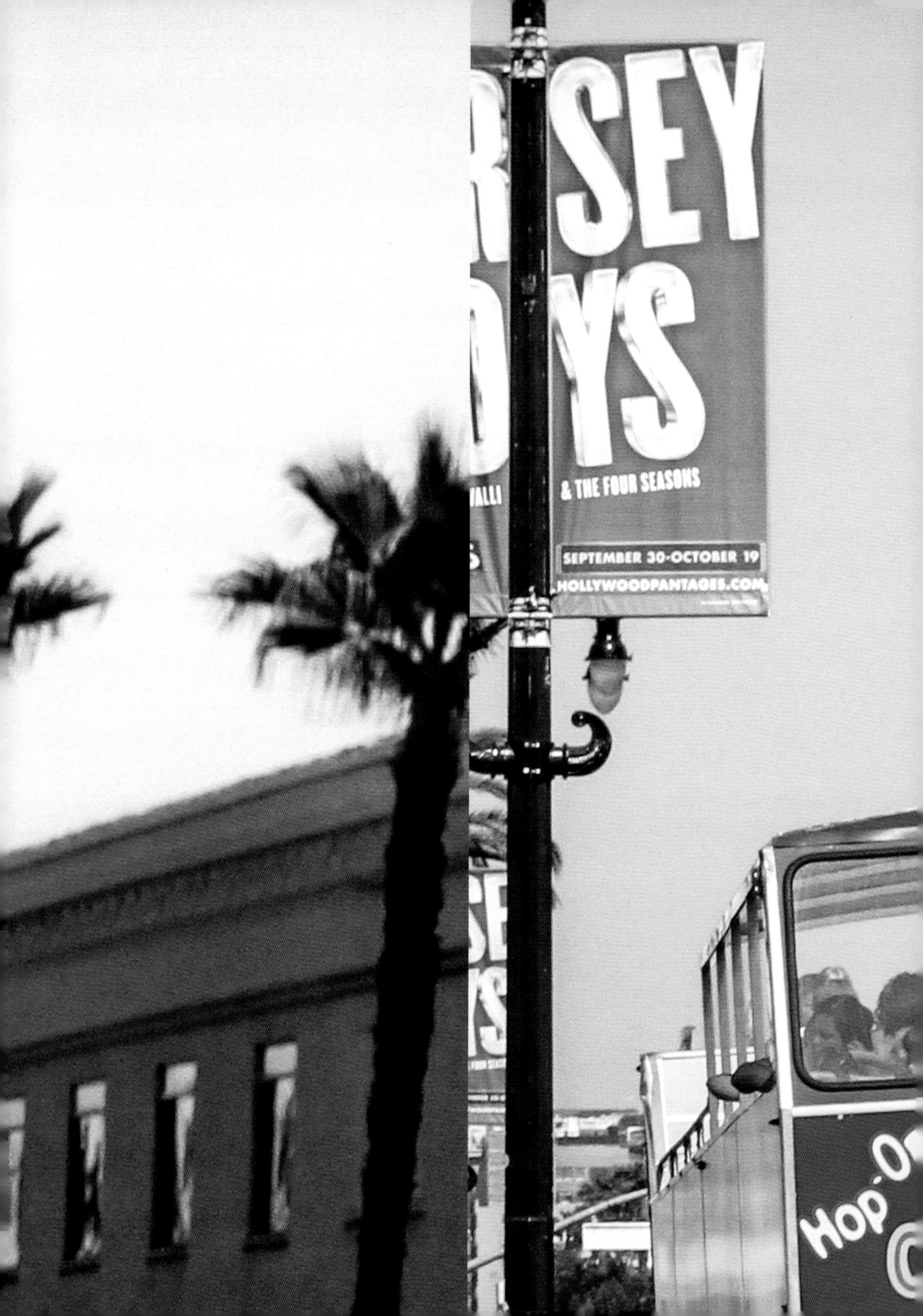

R SEY
OYS
VALLI
& THE FOUR SEASONS
SEPTEMBER 30-OCTOBER 19
HOLLYWOODPANTAGES.COM
Hop-O

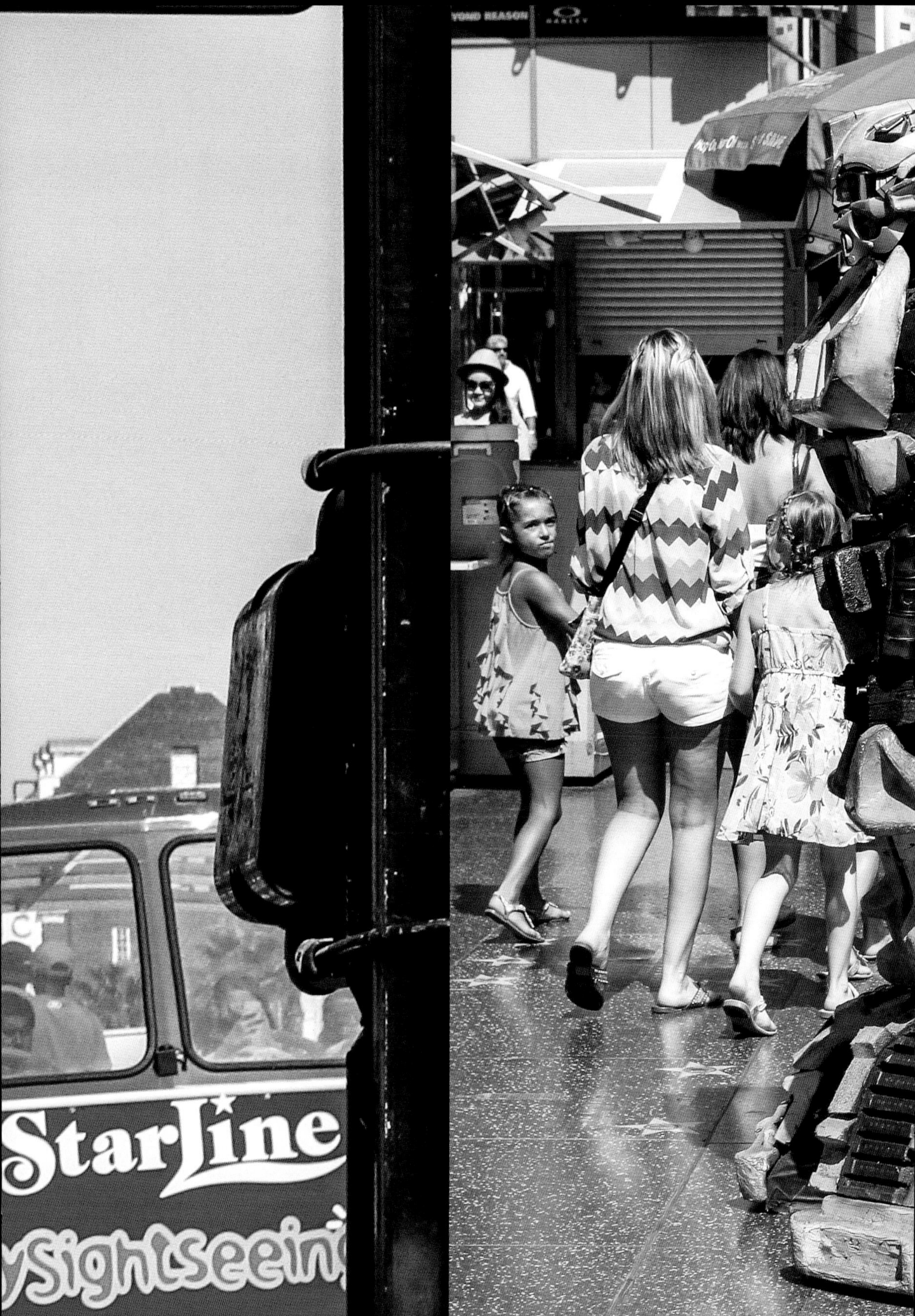
StarJine
Sightseeing

Y
BER 19
IS.COM
Hop-O

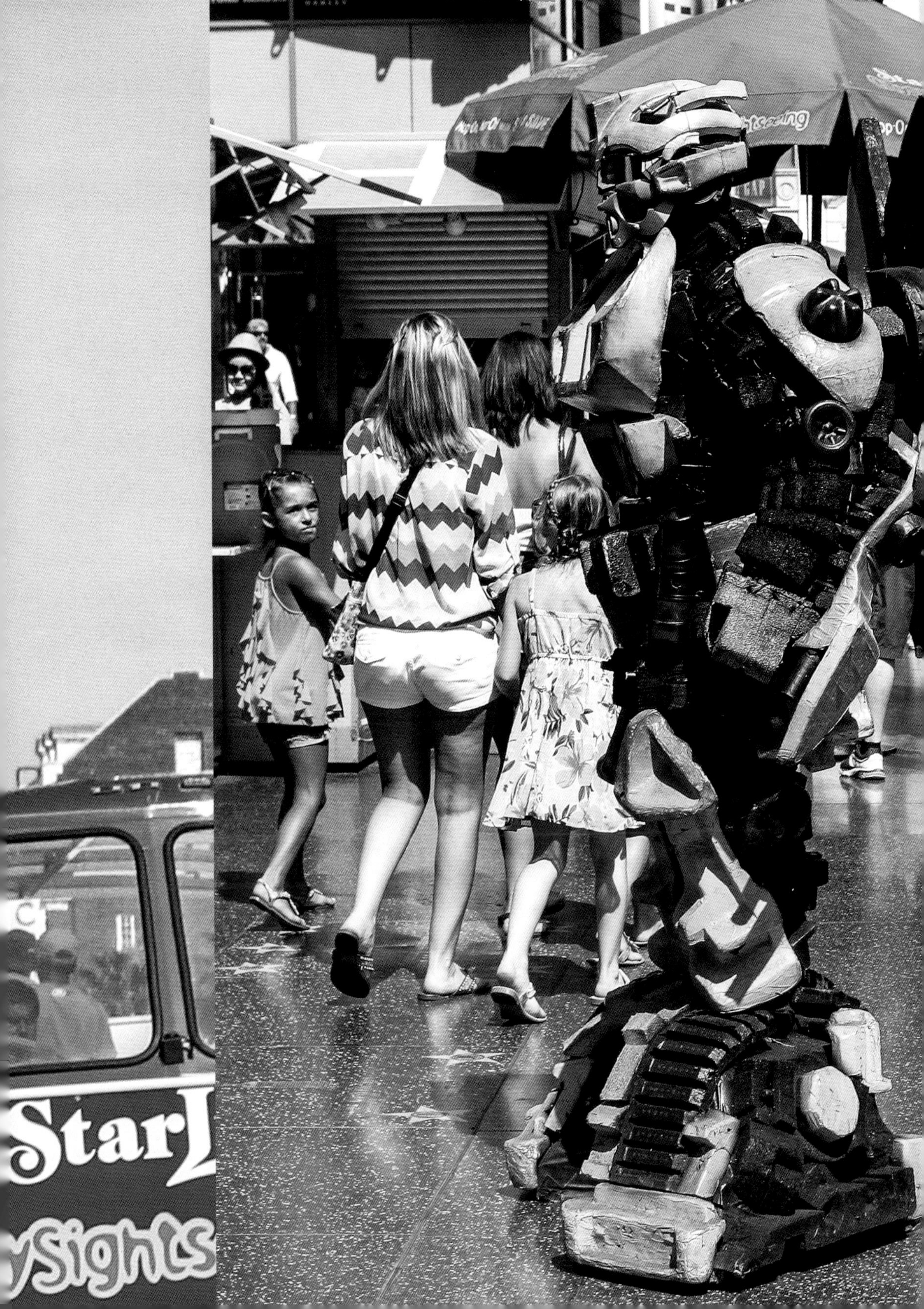
Star1
Sights

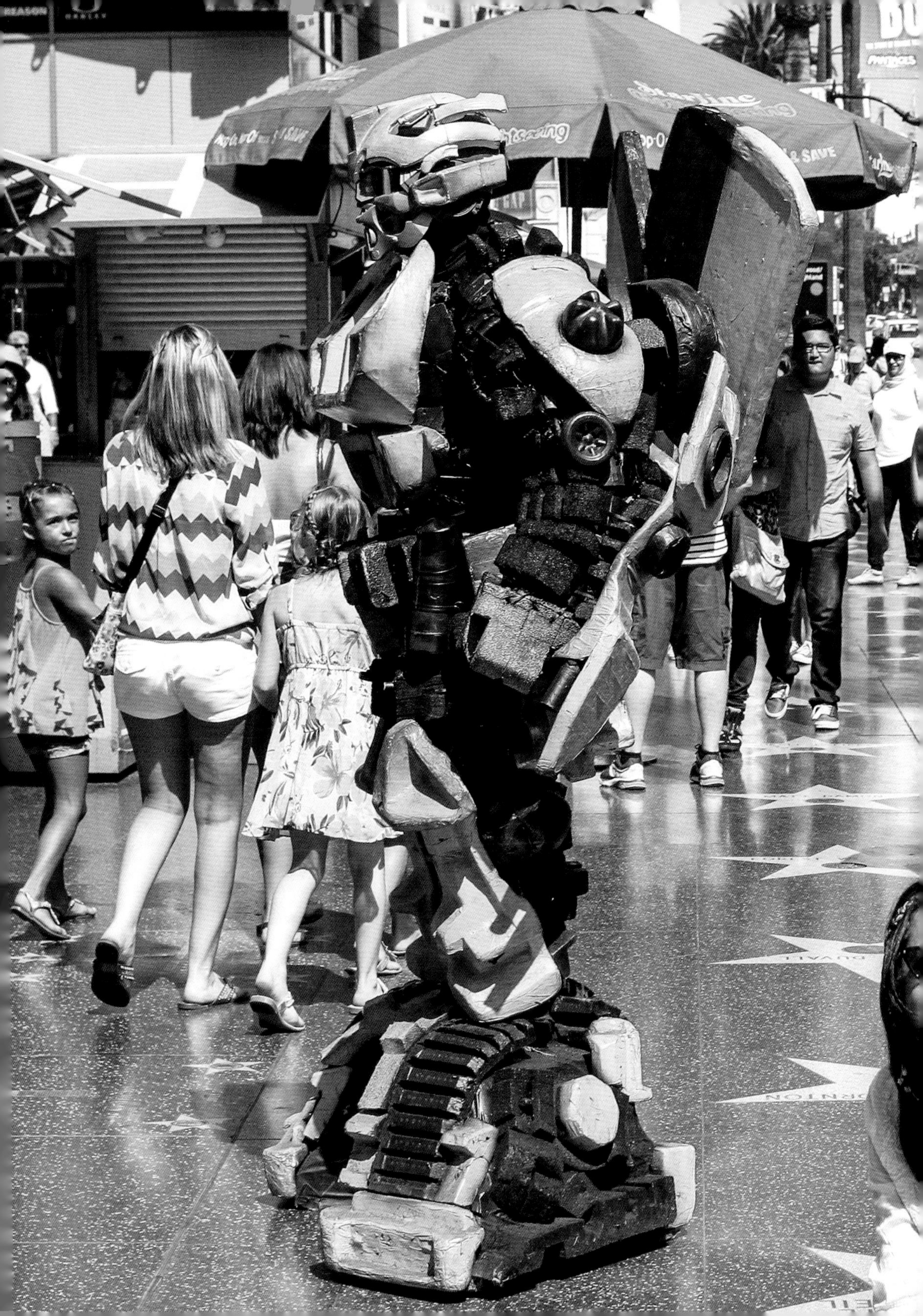

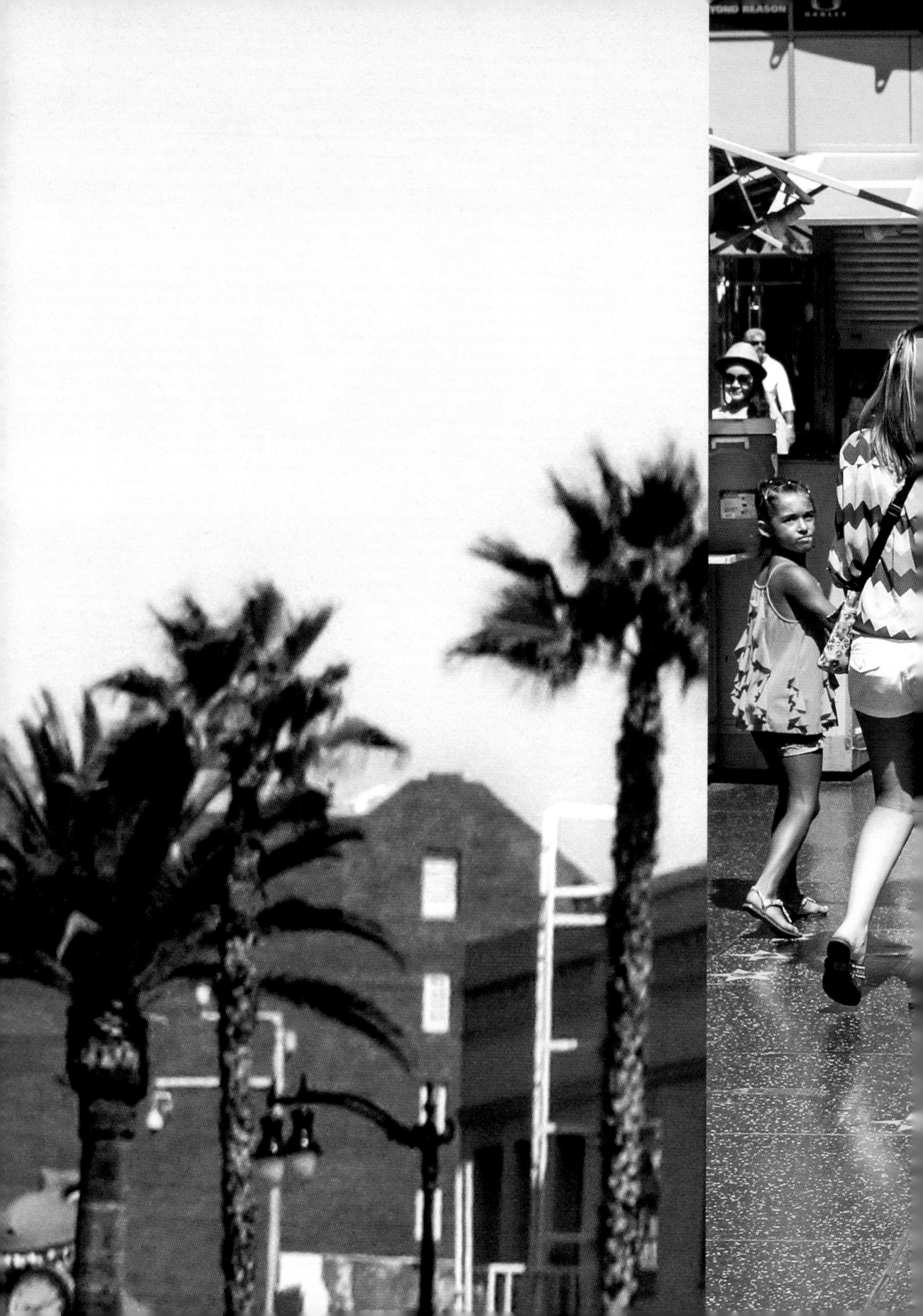

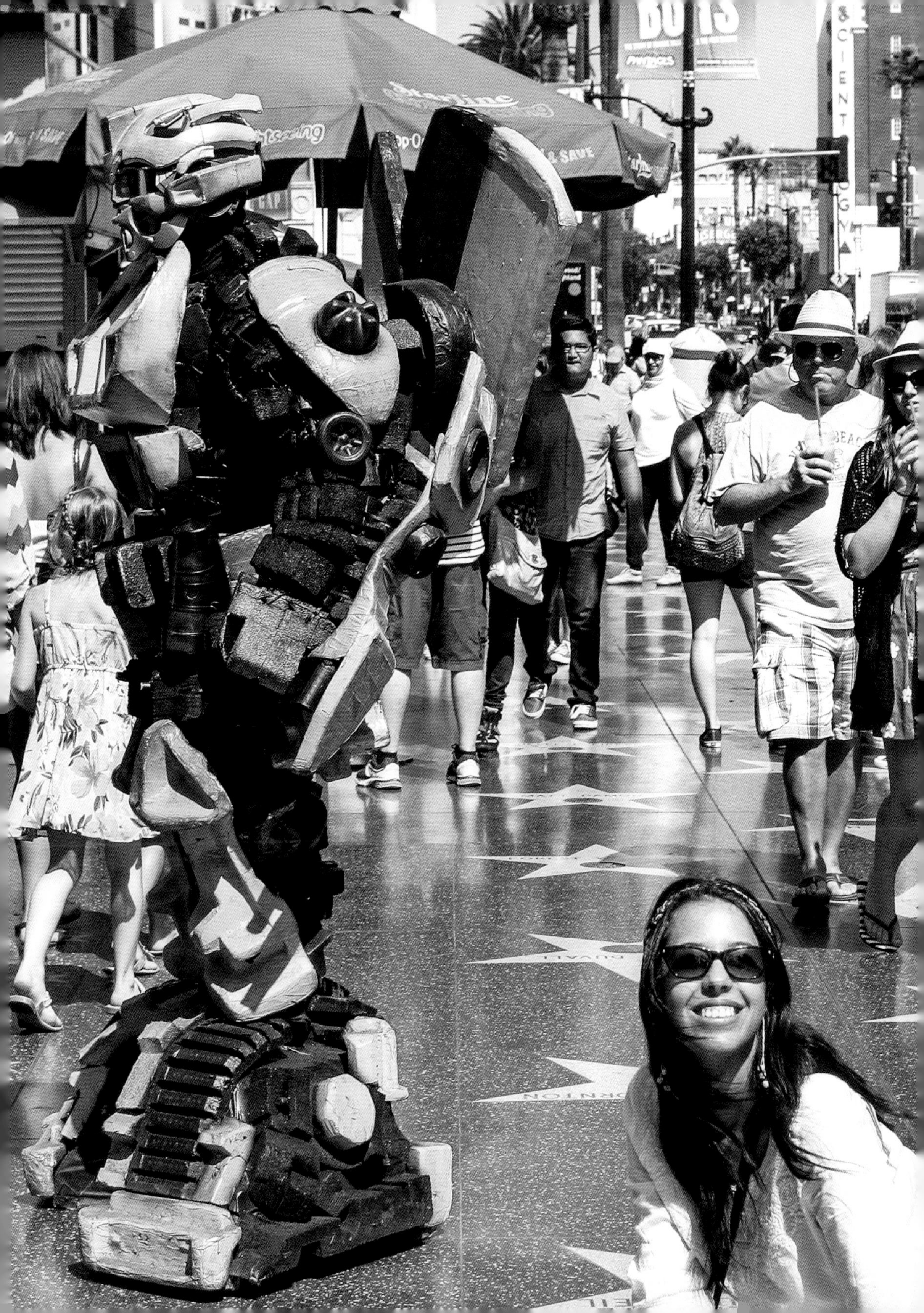

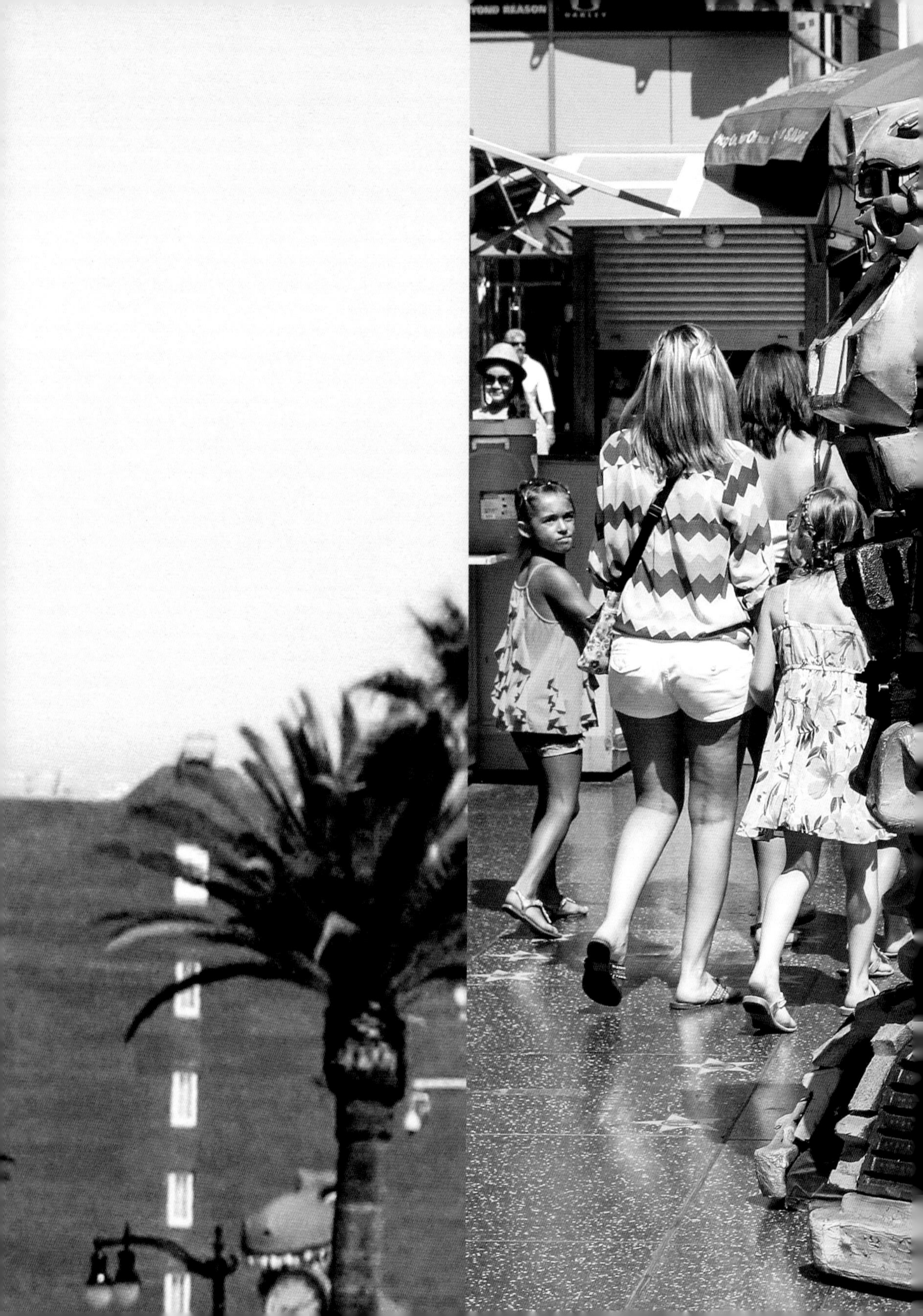

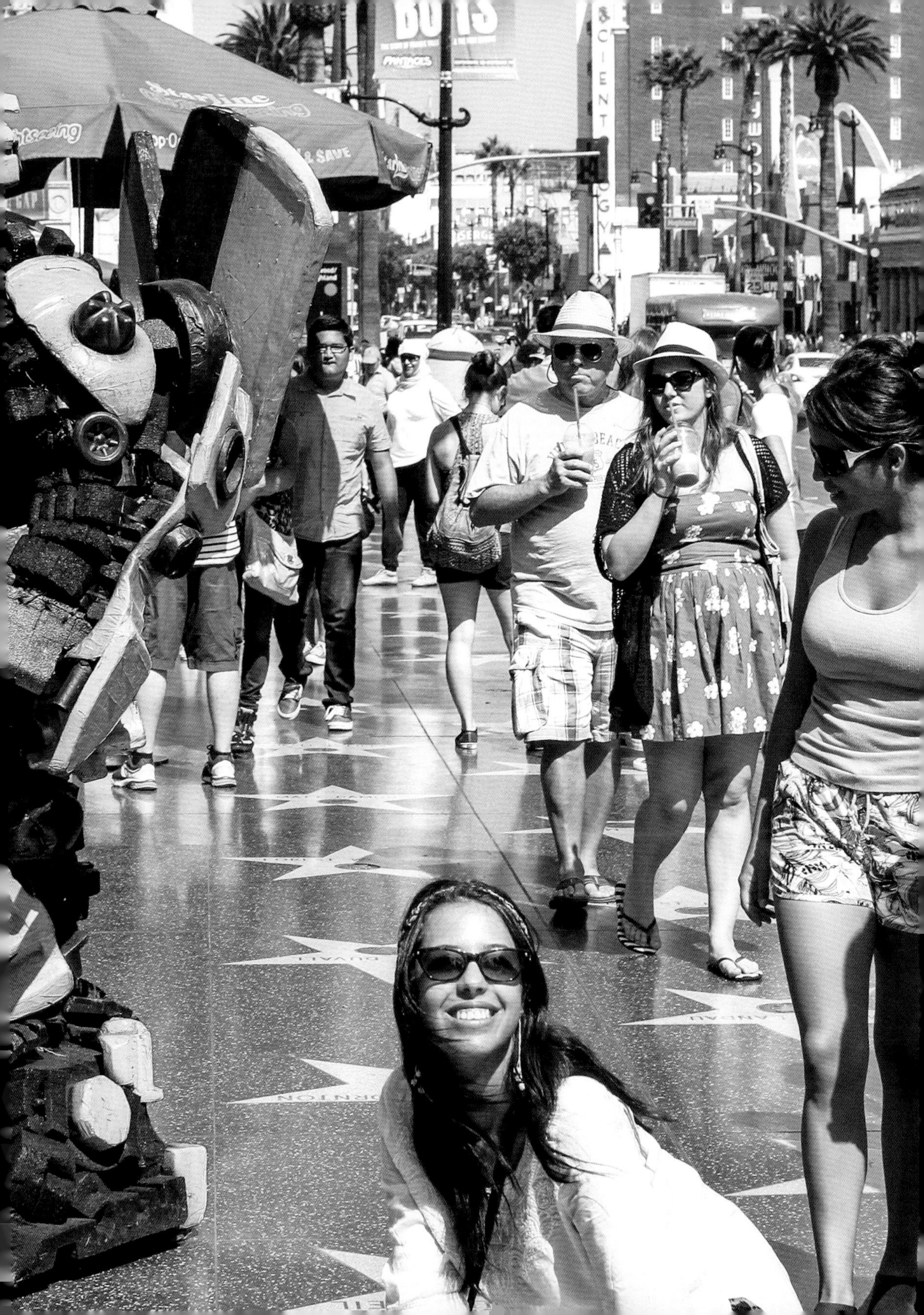

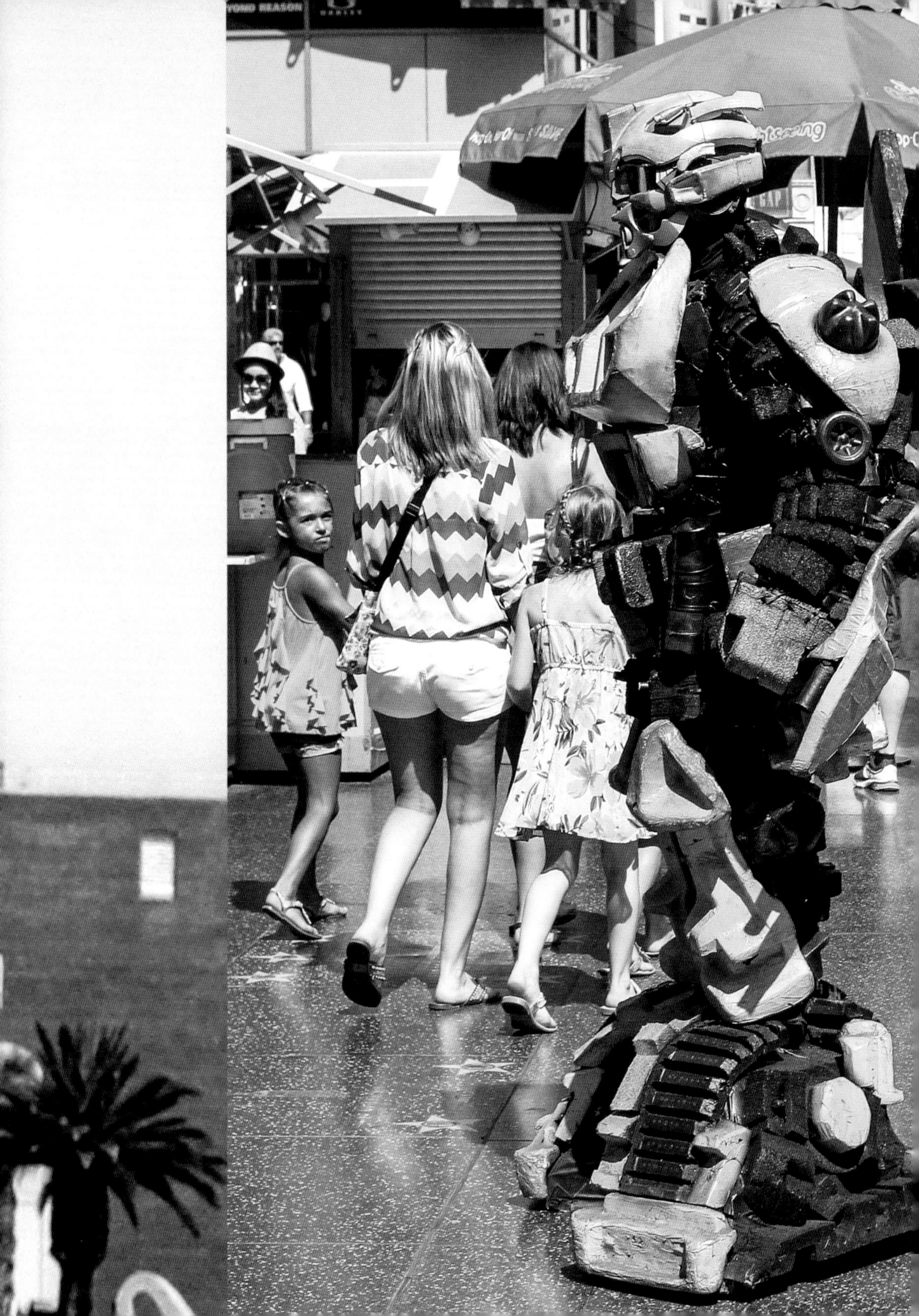

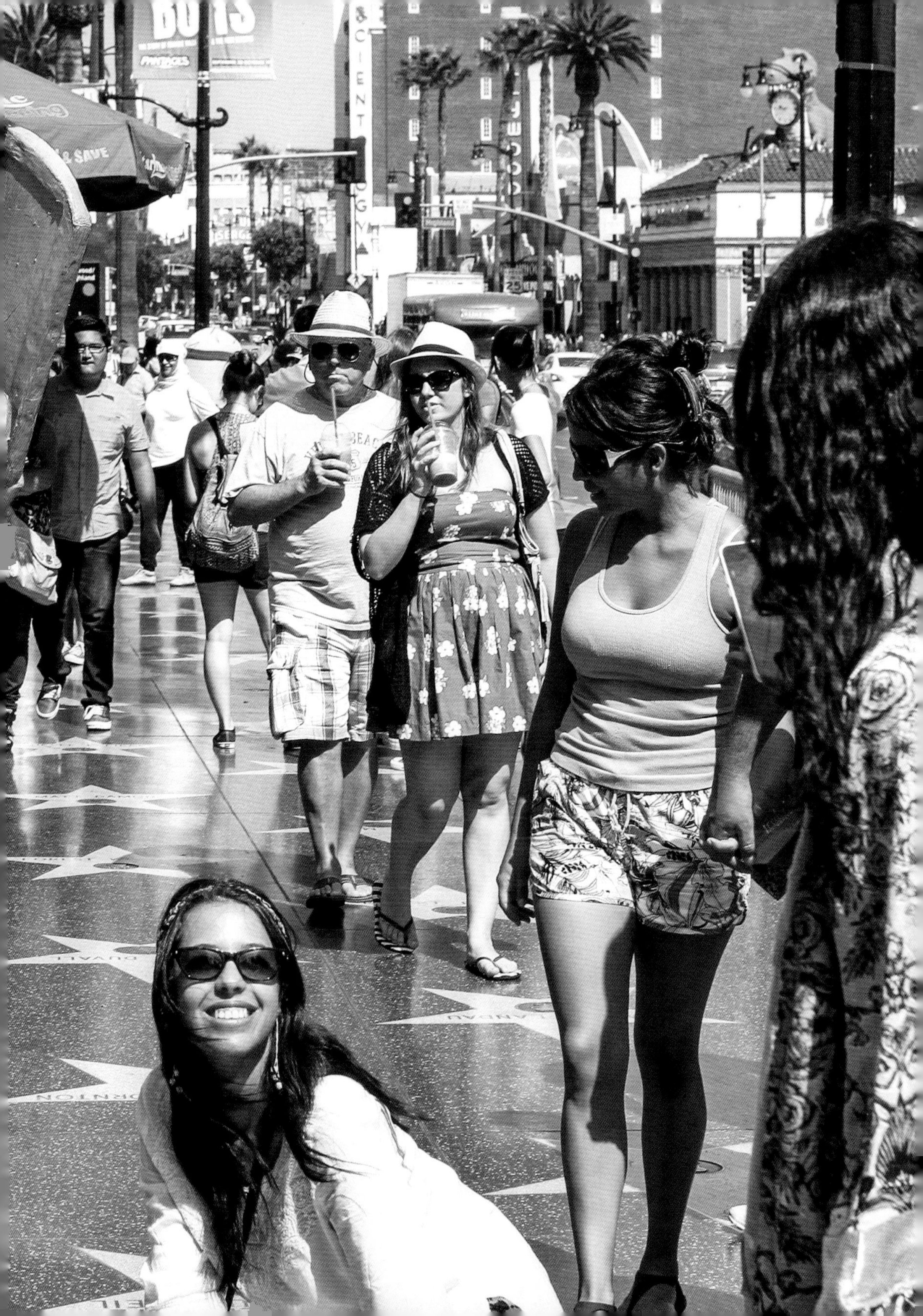

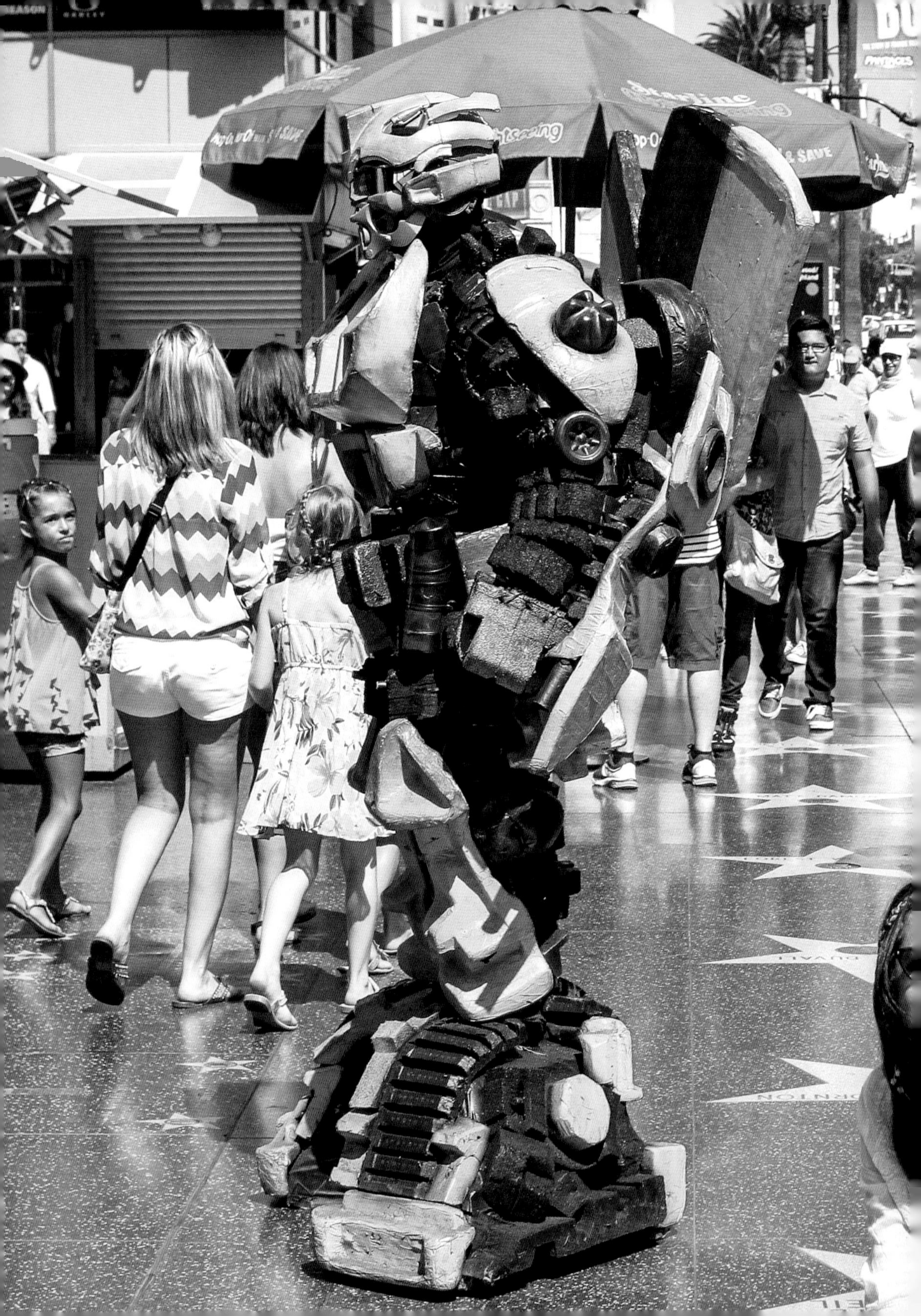

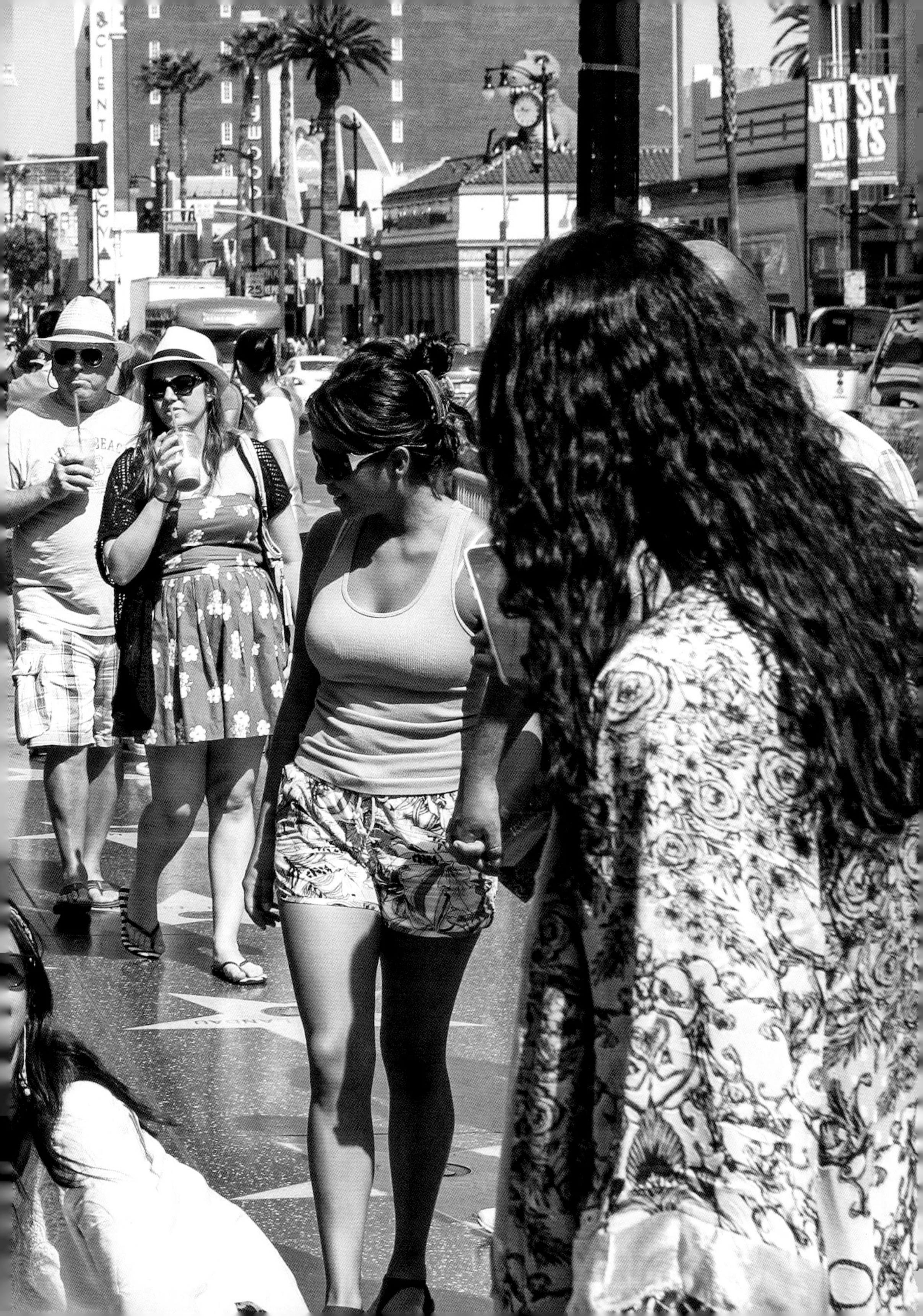

JER SEY
BO YS

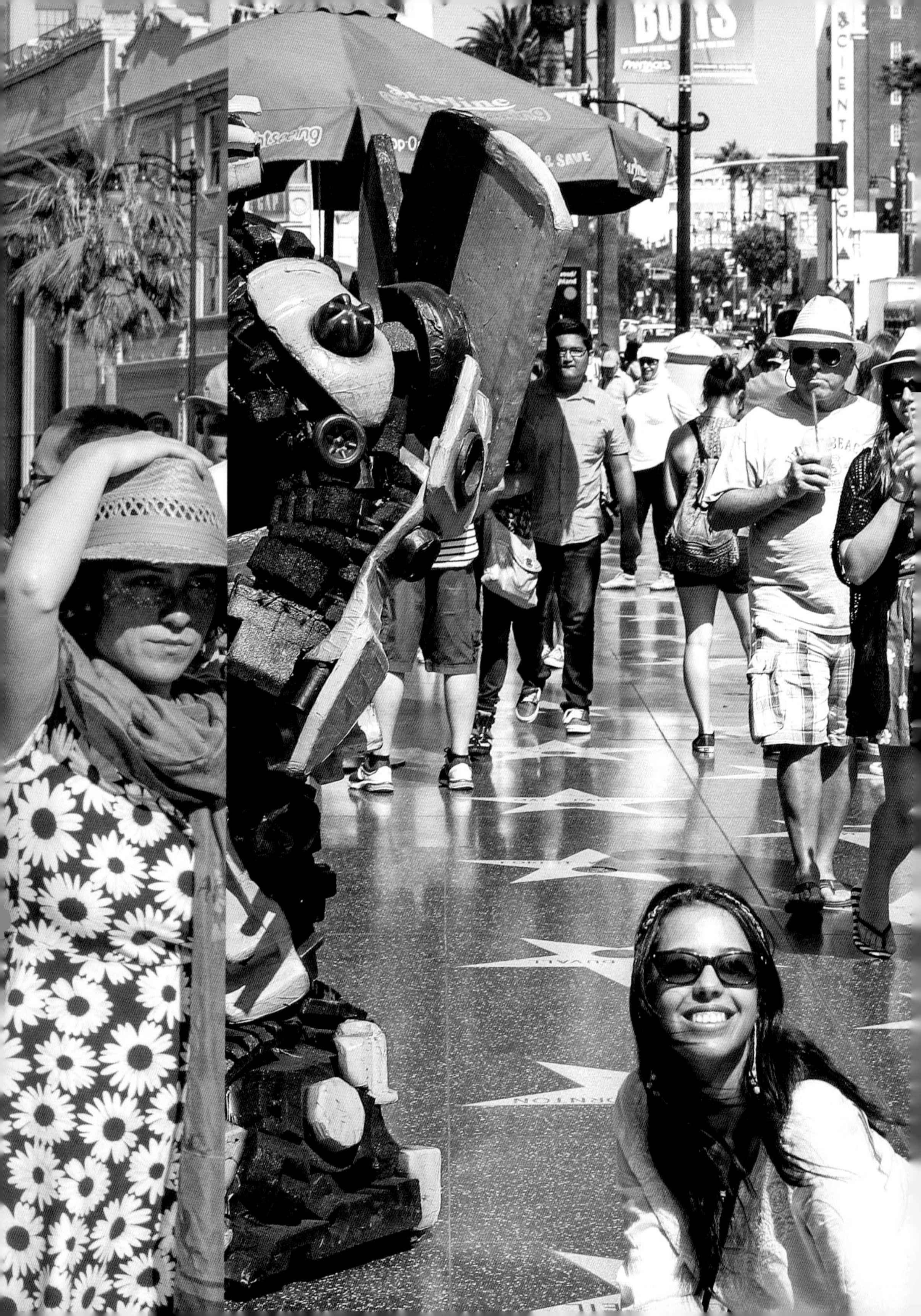

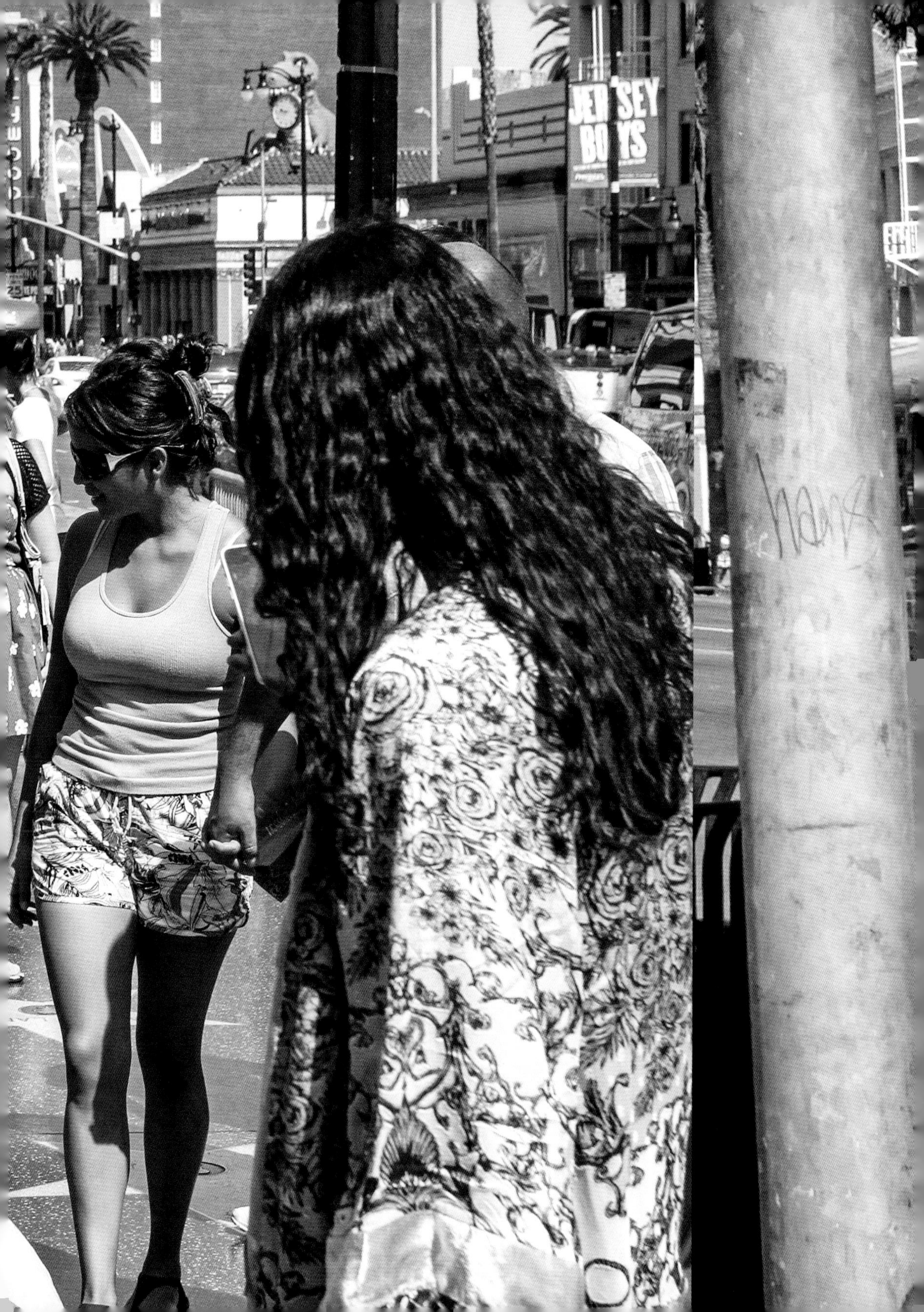

JERSEY
BOYS

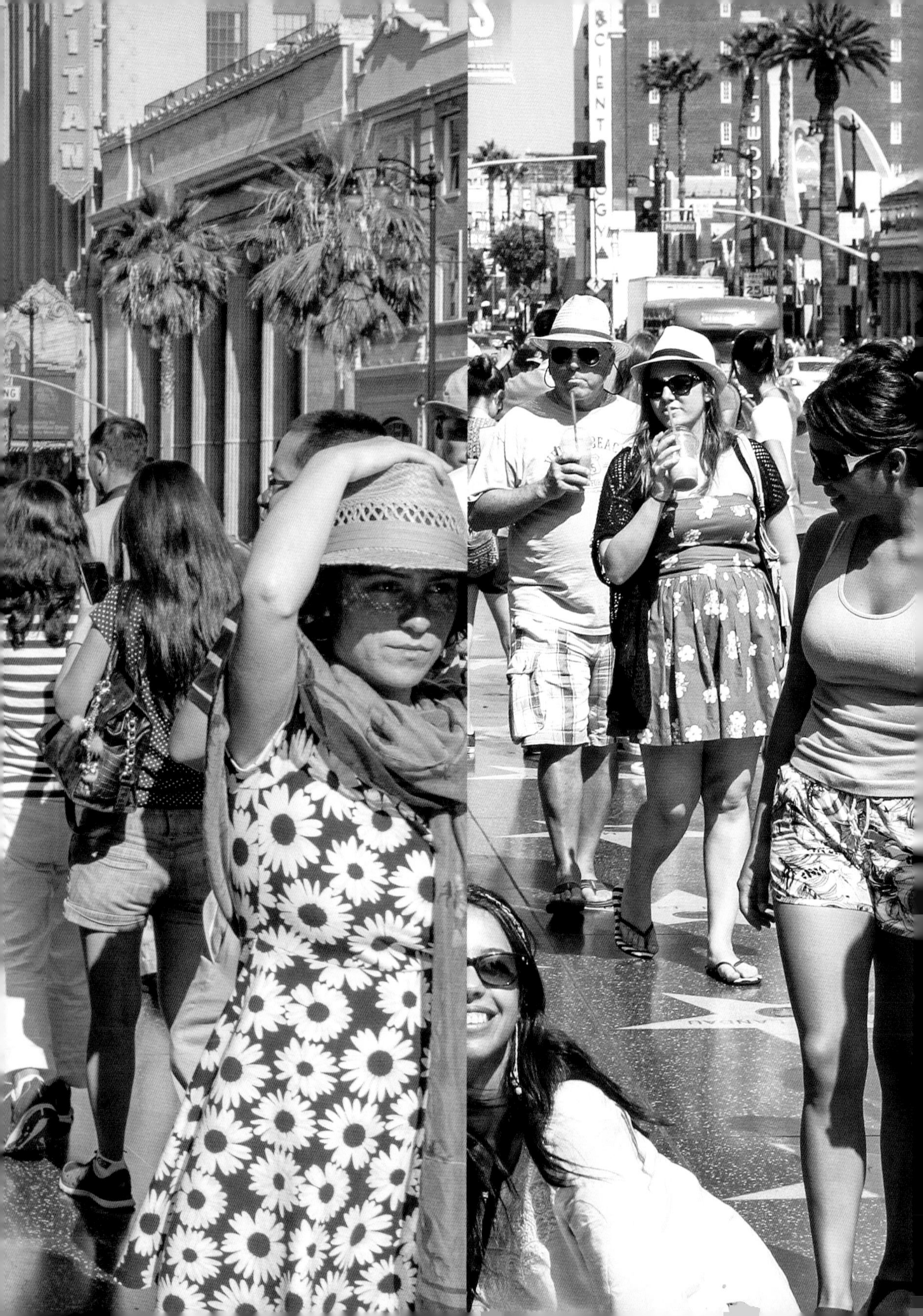

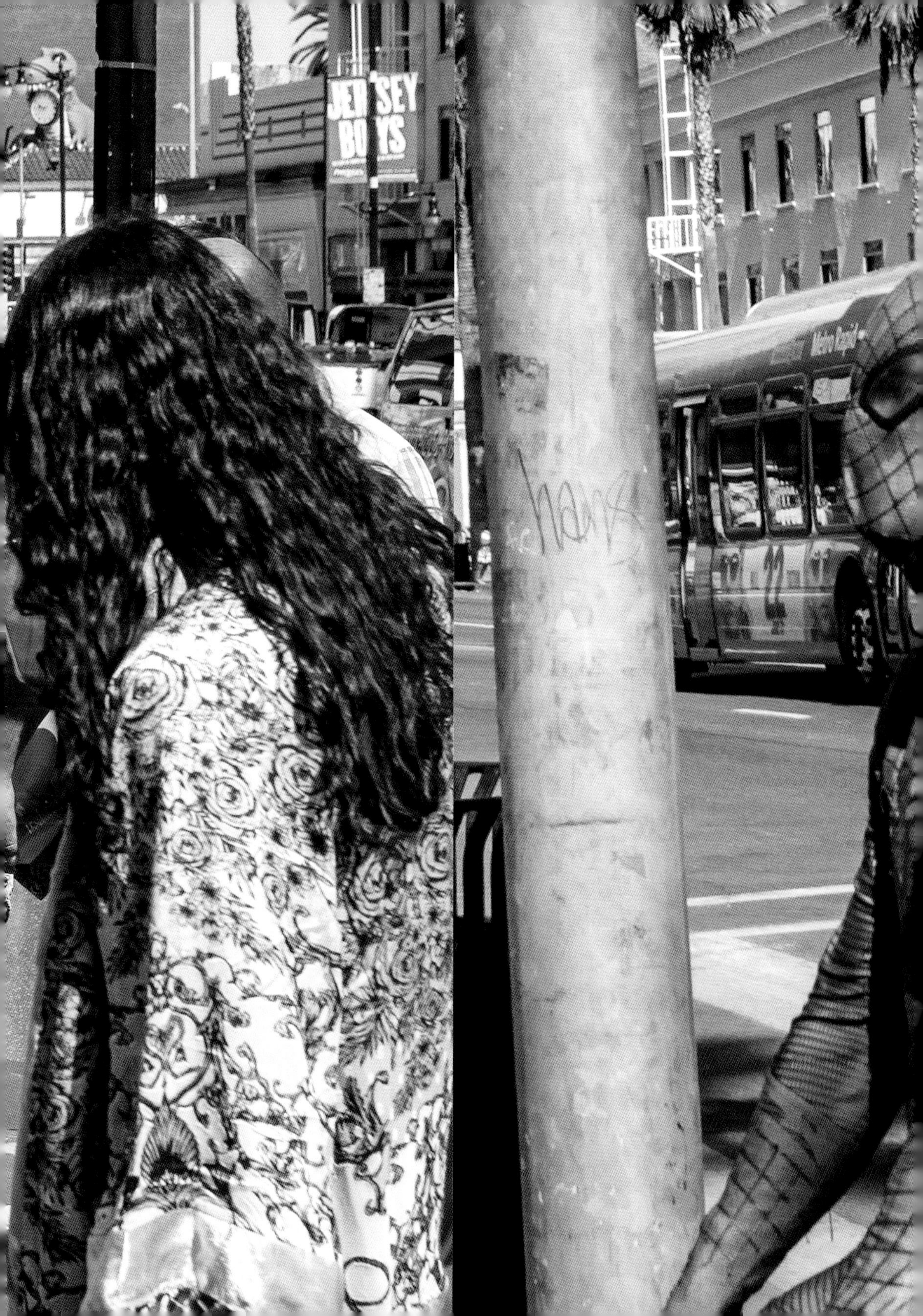
JER SEY
BO YS

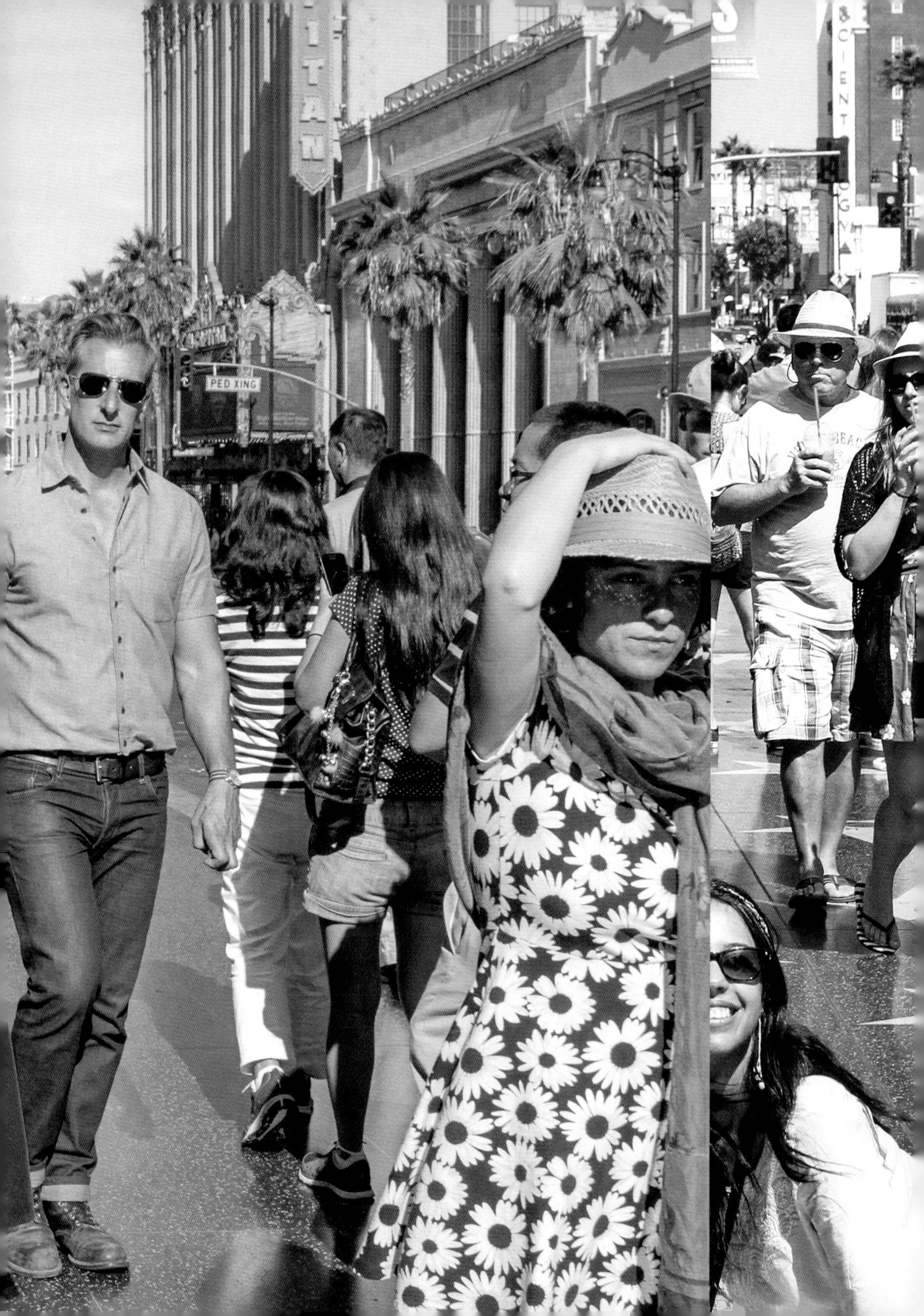

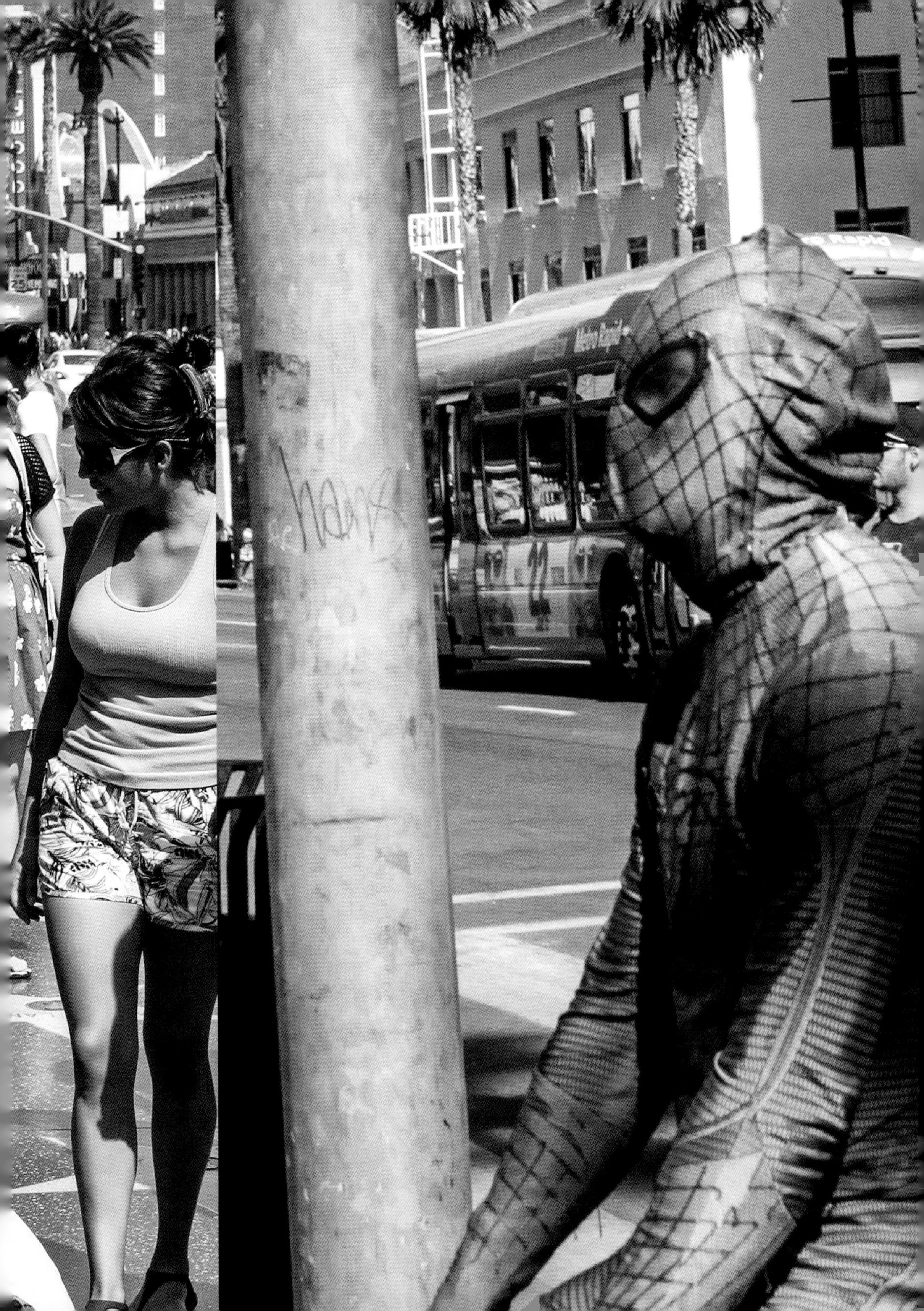
Metro Rapid

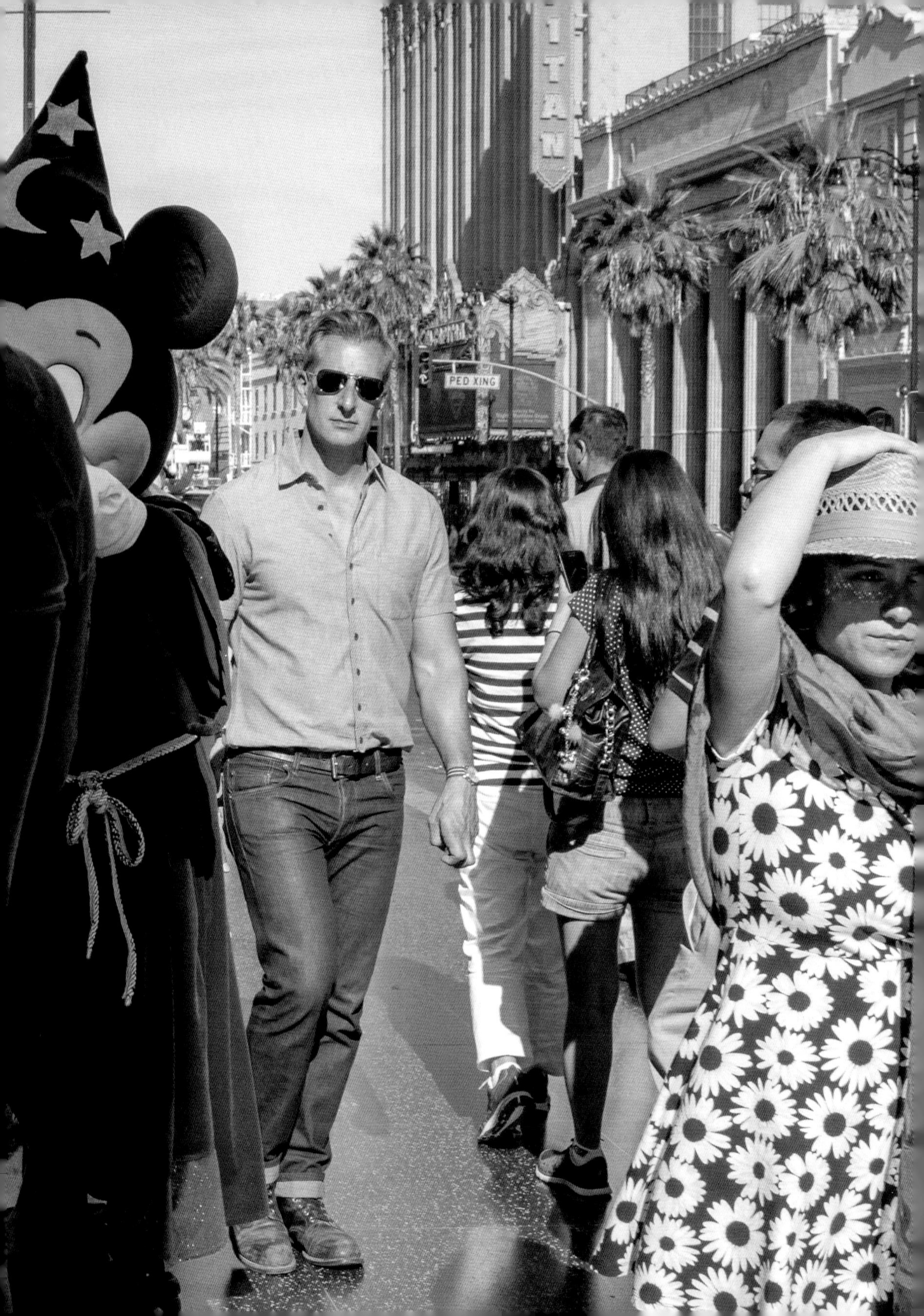
PED XING

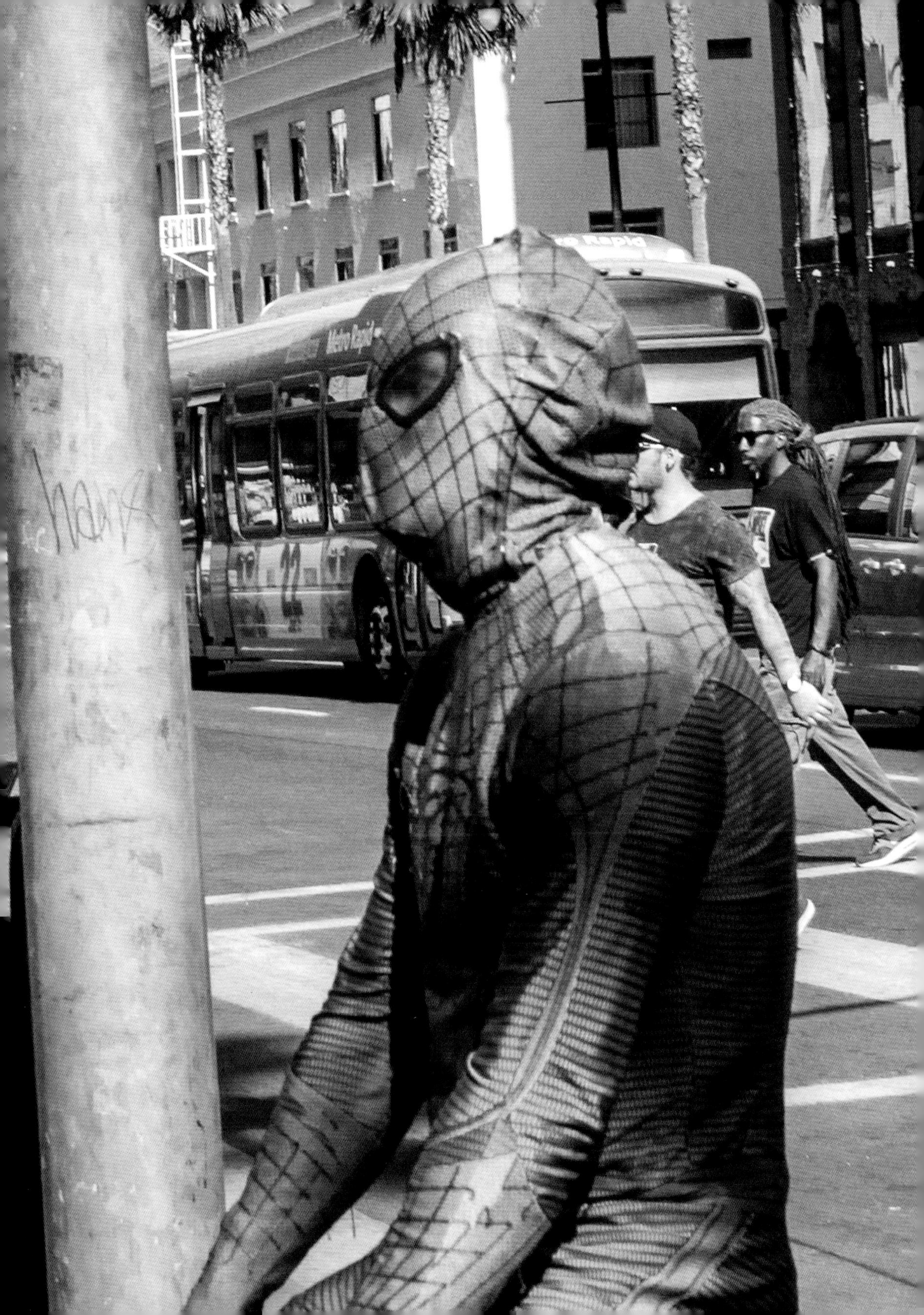

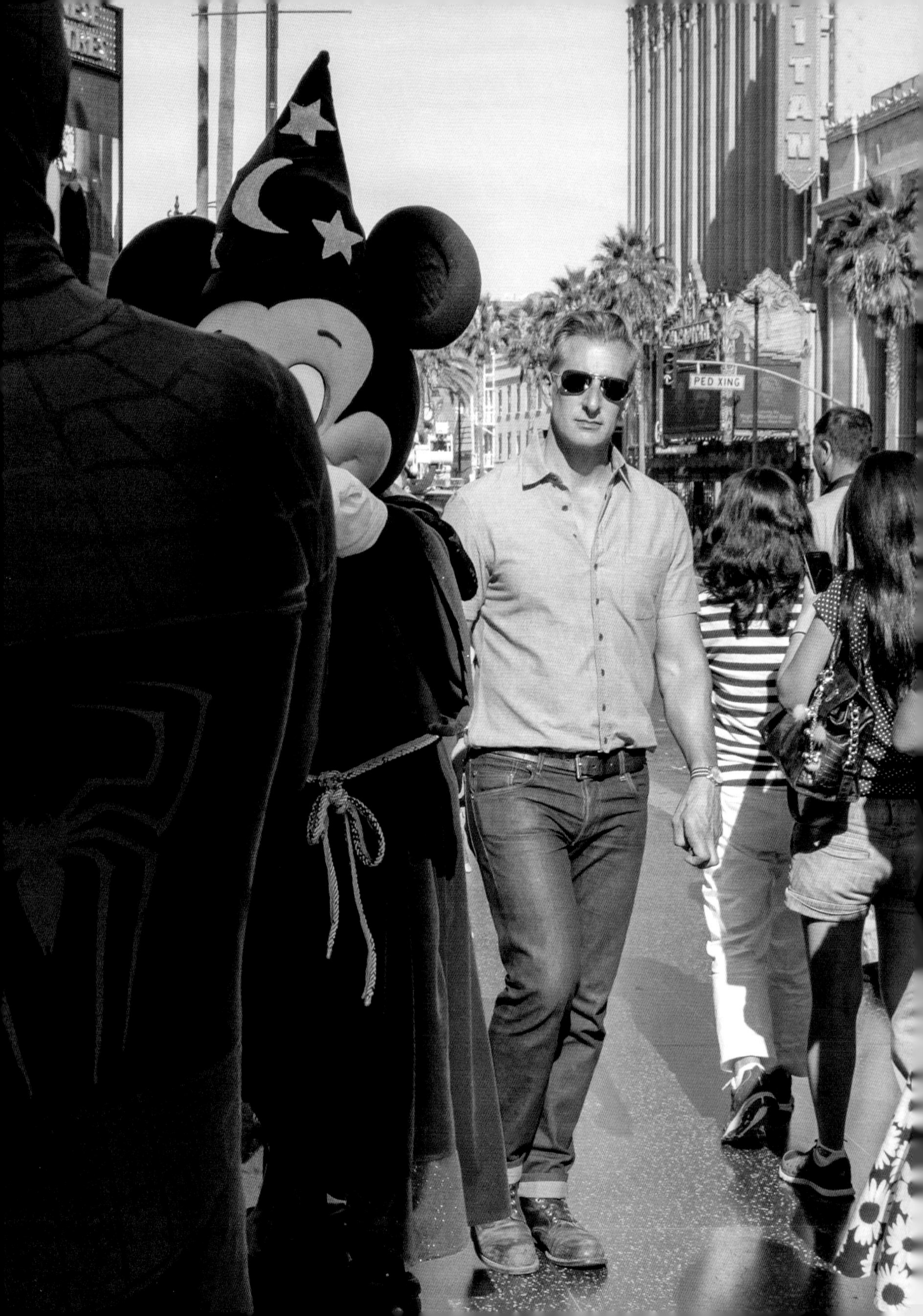

PED XING

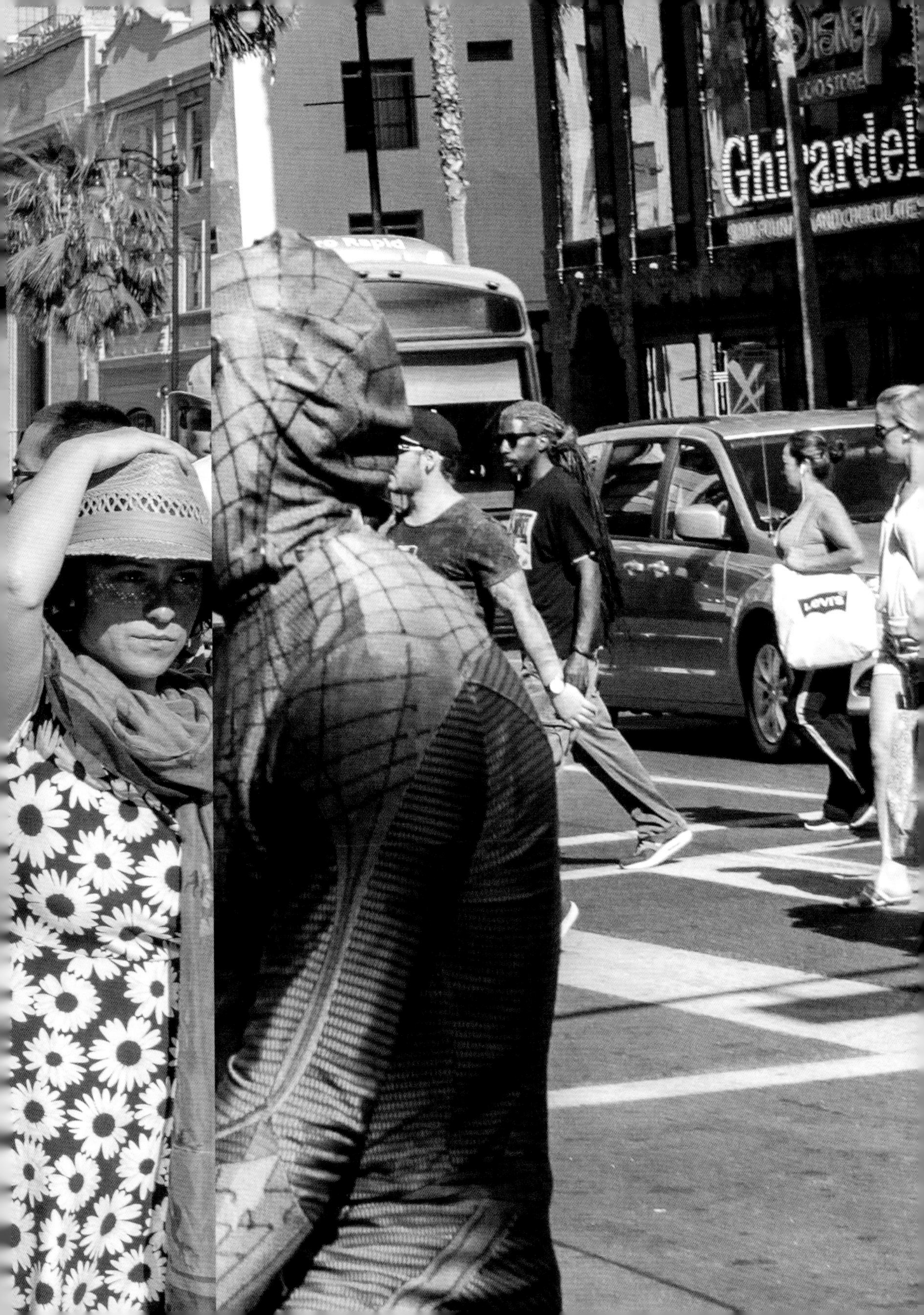

Ghirardel
AND CHOCOLATE
STORE

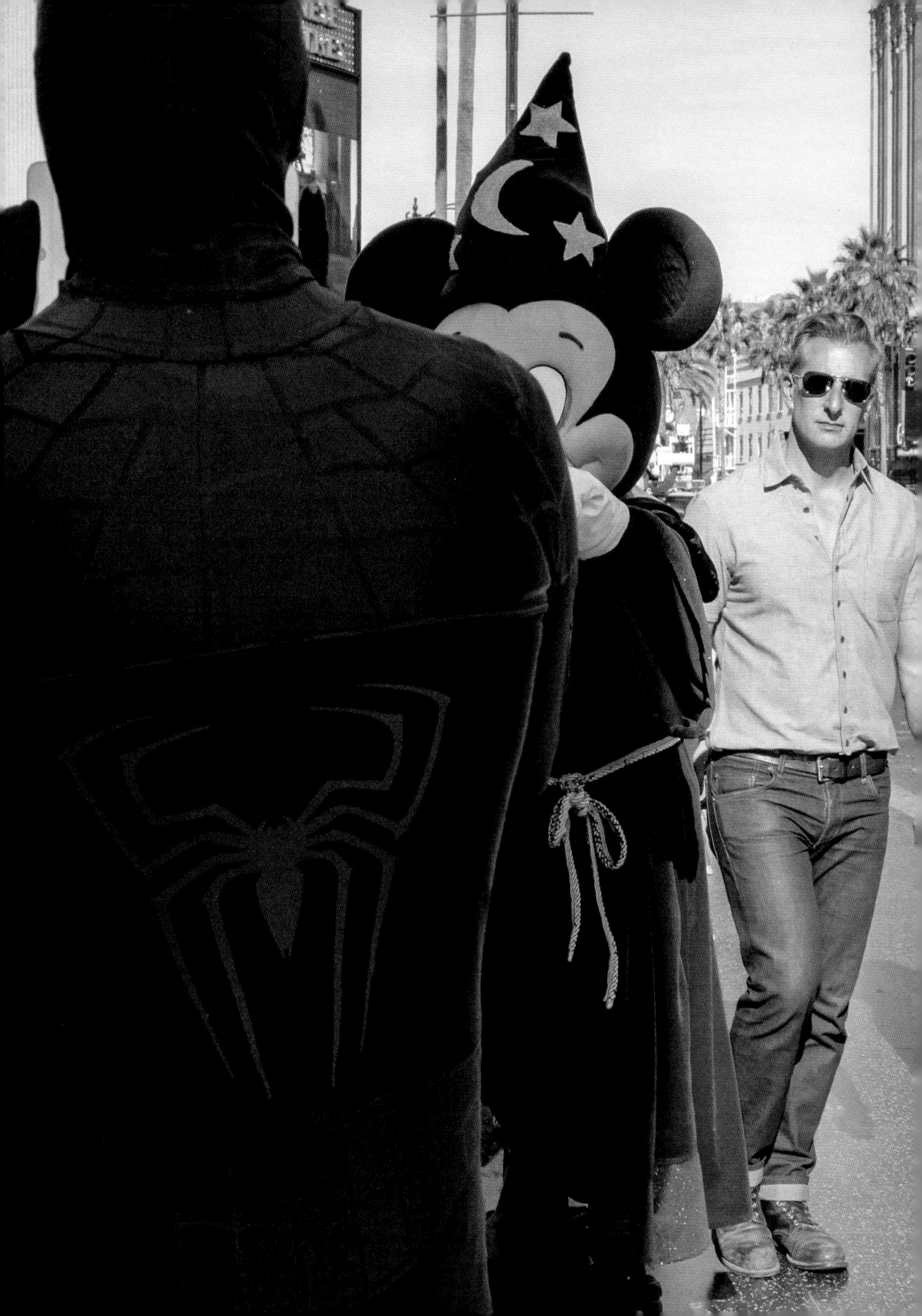

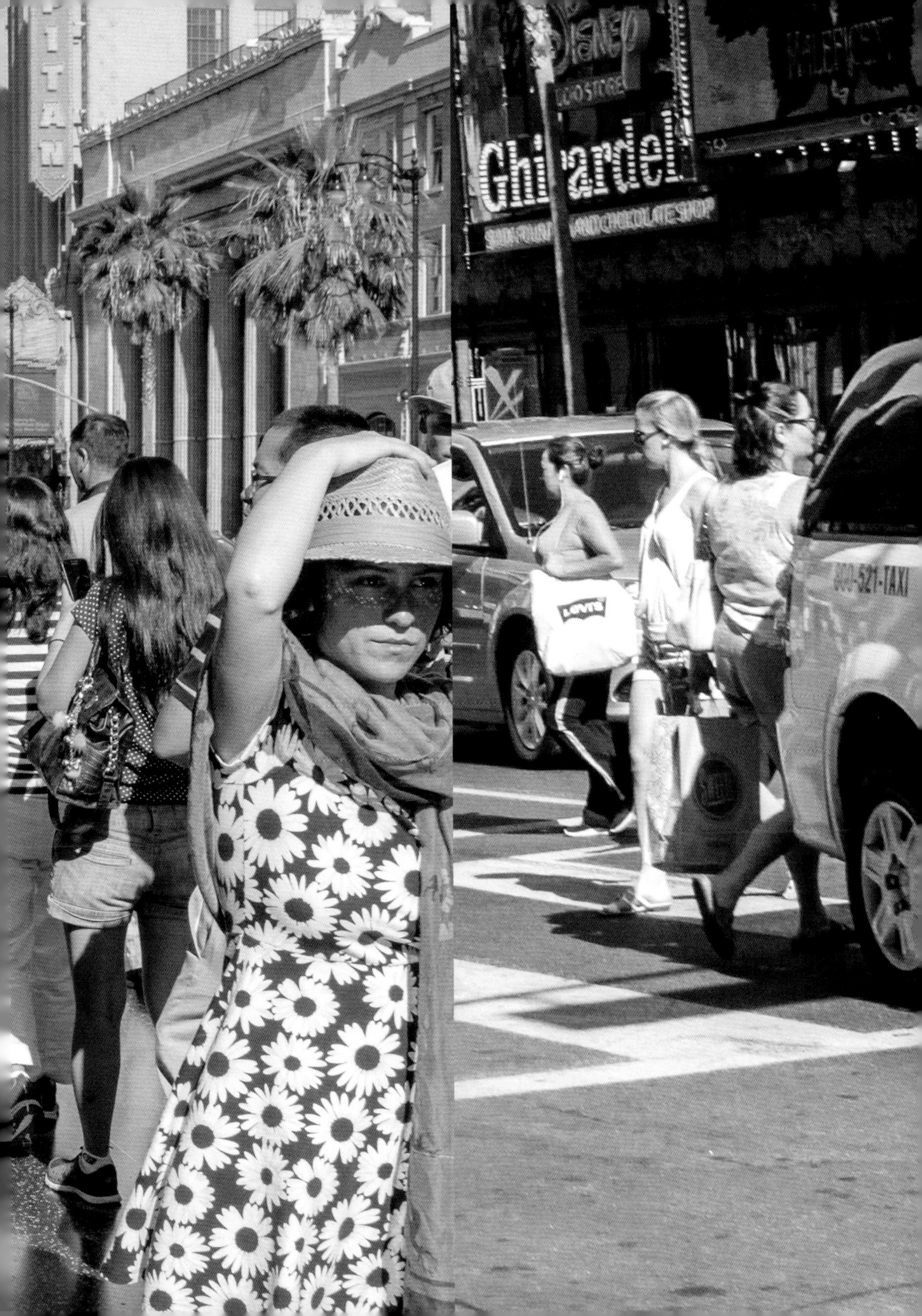
TITAN
Disney
Ghirardelli
SOUVENIR AND CHOCOLATE SHOP
Levi's
800-521-TAXI

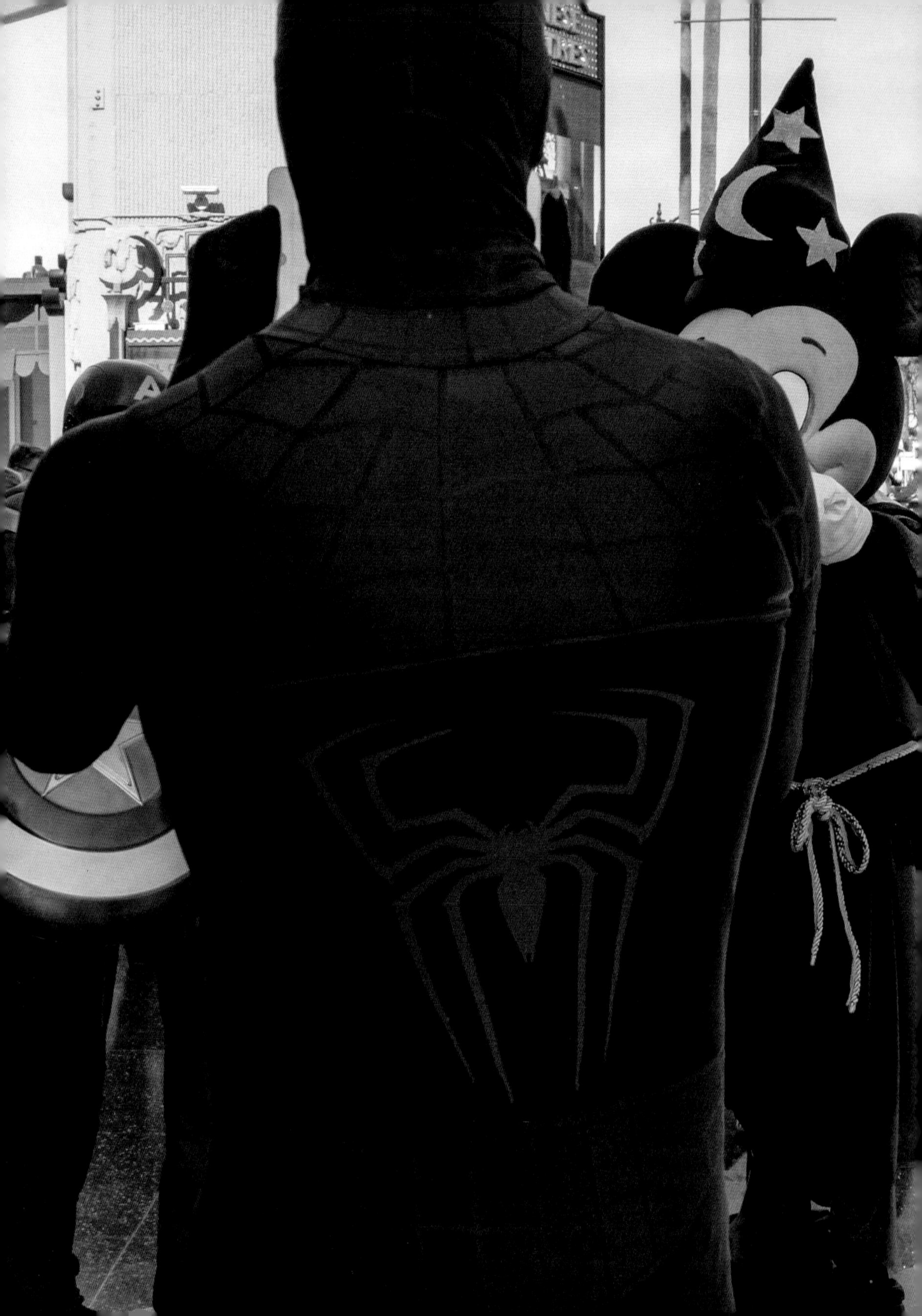

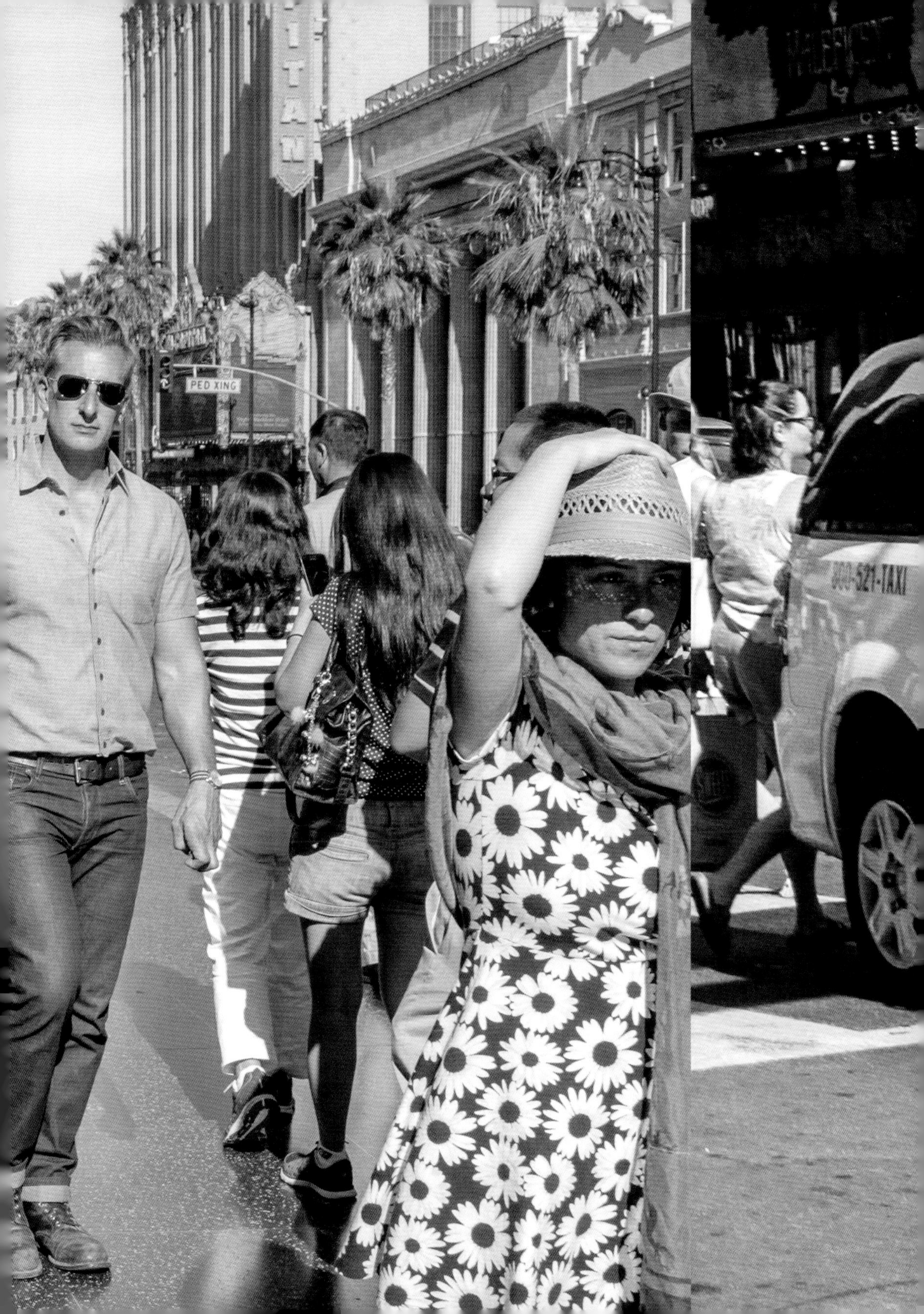

PED XING
800-521-TAXI

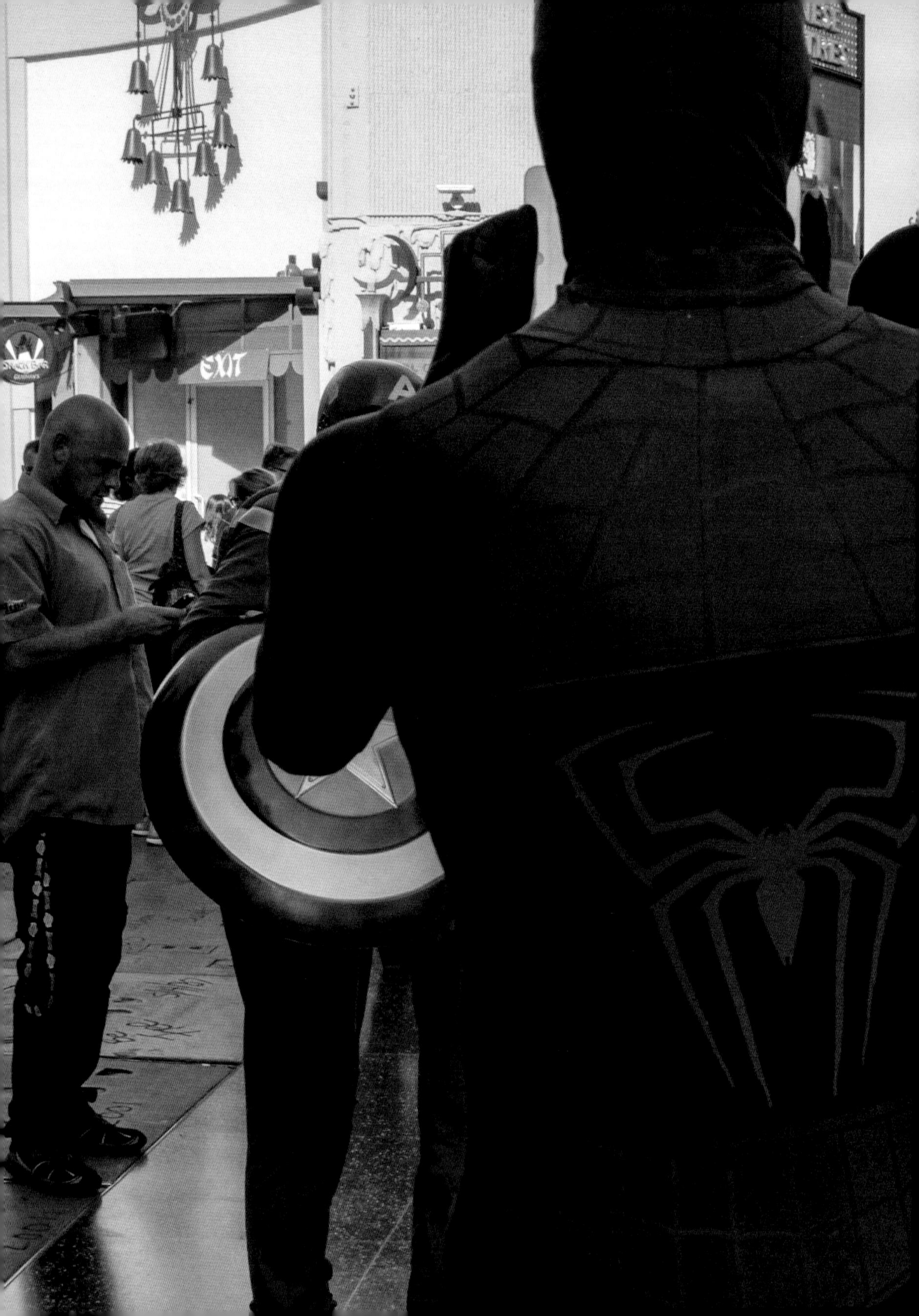

EXIT

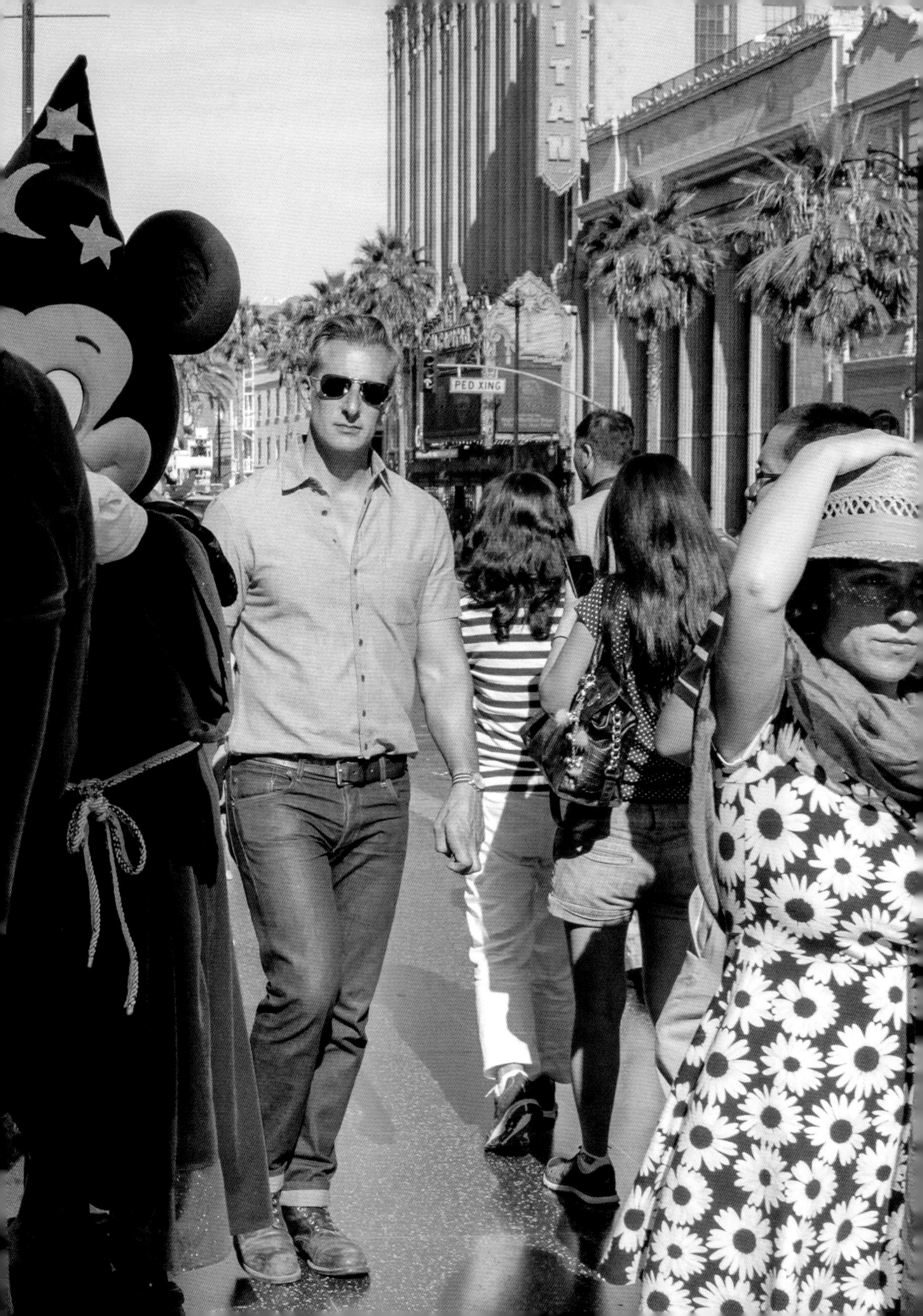

PED XING

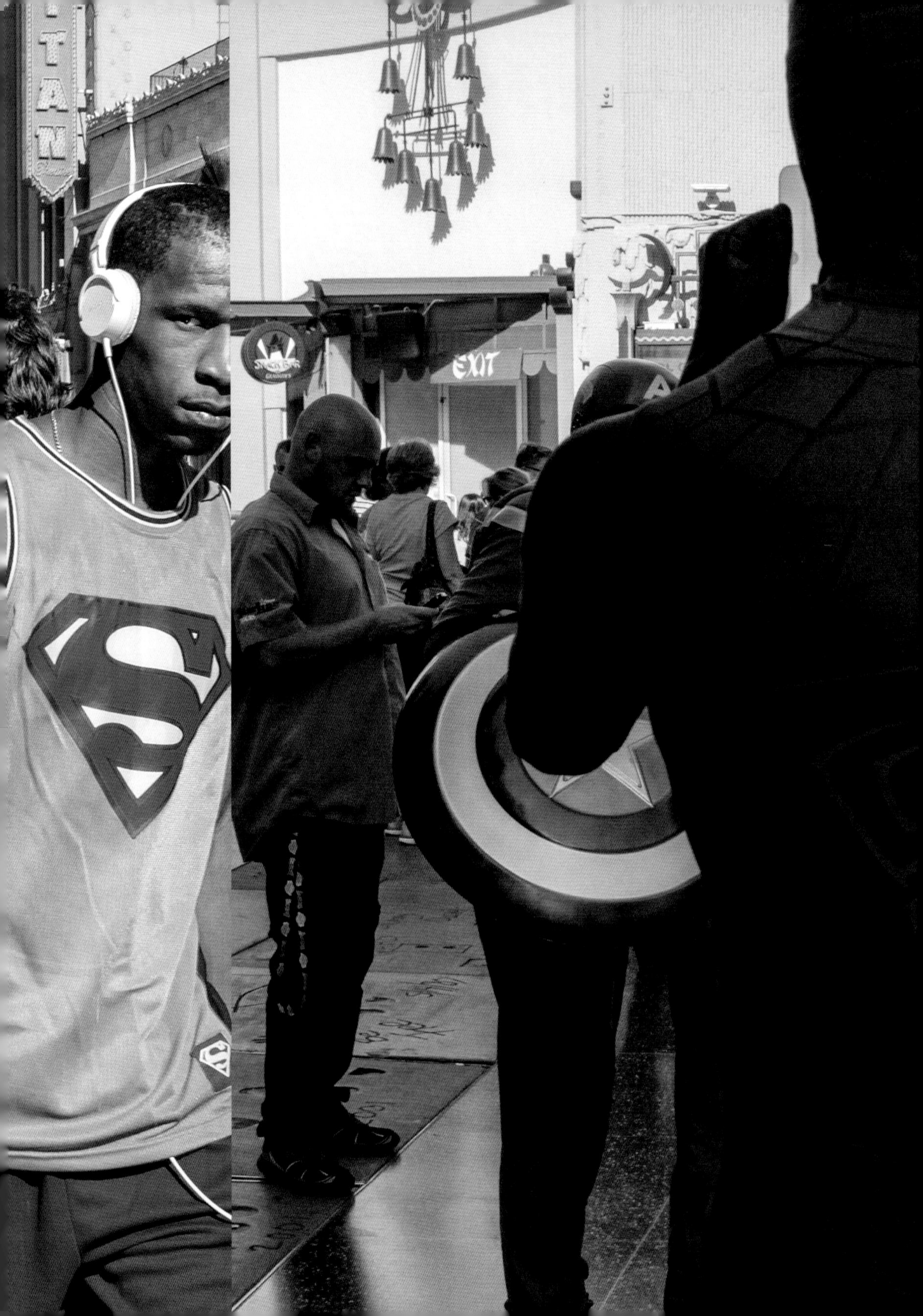
TAN
EXIT

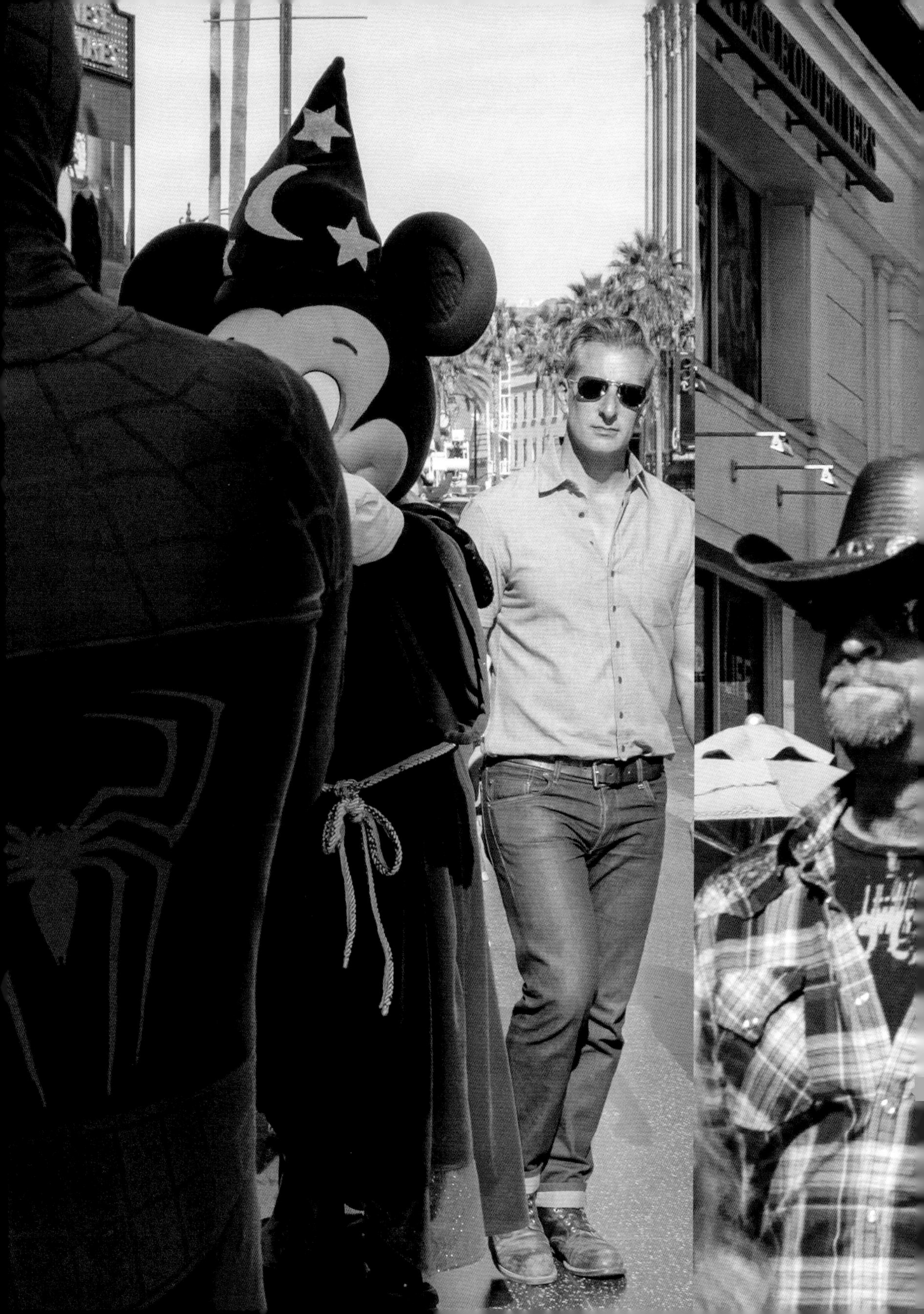

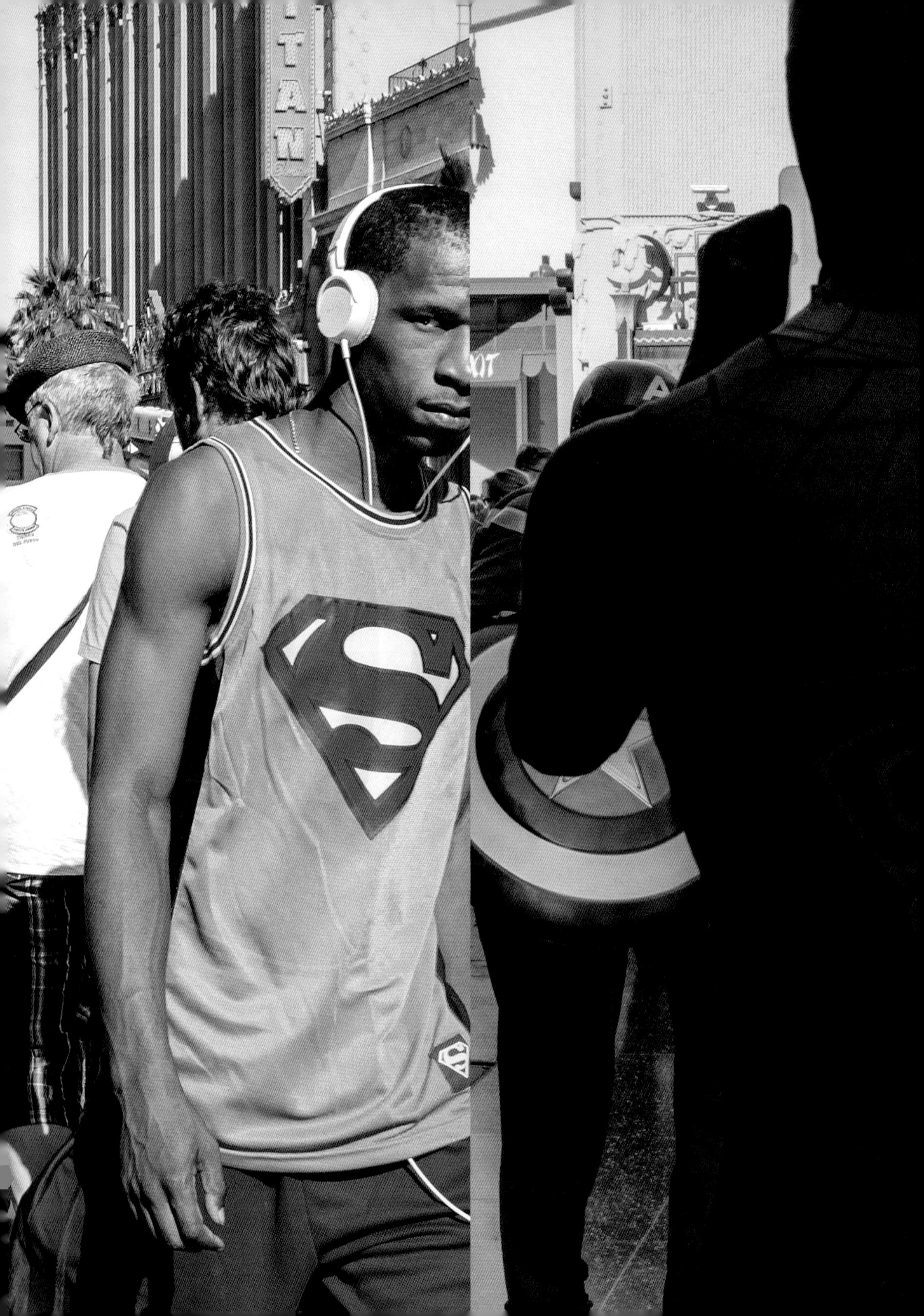

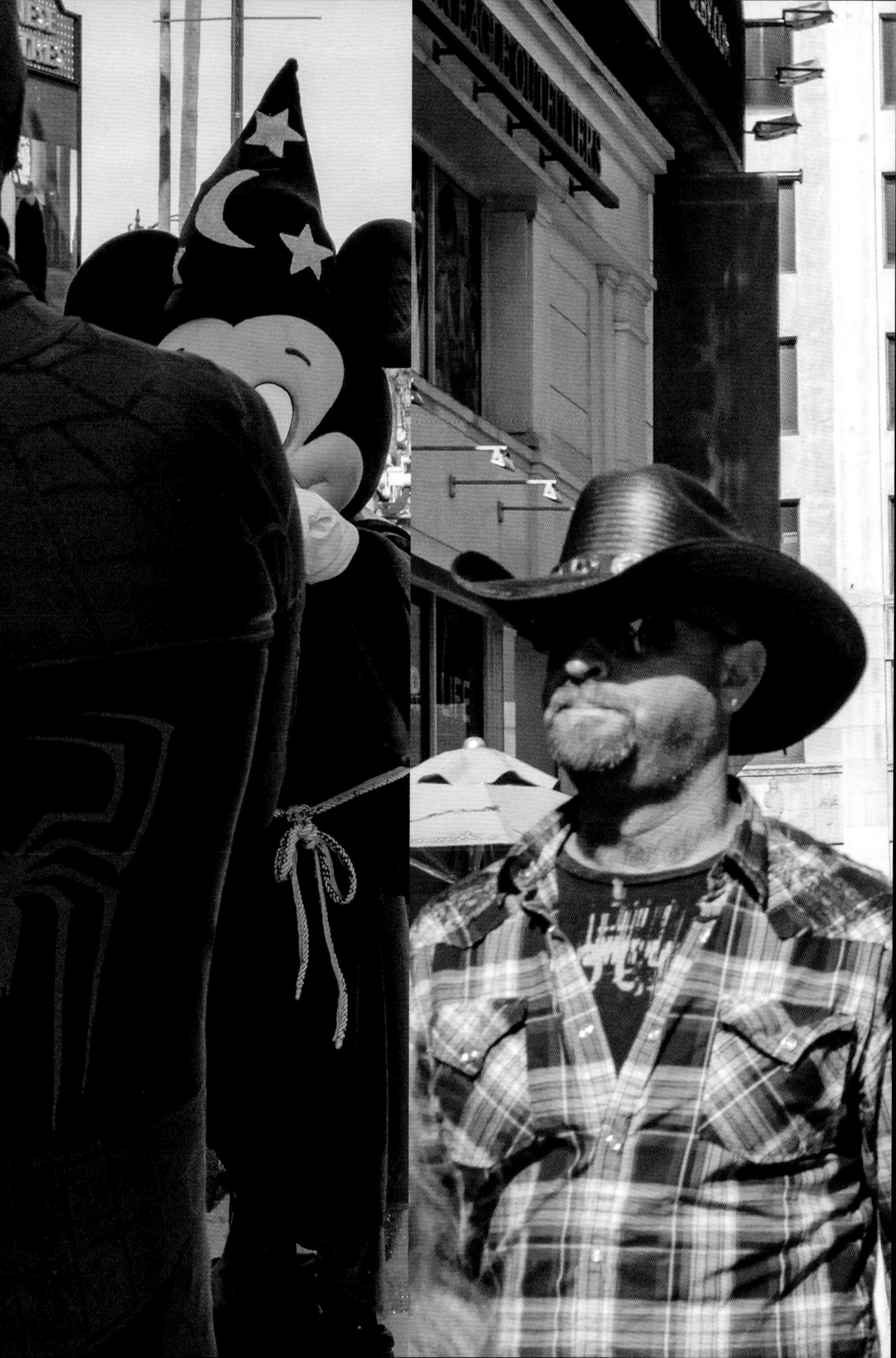

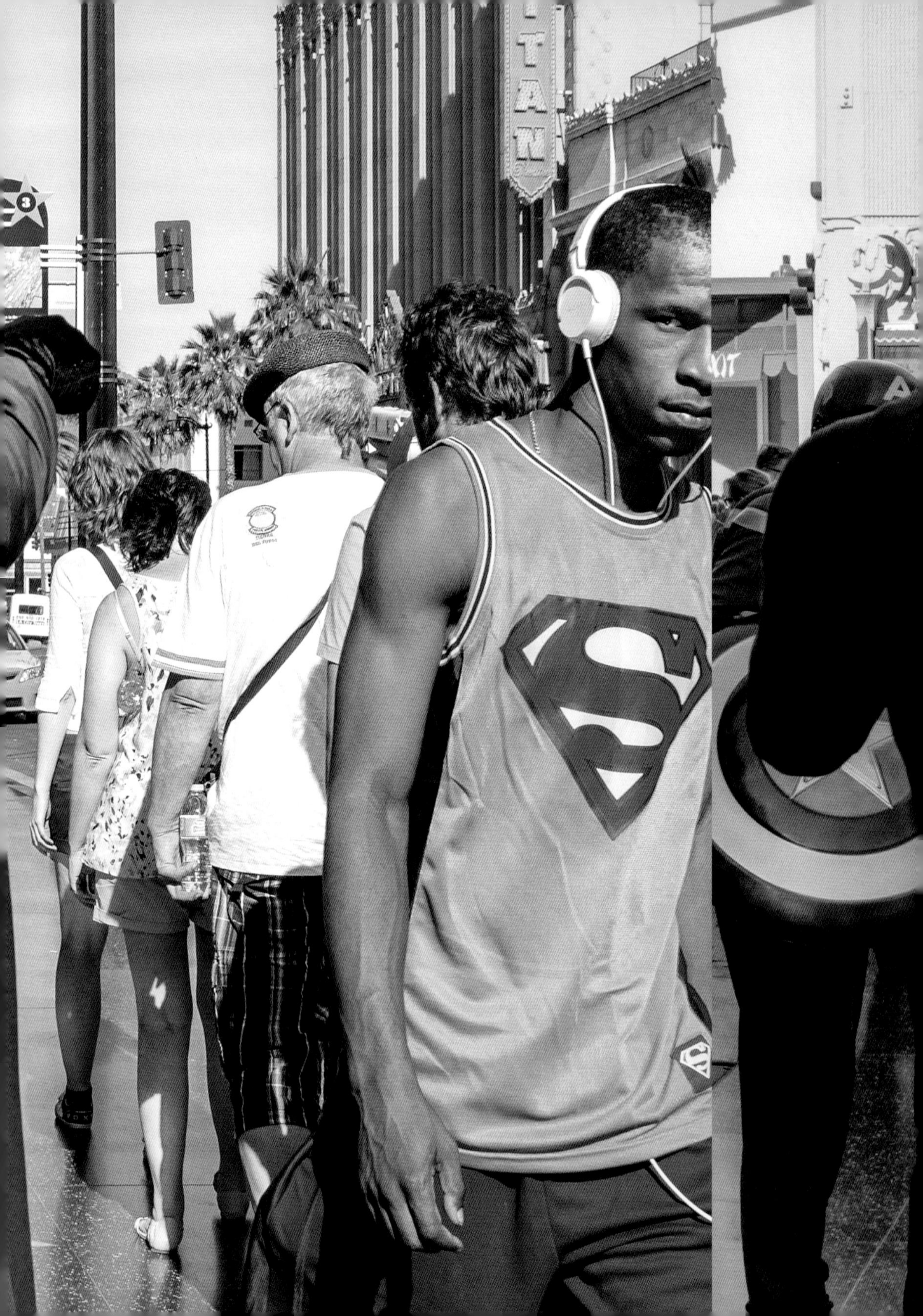

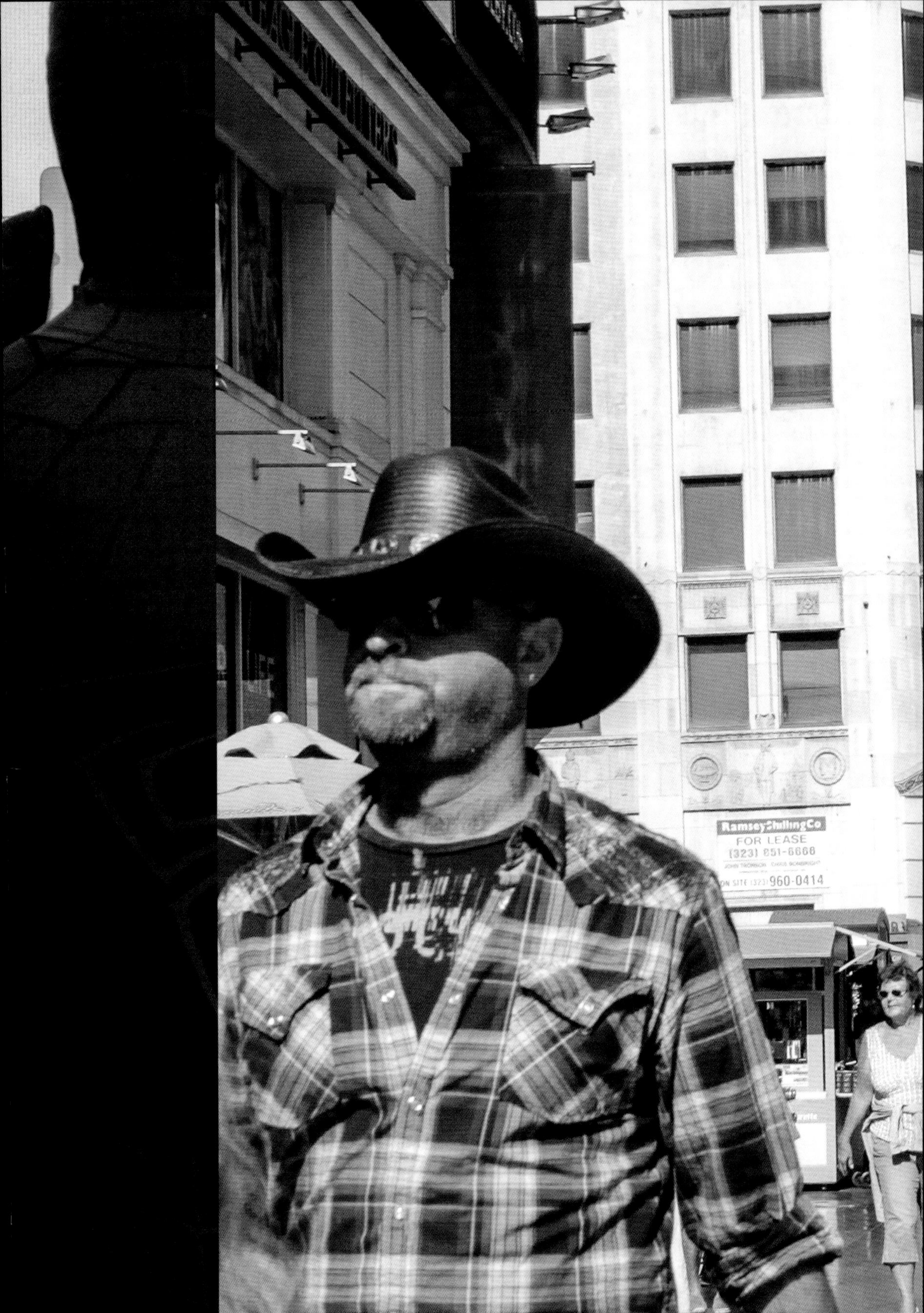

RamseyShillingCo
FOR LEASE
(323) 651-6666
JOHN THOMSON CHRIS BOABRIGHT
ON SITE (323) 960-0414

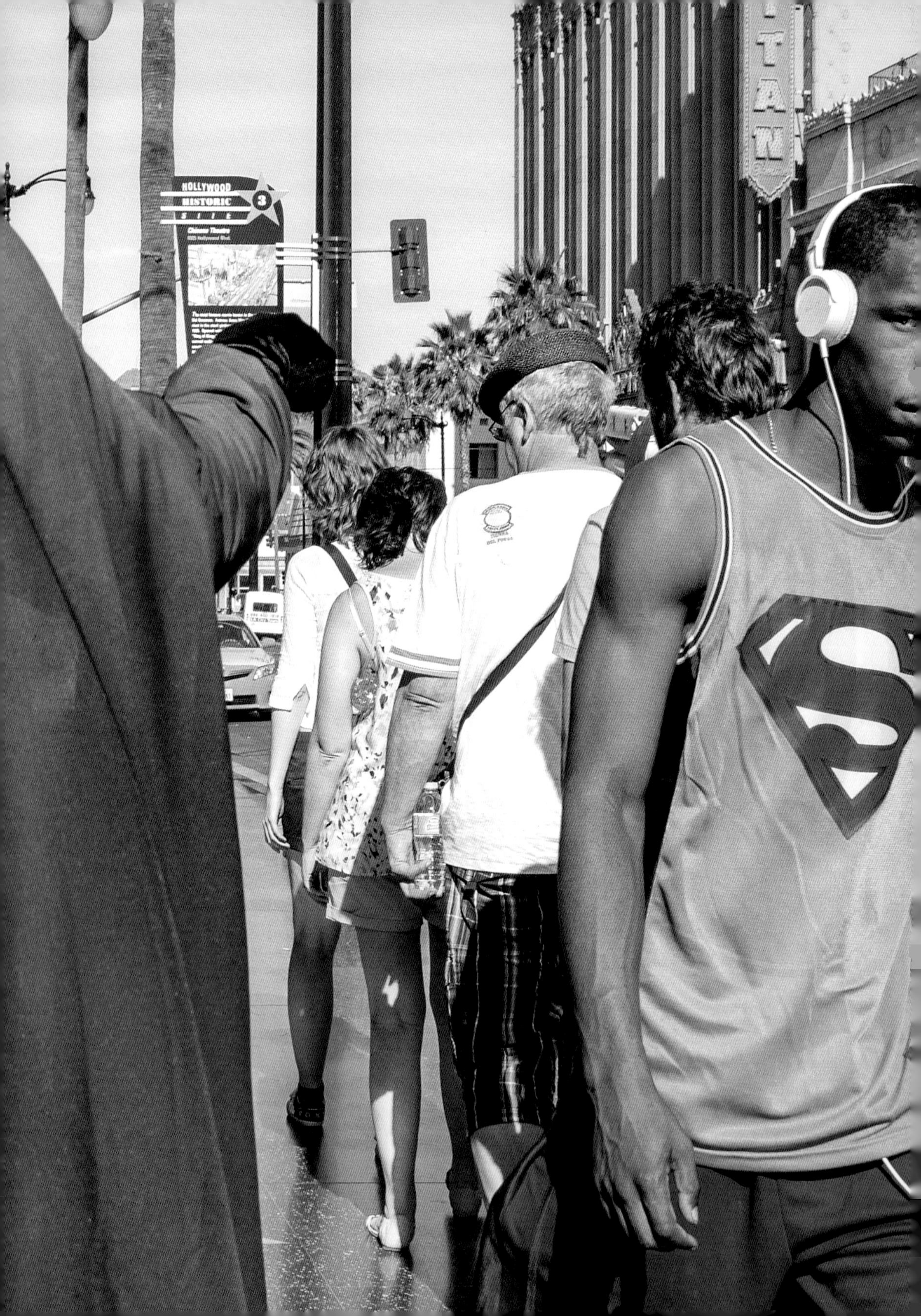
HOLLYWOOD
HISTORIC
SITE

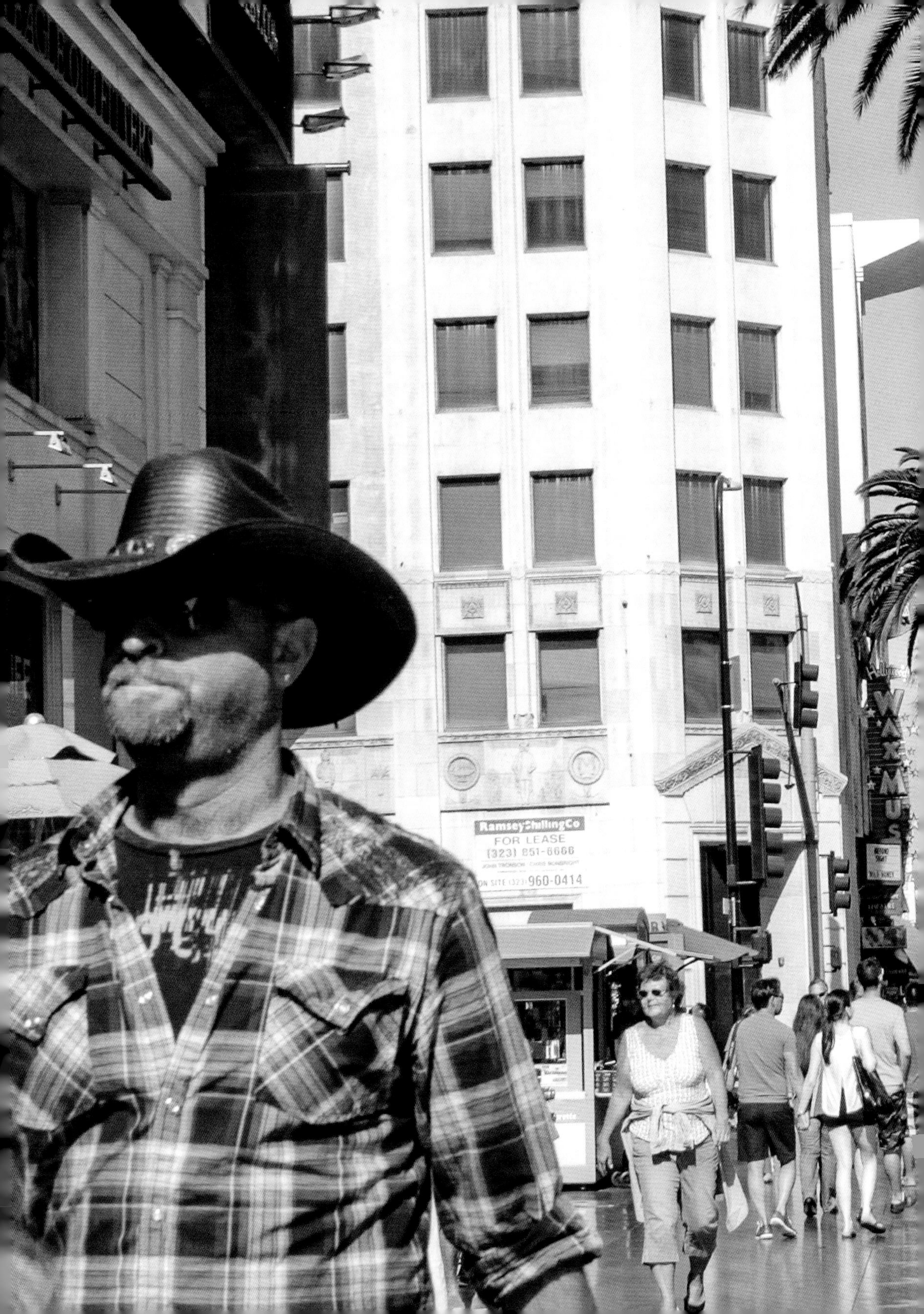
Ramsey-Shilling Co
FOR LEASE
(323) 851-6666
ON SITE (323) 960-0414

HOLLYWOOD
HISTORIC
SITE

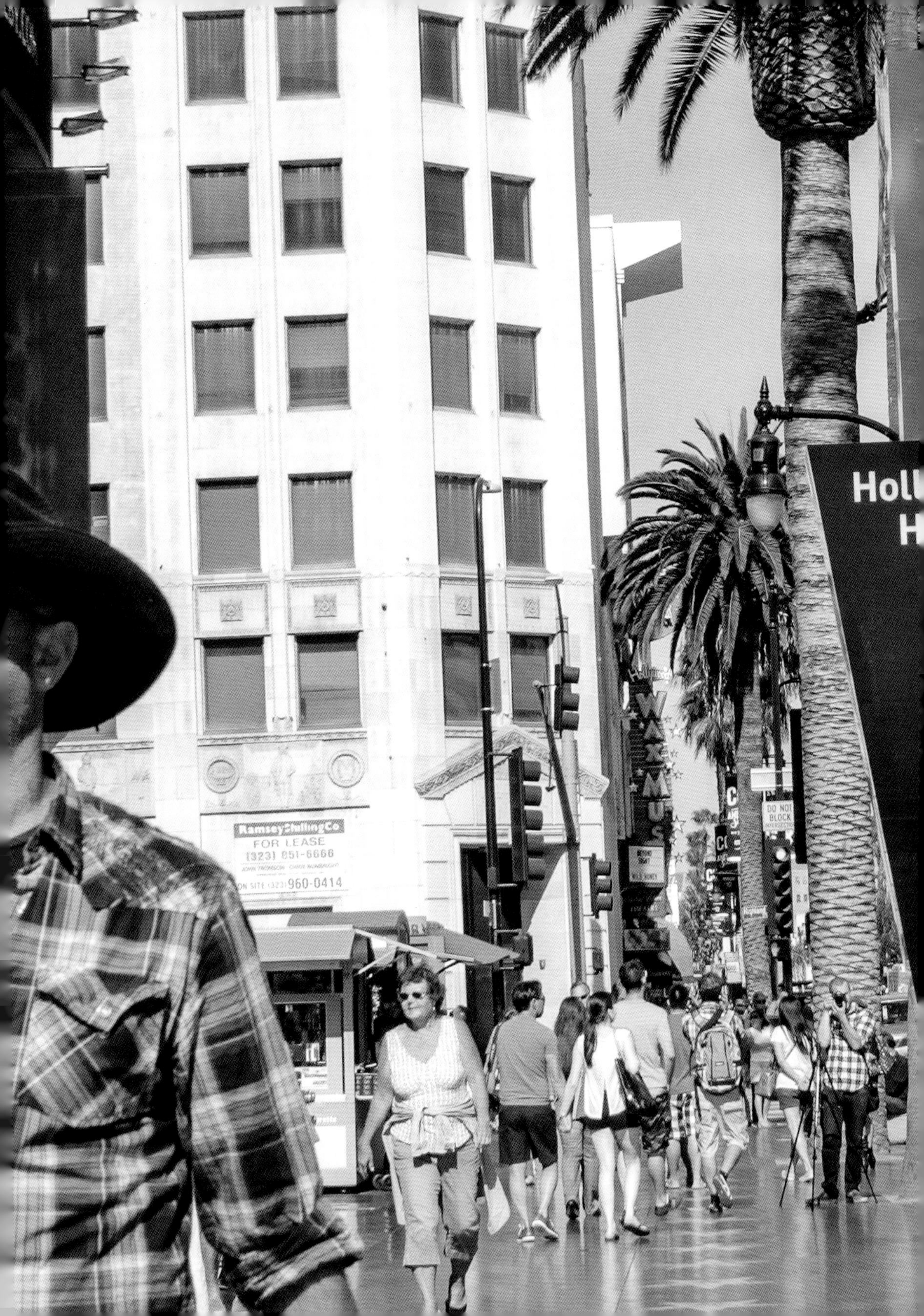
RamseyShillingCo
FOR LEASE
(323) 851-6666
JOHN THOMSON CHRIS MUNDRIGHT
ON SITE (323) 960-0414
Holl
H
DO NOT
BLOCK
INTERSECTION

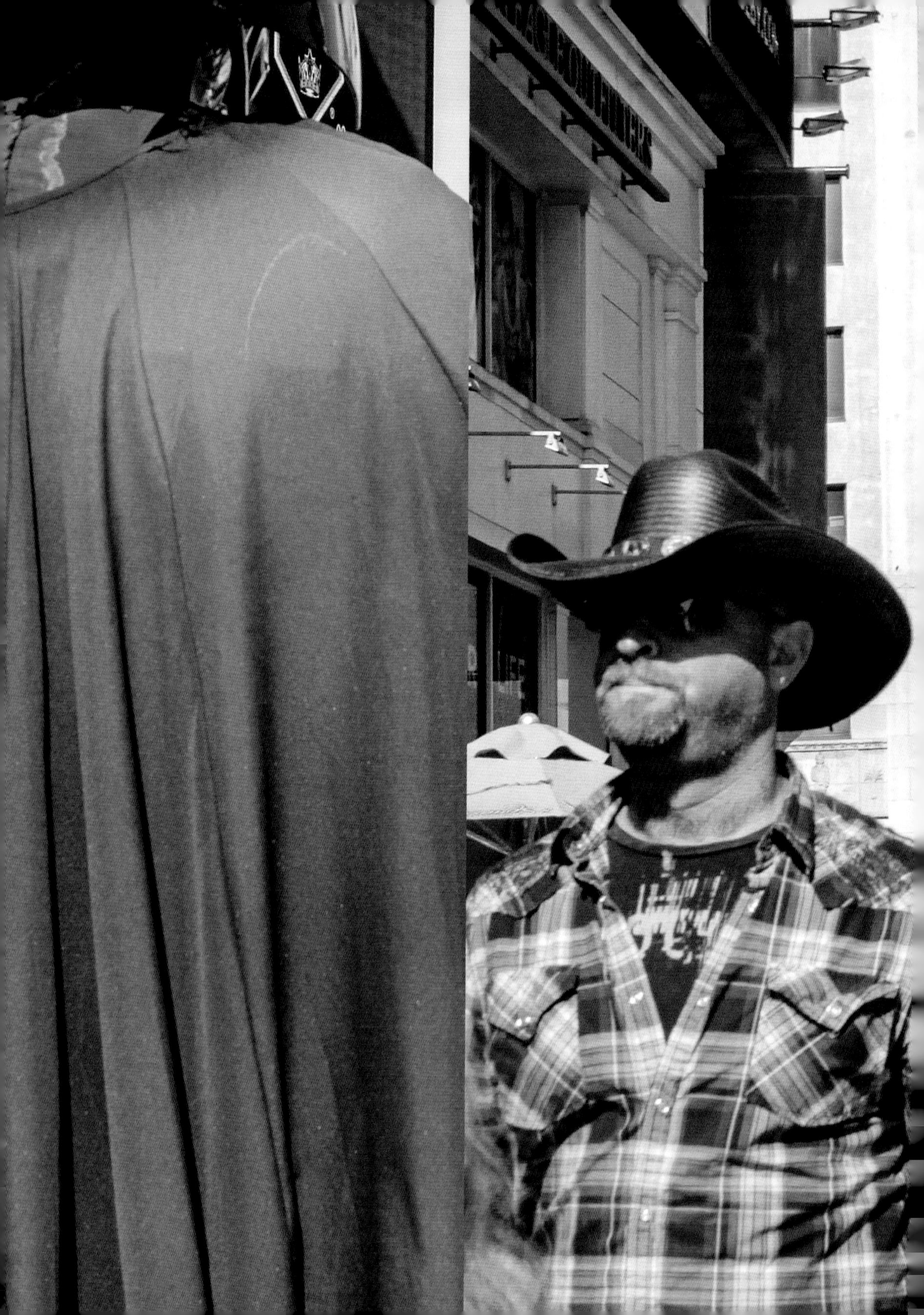

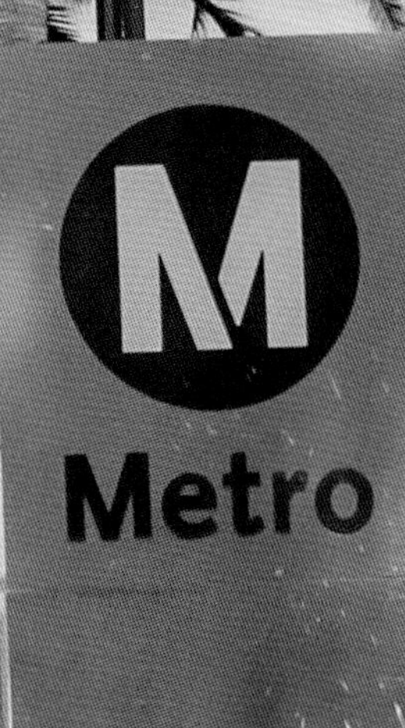

M
Metro
Hollywood/
Highland
FOR LEASE
(323) 851-6666
(323) 960-0414
DO NOT
BLOCK
INTERSECTION

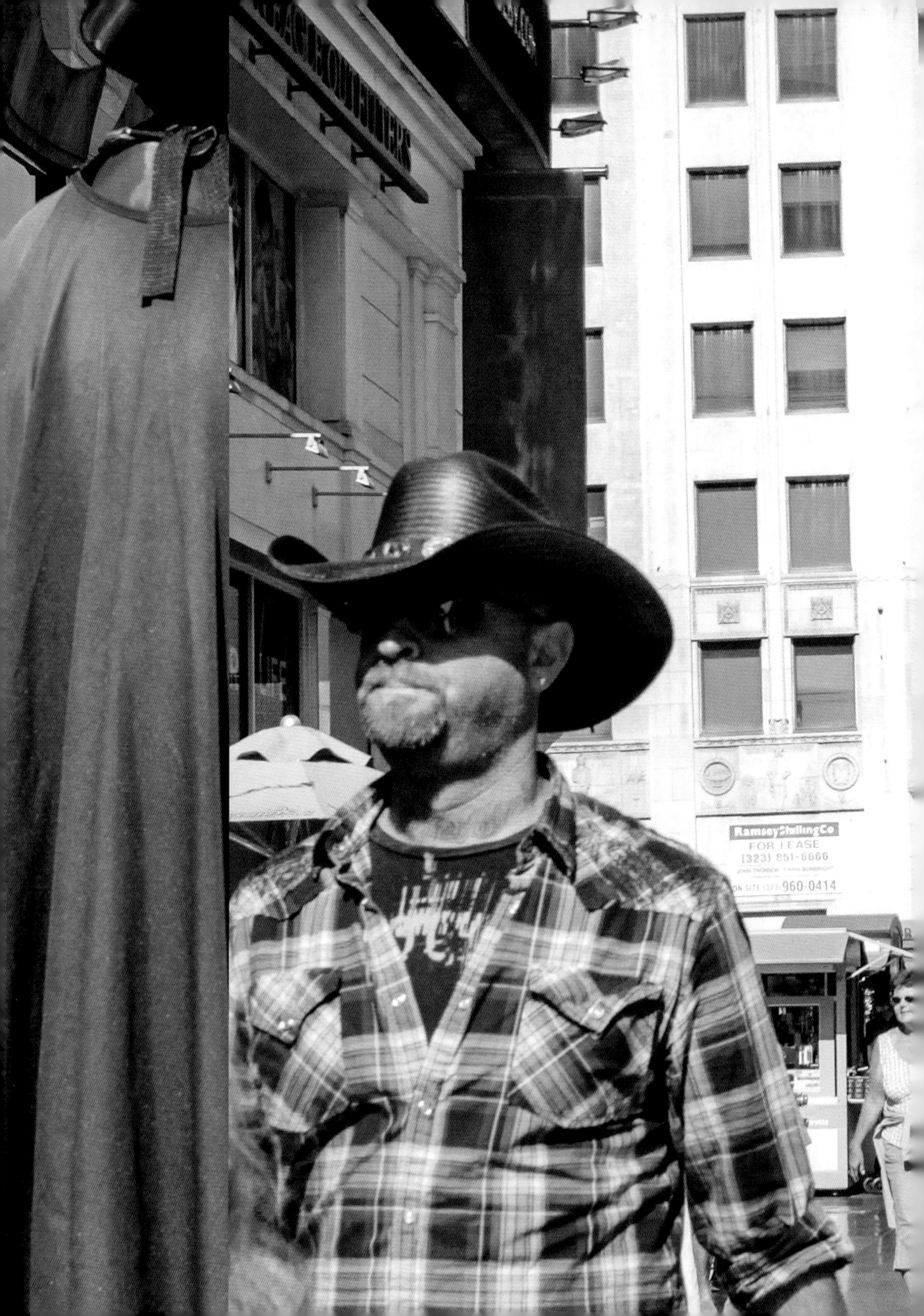
Ramsey Shilling Co
FOR LEASE
(323) 851-8666
ON SITE (323) 960-0414

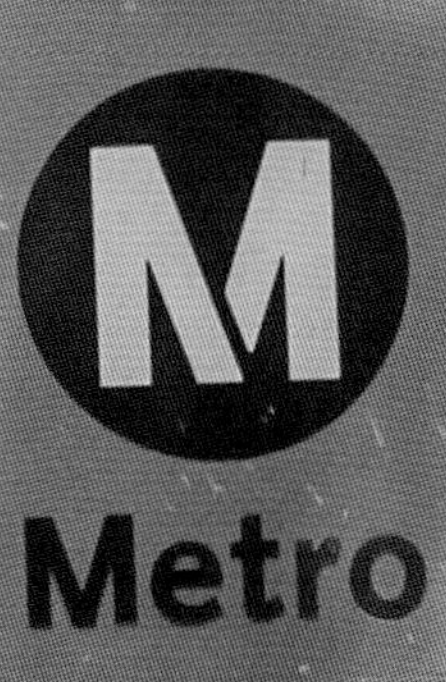
M
Metro

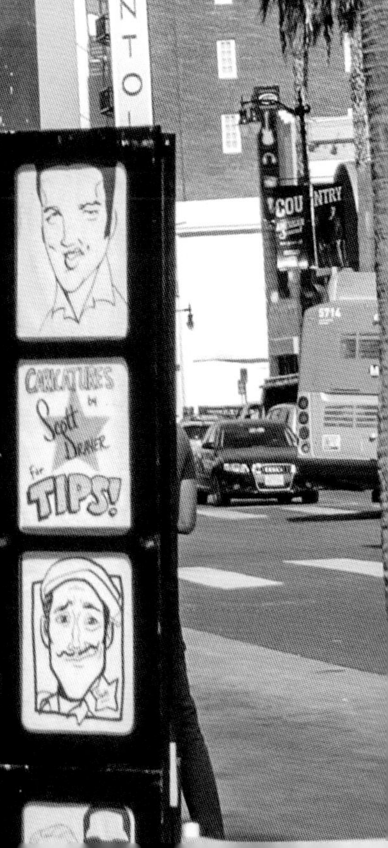
Hollywood/
Highland

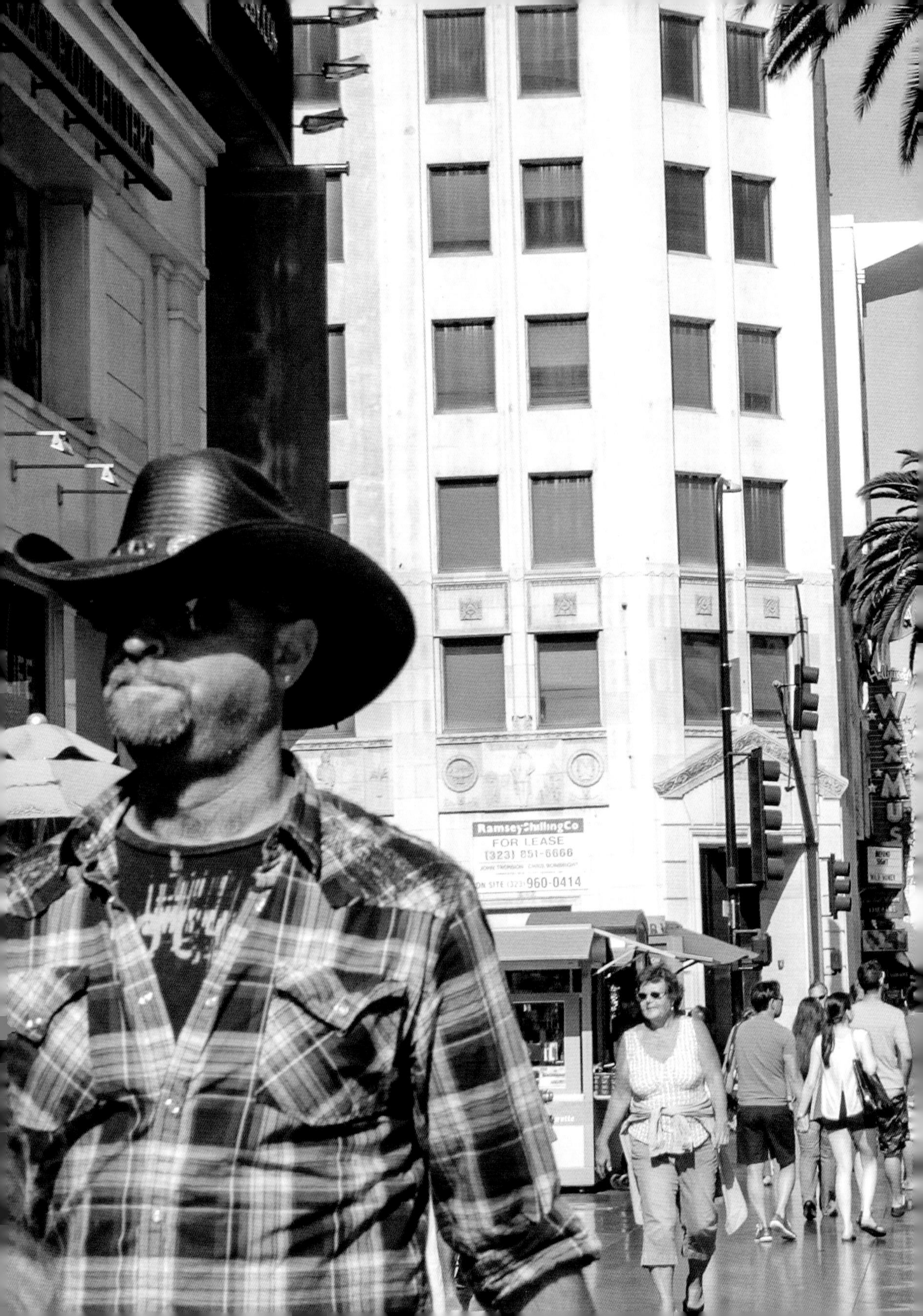
RamseyShillingCo
FOR LEASE
(323) 851-6666
JOHN THORSON   CHRIS BOMBRIGHT
ON SITE (323) 960-0414

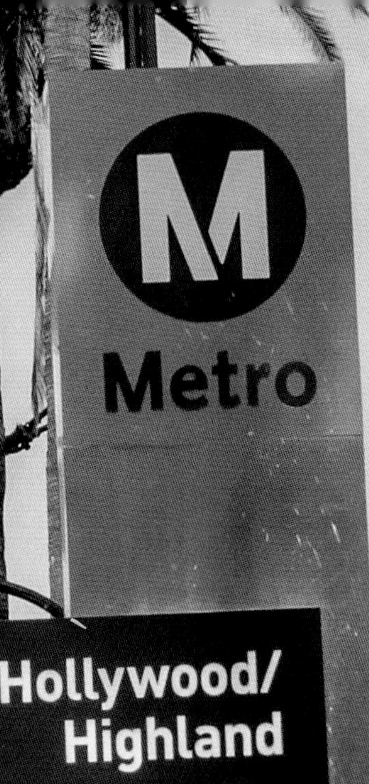

M
Metro

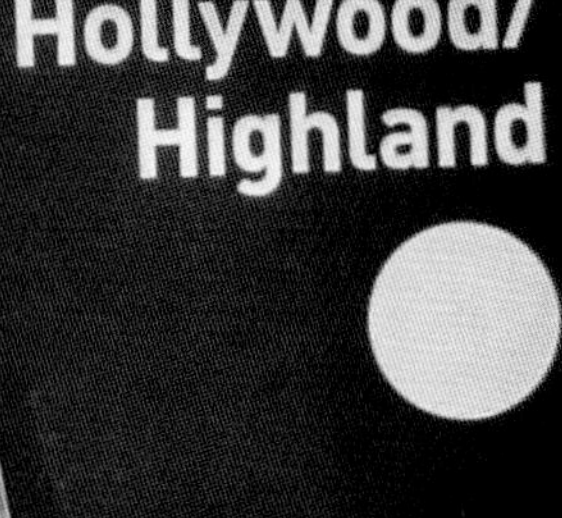

Hollywood/
Highland

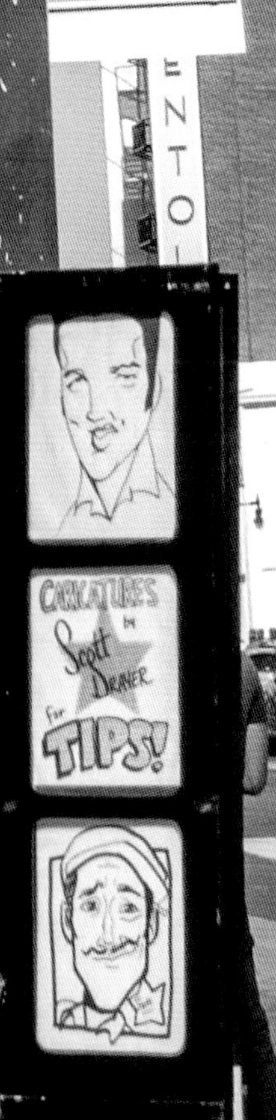

CARICATURES by
Scott
Draper
For
TIPS!

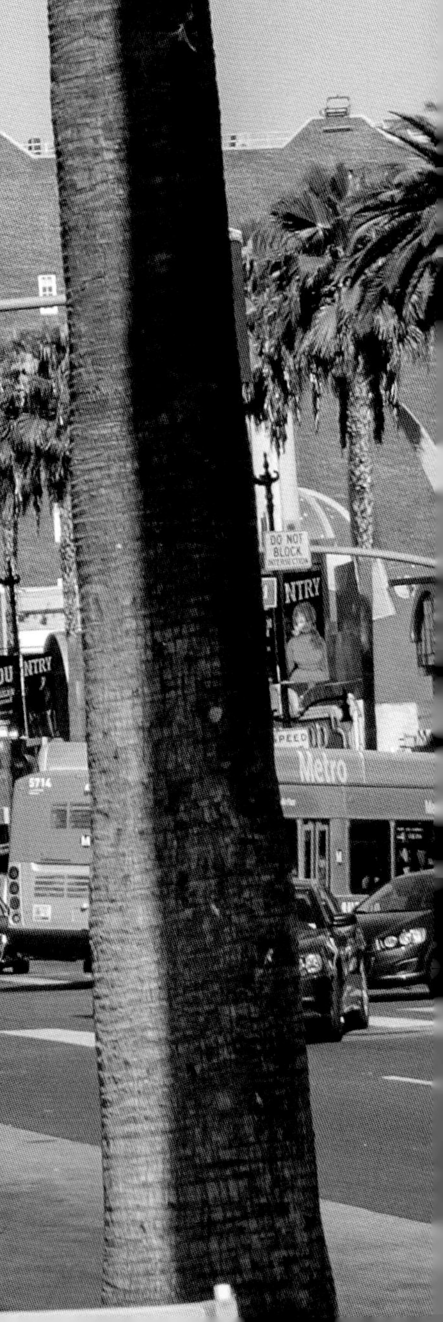

DO NOT
BLOCK
INTERSECTION
Metro

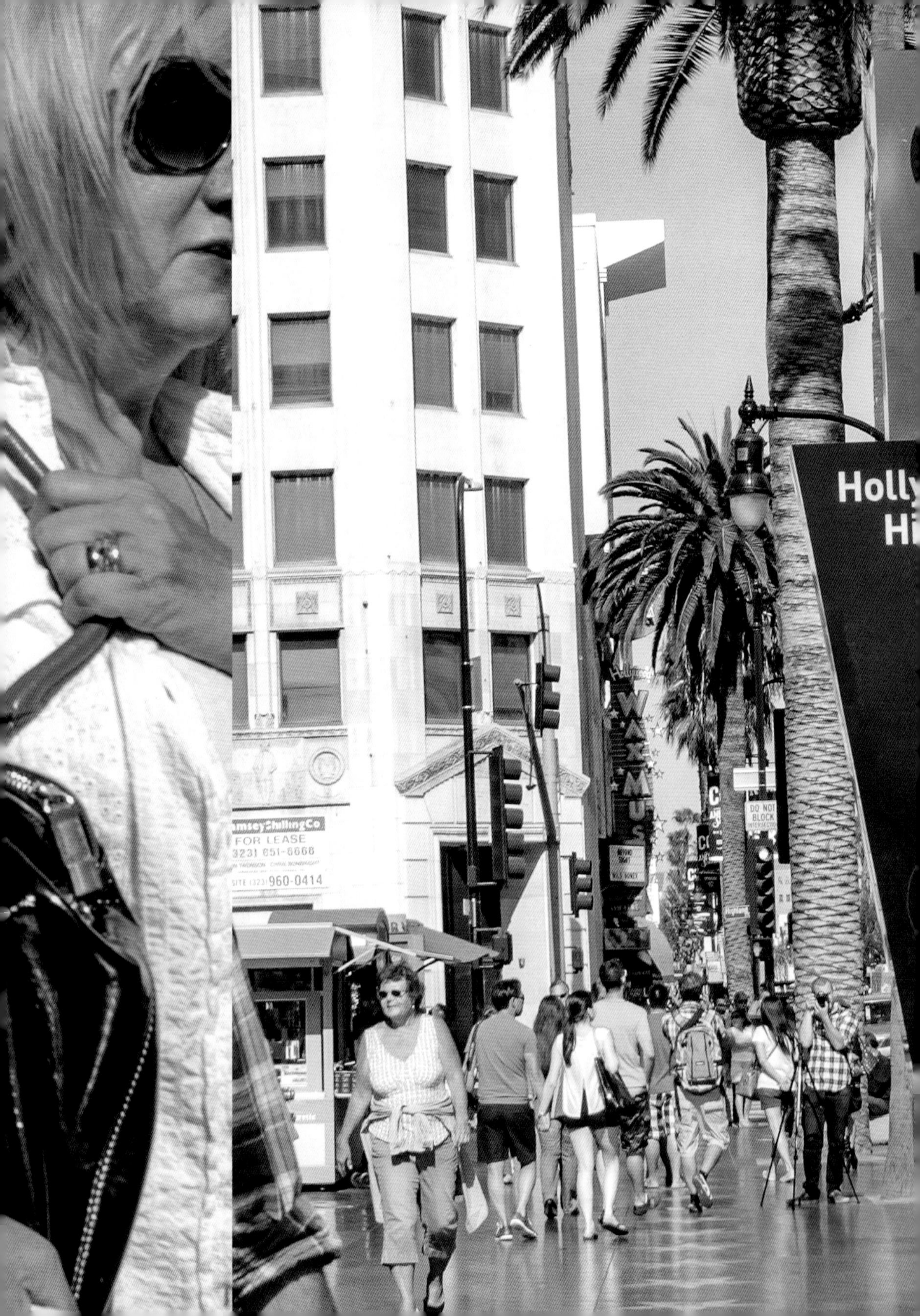

FOR LEASE
3231 651-6666
SITE (323) 960-0414
Holly
Hi
DO NOT
BLOCK
INTERSECTION

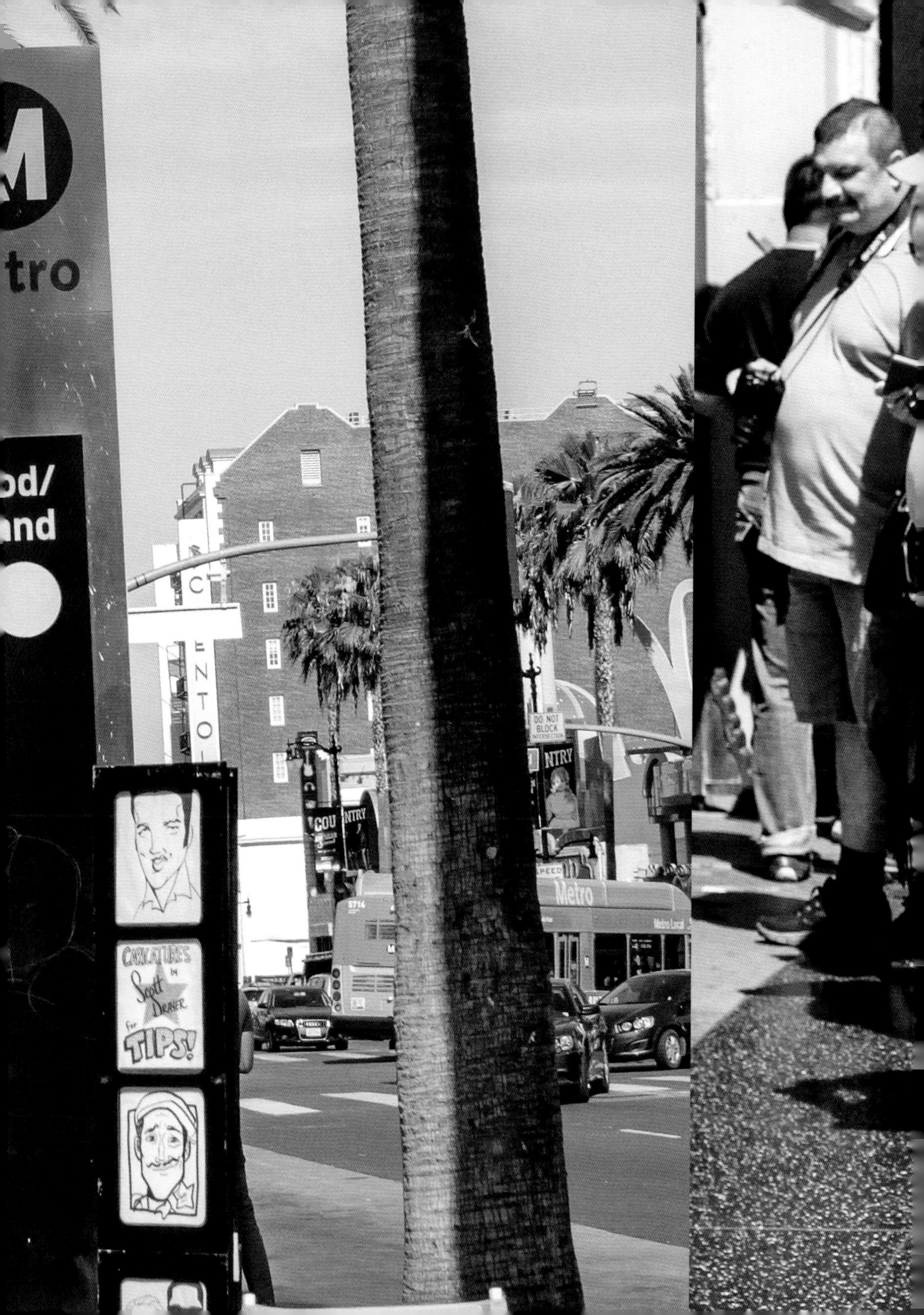

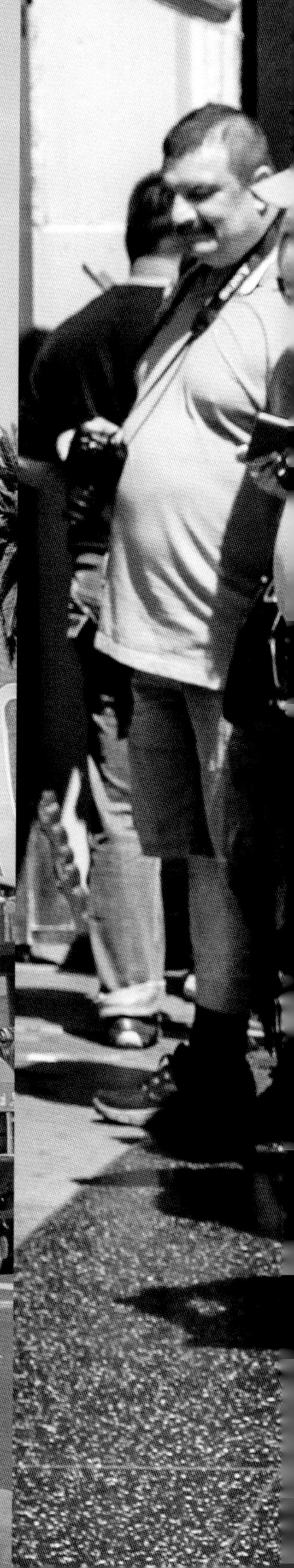
M
tro
od/
and
C
ENTO
COUNTRY
DO NOT
BLOCK
INTERSECTION
NTRY
SPEED
Metro
Metro Local
5714
CARICATURES
by
Scott
Draper
For
TIPS!

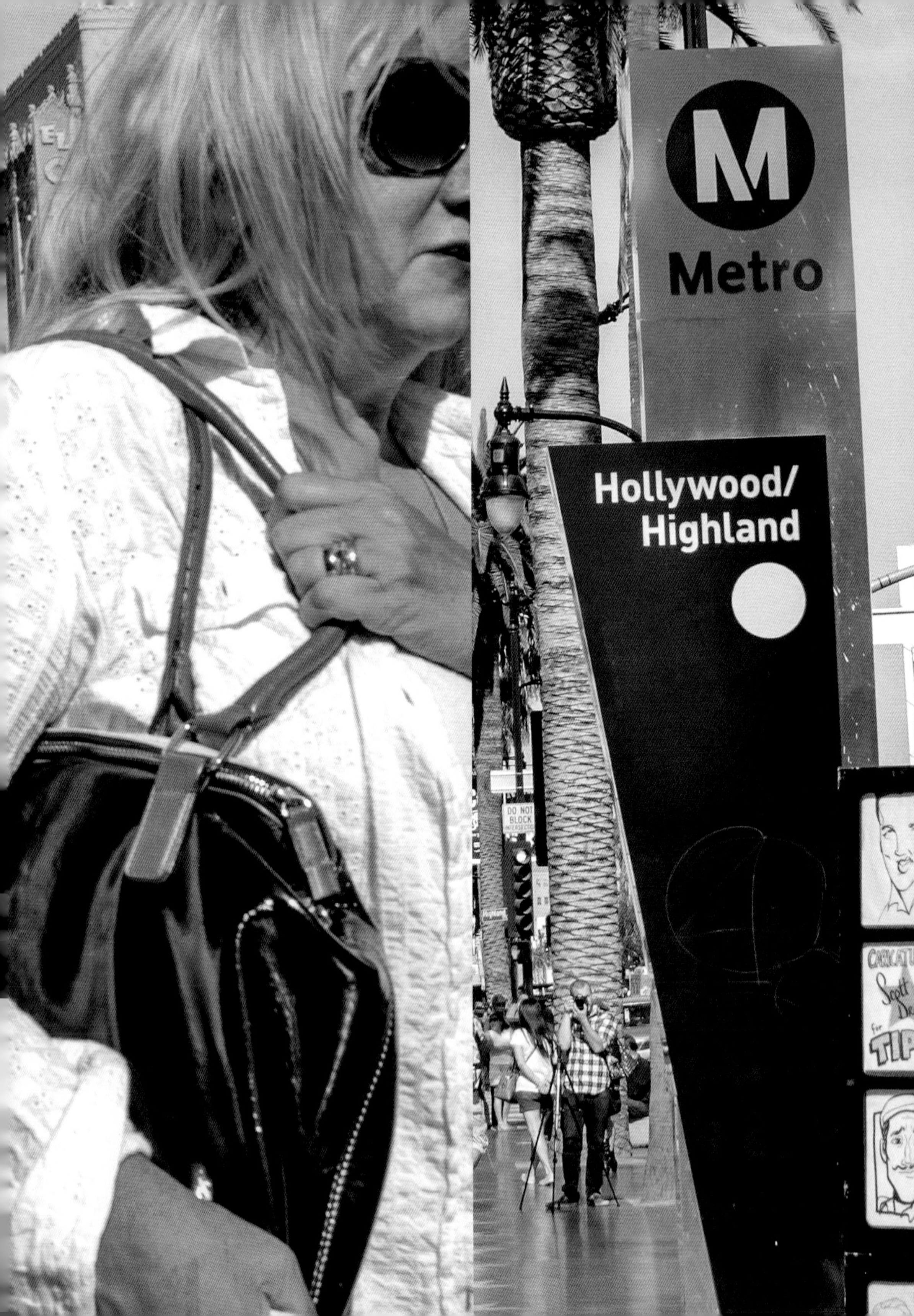

M
Metro
Hollywood/
Highland
DO NOT
BLOCK
INTERSECTION

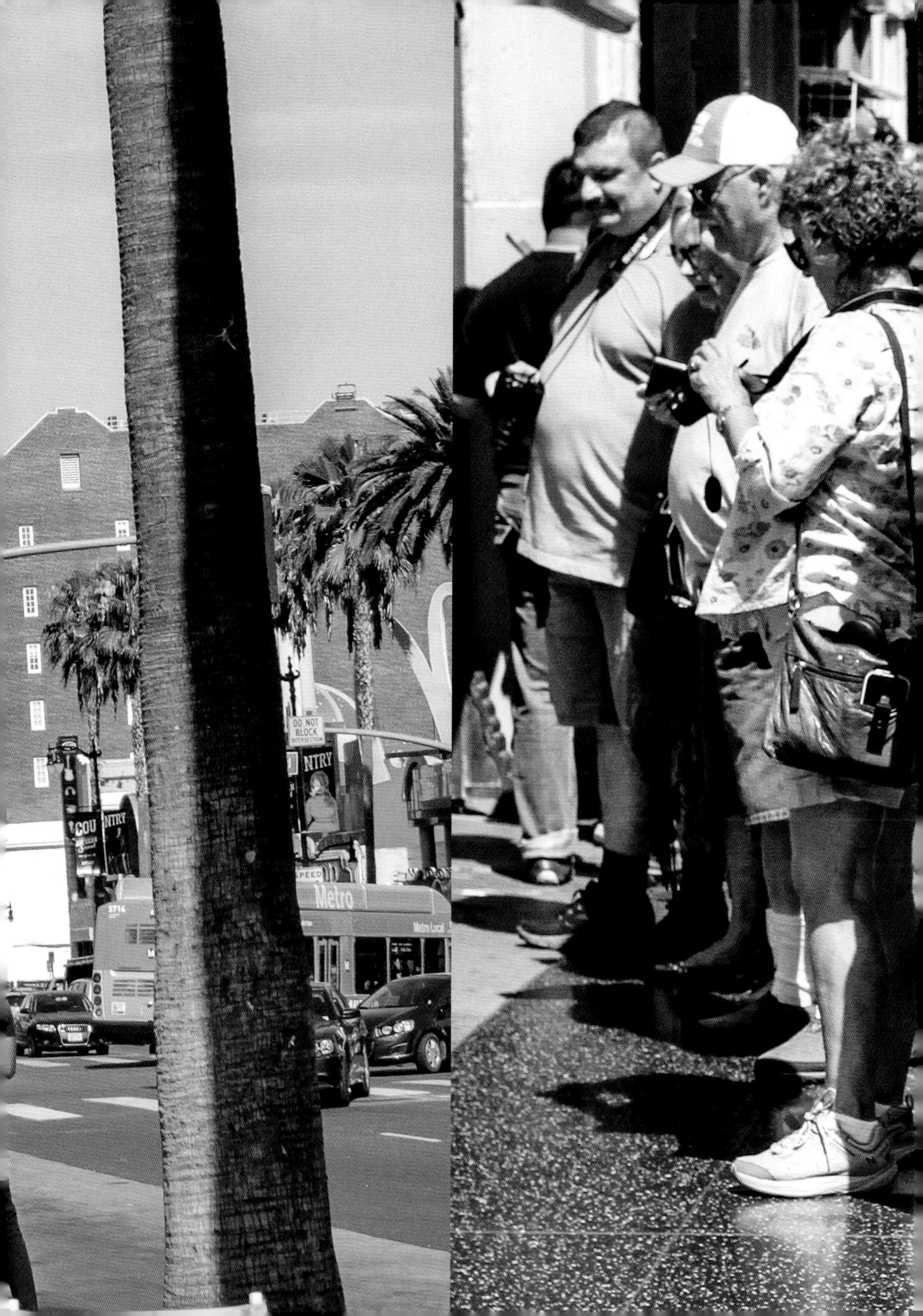

DO NOT
BLOCK
INTERSECTION
NTRY
COU
COUNTRY
Metro
Metro Local
5714

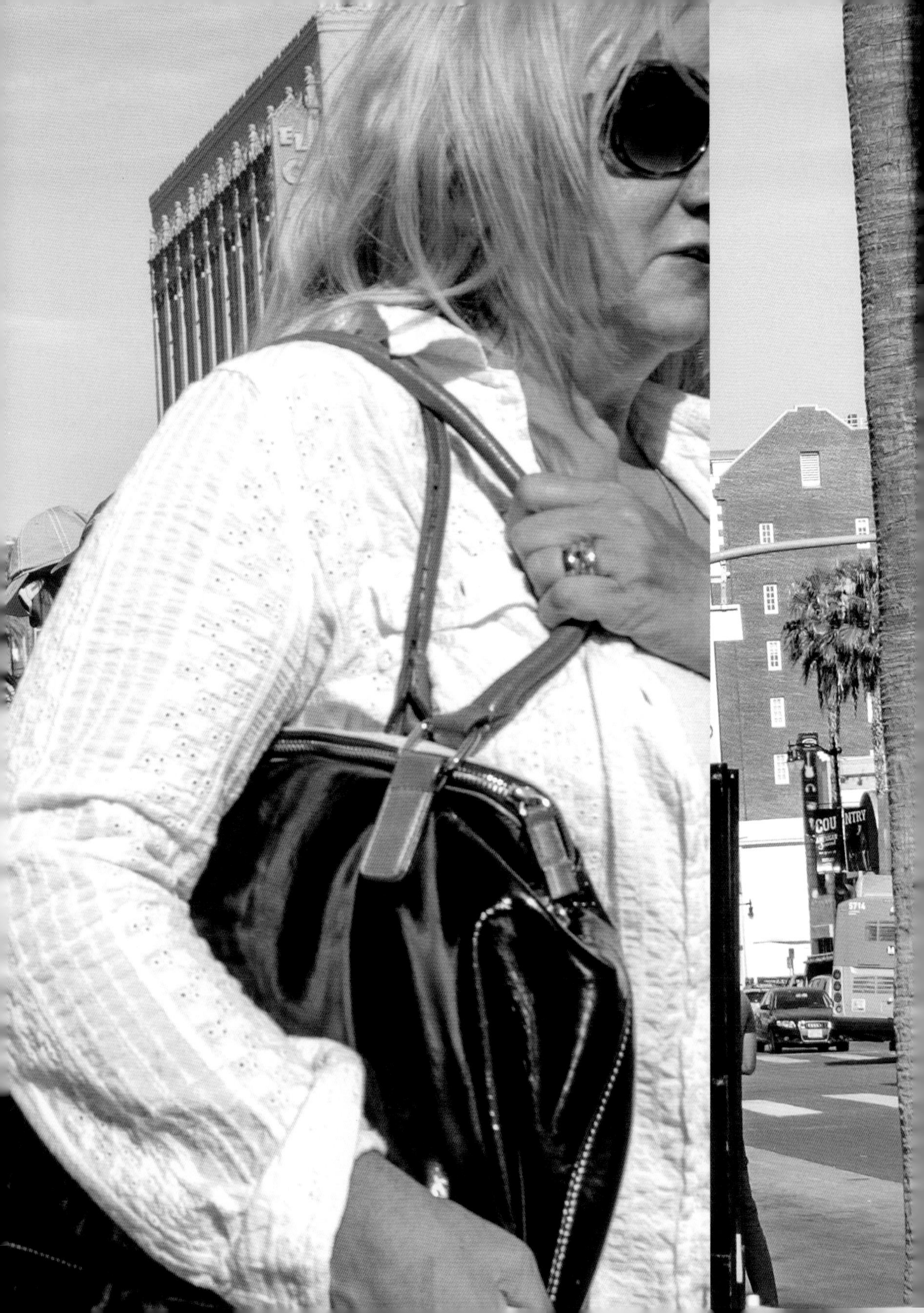

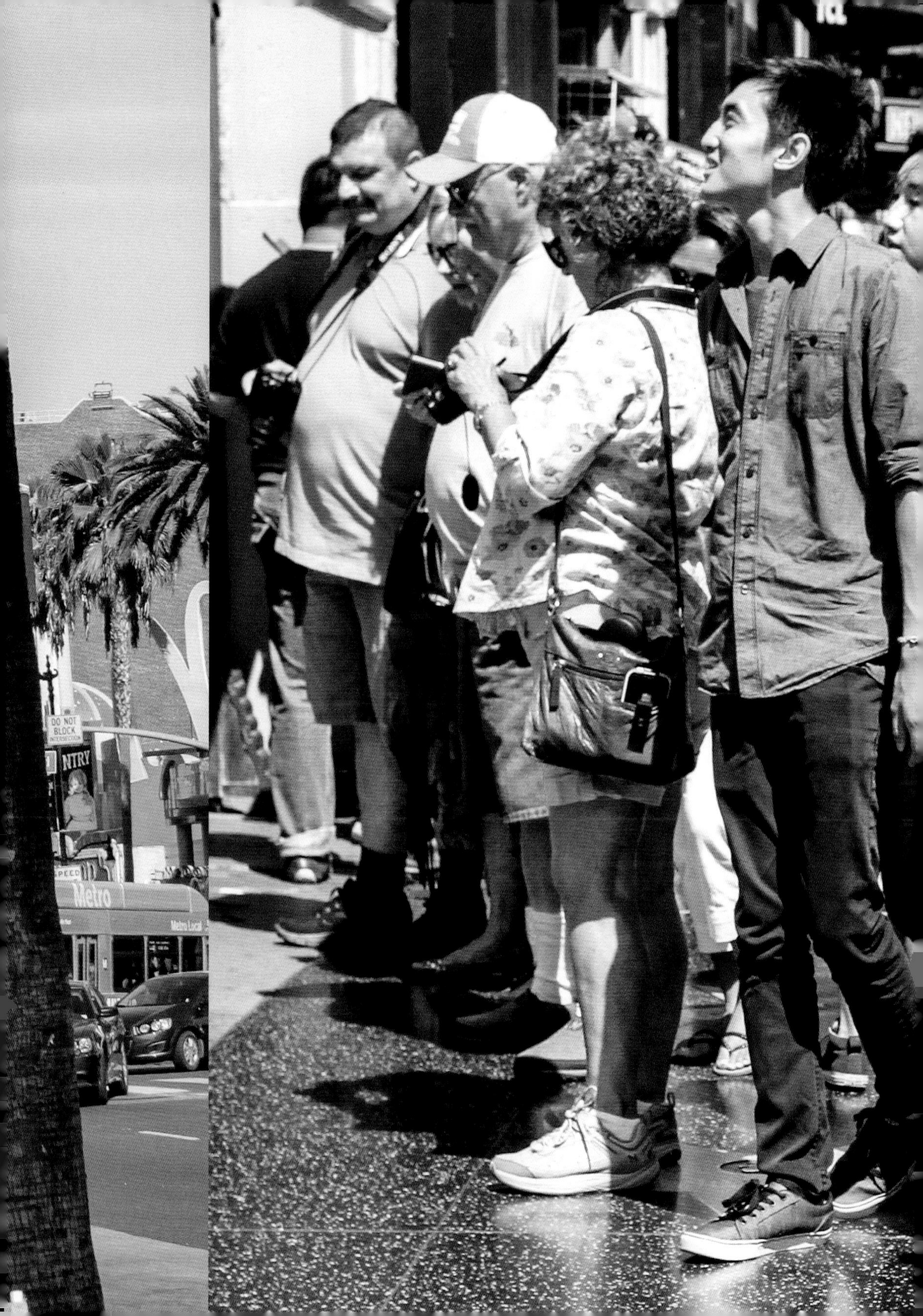

DO NOT
BLOCK
INTERSECTION
NTRY
Metro
Metro Local

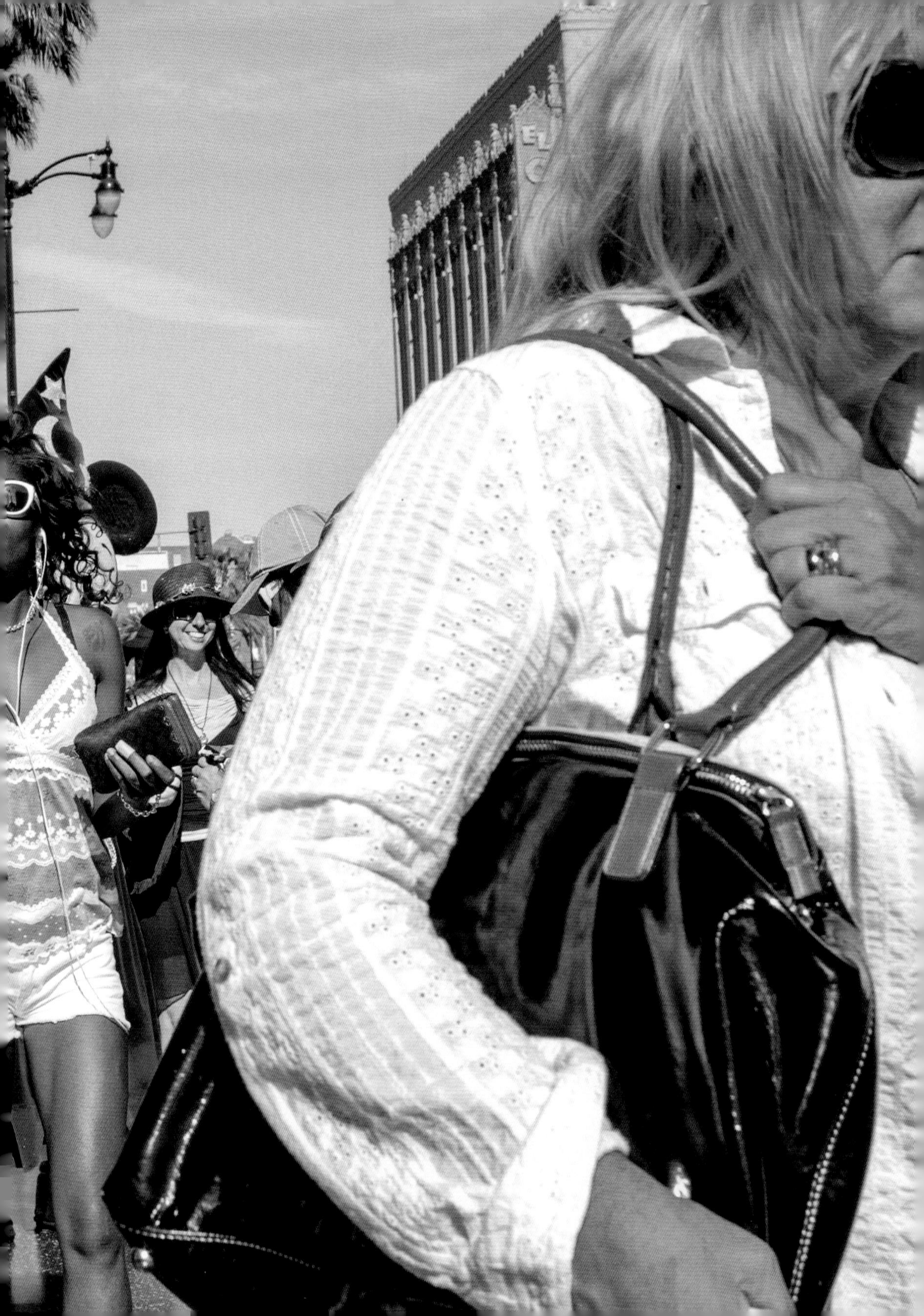

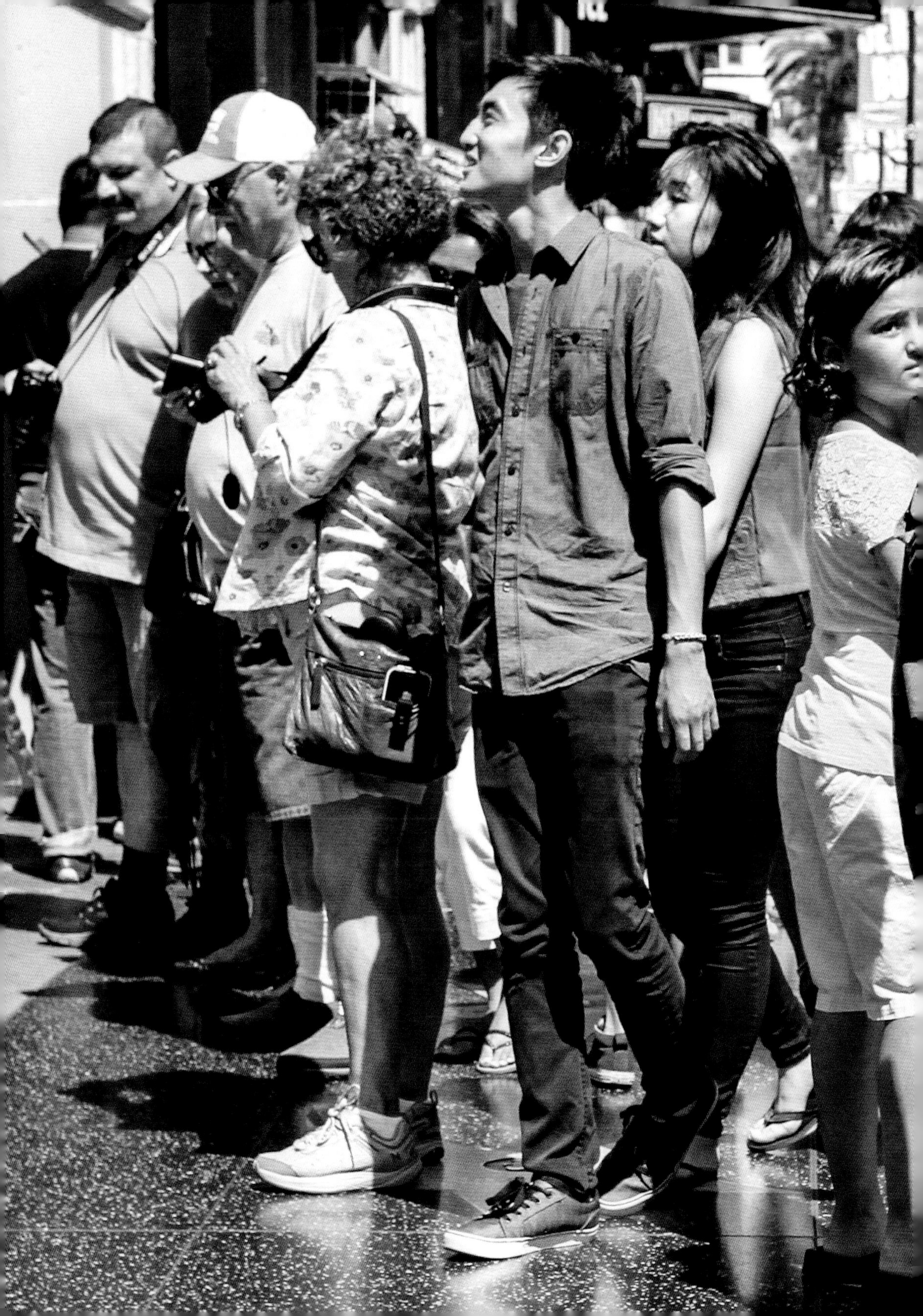

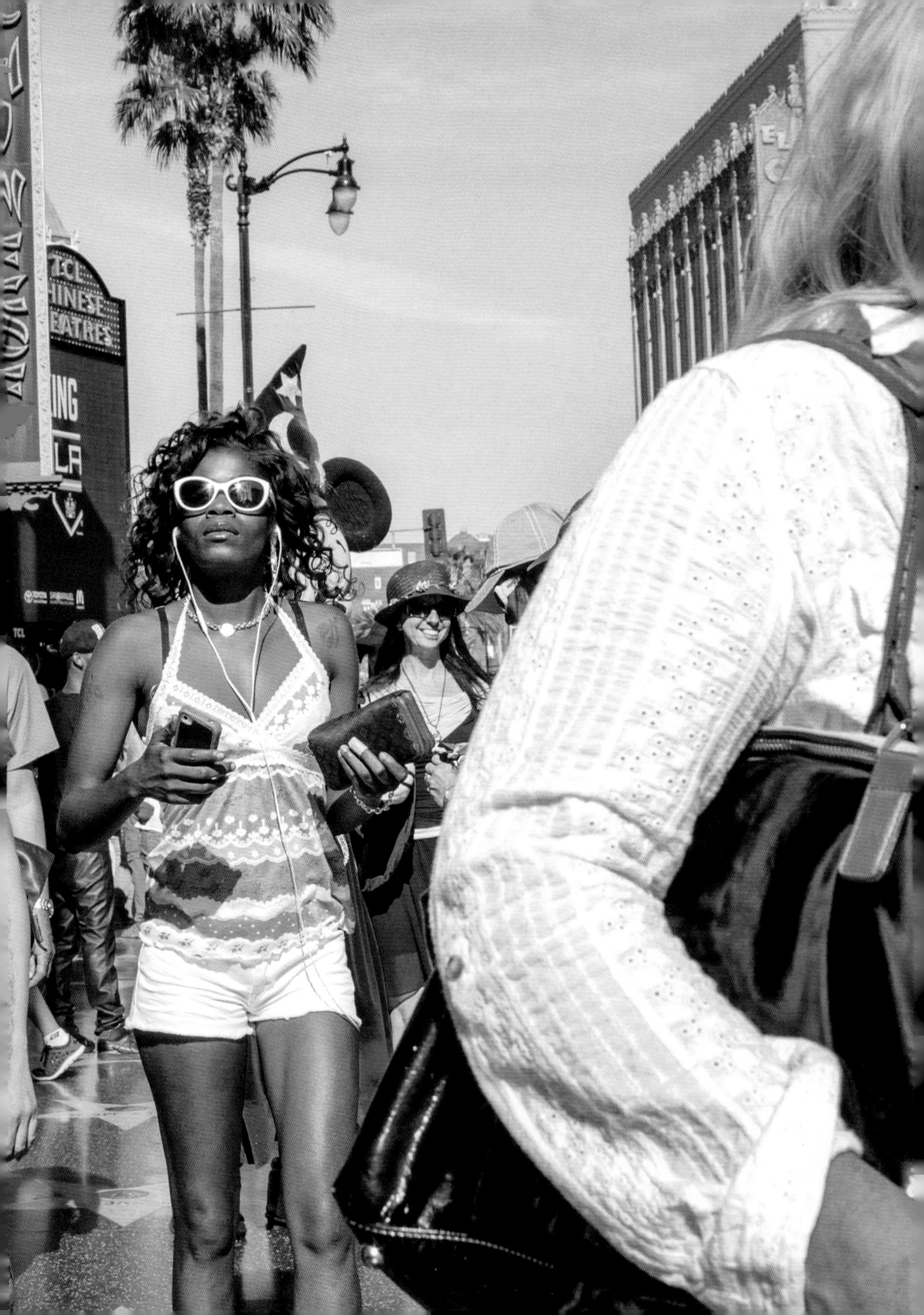

TCL
CHINESE
THEATRES
ING
LA
EL
C

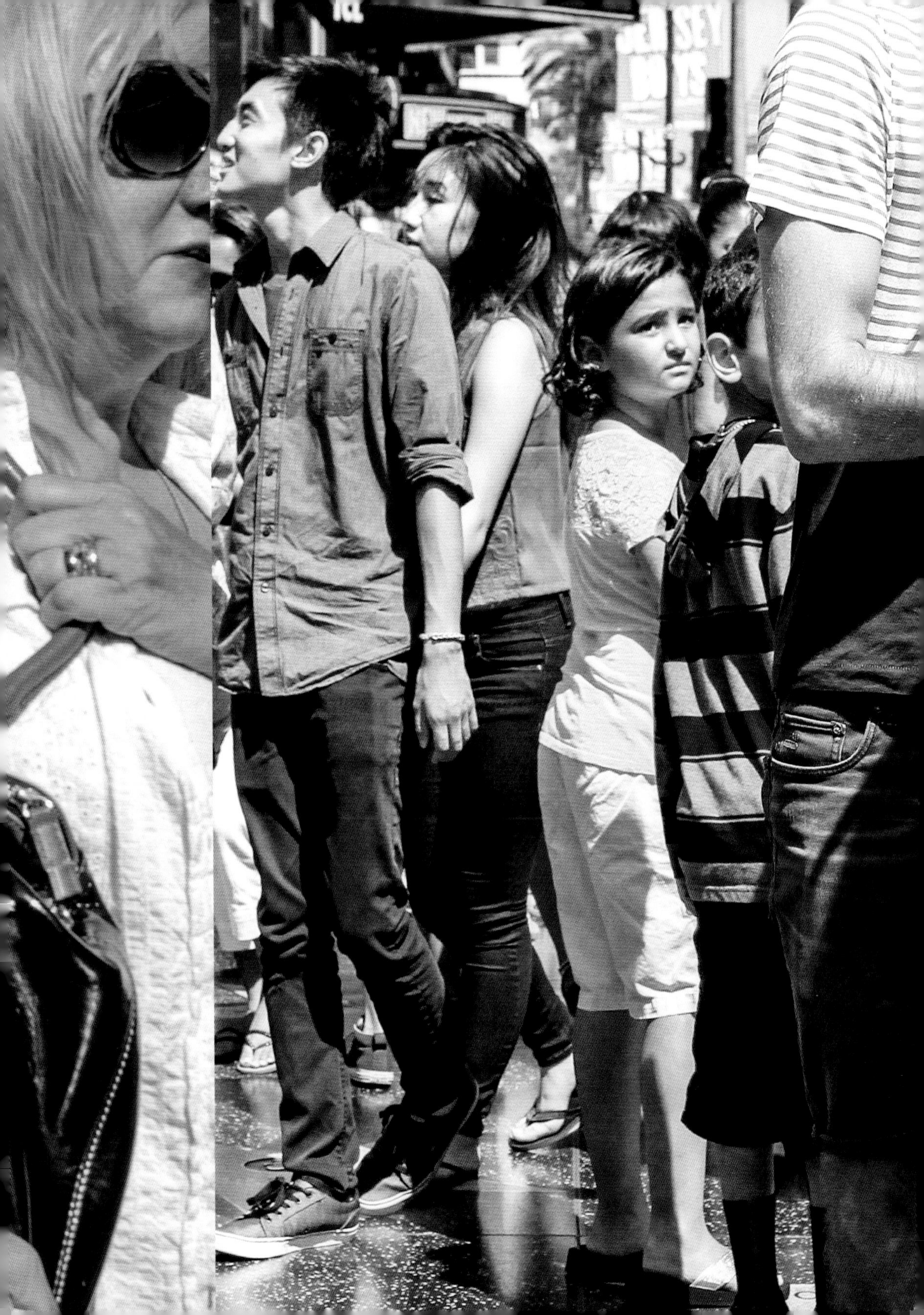

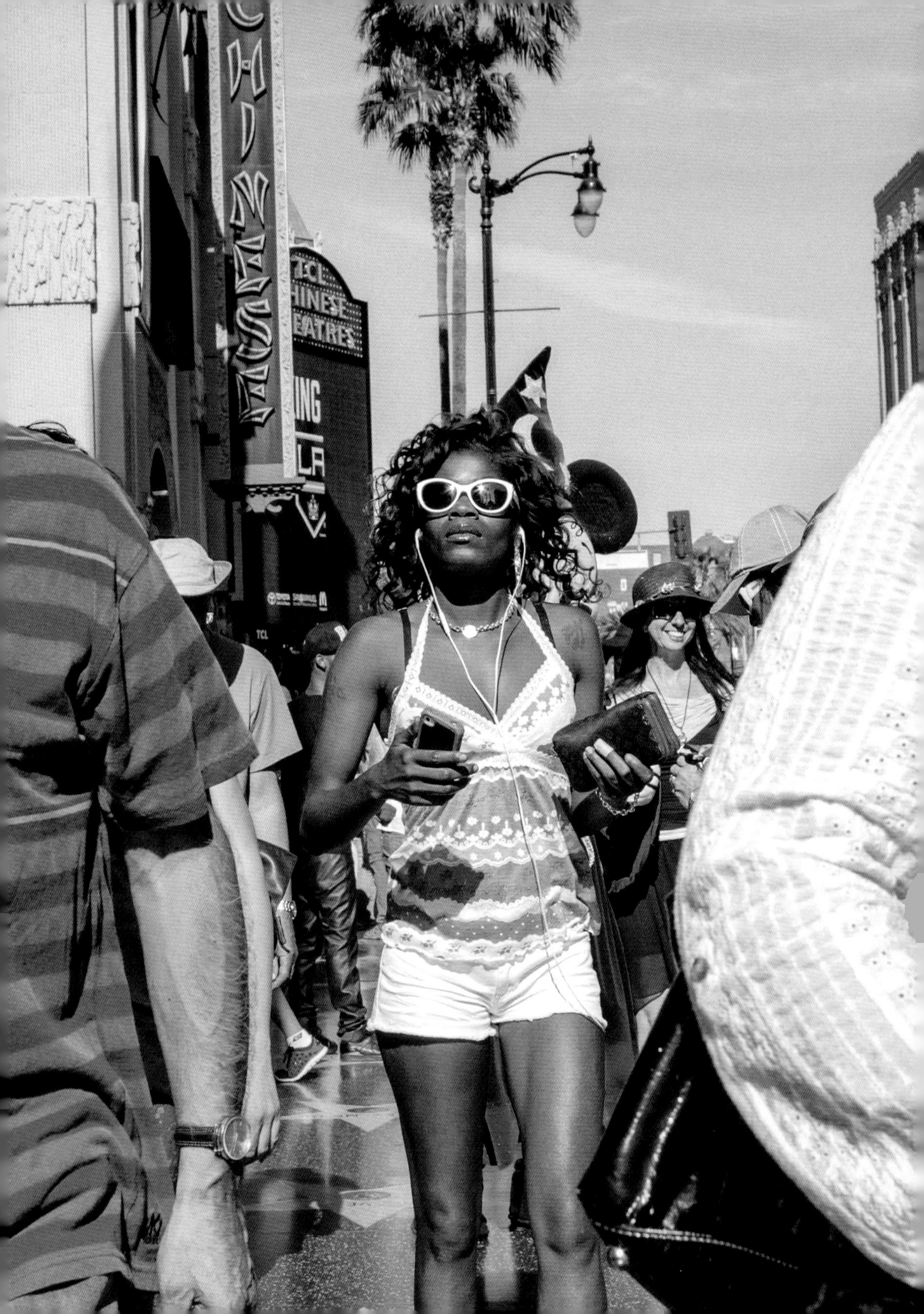

TCL
CHINESE
THEATRES

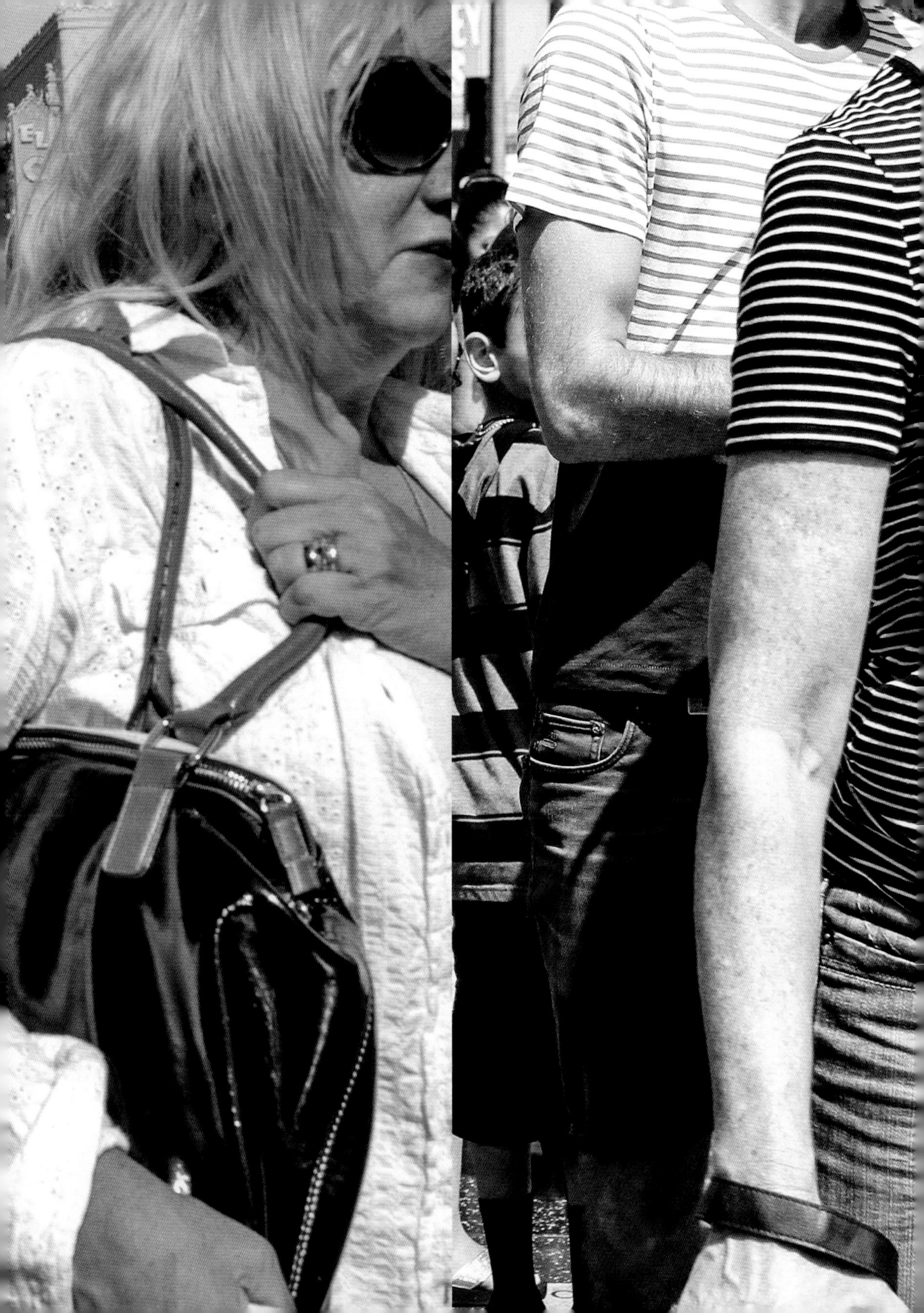

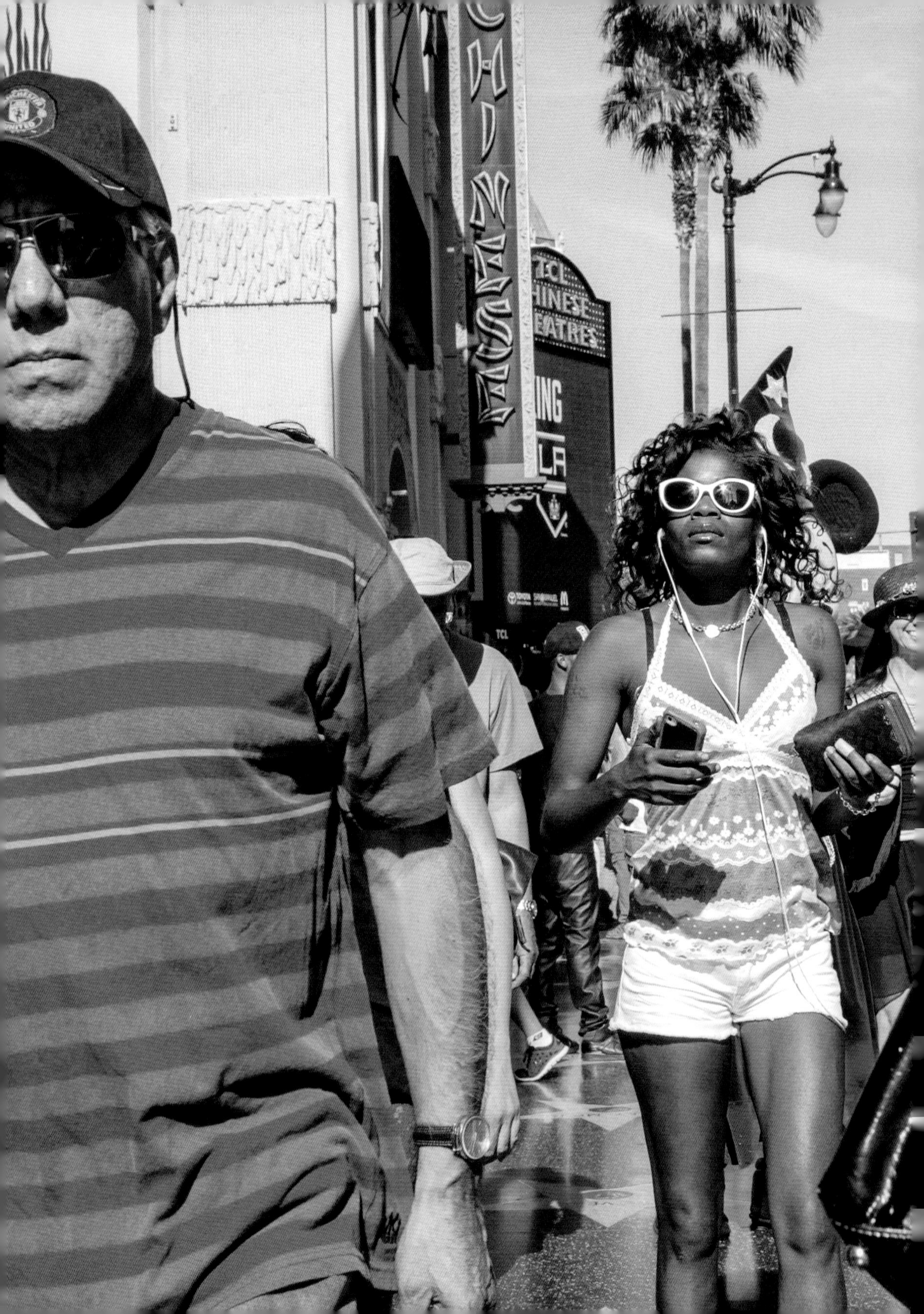

TCL
CHINESE
THEATRES
ING
LA

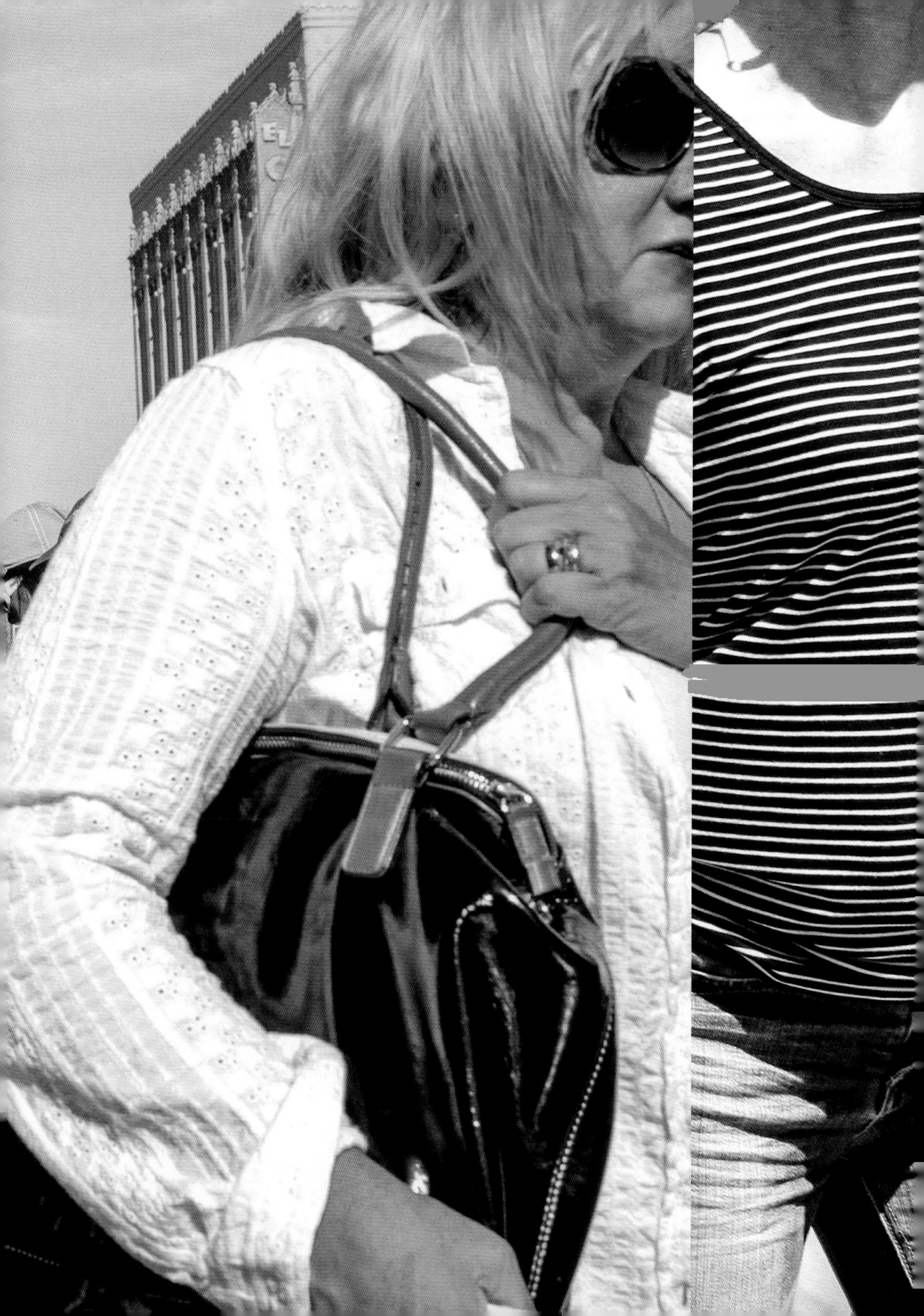

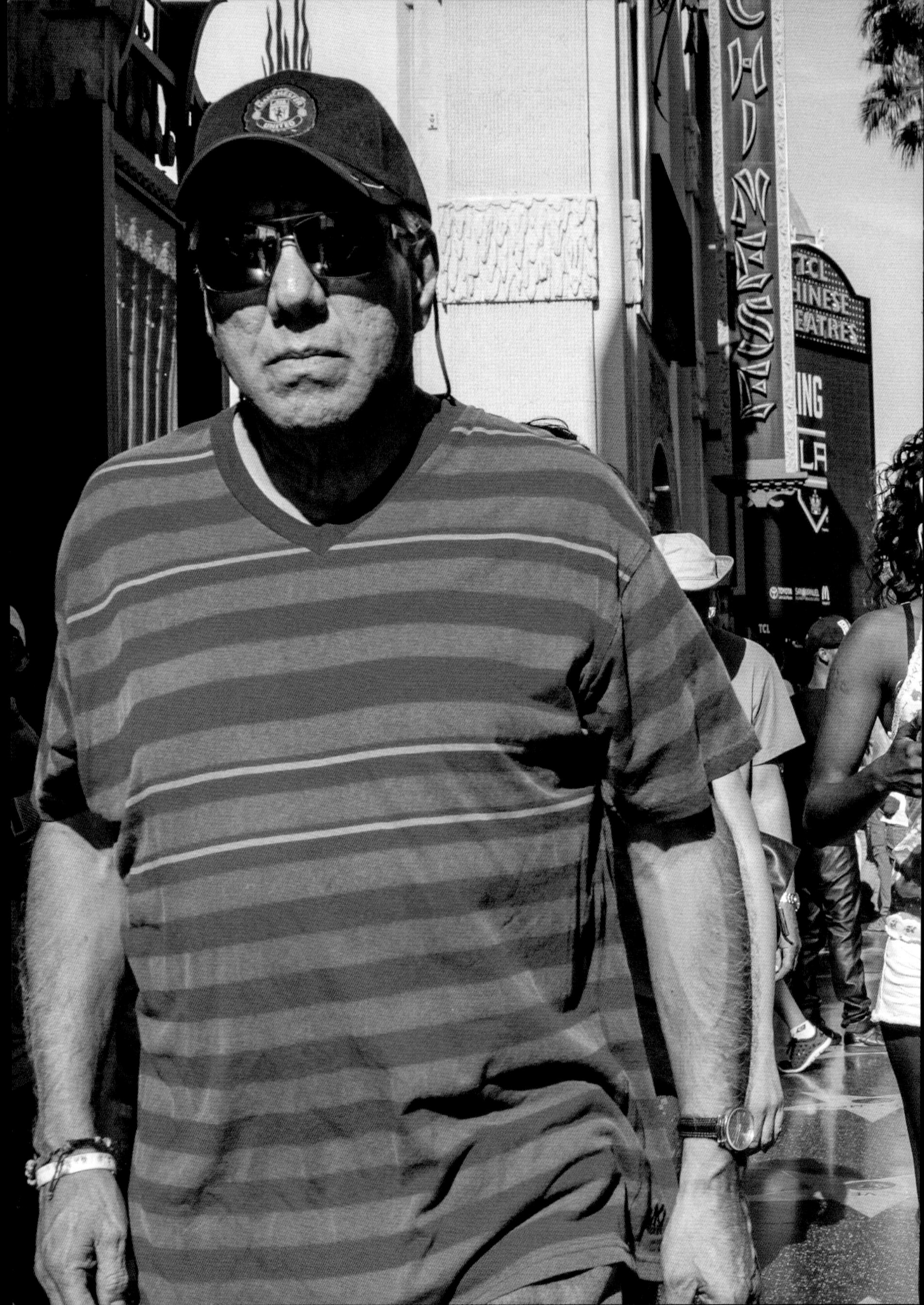

CHINA
TCL
CHINESE
THEATRES
ING
LA

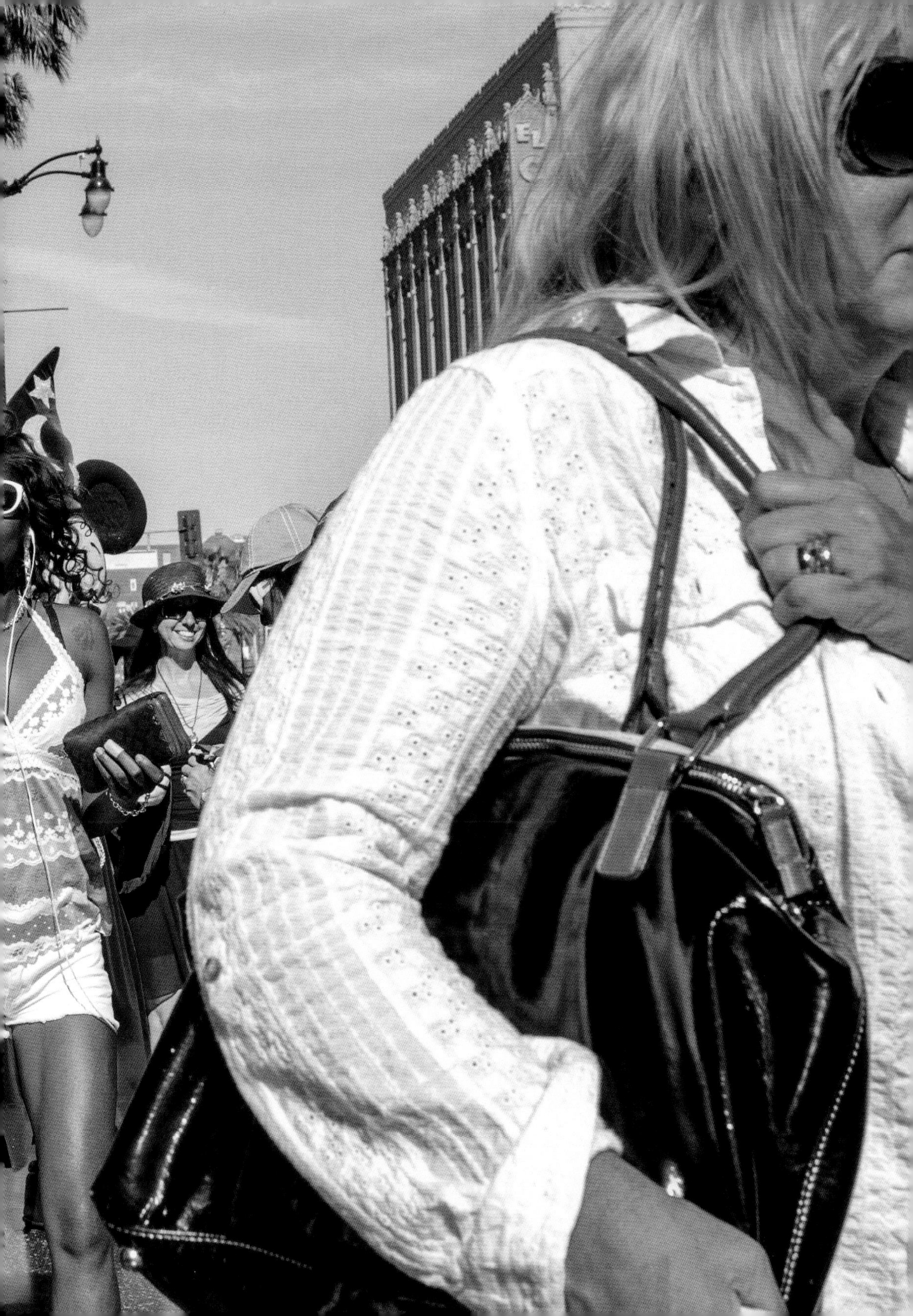

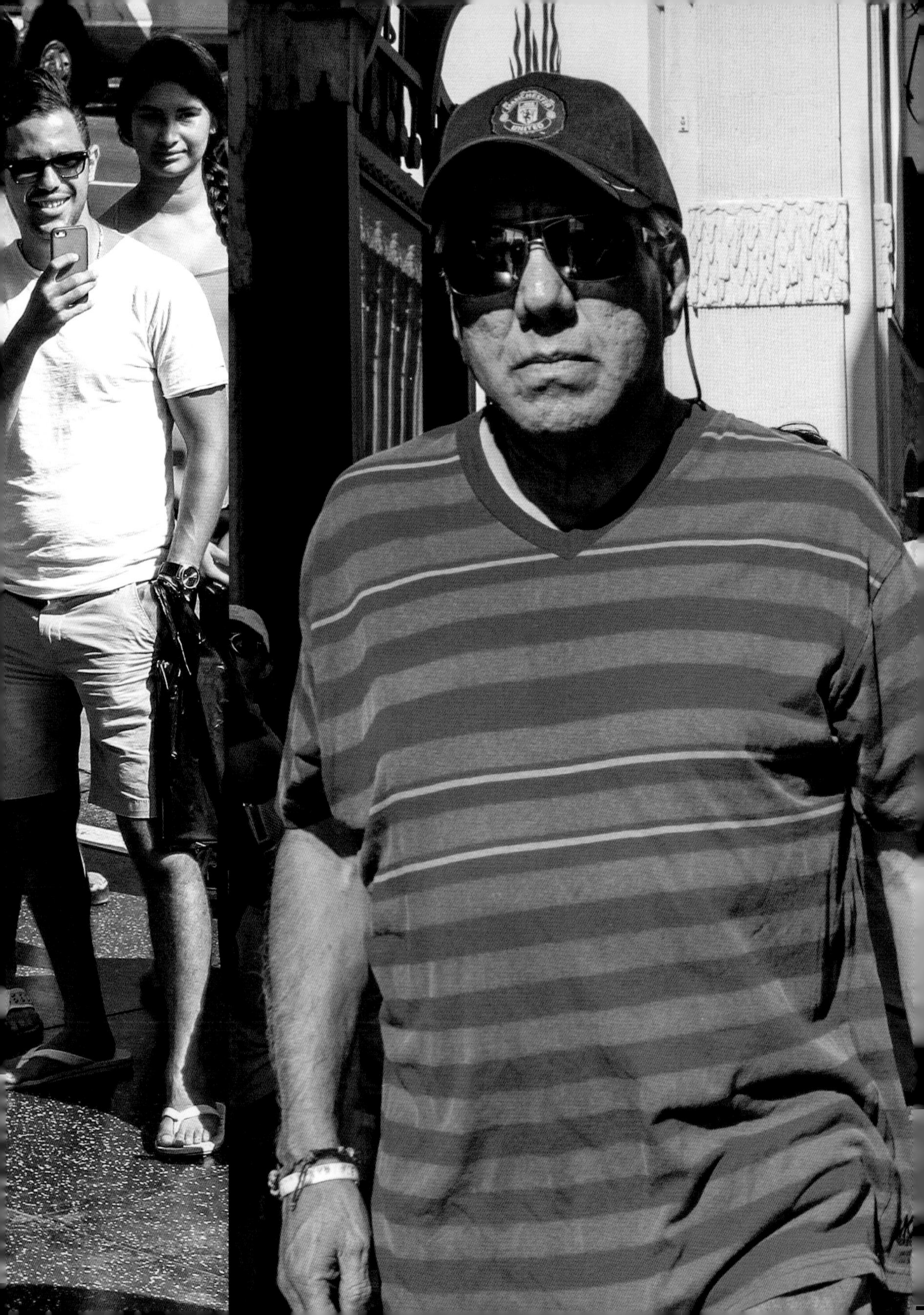

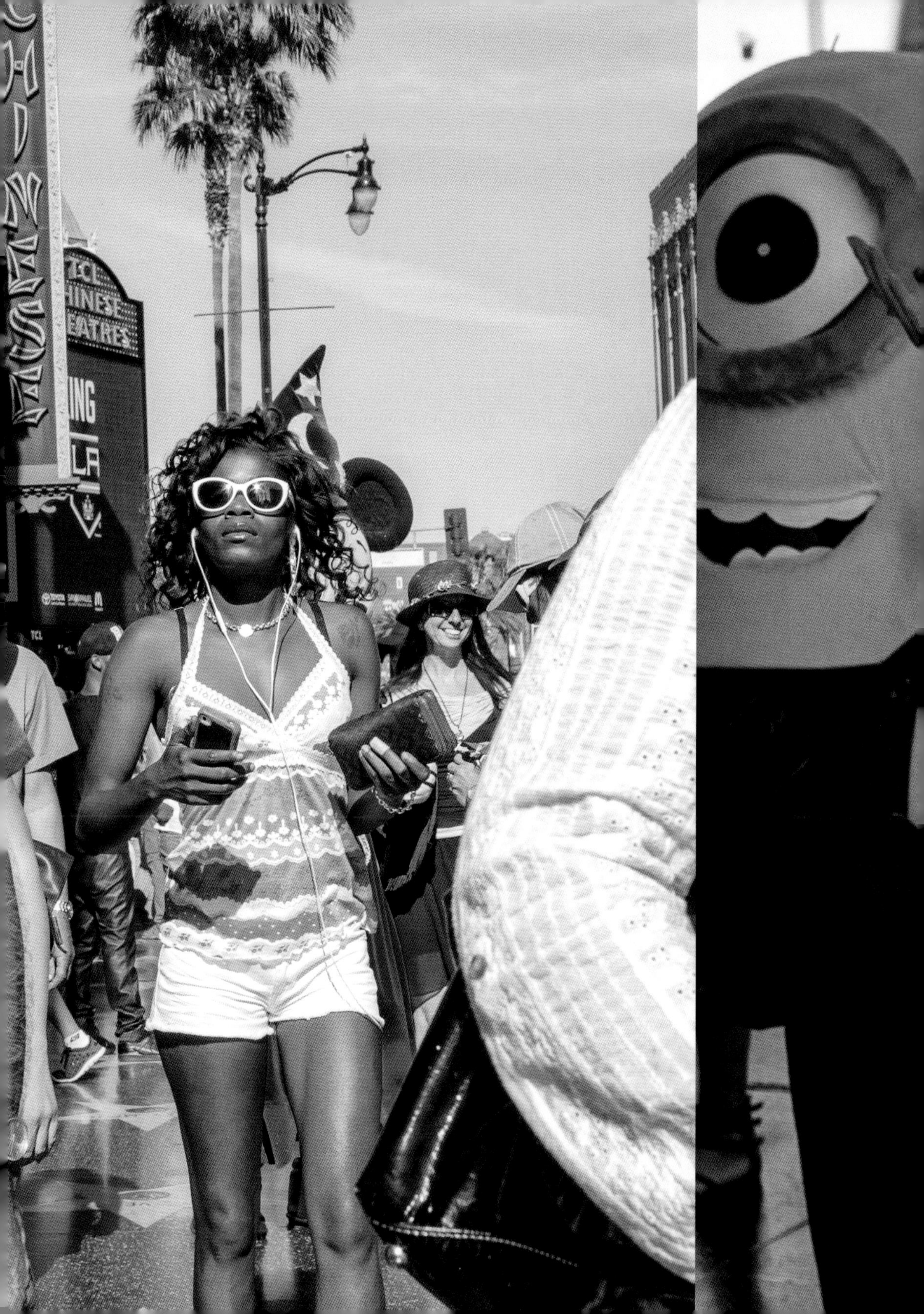

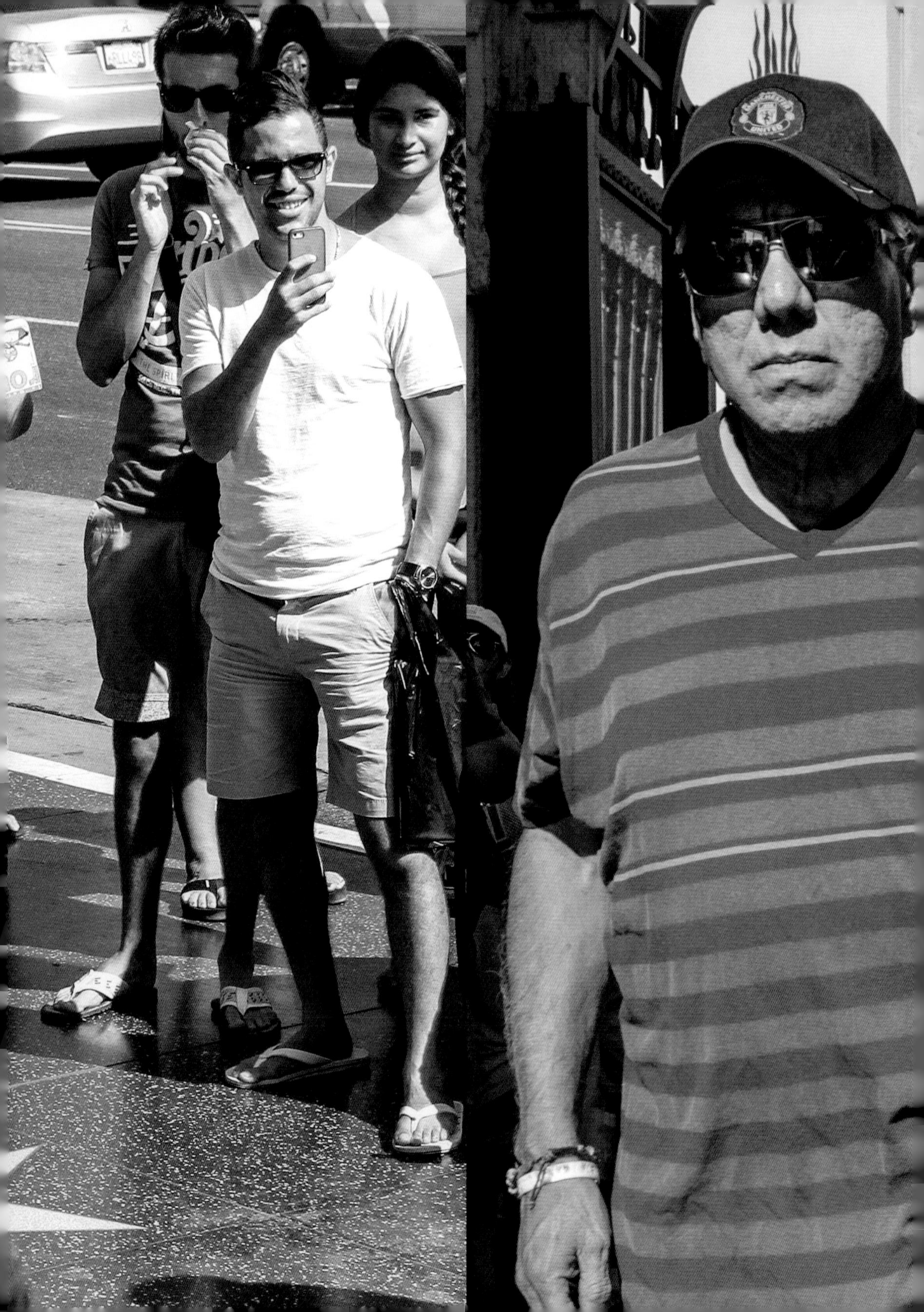

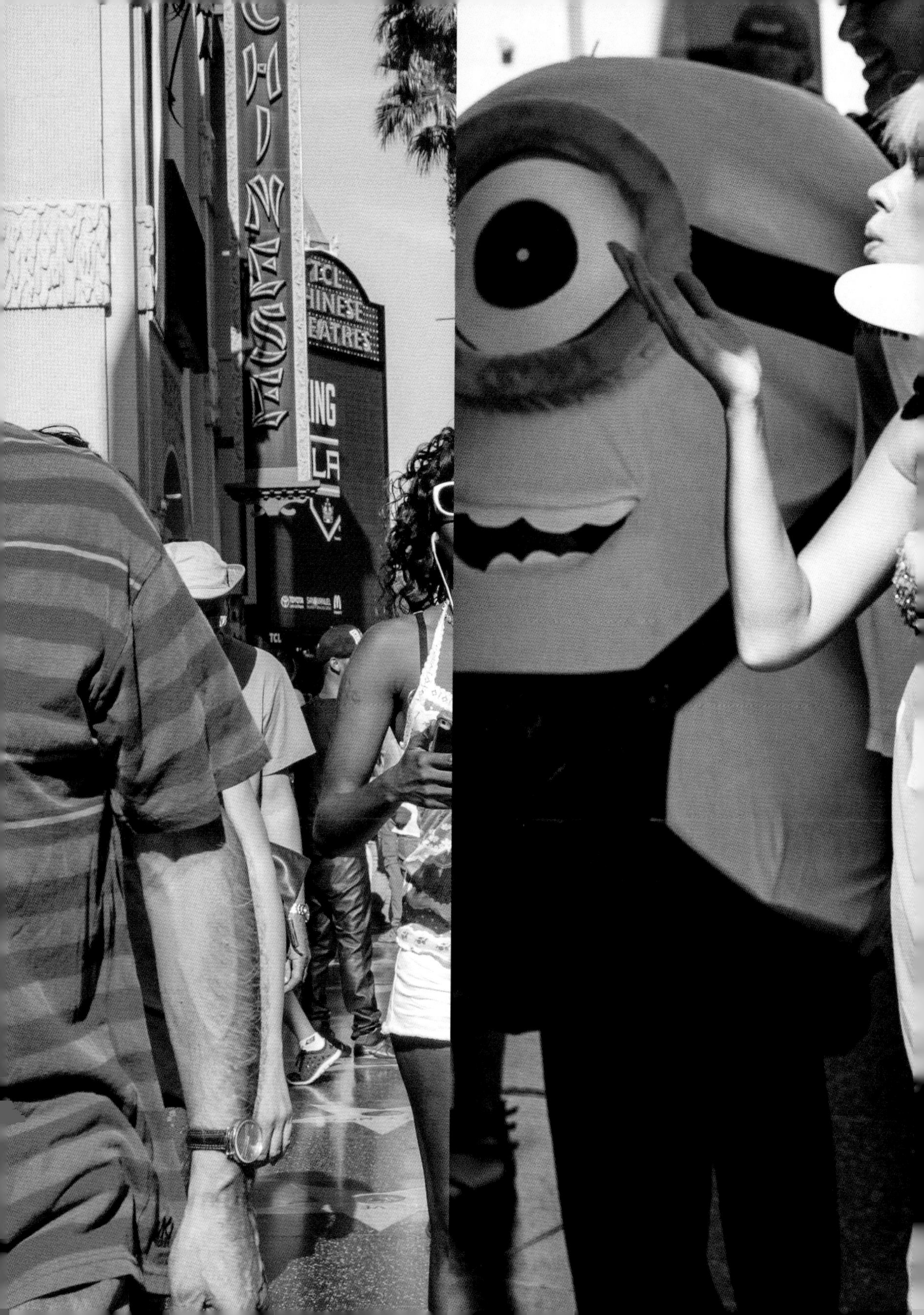

CHINESE
TCL
CHINESE
THEATRES
TCL

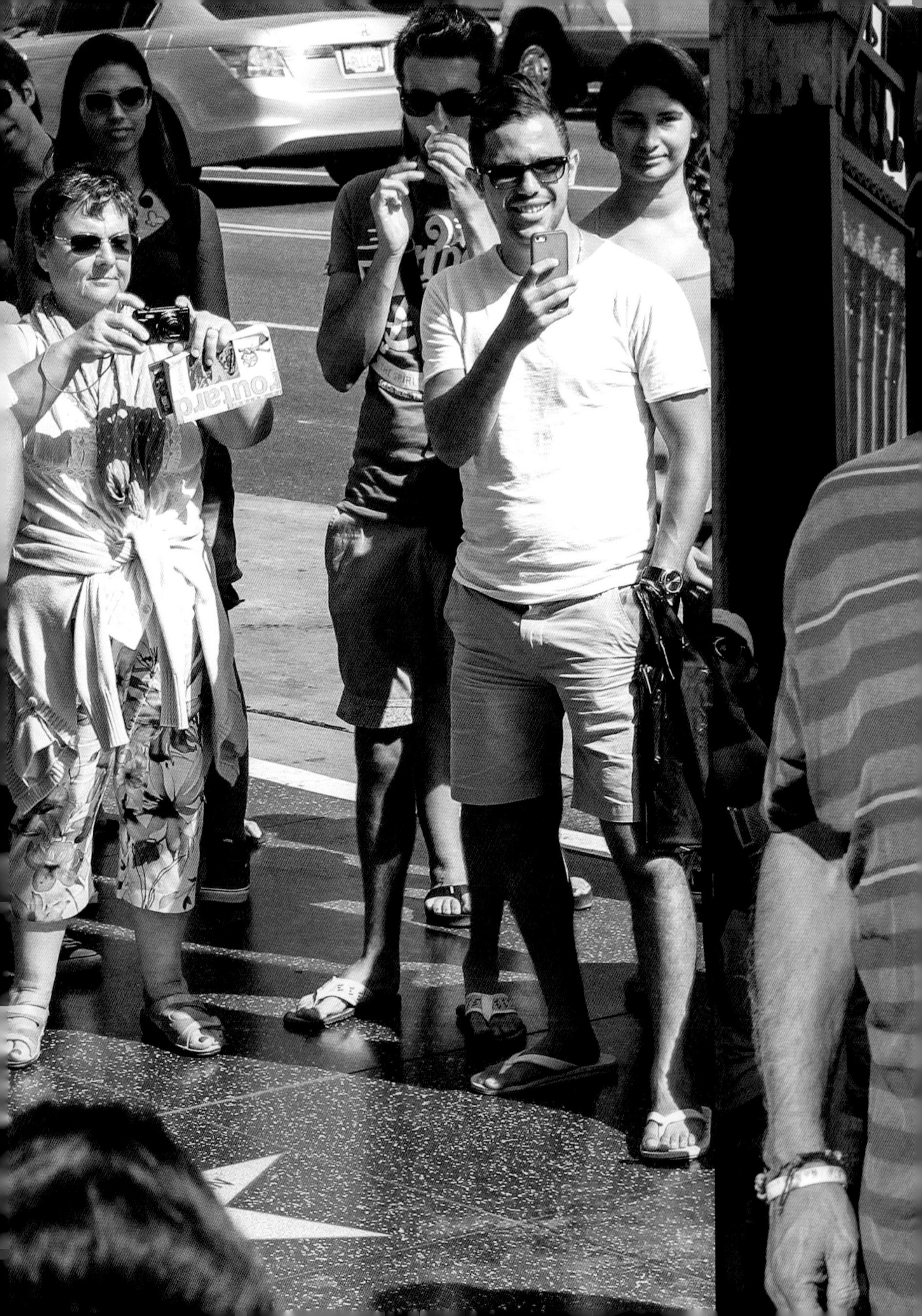

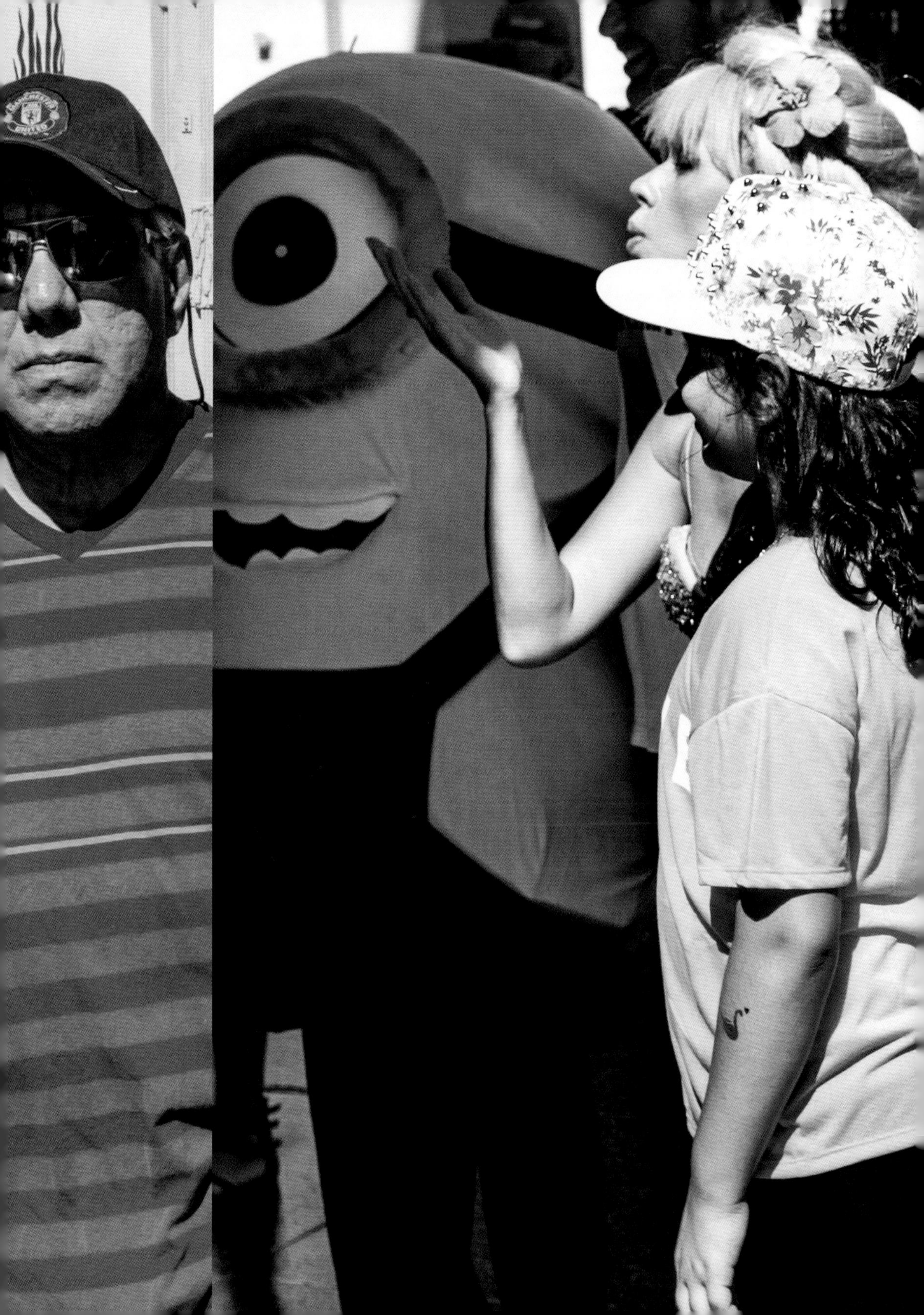

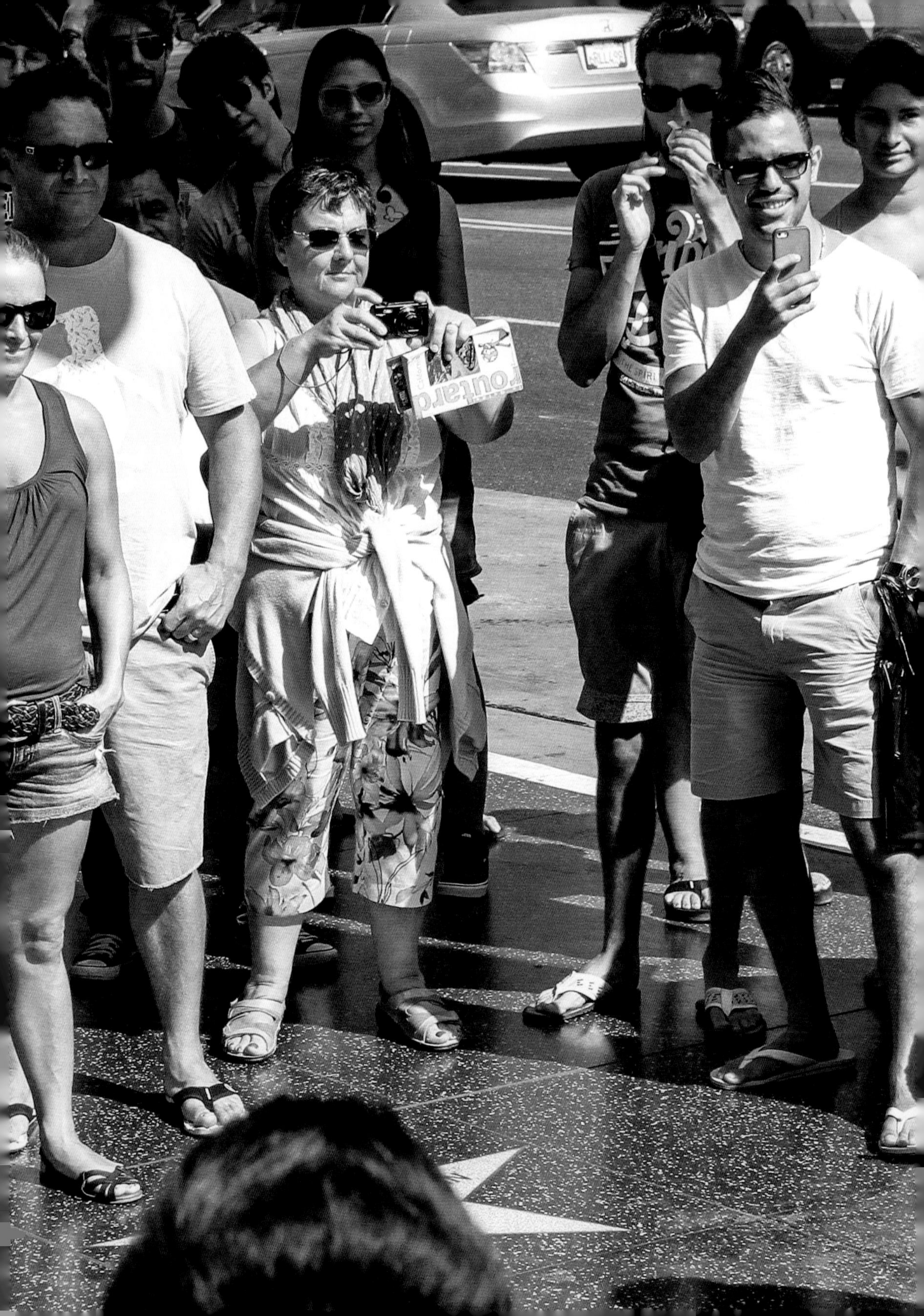

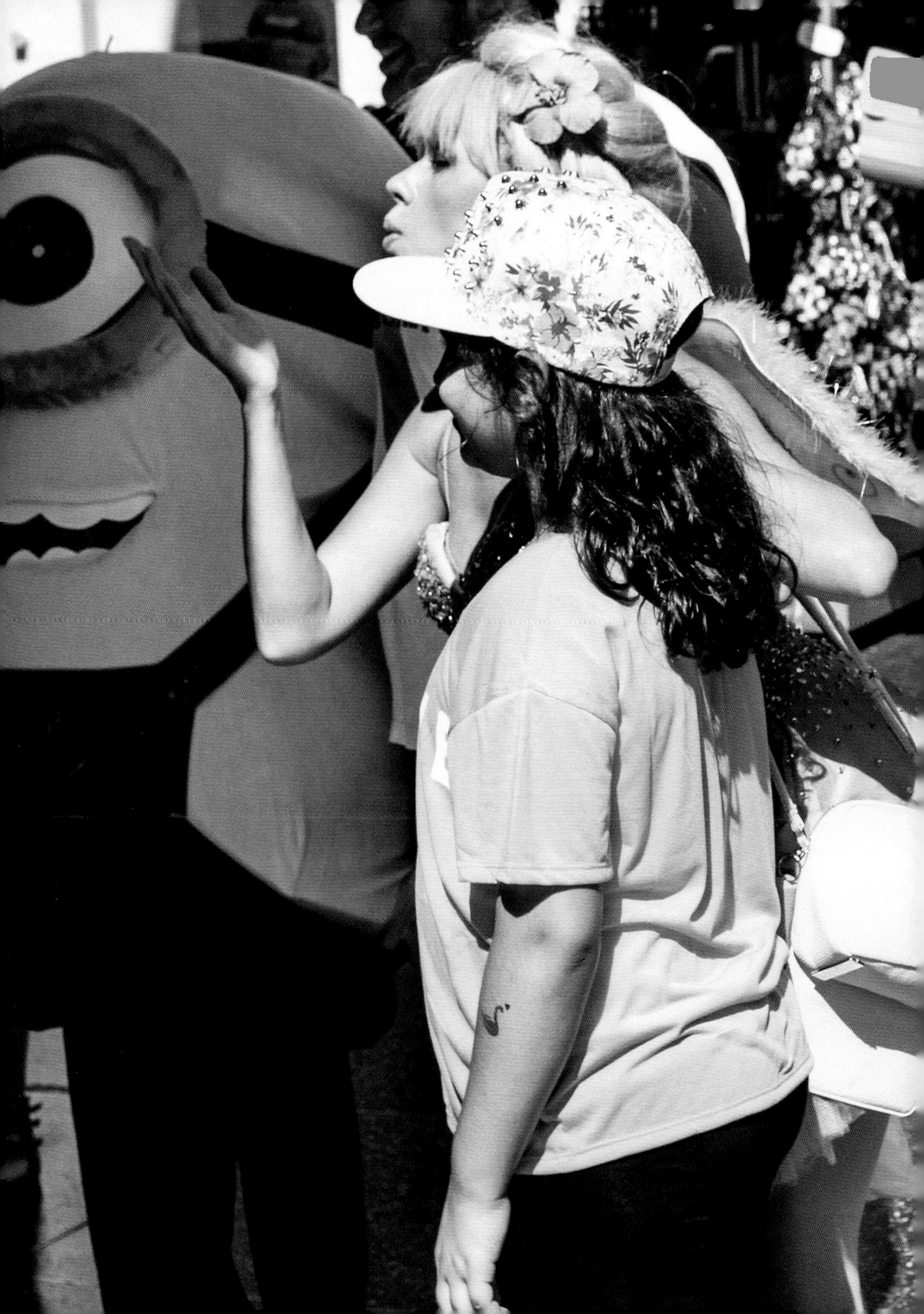

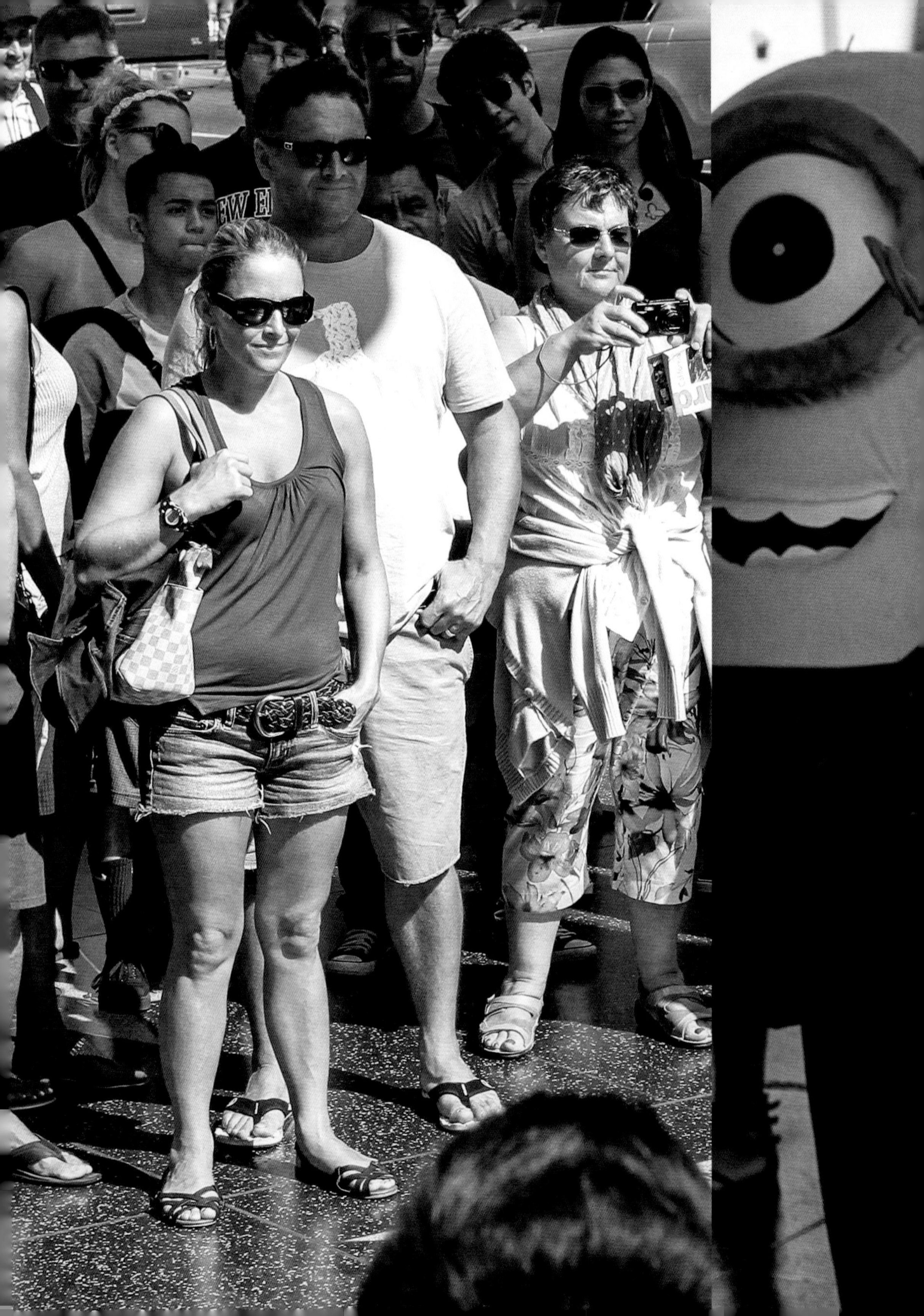

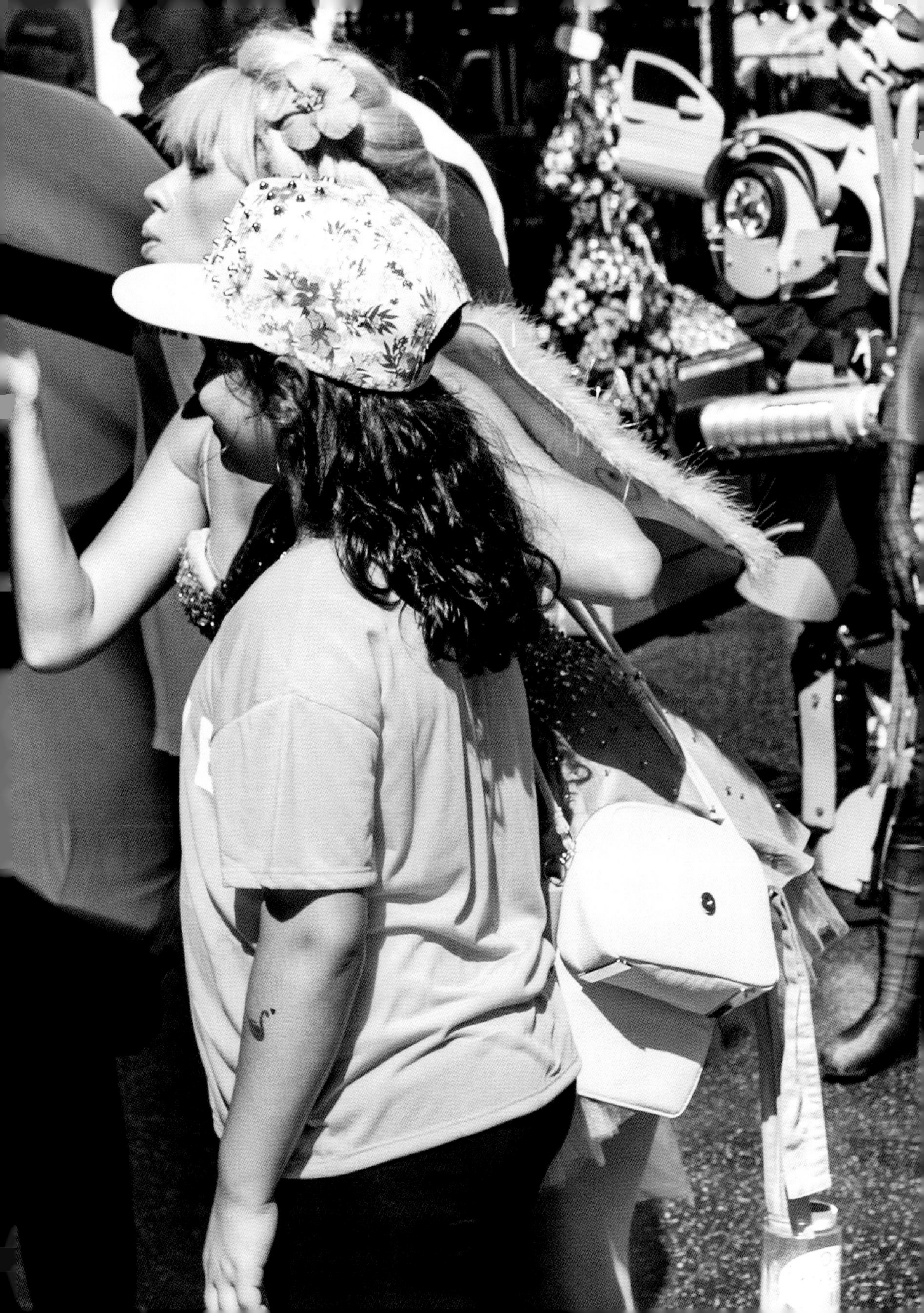

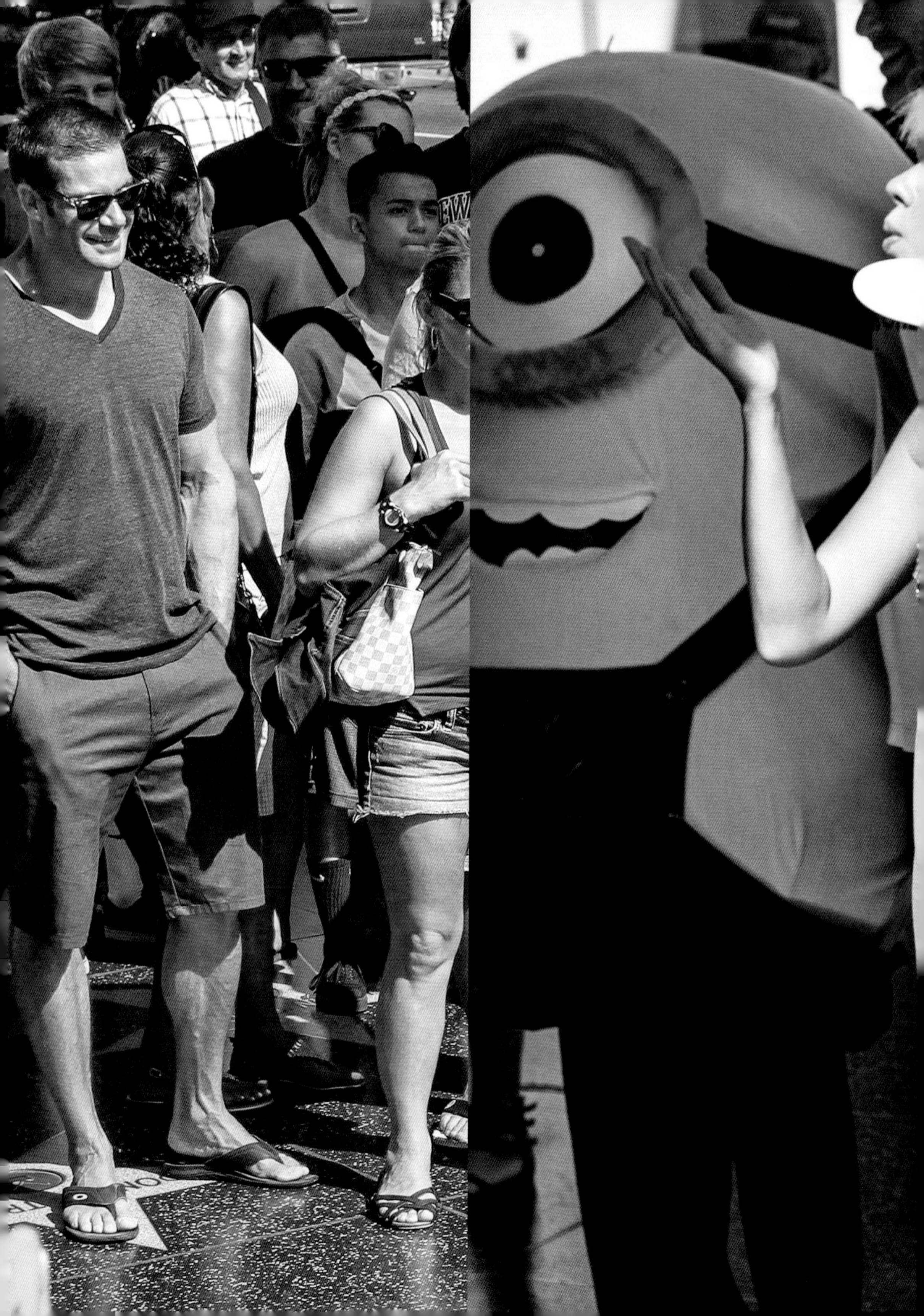

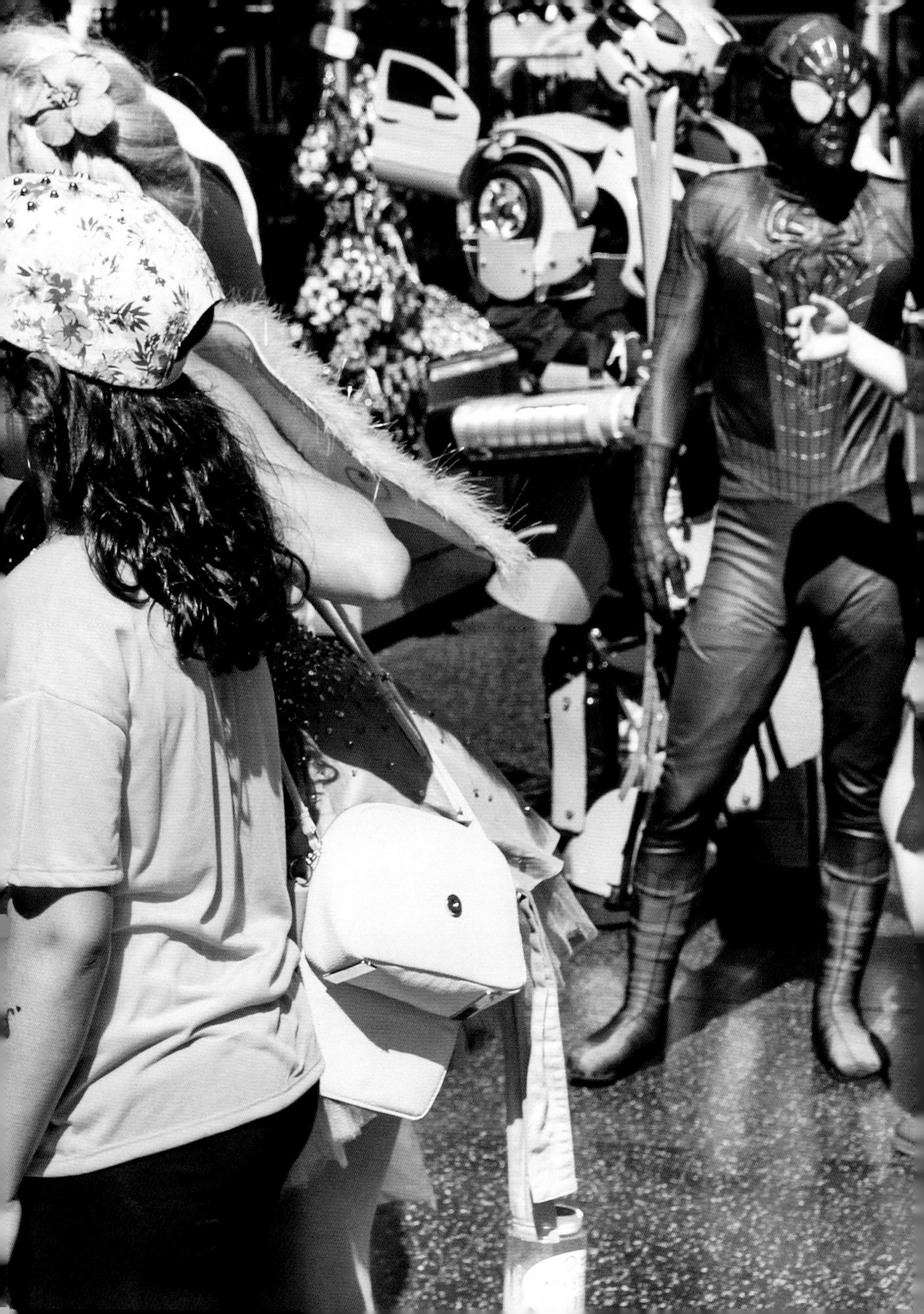

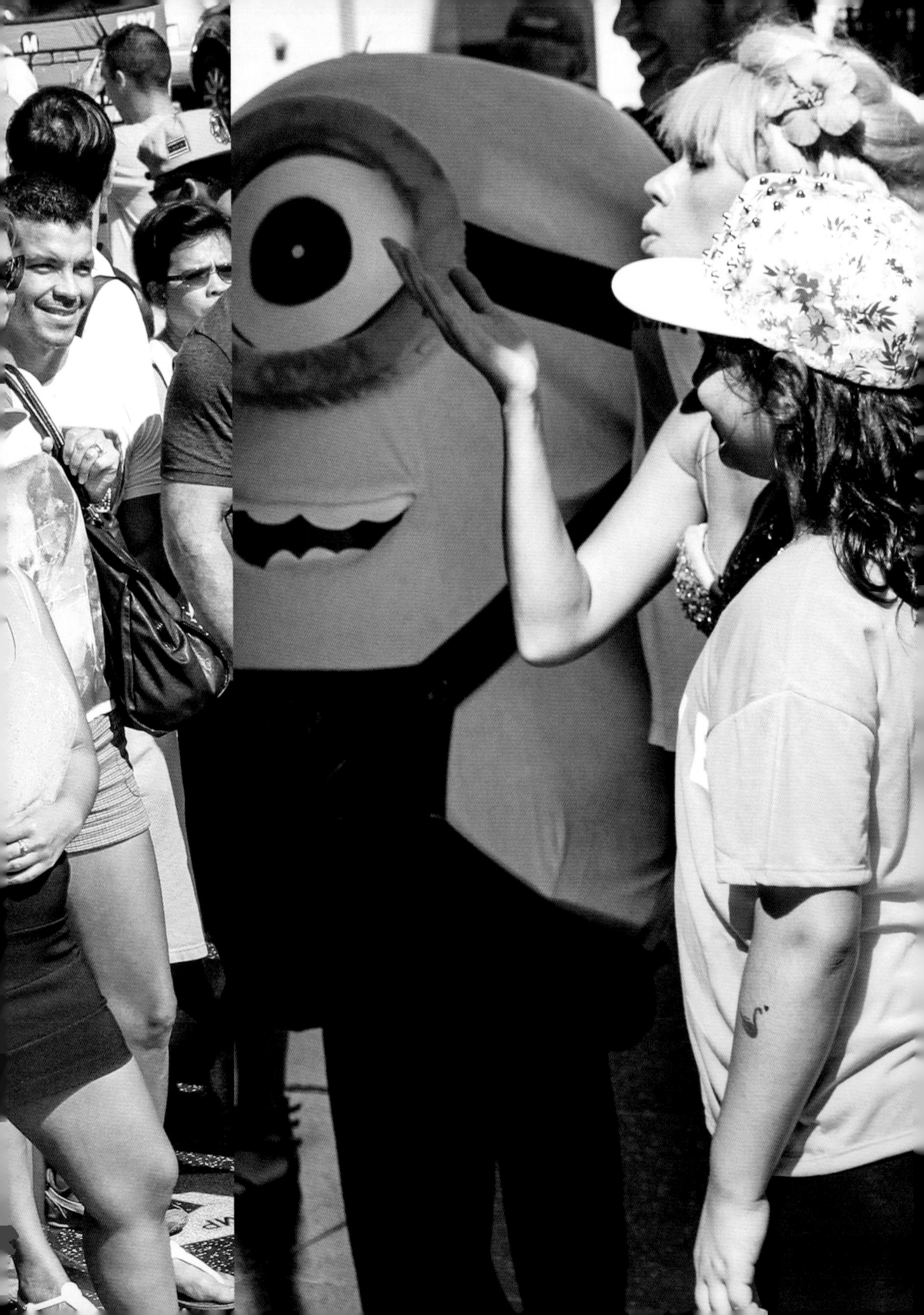

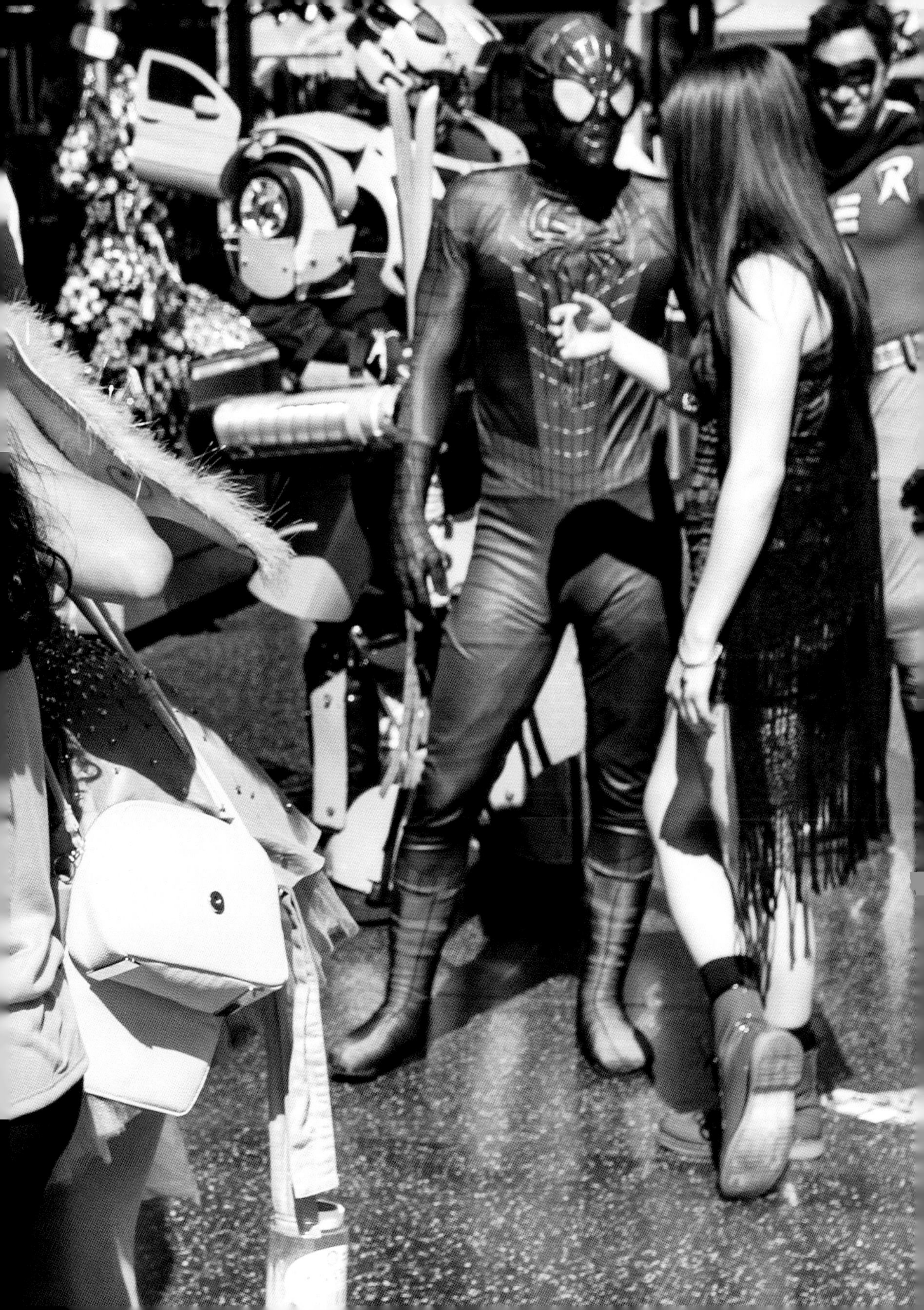

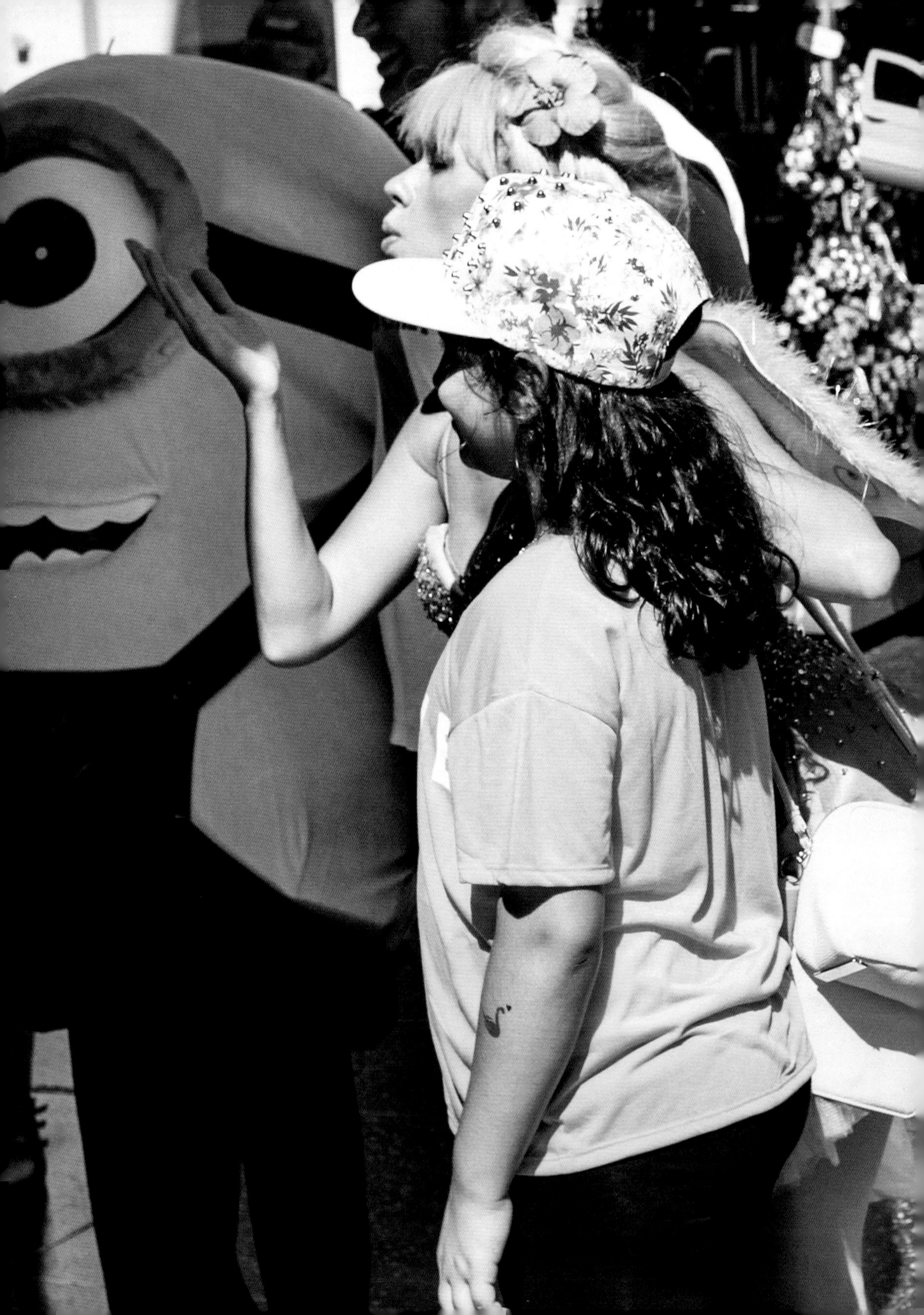

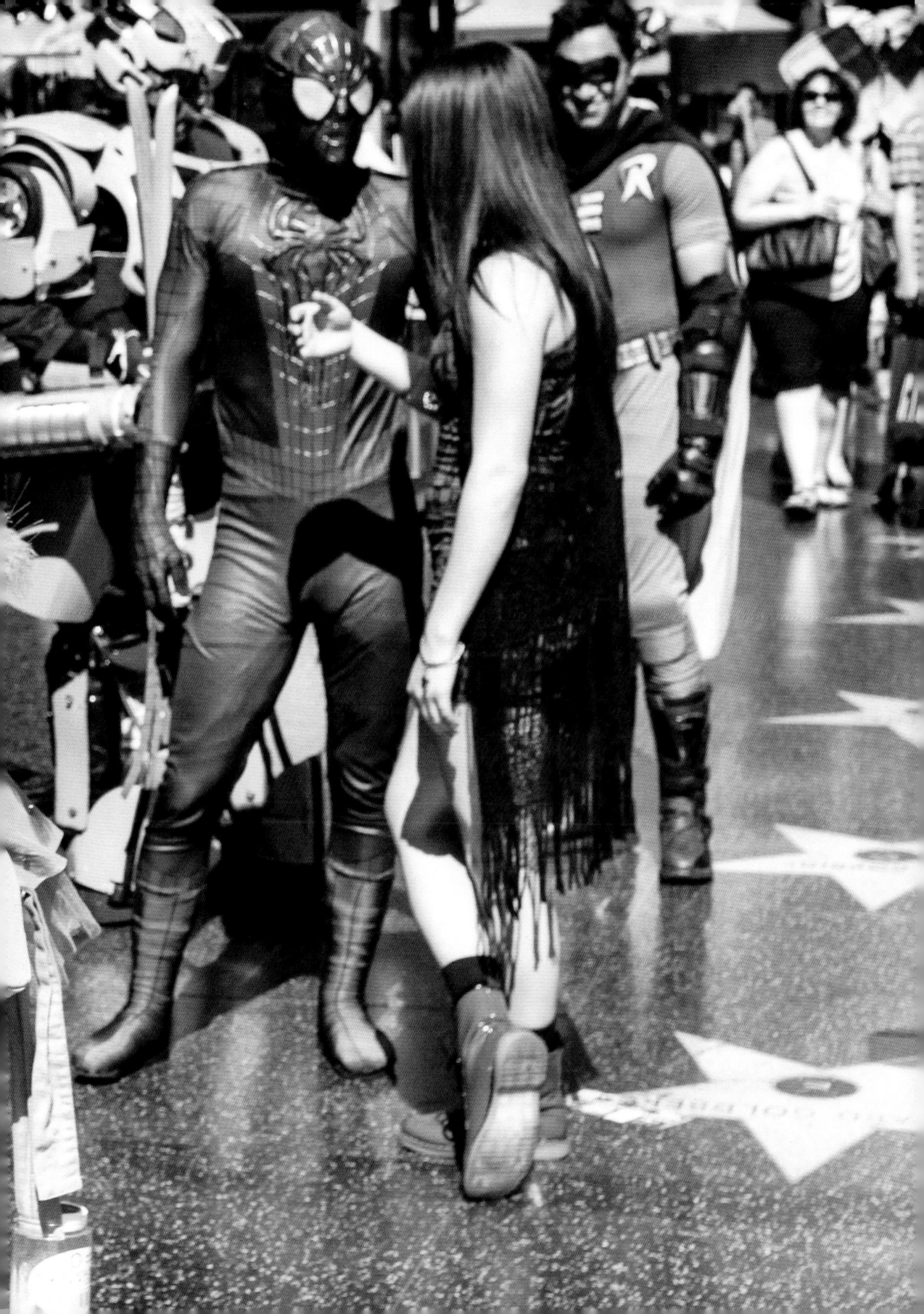

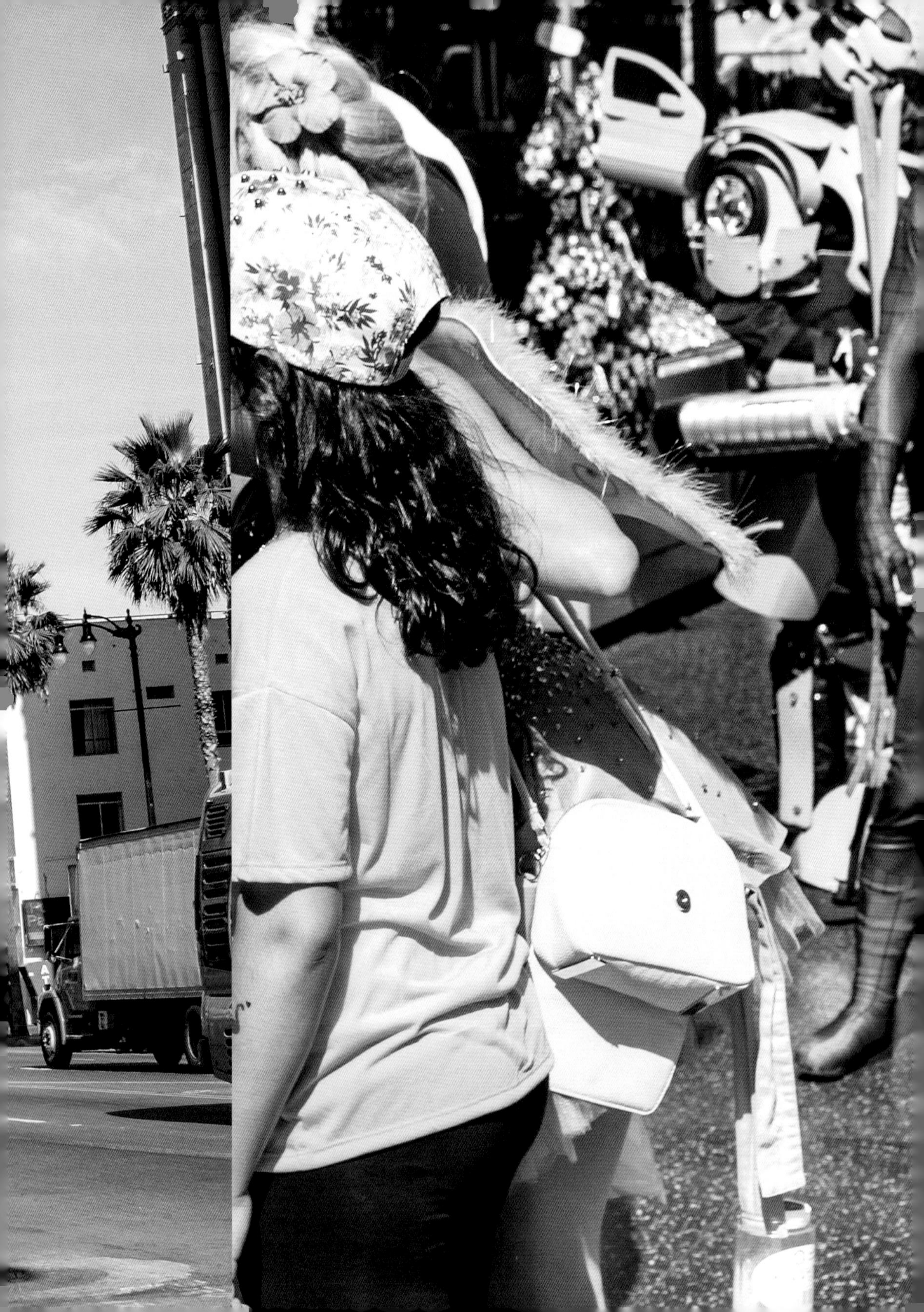

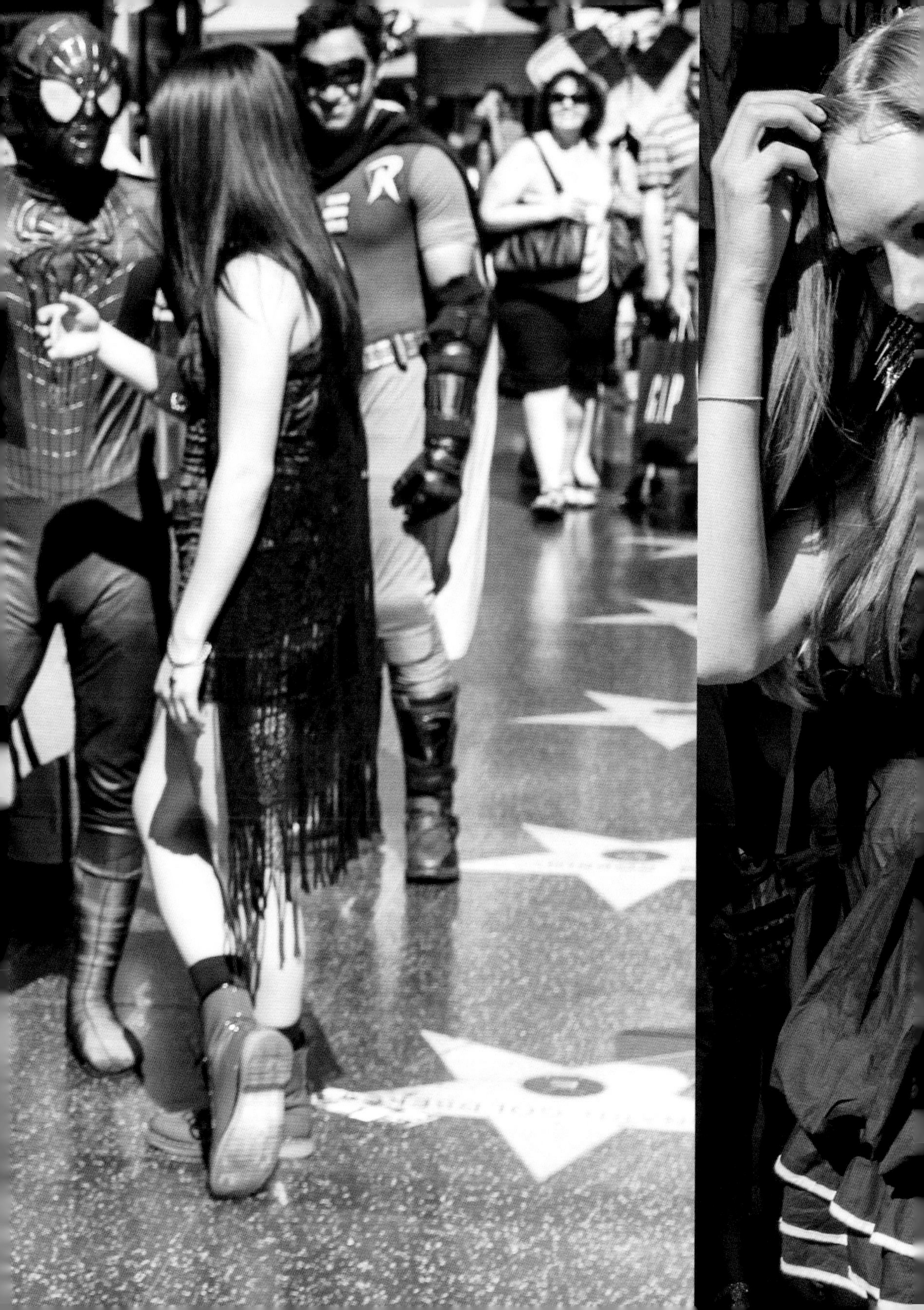

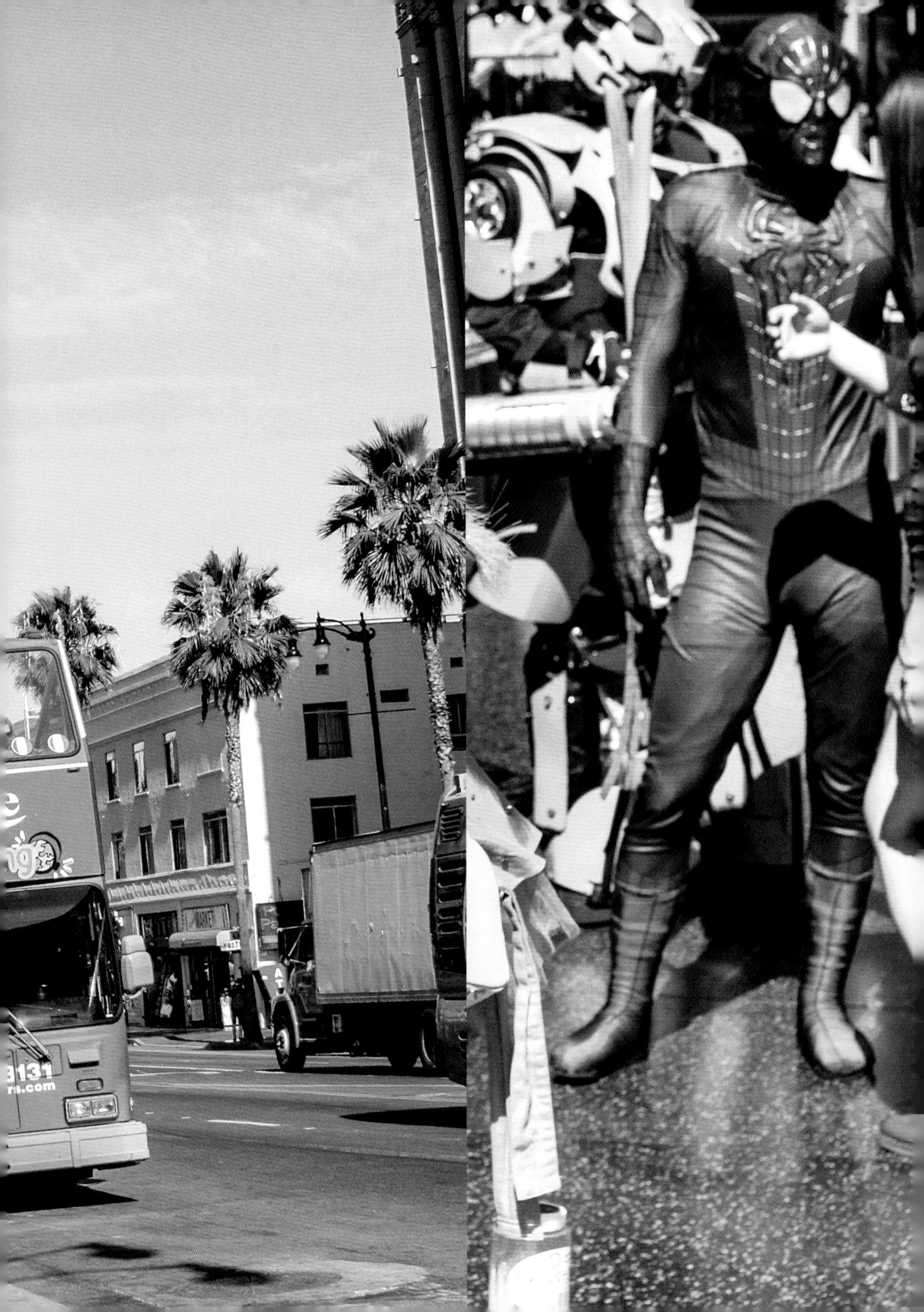

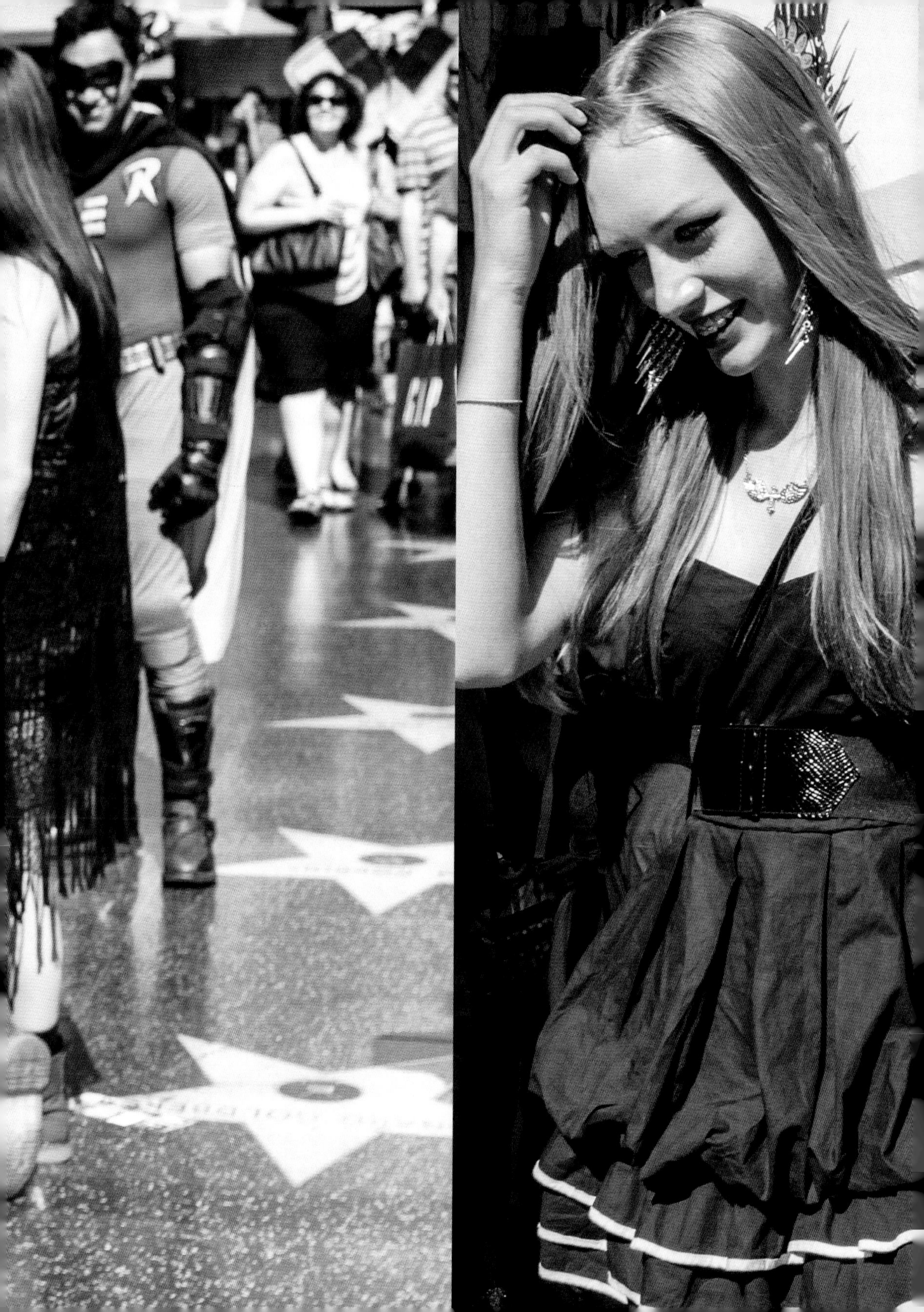

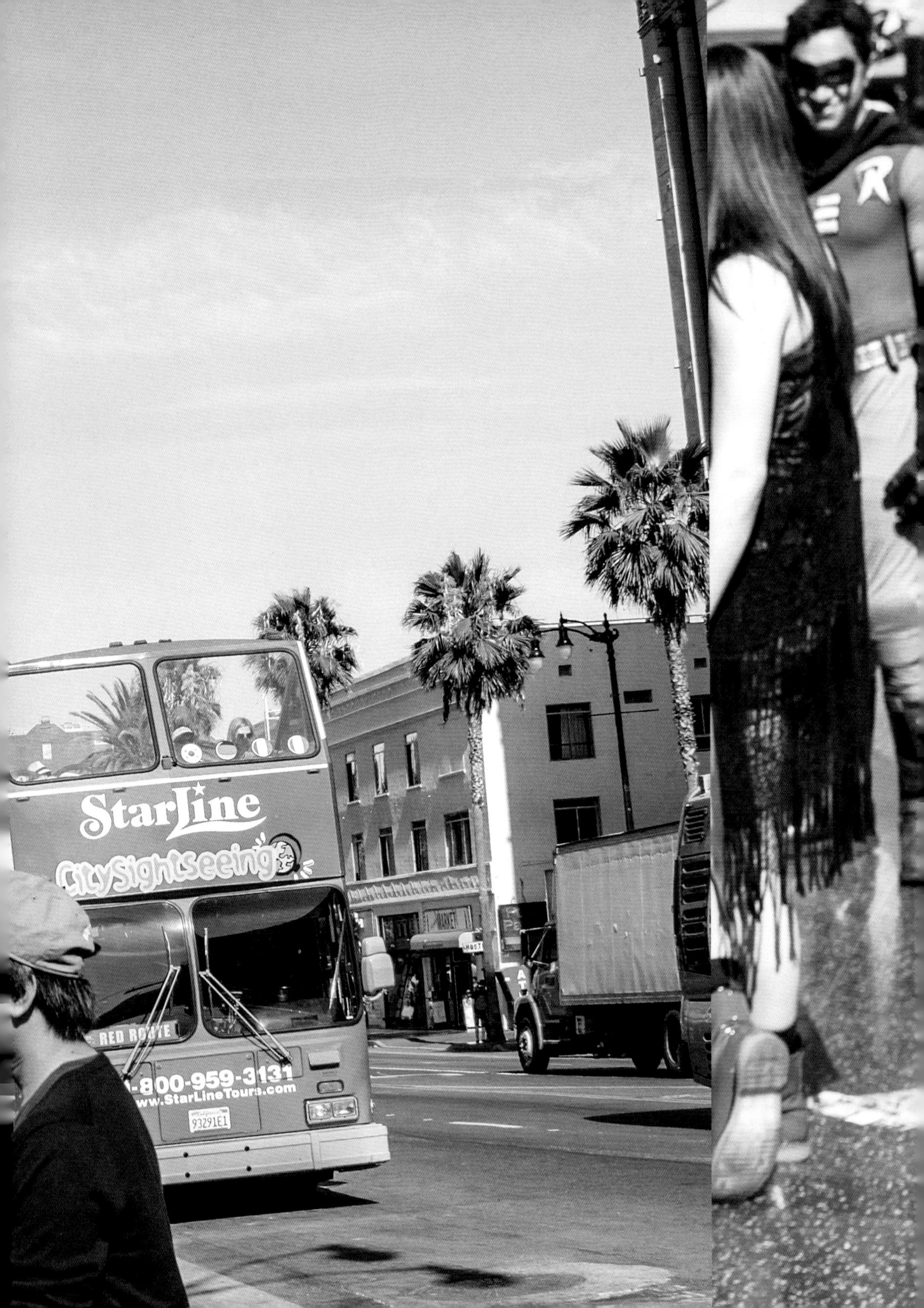
StarLine
CitySightseeing
RED ROUTE
1-800-959-3131
www.StarLineTours.com
93291E1

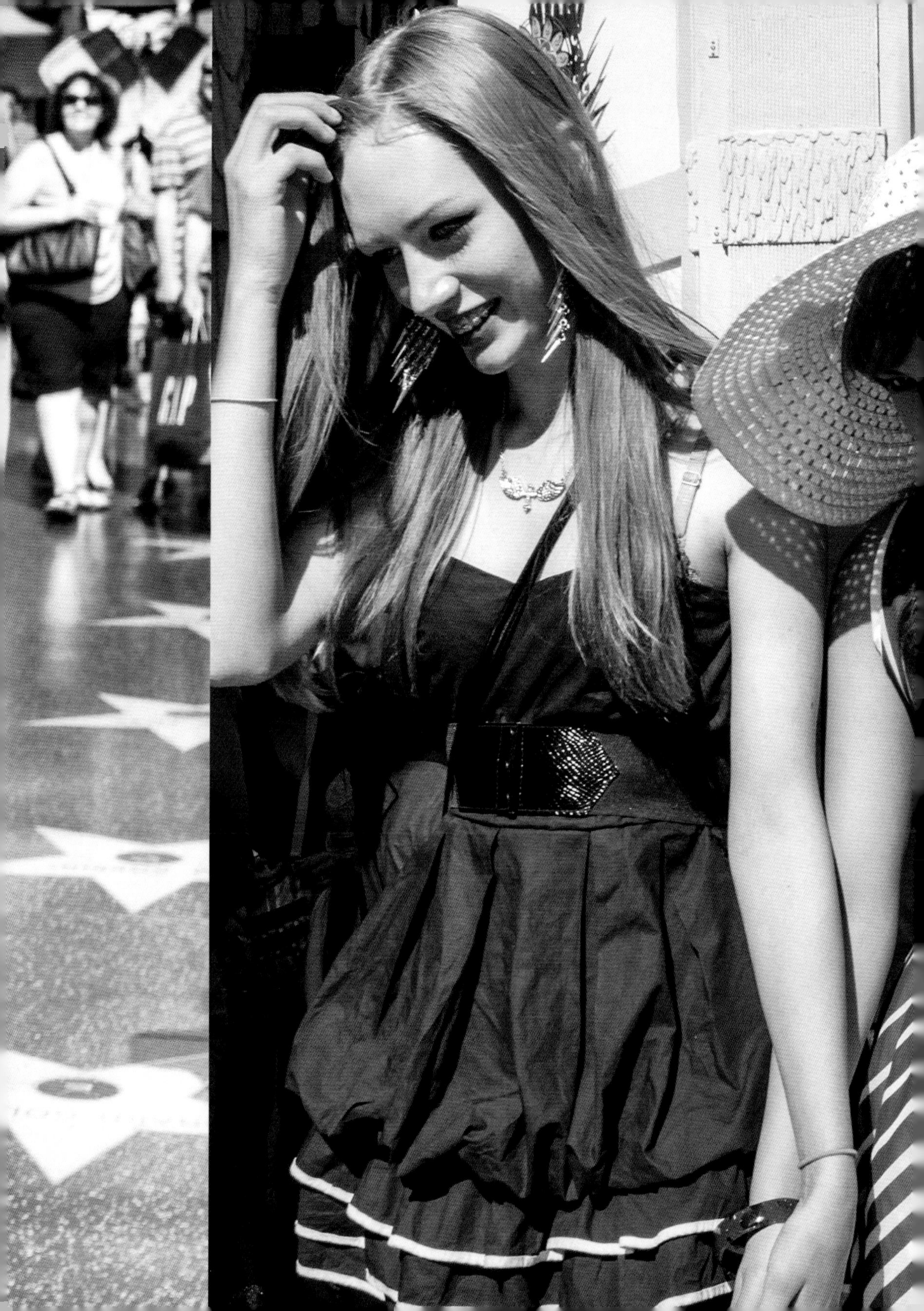

StarLine
City Sightseeing
RED ROUTE
1-800-959-3131
www.StarLineTours.com
93291E1

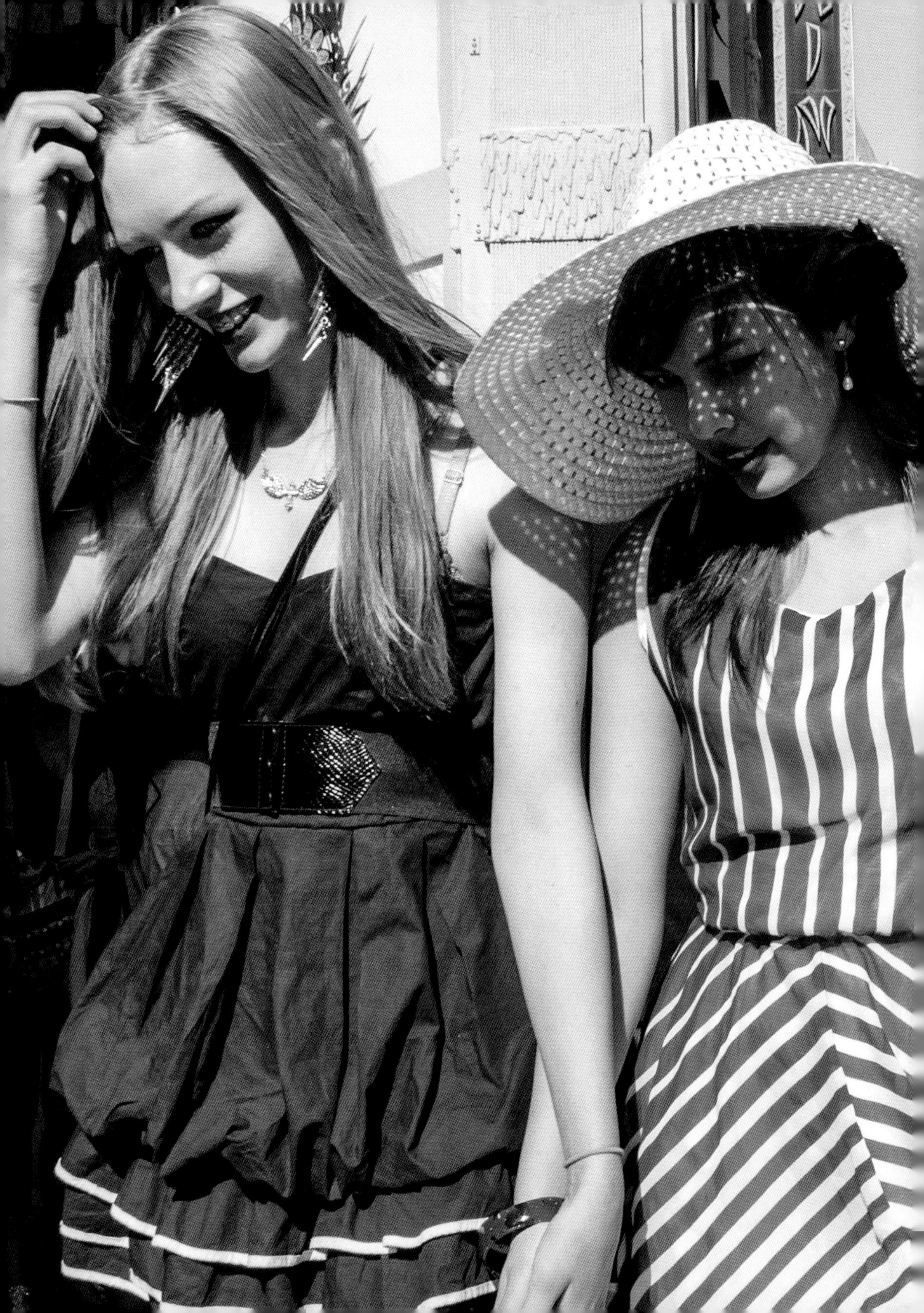

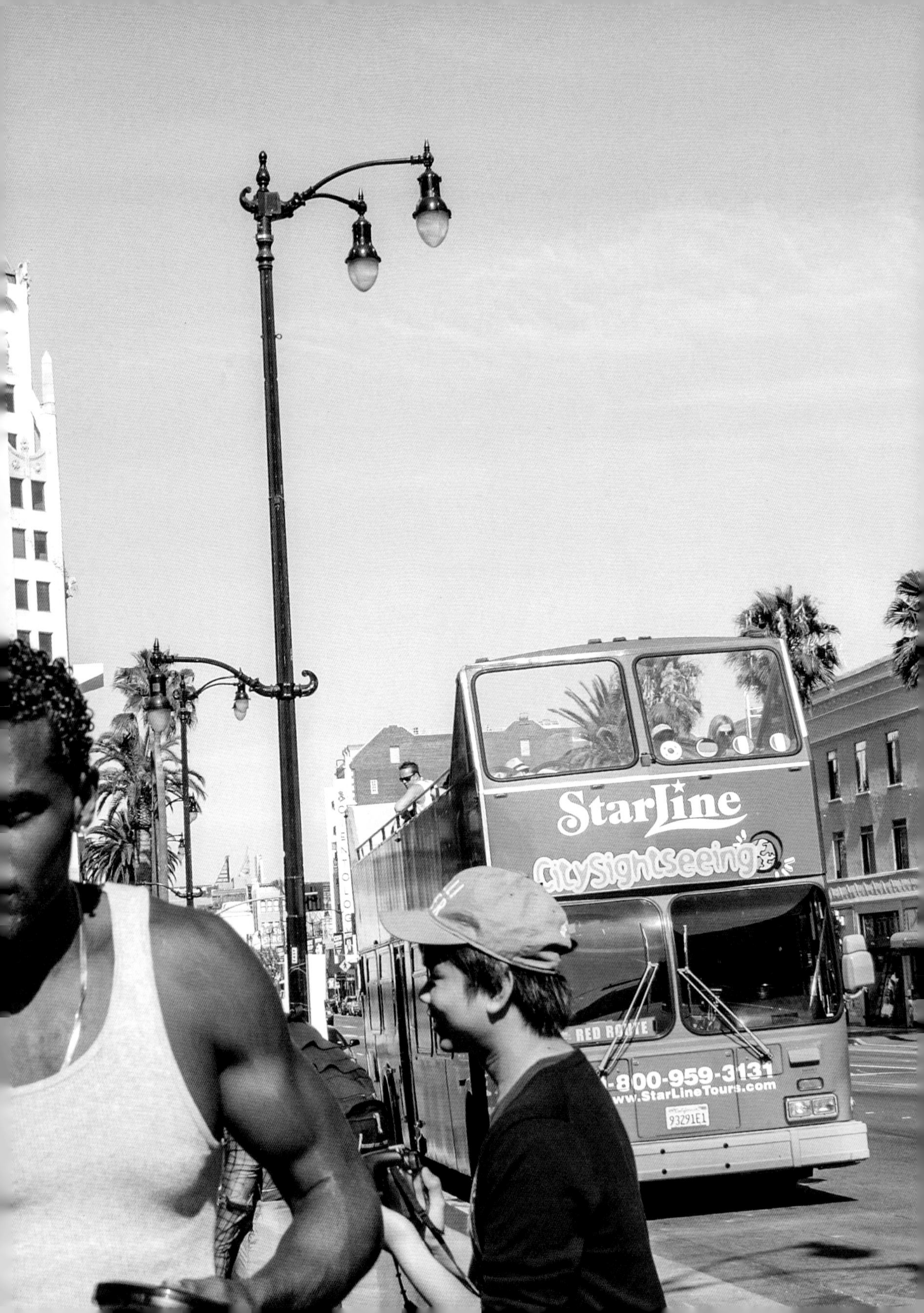

StarLine
CitySightseeing
RED ROUTE
1-800-959-3131
www.StarLineTours.com
93291E1

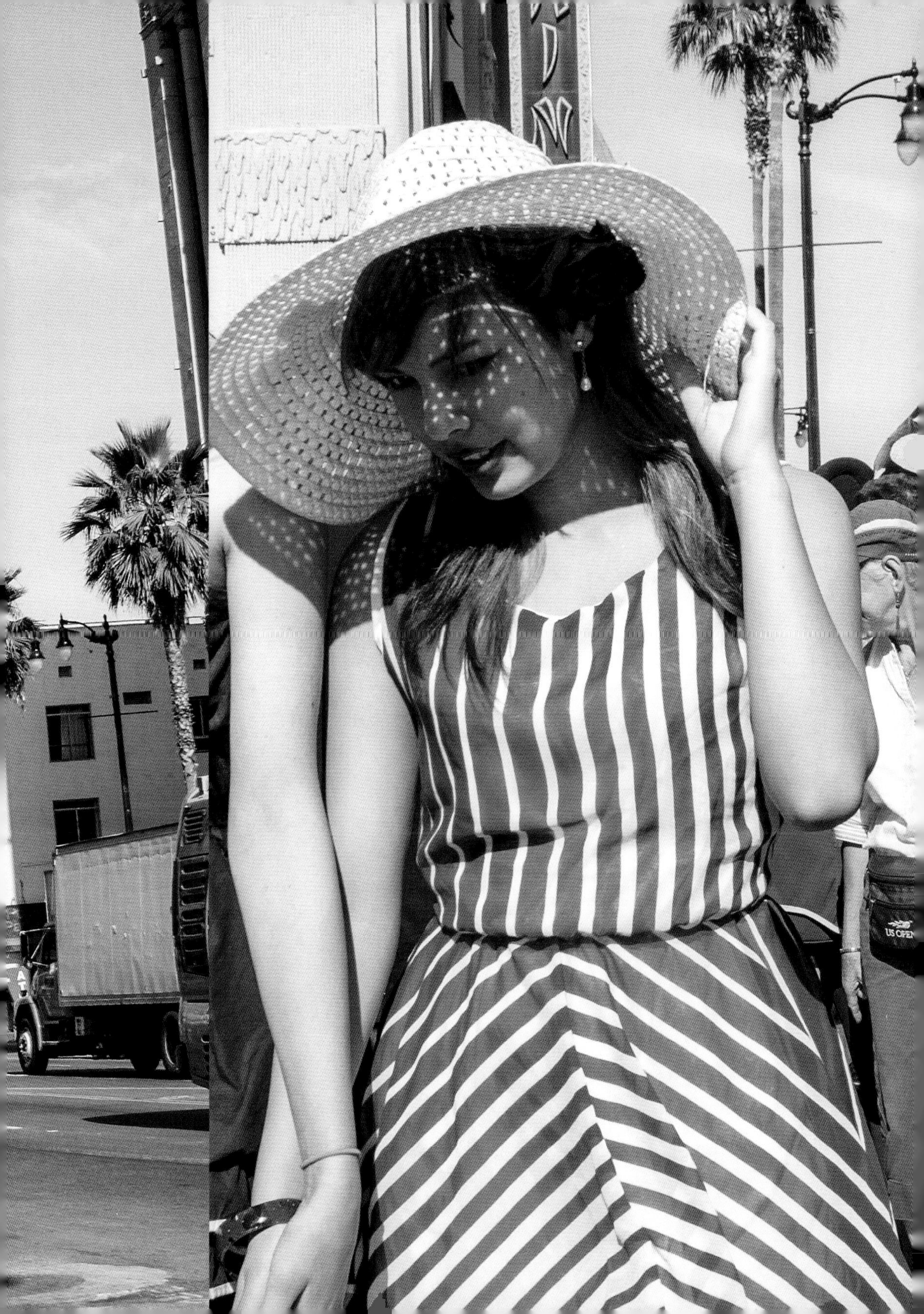
US OPEN

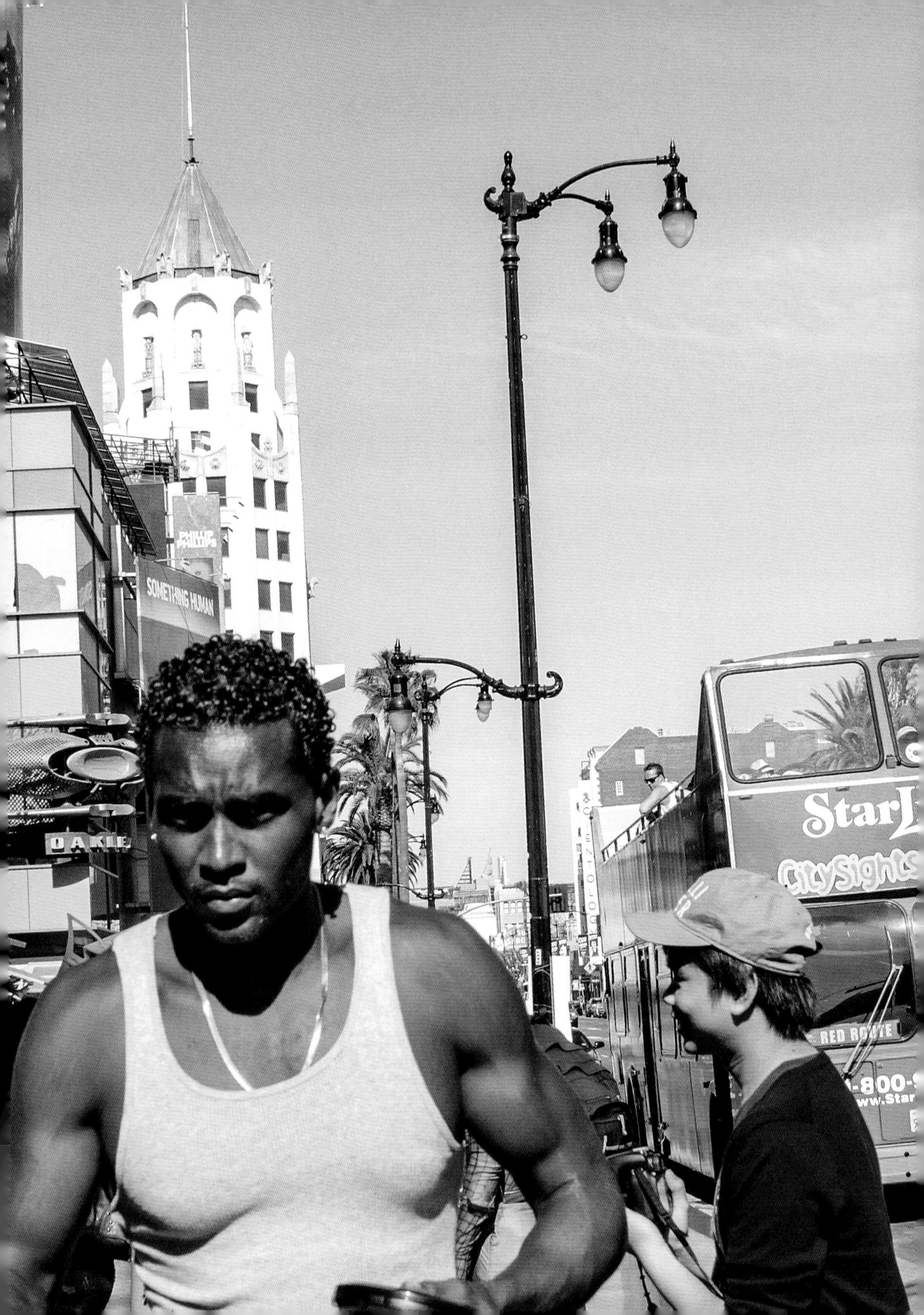

SOMETHING HUMAN
OAKLE
StarL
CitySights
RED ROUTE
1-800-
ww.Star

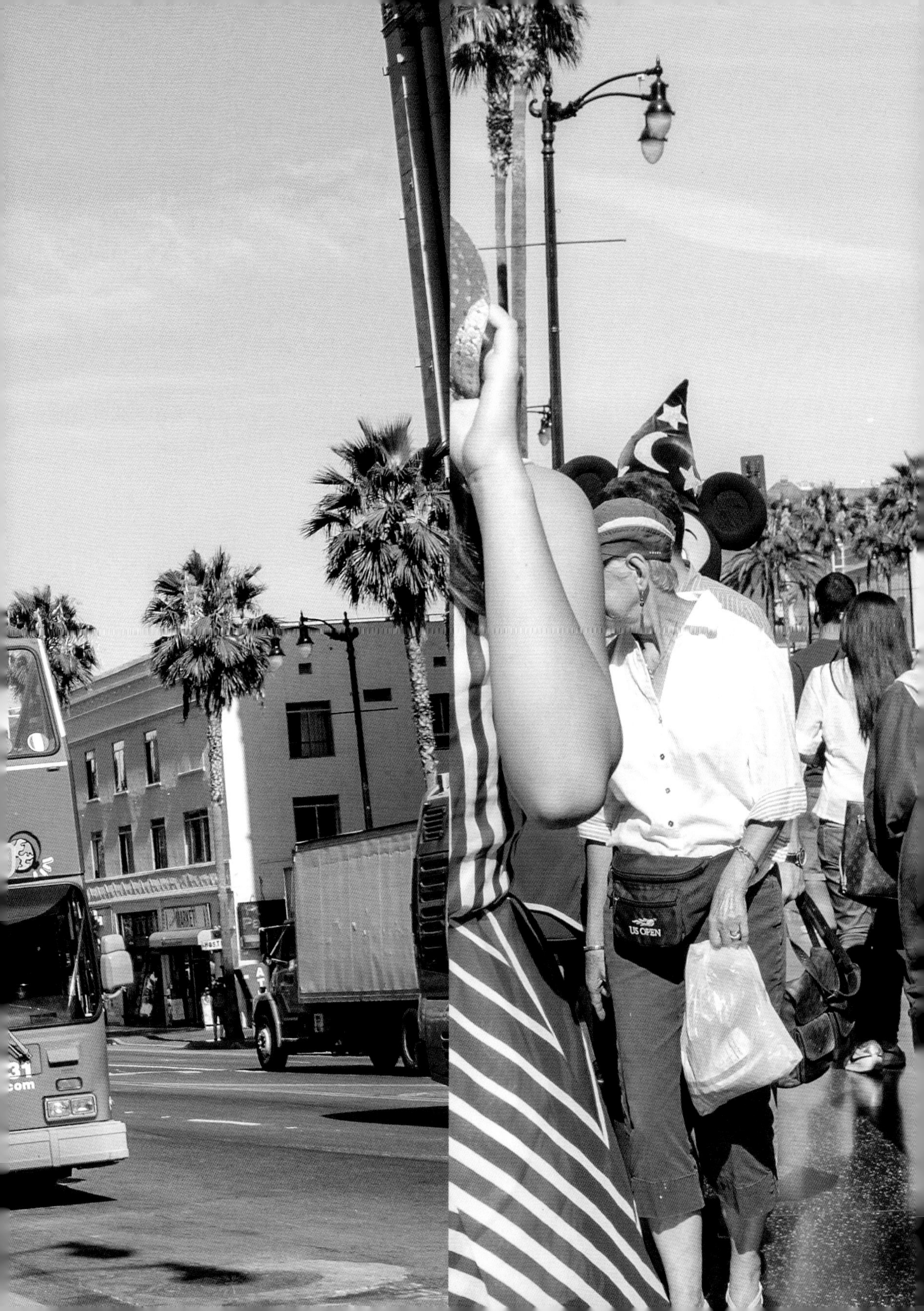

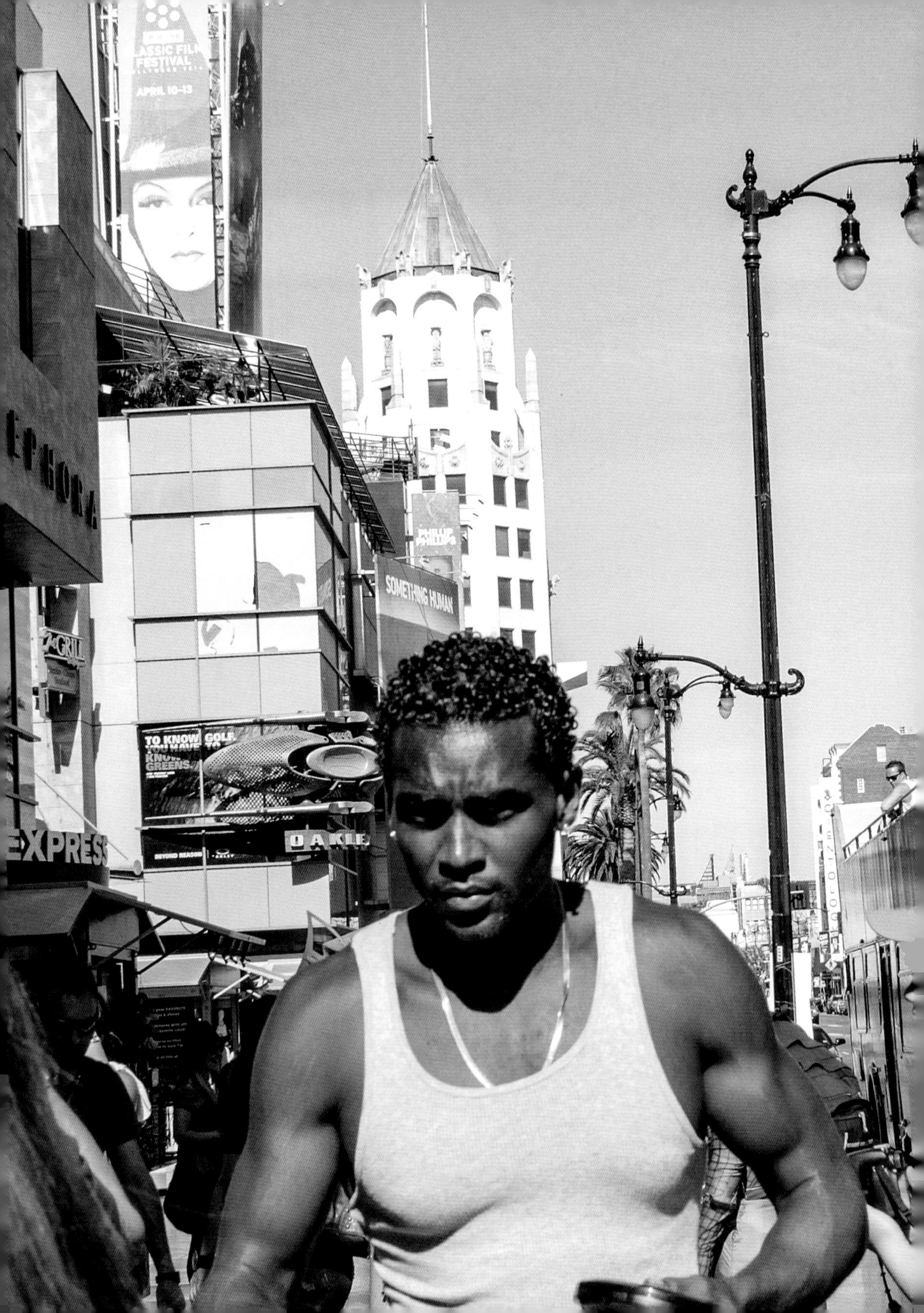
CLASSIC FILM
FESTIVAL
APRIL 10–13
SEPHORA
GRILL
EXPRESS
TO KNOW GOLF
YOU HAVE YO
KNOW
GREENS
OAKLEY
PHILLIP
PHILLIPS
SOMETHING HUMAN

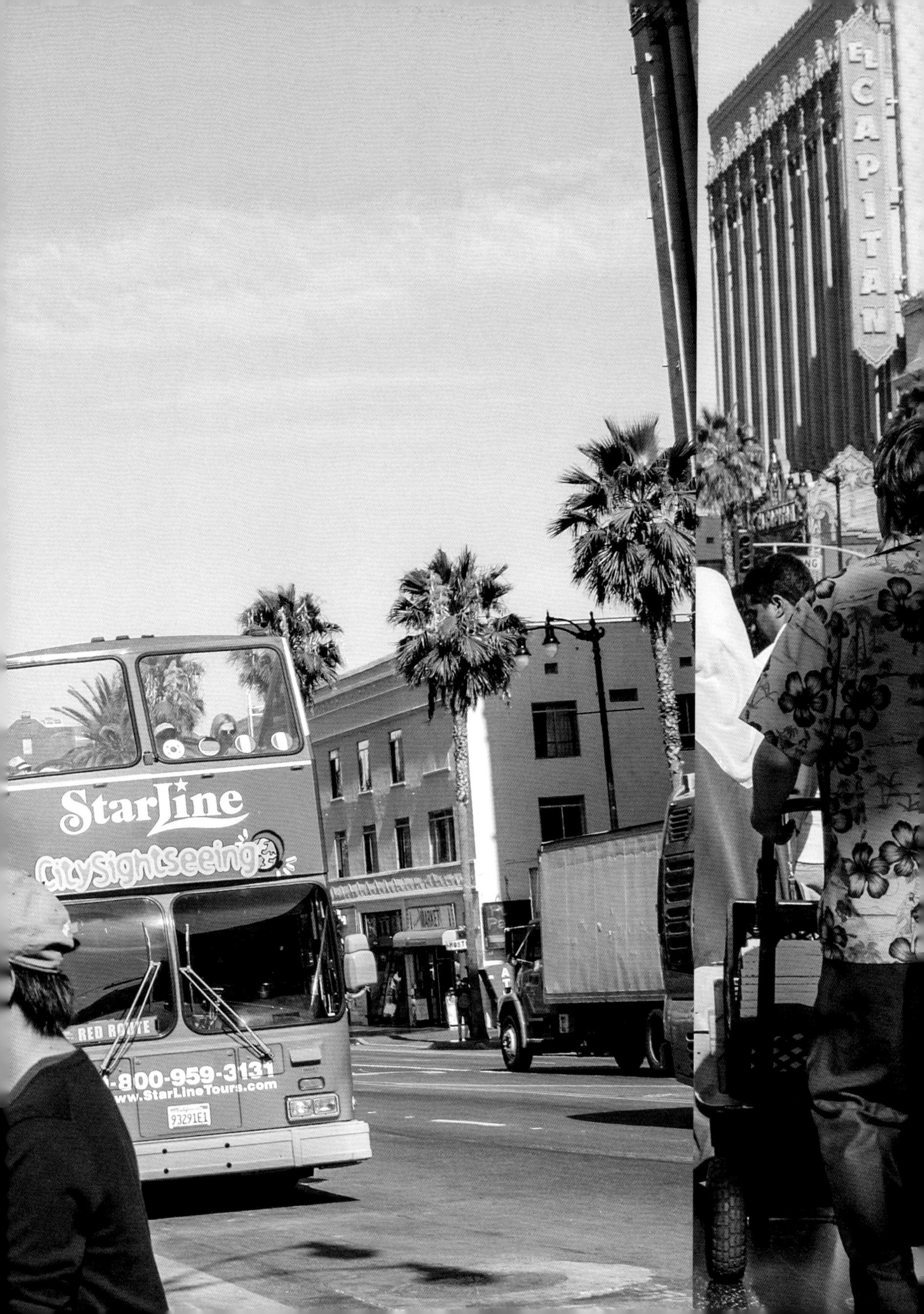

EL CAPITAN
StarLine
City Sightseeing
RED ROUTE
1-800-959-3131
www.StarLineTours.com
93291E1

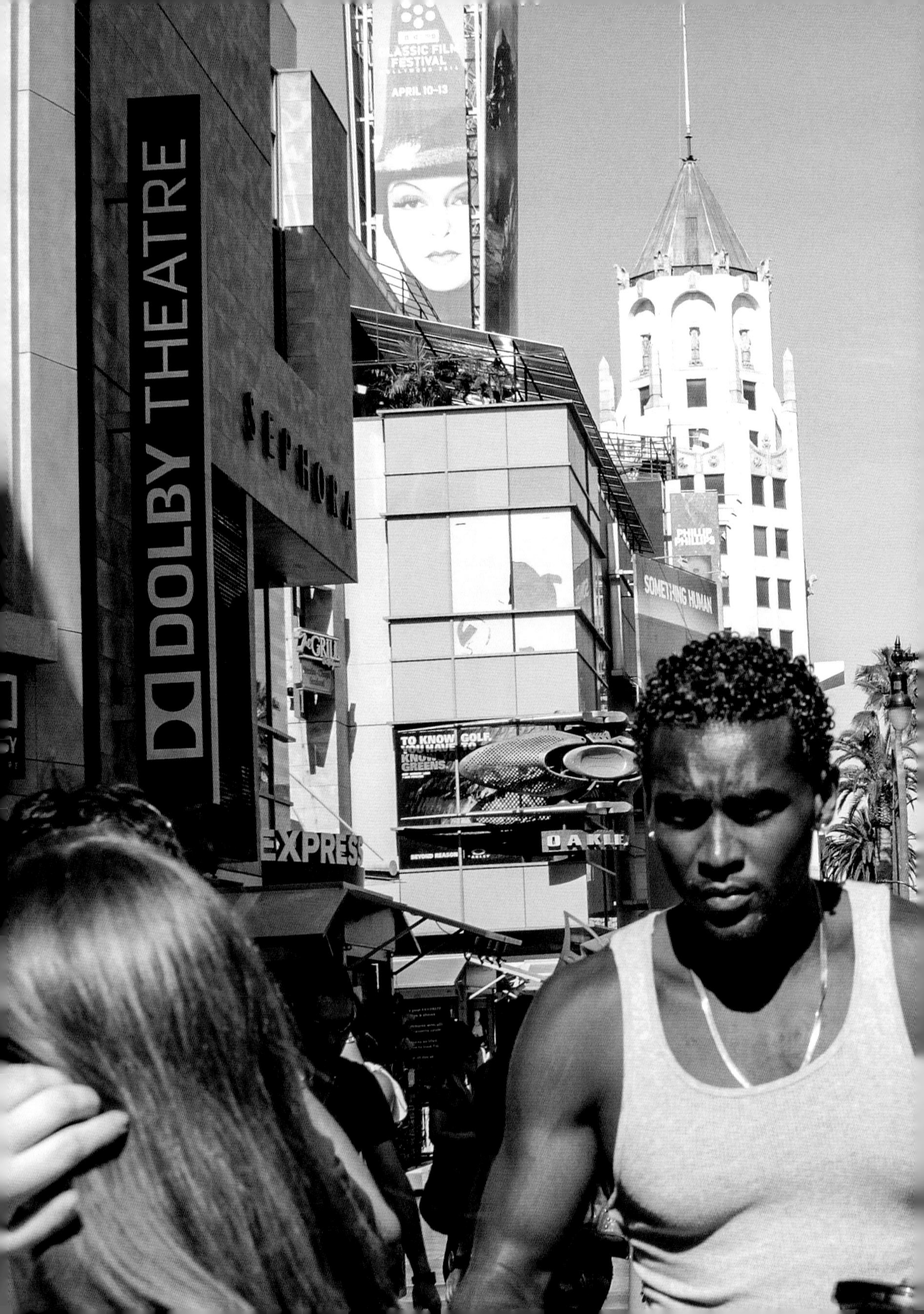

CLASSIC FILM
FESTIVAL
APRIL 10-13
DOLBY THEATRE
DOLBY
SEPHORA
GRILL
EXPRESS
PHILLIP PHILLIPS
SOMETHING HUMAN
TO KNOW GOLF
YOU HAVE TO
KNOW
GREENS
OAKLE

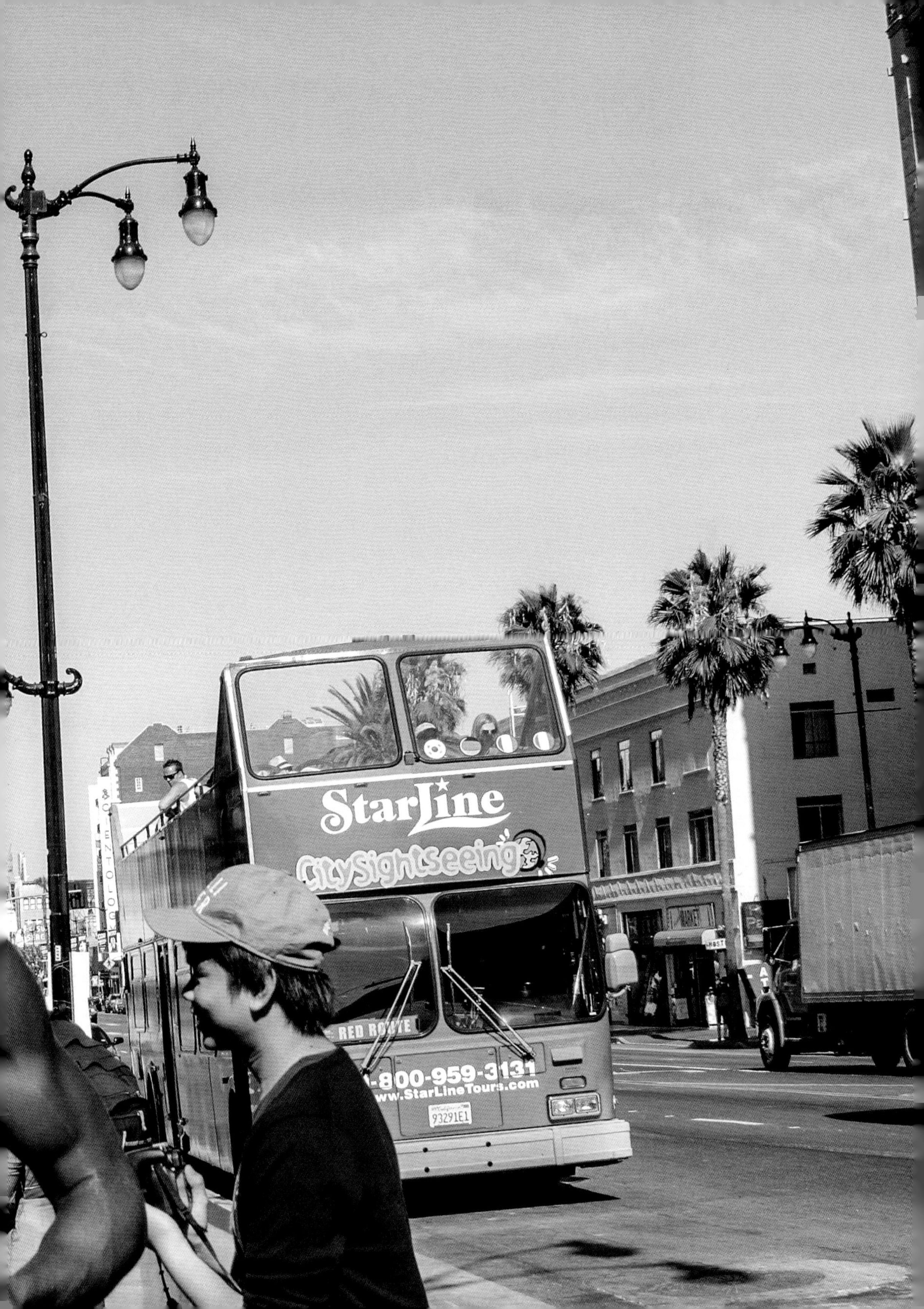

StarLine
CitySightseeing
RED ROUTE
1-800-959-3131
www.StarLineTours.com
93291E1

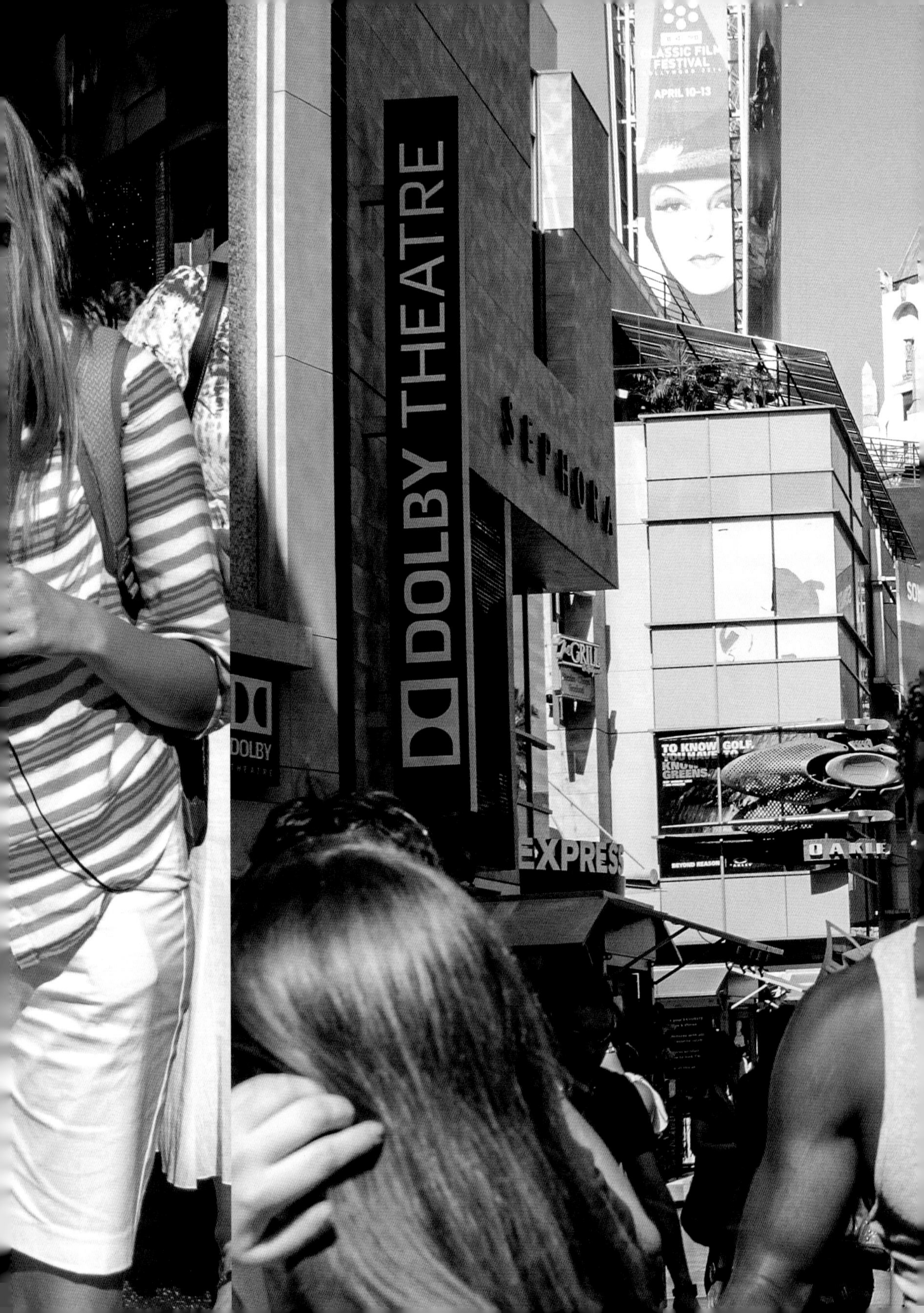

DOLBY THEATRE
DOLBY
DOLBY
THEATRE
SEPHORA
CLASSIC FILM
FESTIVAL
APRIL 10–13
GRILL
EXPRESS
TO KNOW GOLF
YOU HAVE TO
KNOW
GREENS
BEYOND REASON
OAKLE

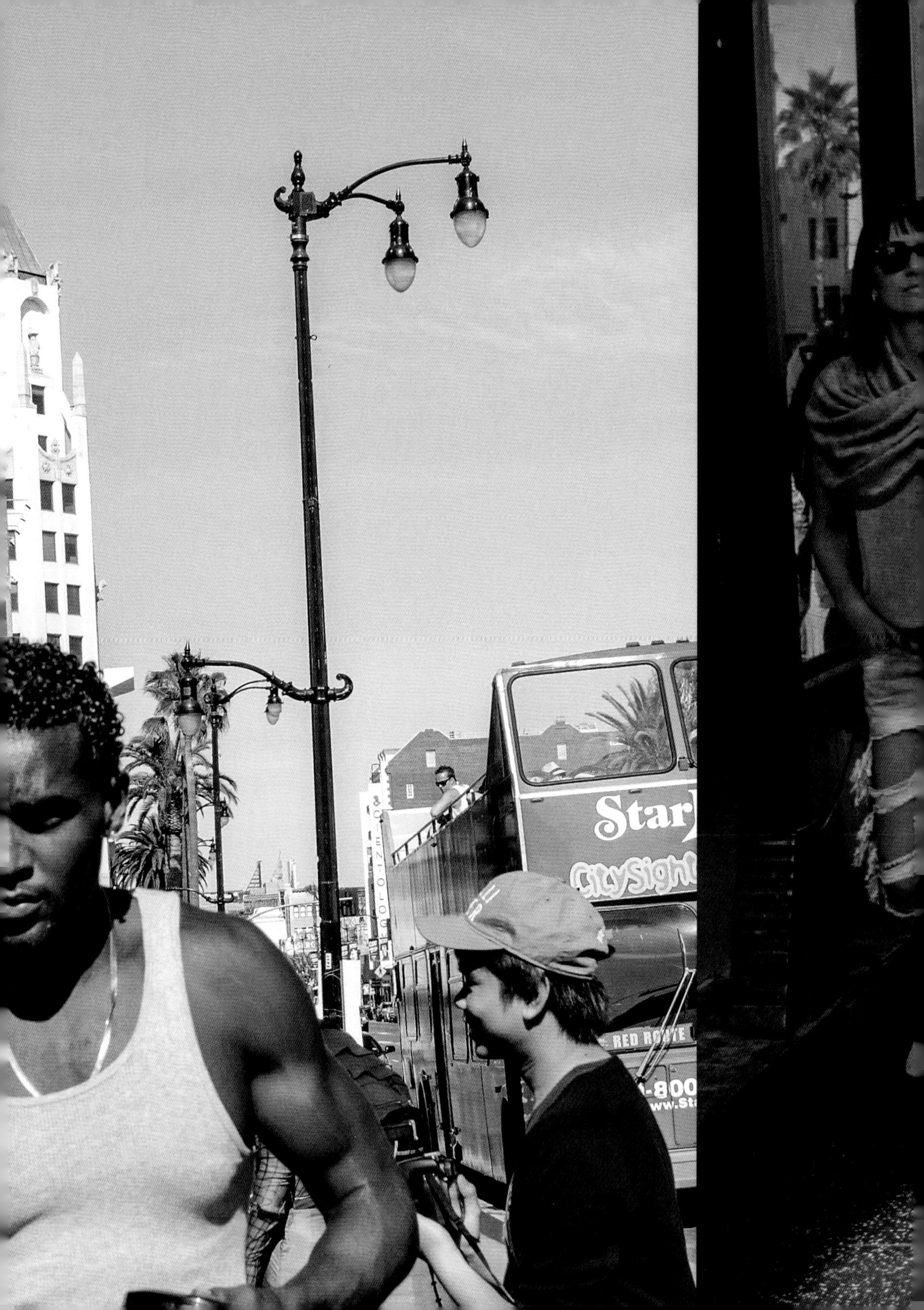
Star
CitySight
RED ROUTE
-800
www.Sta

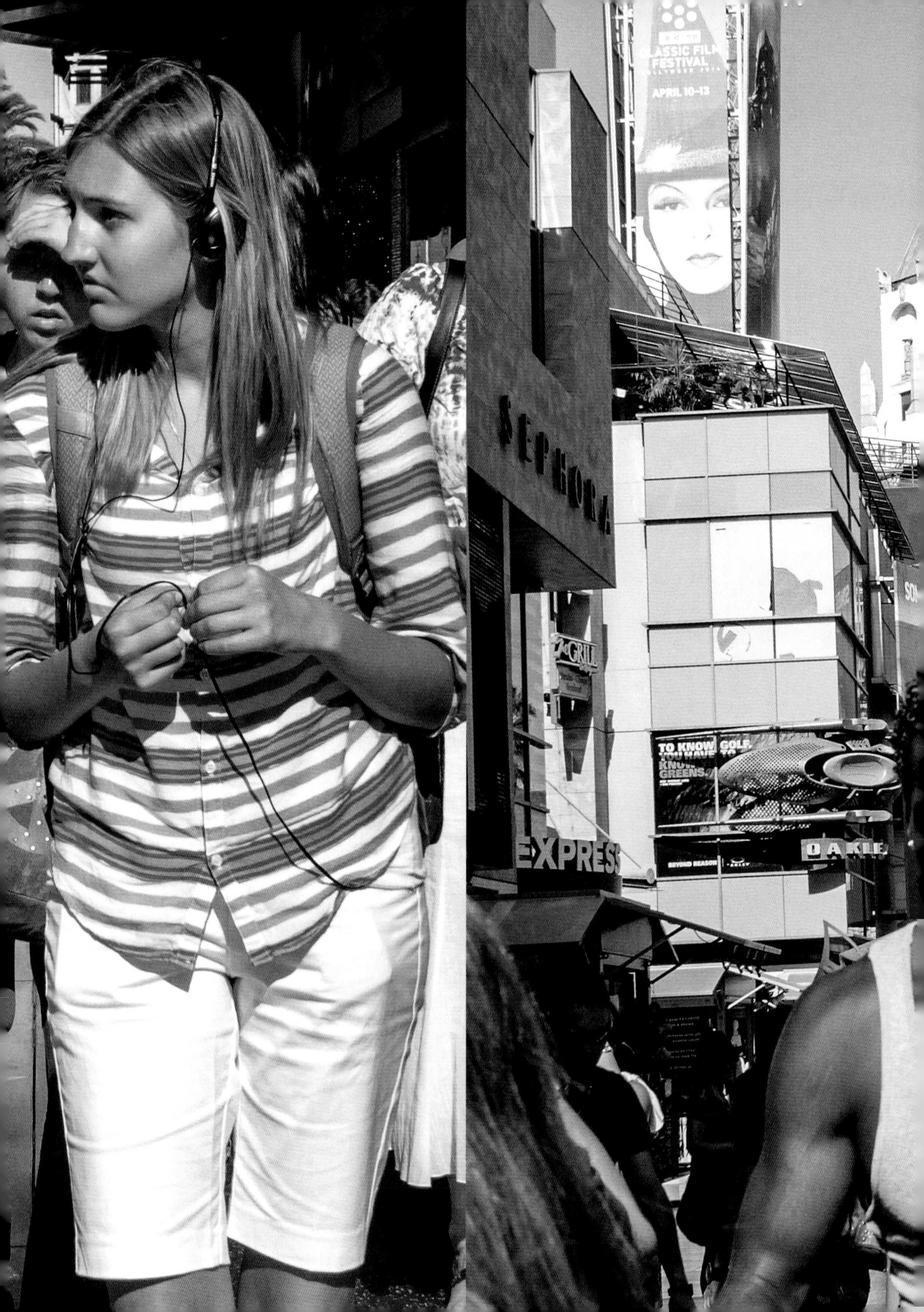
CLASSIC FILM FESTIVAL
APRIL 10-13
SEPHORA
GRILL
TO KNOW GOLF
YOU HAVE TO
KNOW
GREENS
BEYOND REASON
EXPRESS
OAKLE

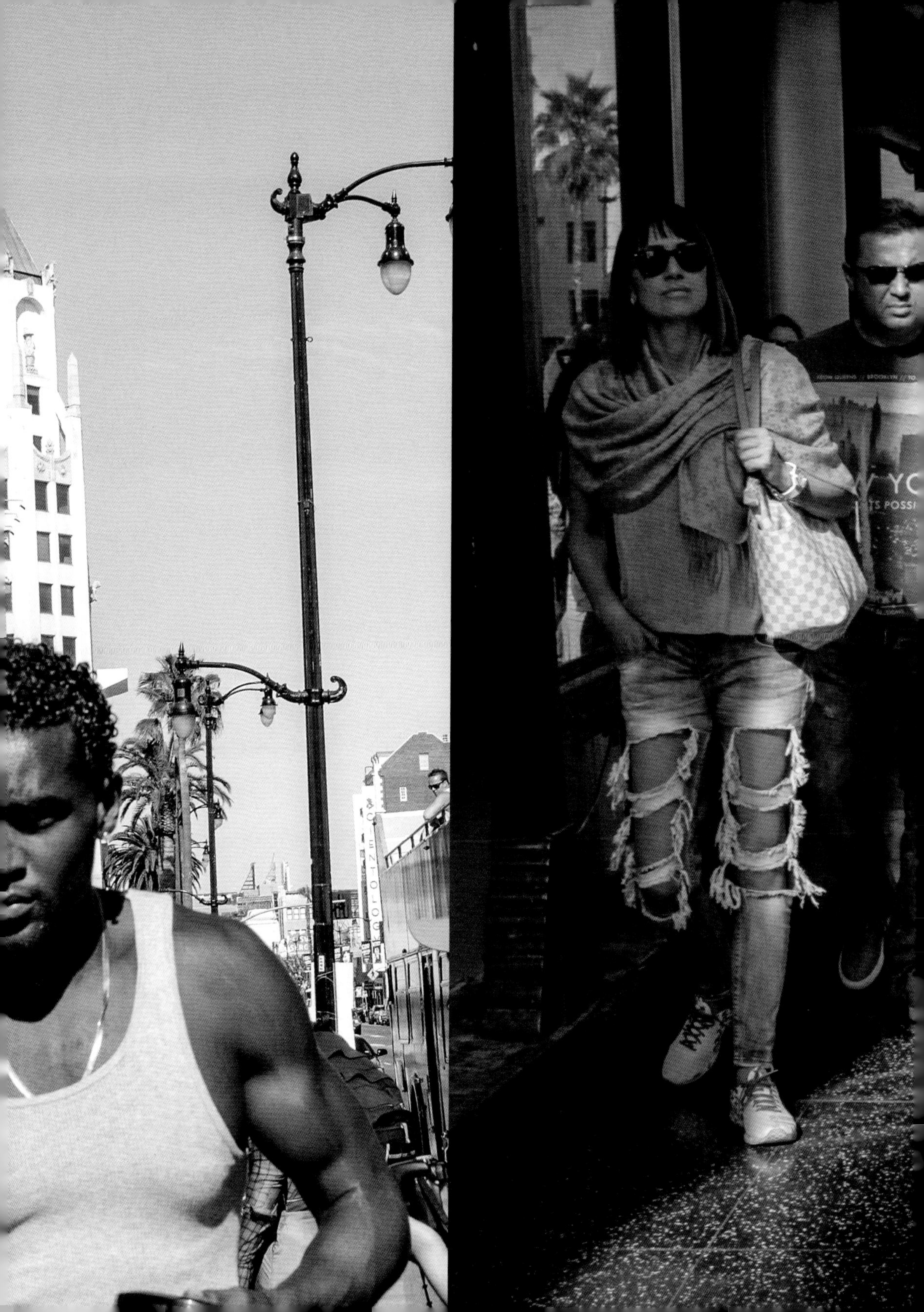

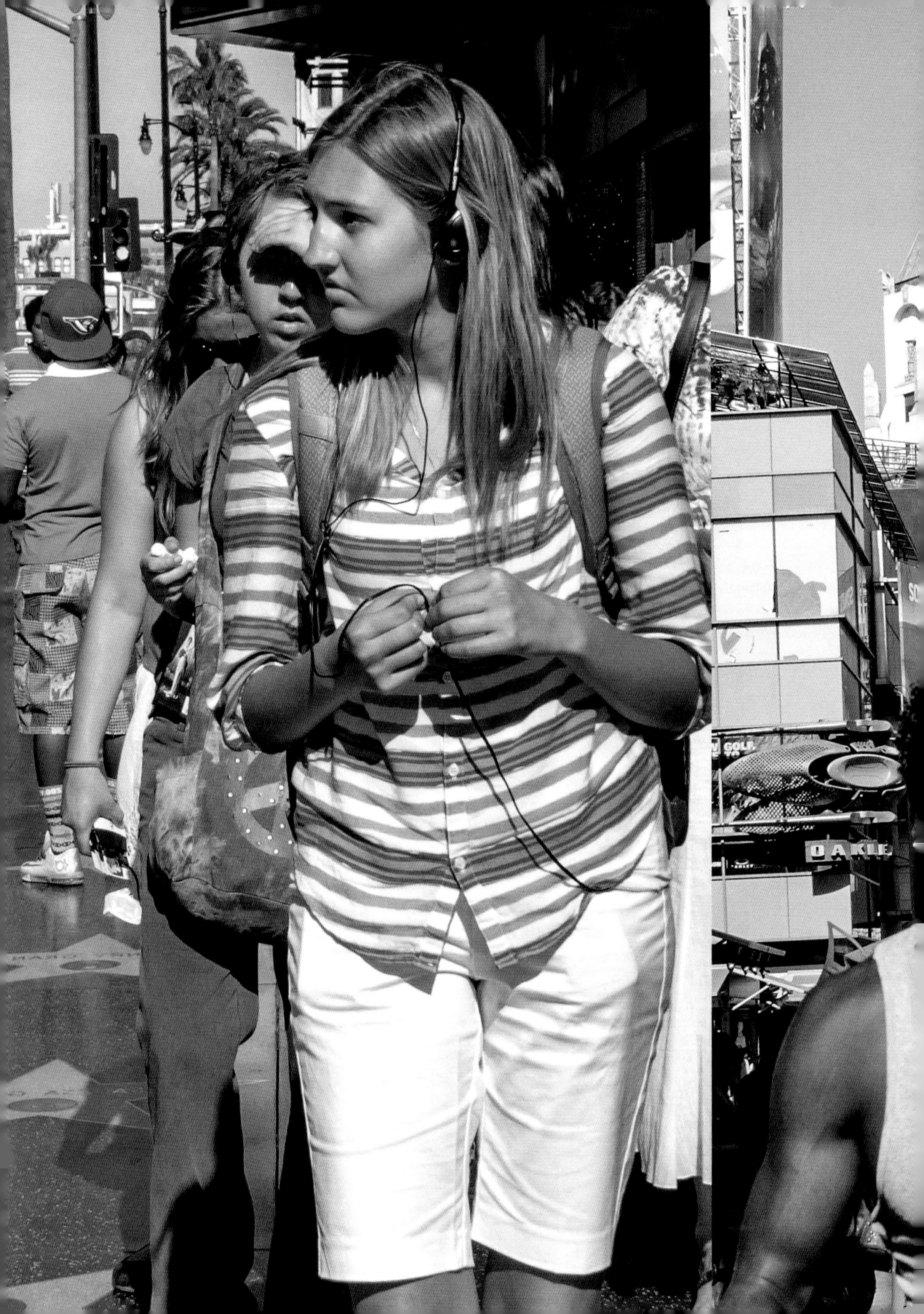

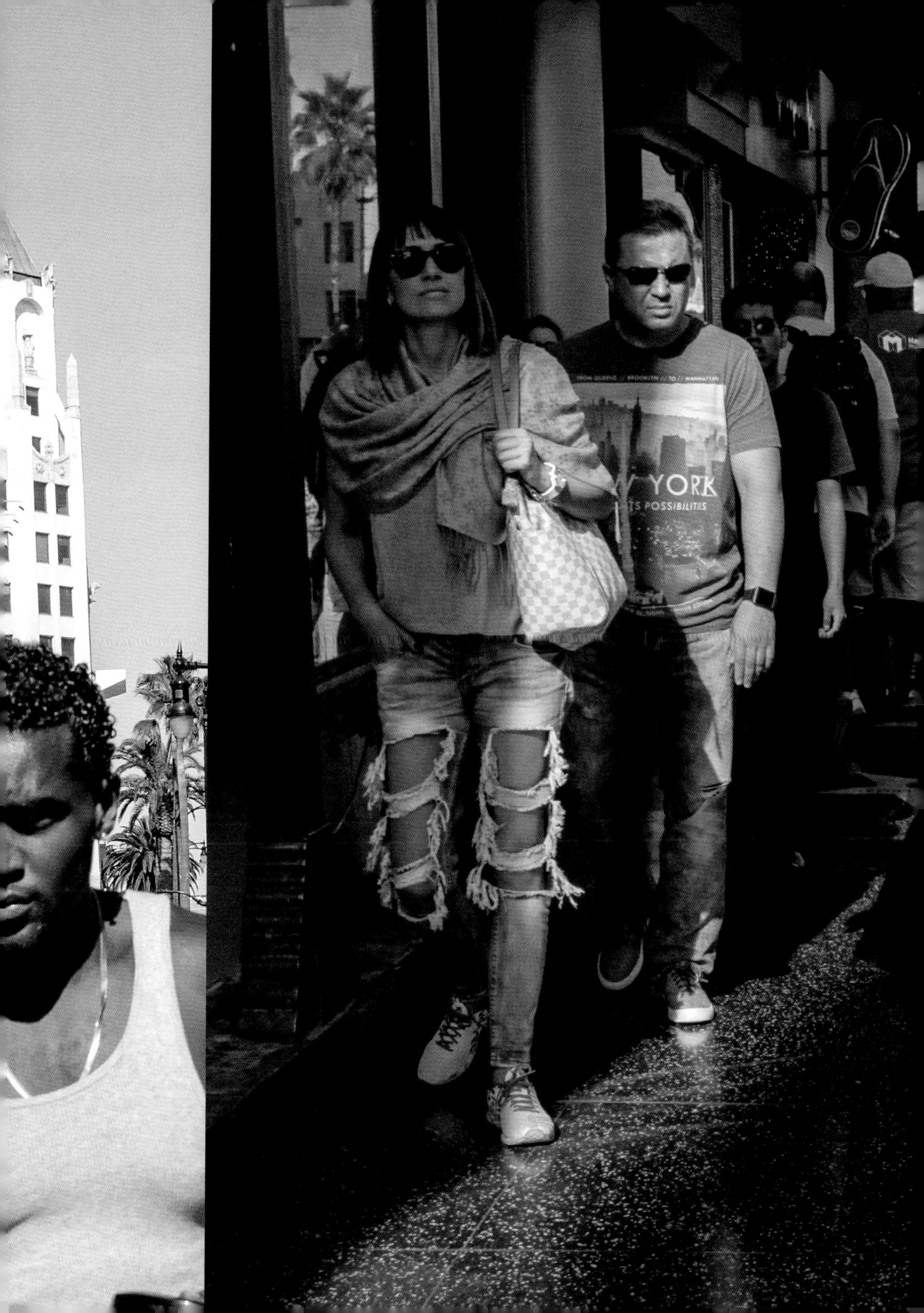
NEW YORK
ITS POSSIBILITIES

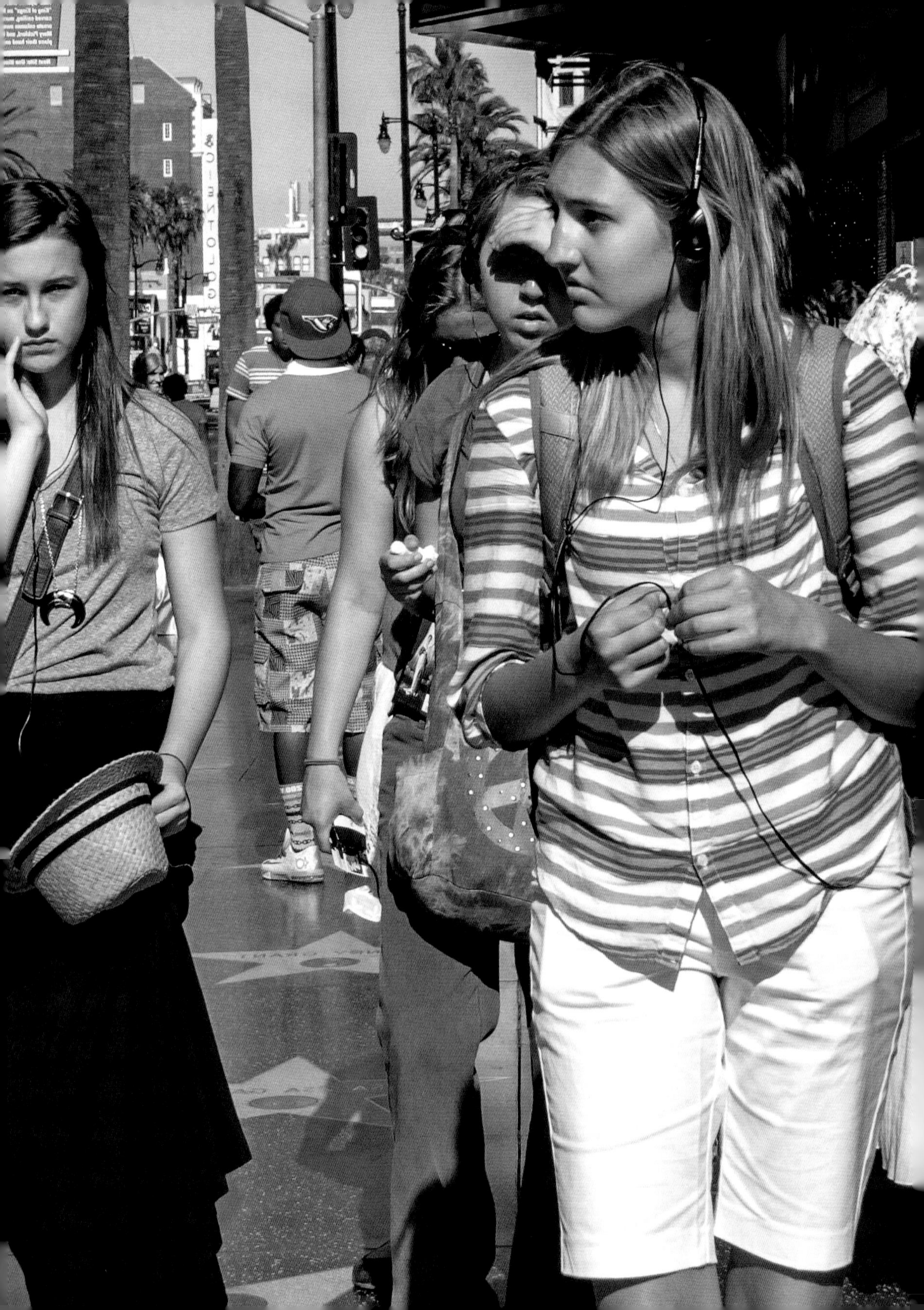

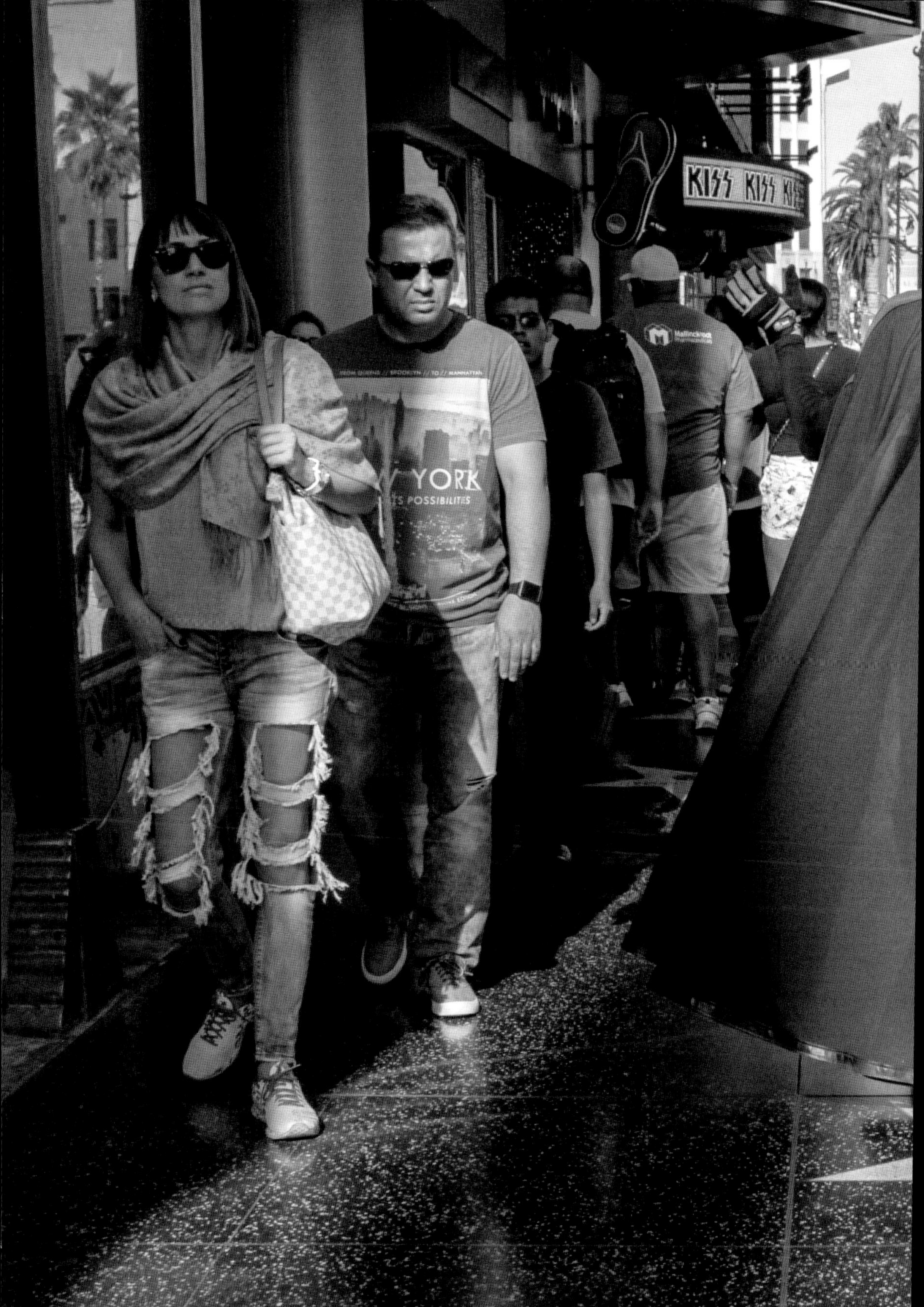

KISS KISS KISS
NEW YORK
ITS POSSIBILITIES

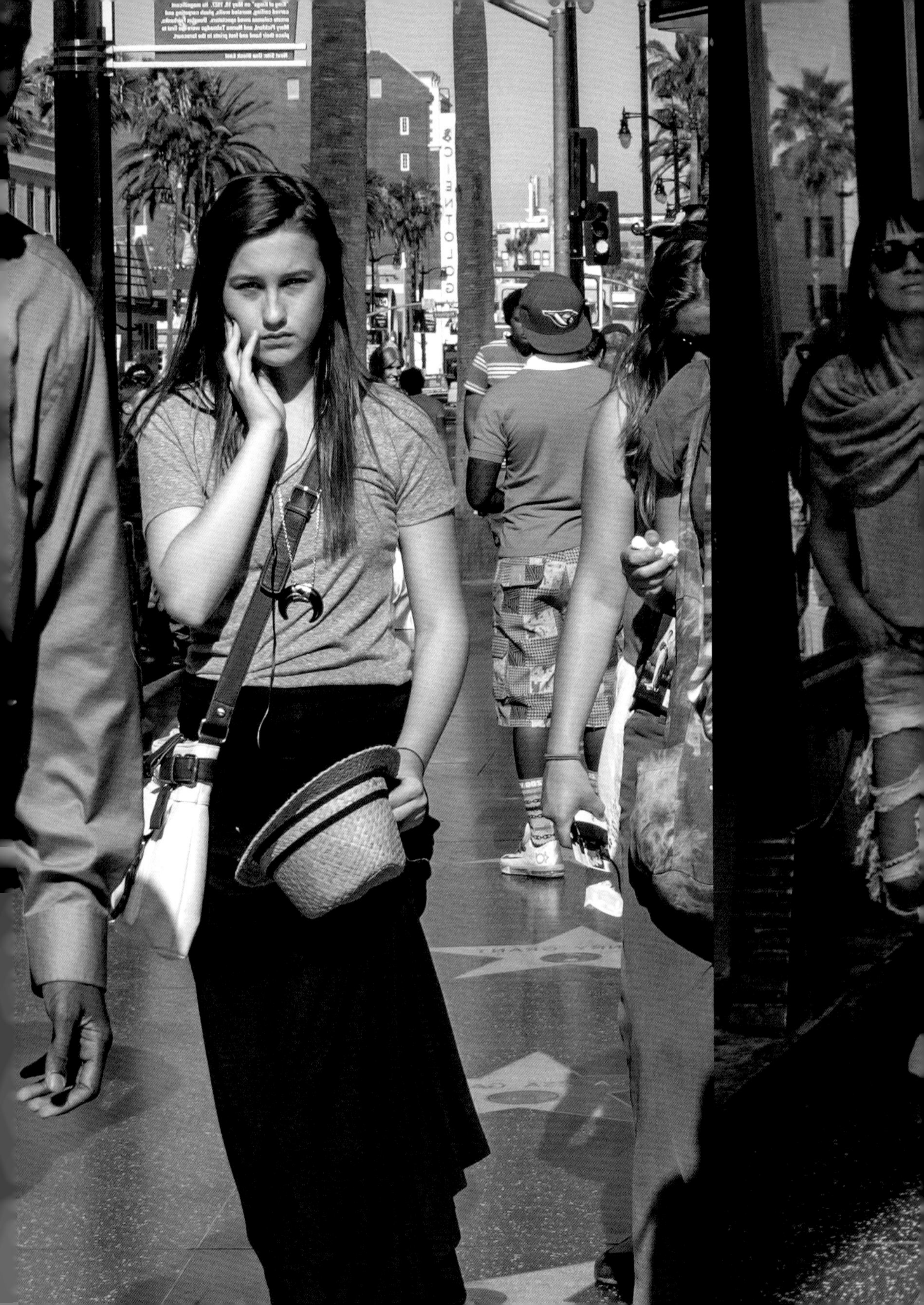

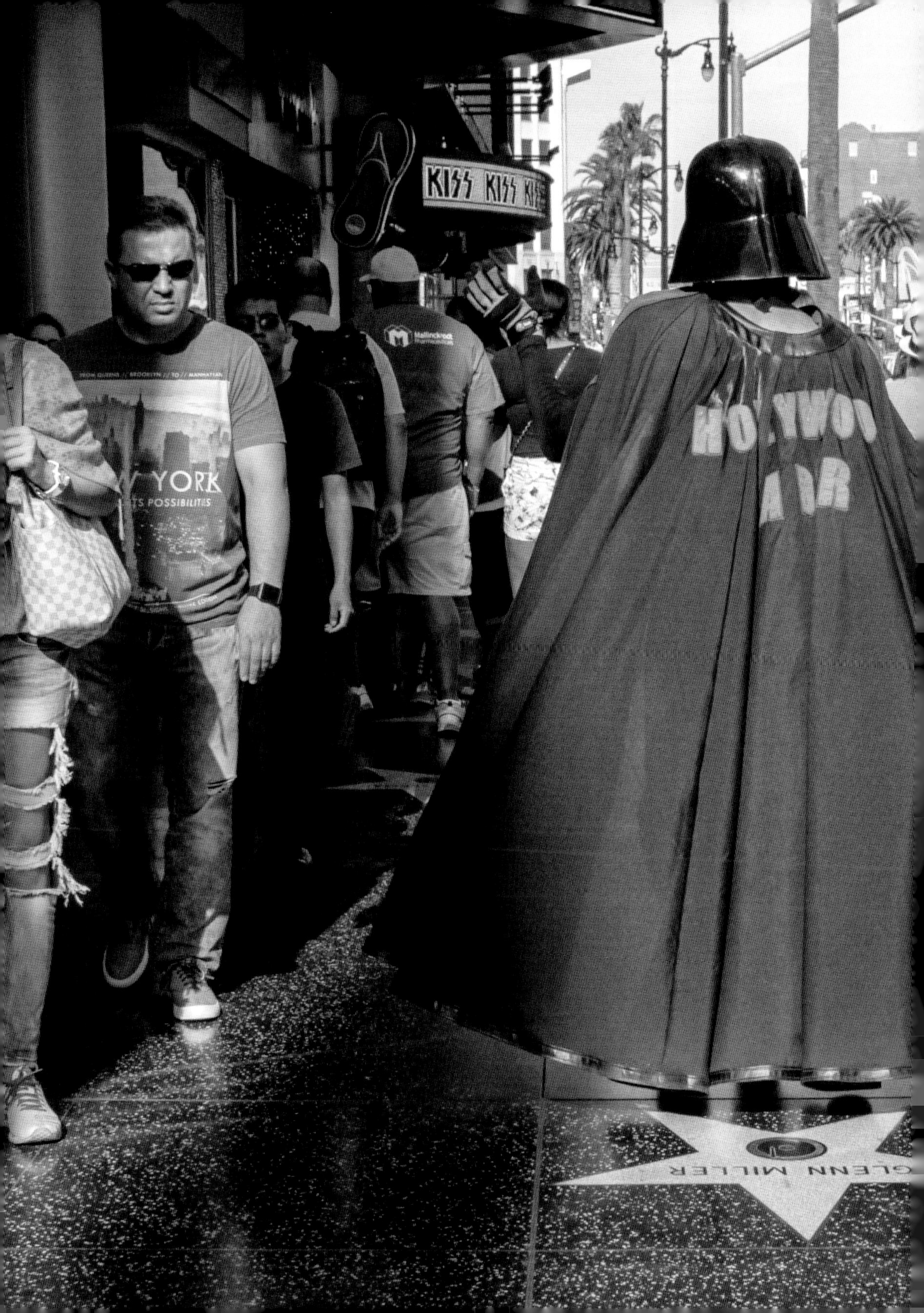

KISS KISS KISS
NEW YORK
TS POSSIBILITIES
HOLLYWOOD VADAR
GLENN MILLER

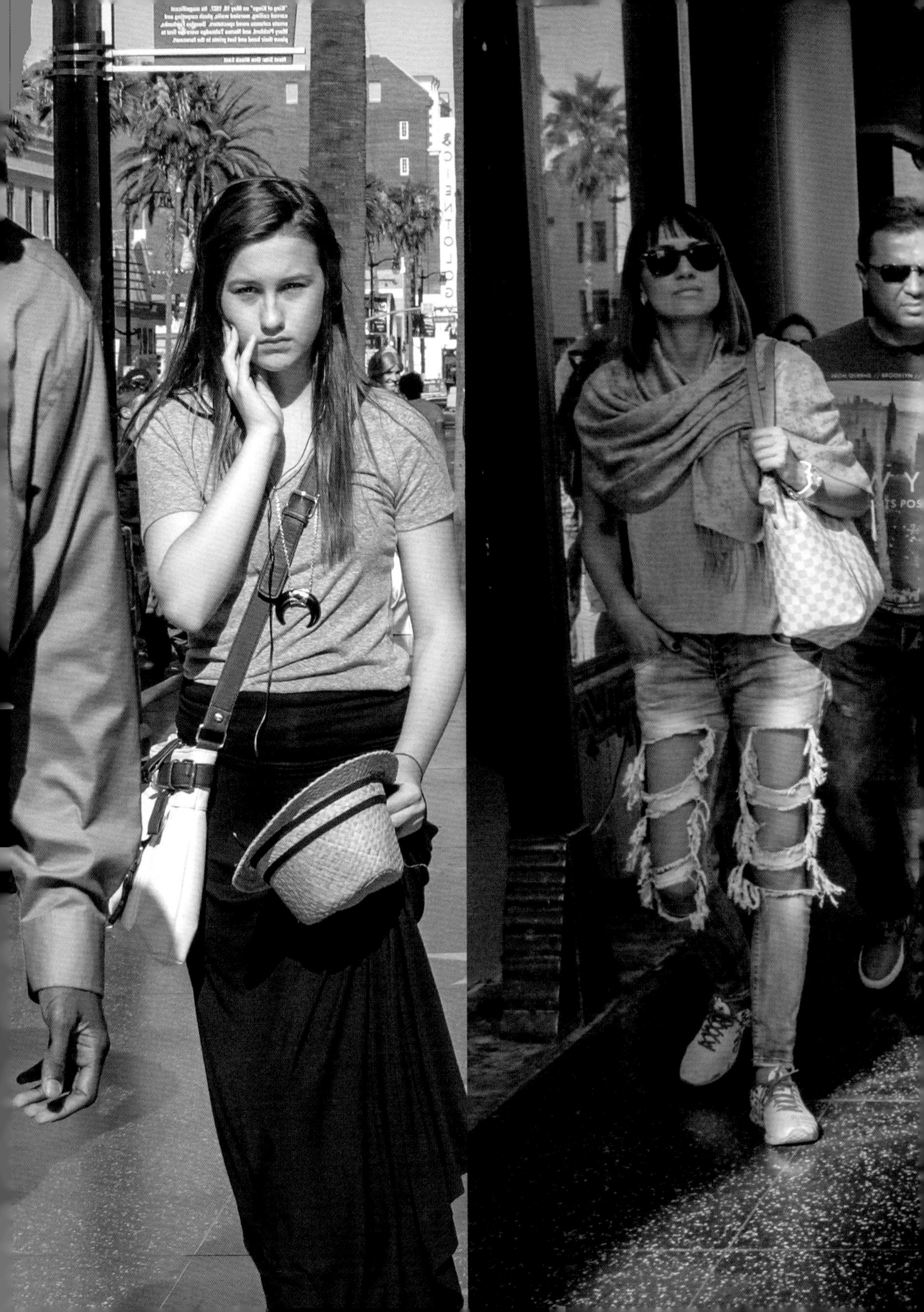

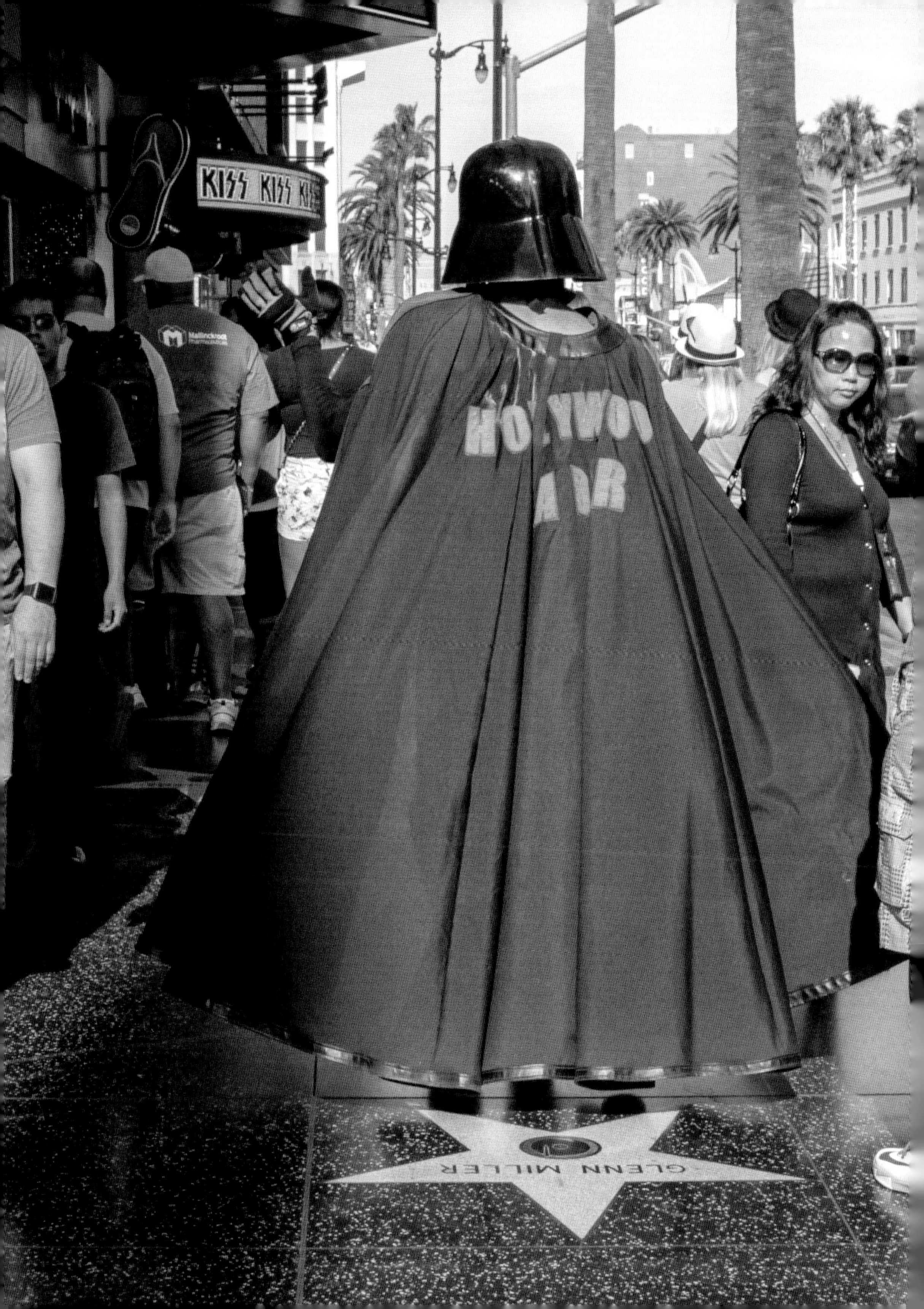

KISS KISS KI
HOLLYWOOD
STAR
GLENN MILLER

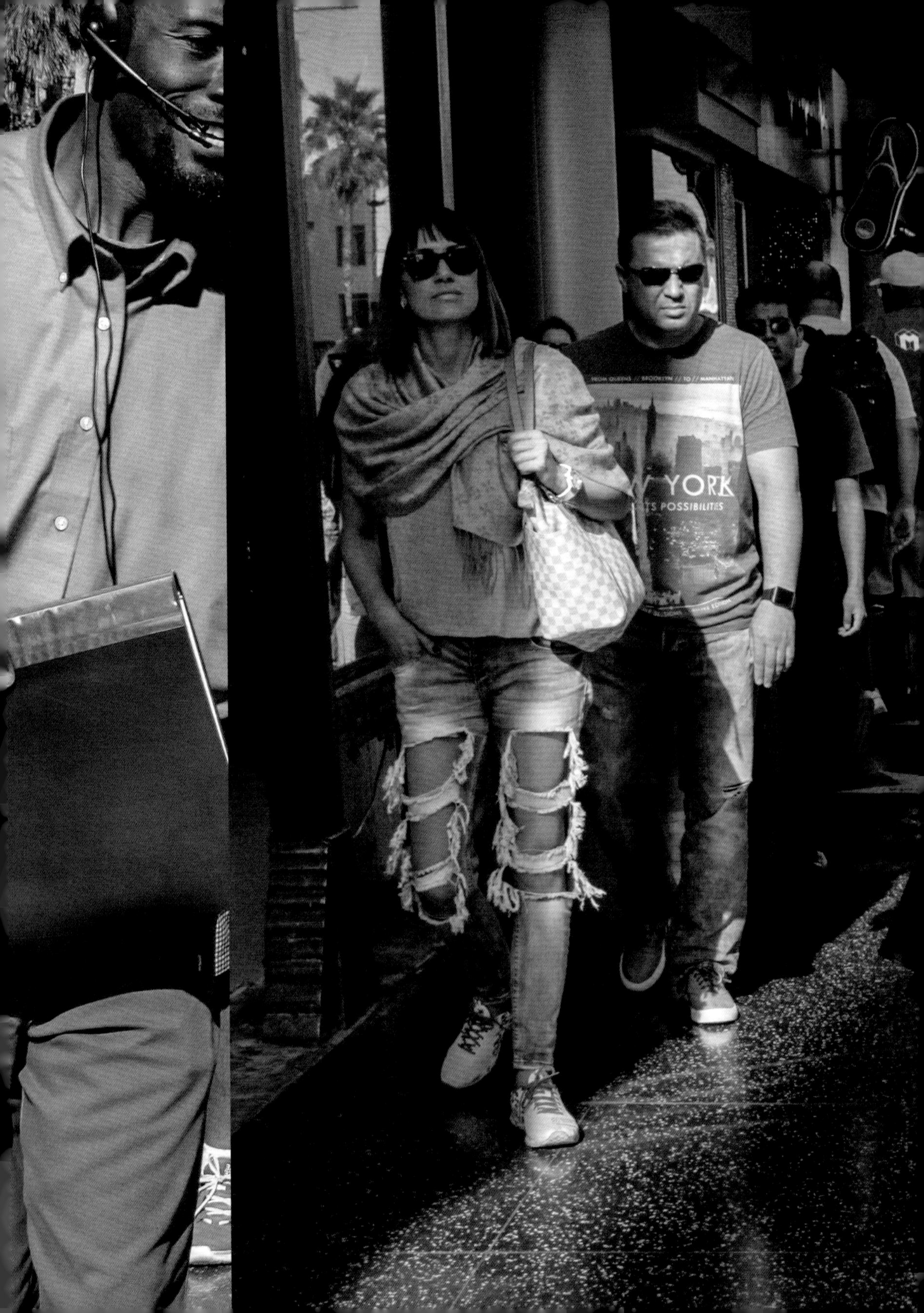

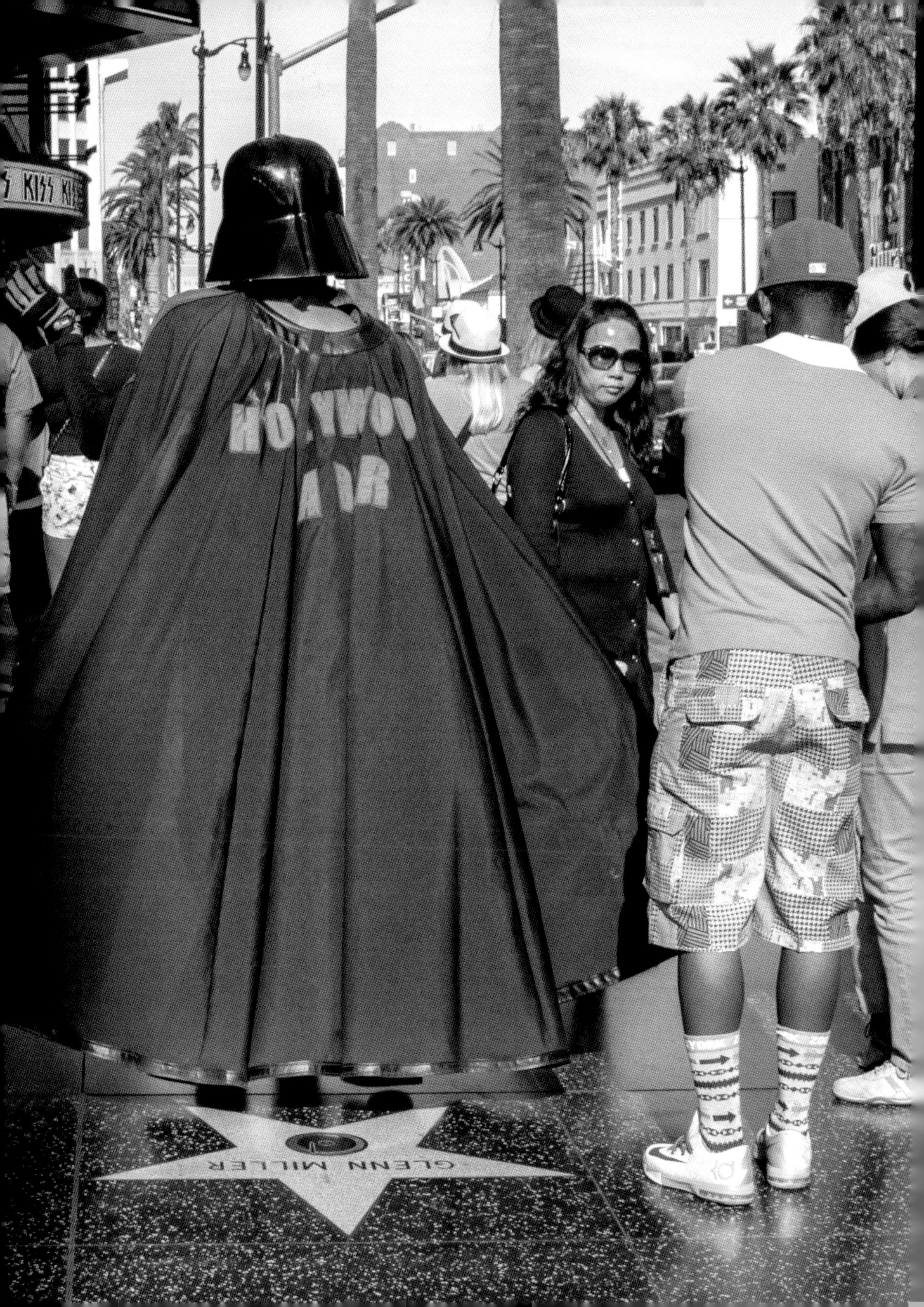

HOLLYWOOD
KISS KISS
GLENN MILLER

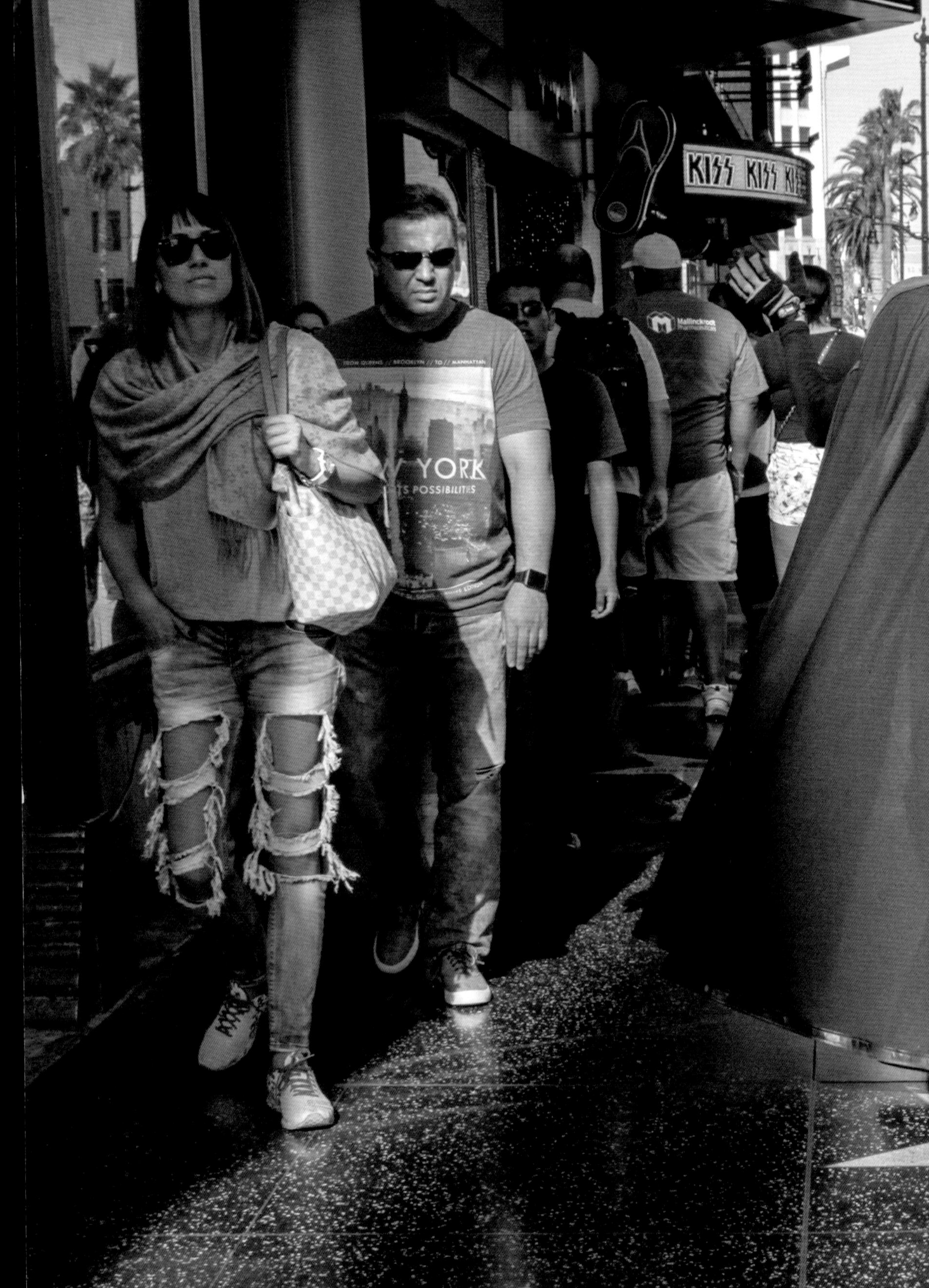

KISS KISS KI
NEW YORK
TS POSSIBILITIES

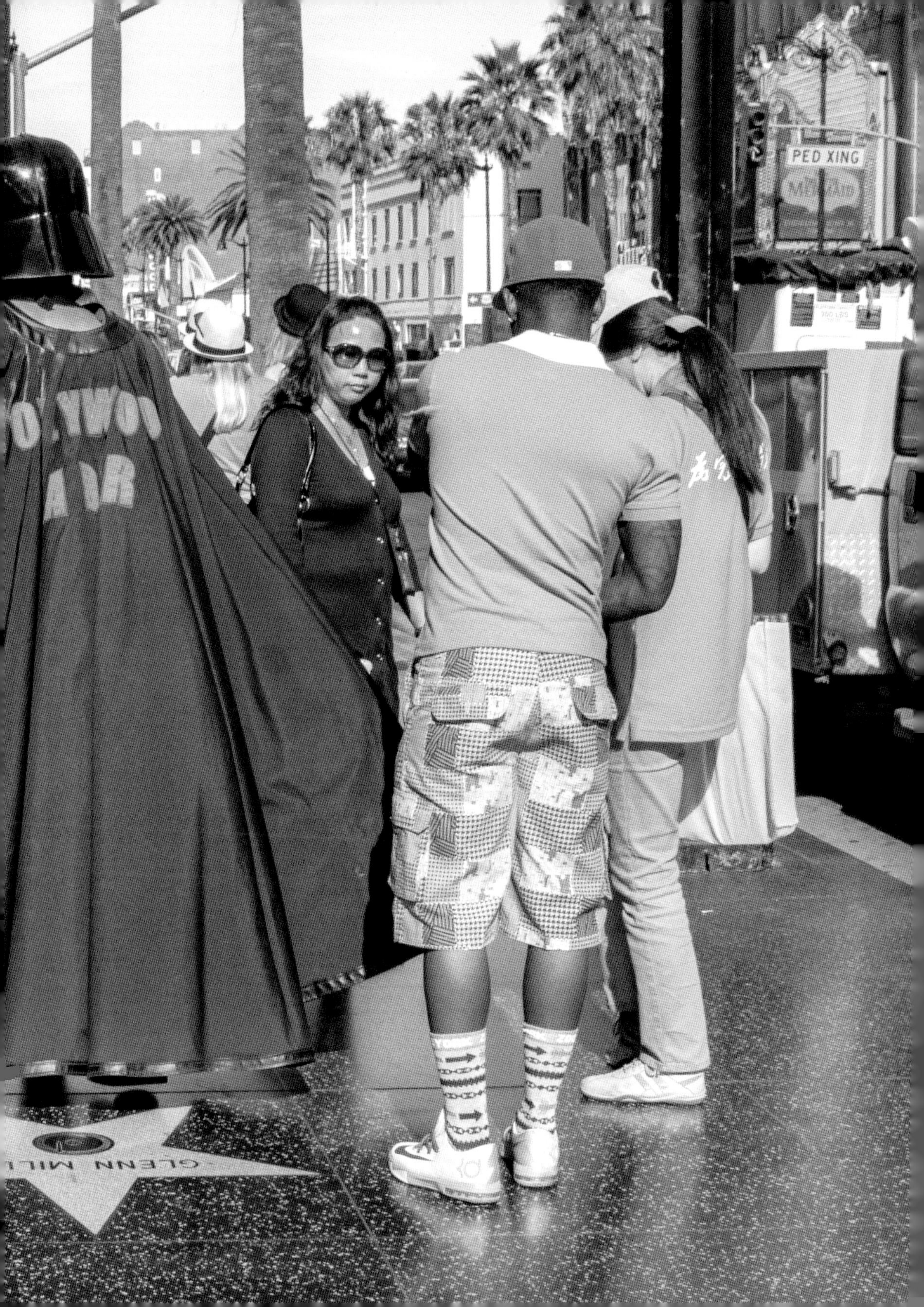

PED XING
GLENN MIL

与蔡秉桥联合策划展览

心举办之际
月9日

鲁斯、尤伦斯当代艺术
uchhandlung Walther
所属。未经出版商授权，
擅自对本出版物进行
版和使用，翻印必究。

、布莱恩·勒廷格

科森蒂诺
罗内

中心

(UCCA)
8艺术区

0224
0220

627-9

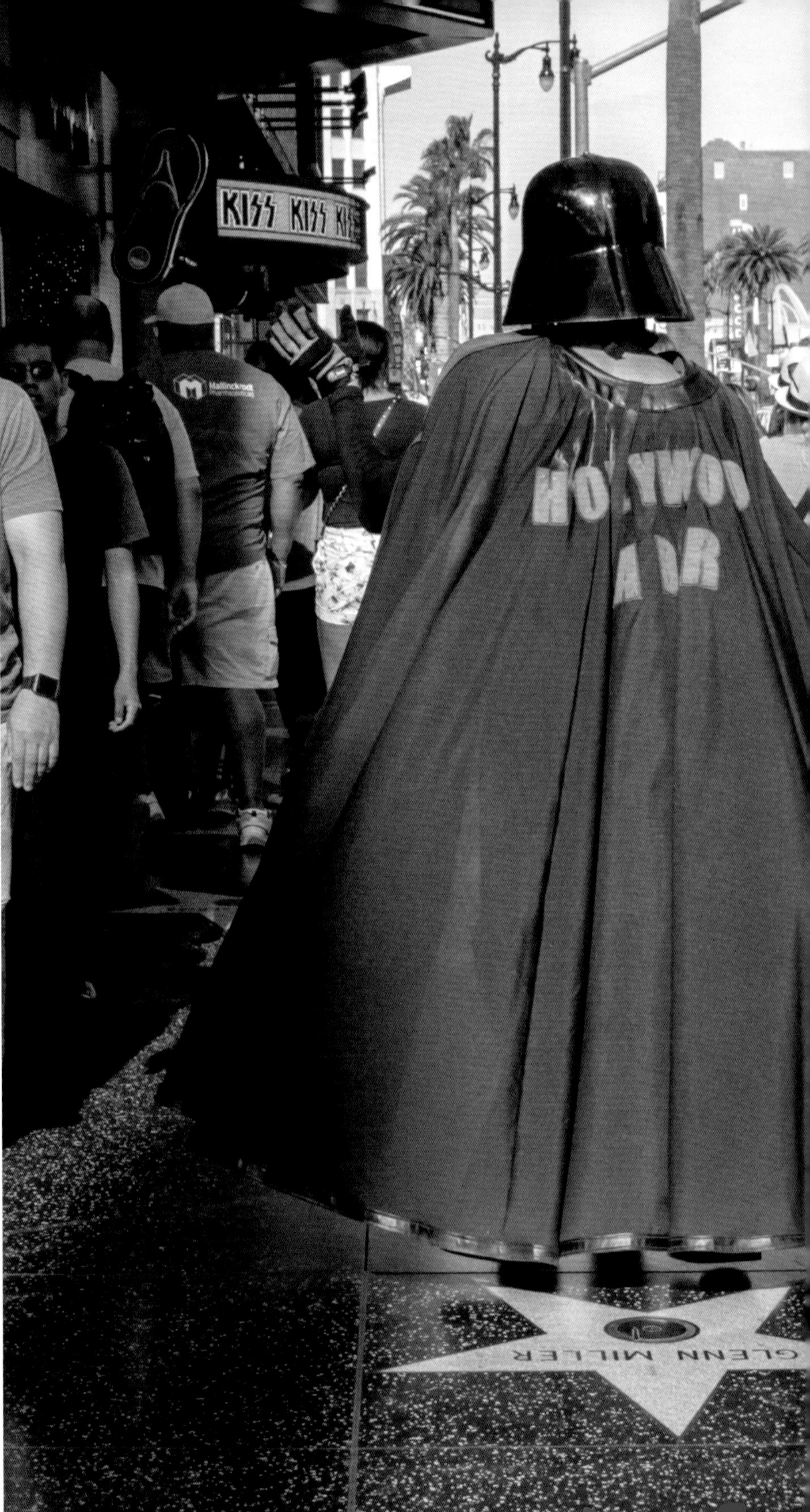

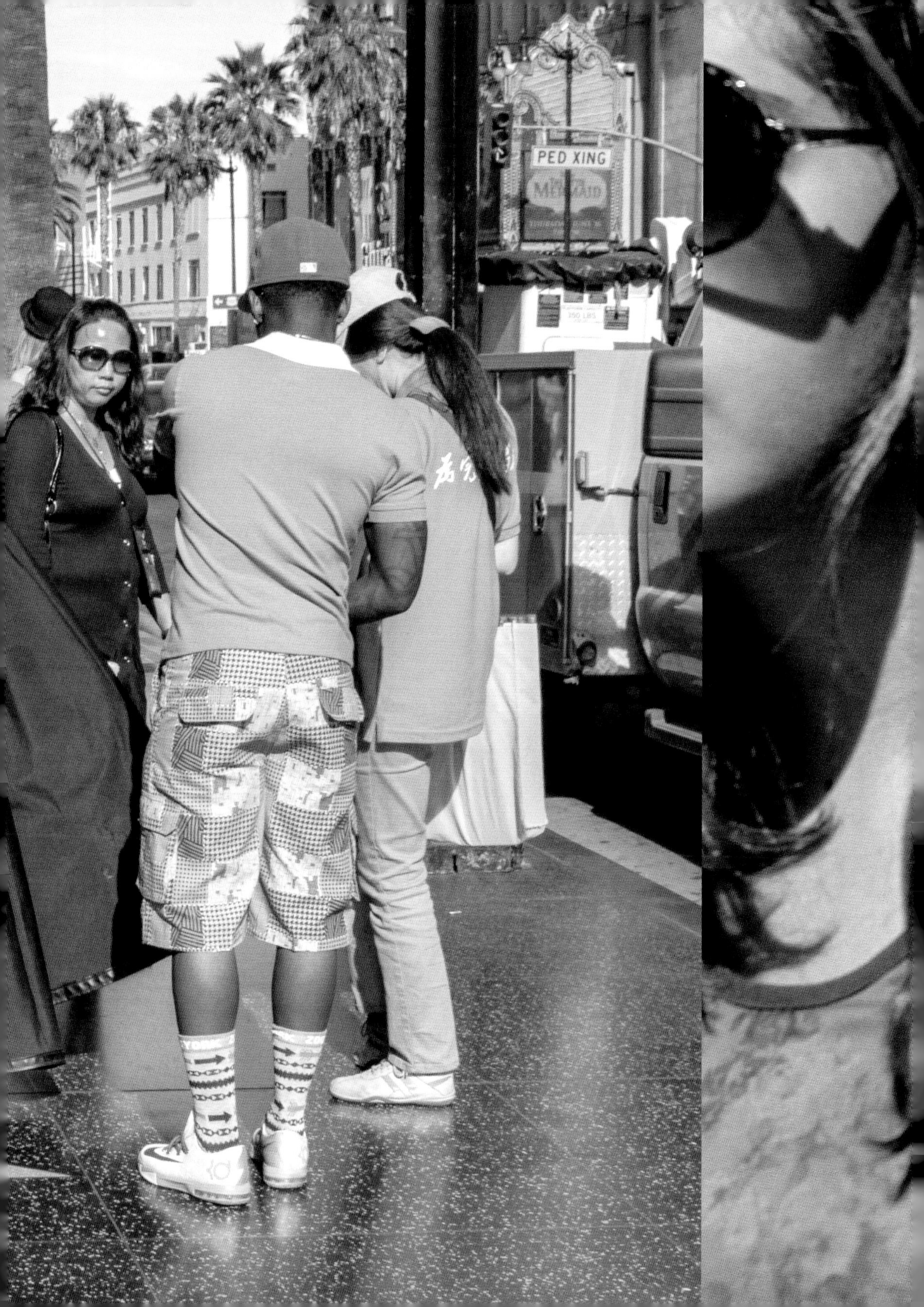
PED XING

凯瑟琳·安德鲁斯
条带

本书出版于由田霏宇与蔡秉桥联合策划展览
洛杉矶计划：
凯瑟琳·安德鲁斯
阿龙·柯里
亚历克斯·以色列
马修·莫纳汉
斯特林·鲁比
莱恩·特里卡丁
卡里·厄普森
在尤伦斯当代艺术中心举办之际
2014年9月13日至11月9日

主编：凯伦·玛尔塔、布莱恩·勒廷格
筹划：蔡秉桥
出版统筹：达斯汀·科森蒂诺
编辑助理：大卫·托罗内

出版：
北京尤伦斯当代艺术中心
伦敦Koenig Books

发行：
尤伦斯当代艺术中心 (UCCA)
中国北京市朝阳区798艺术区
酒仙桥路4号100015
电话：+86 10 57800224
传真：+86 10 57800220
www.ucca.org.cn

ISBN 978-3-86335-627-9

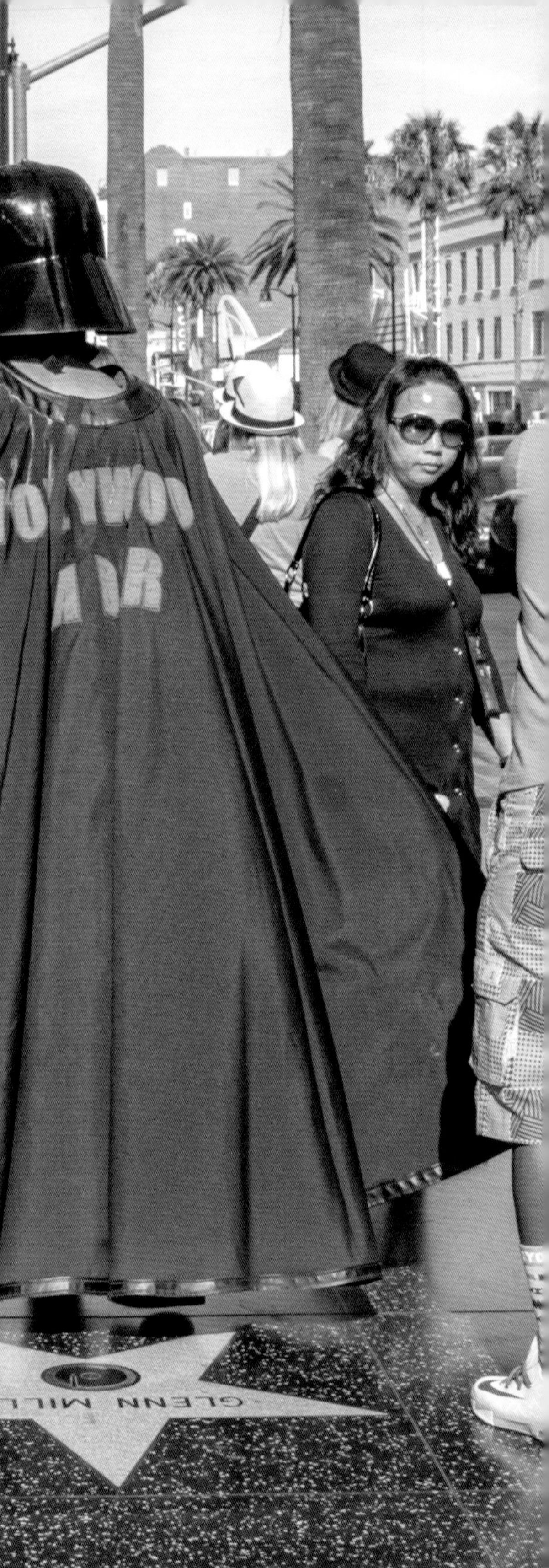

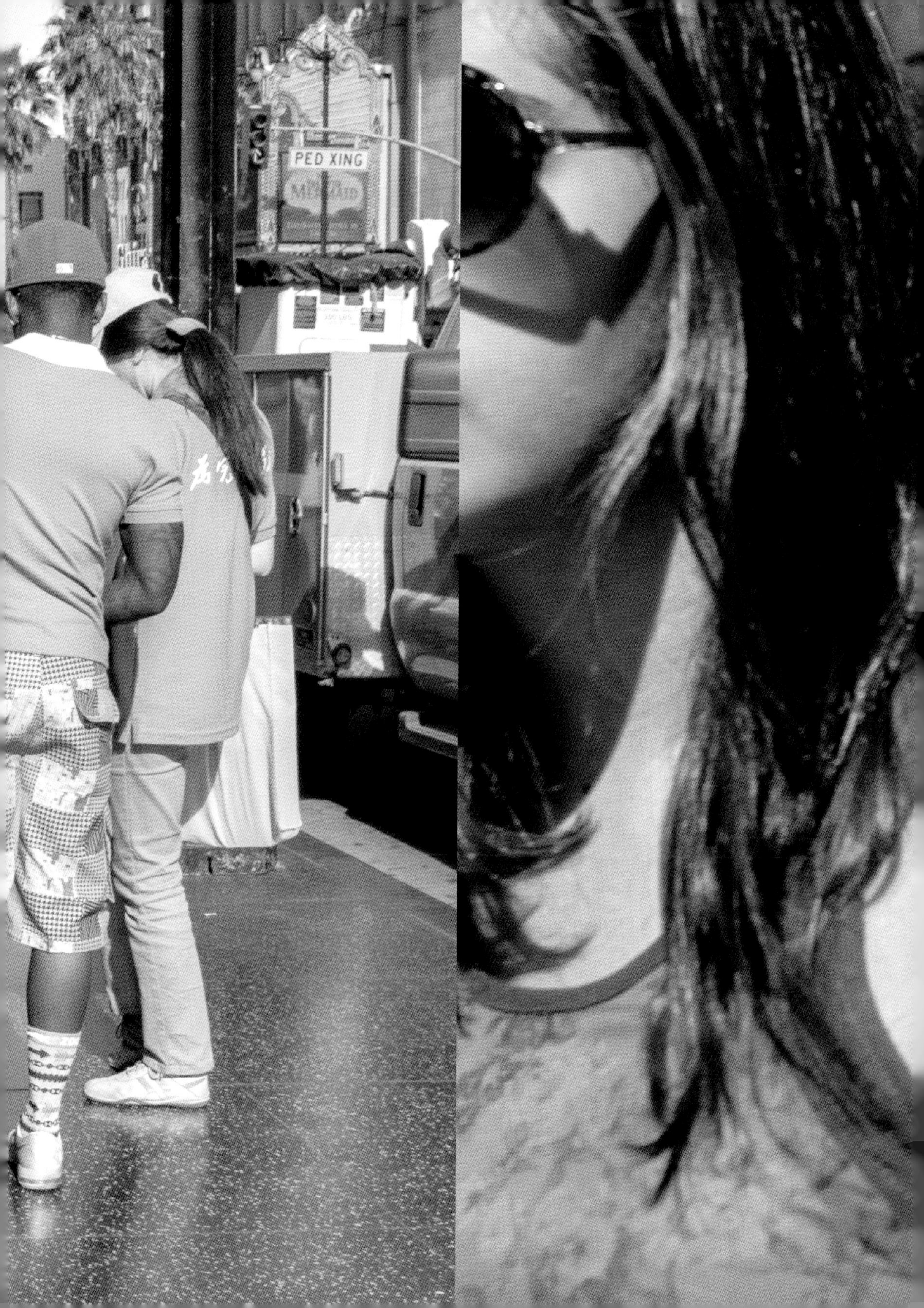
PED XING

凯瑟琳·安德鲁斯
条带

本书出版于由田霏宇与蔡秉桥联合策划展览
洛杉矶计划：
凯瑟琳·安德鲁斯
阿龙·柯里
亚历克斯·以色列
马修·莫纳汉
斯特林·鲁比
莱恩·特里卡丁
卡里·厄普森
在尤伦斯当代艺术中心举办之际
2014年9月13日至11月9日

2014 凯瑟琳·安德鲁斯、尤伦斯当代艺术
中心、Verlag der Buchhandlung Walther
König, Cologne版权所属。未经出版商授权，
任何单位和个人不得擅自对本出版物进行
复制、销售、翻译出版和使用，翻印必究。

主编：凯伦·玛尔塔、布莱恩·勒廷格
筹划：蔡秉桥
出版统筹：达斯汀·科森蒂诺
编辑助理：大卫·托罗内

出版：
北京尤伦斯当代艺术中心
伦敦Koenig Books

发行：
尤伦斯当代艺术中心 (UCCA)
中国北京市朝阳区798艺术区
酒仙桥路4号100015
电话：+86 10 57800224
传真：+86 10 57800220
www.ucca.org.cn

ISBN 978-3-86335-627-9
版权所有 翻印必究

Distribution:

Germany & Europe
Buchhandlung Walther König, Köln
Ehrenstr. 4, 50672 Köln
Tel. +49 (0) 221 / 20 59 6-53
Fax +49 (0) 221 / 20 59 6-60
verlag@buchhandlung-walther-koenig.de

UK & Ireland
Cornerhouse Publications
70 Oxford Street
GB-Manchester M1 5NH
Tel. +44 (0) 161 200 15 03
Fax +44 (0) 161 200 15 04
publications@cornerhouse.org

Outside Europe
D.A.P. / Distributed Art Publishers, Inc.
155 6th Avenue, 2nd Floor
USA-New York, NY 10013
Tel. +1 (0) 212 627 1999
Fax +1 (0) 212 627 9484
eleshowitz@dapinc.com

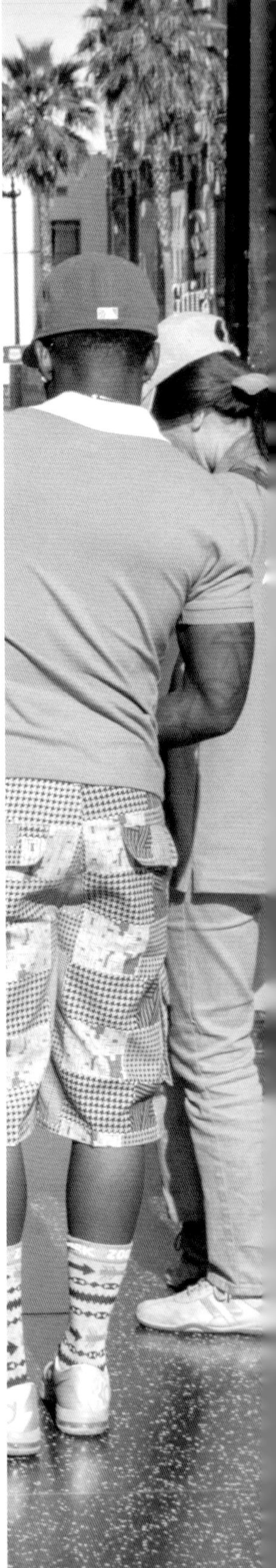

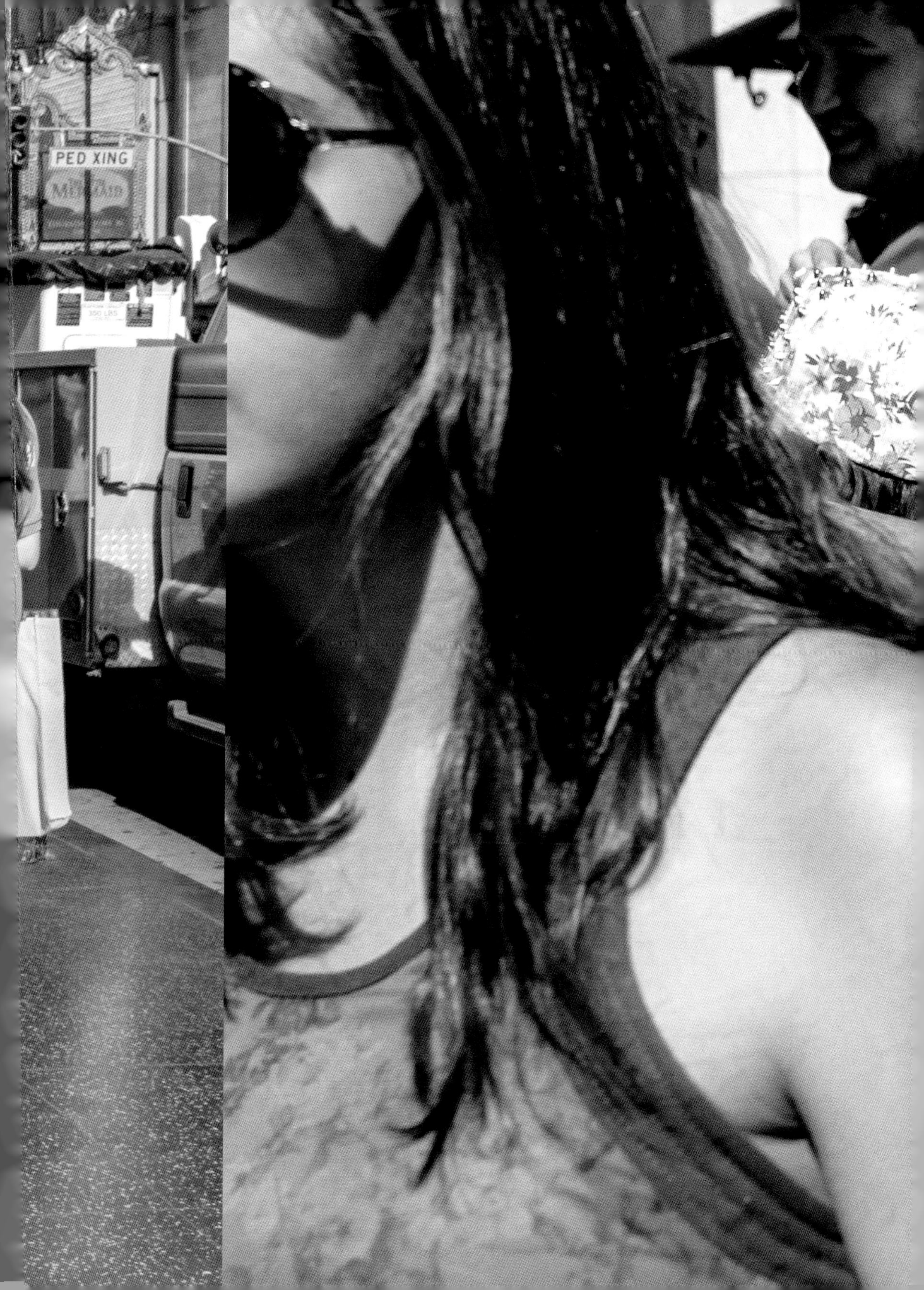
PED XING

KATHRYN ANDREWS
STRIP

Published on the occasion of the exhibition
*The Los Angeles Project: Kathryn Andrews,
Aaron Curry, Alex Israel, Matthew Monahan,
Sterling Ruby, Ryan Trecartin, and Kaari
Upson,* curated by Philip Tinari and Paula
Tsai at Ullens Center for Contemporary Art
(Beijing), 13 September–9 November 2014.

Project Editors: Karen Marta,
　Brian Roettinger
Project Manager: Paula Tsai
Distribution Coordinator: Dustin Cosentino
Editorial Assistant: David Torrone

Many thanks to Amy Harrington, Ahrum
Hong, Franz König, David Kordansky
Gallery, Elisa Leshowitz, and Hans-Peter
Thomas, as well as Philip Tinari, Guy and
Myriam Ullens, everyone at the UCCA, and
Artron Art Group for their enthusiastic
support of the project.

First published by Ullens Center for
Contemporary Art, Beijing, and Koenig
Books, London

Koenig Books Ltd
At the Serpentine Gallery
Kensington Gardens
London W2 3XA
www.koenigbooks.co.uk

Printed by Artron
Printed in China

ISBN 978-3-86335-627-9

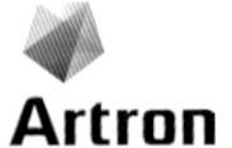

Koenig Books, London

Distribution:

Germany & Europe
Buchhandlung Walther König, Köln
Ehrenstr. 4, 50672 Köln
Tel. +49 (0) 221 / 20 59 6-53
Fax +49 (0) 221 / 20 59 6-60
verlag@buchhandlung-walther-koenig.de

UK & Ireland
Cornerhouse Publications
70 Oxford Street
GB-Manchester M1 5NH
Tel. +44 (0) 161 200 15 03
Fax +44 (0) 161 200 15 04
publications@cornerhouse.org

Outside Europe
D.A.P. / Distributed Art Publishers, Inc.
155 6th Avenue, 2nd Floor
USA-New York, NY 10013
Tel. +1 (0) 212 627 1999
Fax +1 (0) 212 627 9484
eleshowitz@dapinc.com

凯瑟琳 · 安德鲁斯
条带

本书出版于由田霏宇与蔡秉桥联合策划展览
洛杉矶计划：
凯瑟琳 · 安德鲁斯
阿龙 · 柯里
亚历克斯 · 以色列
马修 · 莫纳汉
斯特林 · 鲁比
莱恩 · 特里卡丁
卡里 · 厄普森
在尤伦斯当代艺术中心举办之际
2014年9月13日至11月9日

2014 凯瑟琳 · 安德鲁斯、尤伦斯当代艺术
中心、Verlag der Buchhandlung Walther
König, Cologne版权所属。未经出版商授权，
任何单位和个人不得擅自对本出版物进行
复制、销售、翻译出版和使用，翻印必究。

主编：凯伦 · 玛尔塔、布莱恩 · 勒廷格
筹划：蔡秉桥
出版统筹：达斯汀 · 科森蒂诺
编辑助理：大卫 · 托罗内

出版：
北京尤伦斯当代艺术中心
伦敦Koenig Books

发行：
尤伦斯当代艺术中心（UCCA）
中国北京市朝阳区798艺术区
酒仙桥路4号100015
电话：+86 10 57800224
传真：+86 10 57800220
www.ucca.org.cn

ISBN 978-3-86335-627-9
版权所有 翻印必究